HAROLD

The Last Anglo-Saxon King

To My Mother and Father

HAROLD

The Last Anglo-Saxon King

IAN W. WALKER

SUTTON PUBLISHING

First published in 1997 by
Sutton Publishing Ltd
Thrupp · Stroud · Gloucestershire · GL5 2BU

Paperback edition first published 2000

British Library Cataloguing in Publication Data
A catalogue record for this book is available from the British Library

ISBN 0-7509-2456-X

Typeset in 11/14 pt Bembo.
Typesetting and origination by
Sutton Publishing Limited.
Printed in Great Britain by
Redwood Books, Trowbridge, Wiltshire.

CONTENTS

List of Plates, Illustrations and Maps   vii

Acknowledgements   xi

Family Trees   xiii–xvi

General Maps   xvii–xix

Introduction   xxi

Chapter One   FAMILY ORIGINS   1

Chapter Two   HAROLD, SON OF GODWINE   19

Chapter Three   EXILE AND RETURN   37

Chapter Four   THE LANDS AND WEALTH OF HAROLD   54

Chapter Five   EARL OF WESSEX   74

Chapter Six   WILLIAM OF NORMANDY   91

Chapter Seven   EARL TOSTI   103

Chapter Eight   HAROLD THE MAN   120

Chapter Nine   KING HAROLD   136

Chapter Ten   HARALD OF NORWAY   152

Chapter Eleven   THE LAST CAMPAIGN   166

Chapter Twelve   END OF A DYNASTY   183

Conclusion   199

Appendix One   203

Appendix Two   205

Abbreviations   215

Notes   217

Bibliography   237

Index   245

LIST OF PLATES, ILLUSTRATIONS AND MAPS

PLATES

Between pp. 98 and 99

1. Frontispiece of New Minster *Liber Vitae*. (BL, Stowe MS 944, f. 6)
2. Seal die of Godwine the thegn. (British Museum, MLA 1881, 4-4, 1)
3. Scene depicting shepherds, from an eleventh-century calendar. (BL, MS Cotton Tiberius B.v, f. 5r)
4. Scene depicting reaping, from an eleventh-century calendar. (BL, MS Cotton Tiberius B.v, f. 6v)
5. Harold is handed over to William. (The Bayeux Tapestry – 11th Century. By special permission of the City of Bayeux)
6. The coronation of King Harold. (The Bayeux Tapestry – 11th Century. By special permission of the City of Bayeux)
7. A king and his counsellors. (BL, MS Cotton Claudius B.iv, f. 59)
8. Anglo-Saxon feast. (BL, MS Cotton Claudius B.iv, f. 63v)
9. Scene of hawking, from an eleventh-century calendar. (BL, MS Cotton Tiberius B.v, f. 7v)
10. The death of King Harold. (The Bayeux Tapestry – 11th Century. By special permission of the City of Bayeux)

ILLUSTRATIONS

		page
1.	Anglo-Saxon Chronicle E, the entry for 1009. (The Bodleian Library, Oxford, MS Laud Misc. 636, f. 43v)	2
2.	The will of Atheling Athelstan, 1014. (BL, Stowe Charter 37)	4
3.	Diploma of King Cnut. (BL, Stowe Charter 38)	9
4.	King Edward. (The Bayeux Tapestry – 11th Century. By special permission of the City of Bayeux)	17
5.	Harold at Bosham Church in Sussex. (The Bayeux Tapestry – 11th Century. By special permission of the City of Bayeux)	23
6.	Diploma of King Edward, 1050. (The Dean and Chapter of Exeter)	26

page

7. The lands of King Edward, 1066. (Blackwell Publishers)   28

8. Anglo-Saxon Chronicle E, part of the entry for 1051. (The Bodleian
   Library, Oxford, MS Laud Misc. 636, f. 53v)   31

9. Harold in a foreign palace. (The Bayeux Tapestry – 11th Century.
   By special permission of the City of Bayeux)   42

10. Harold aboard a ship. (The Bayeux Tapestry – 11th Century. By special
    permission of the City of Bayeux)   45

11. Bosham Church, Sussex. (RCHME © Crown Copyright)   48

12. Harold at a feast. (The Bayeux Tapestry – 11th Century. By special
    permission of the City of Bayeux)   52

13. Domesday Book and its chest. (Public Record Office)   55

14. The lands of Earl Harold, 1066. (Blackwell Publishers)   57

15. Domesday Book, the opening page of the entries for Sussex. (Reproduced
    by kind permission of Alecto Historical Editions)   64

16. The seal of Harold's College of Holy Cross at Waltham. (The Dean
    and Chapter of Durham)   71

17. King Edward and Earl Harold. (The Bayeux Tapestry – 11th Century.
    By special permission of the City of Bayeux)   75

18. Writ of King Edward, 1065. (By courtesy of the Dean and
    Chapter of Westminster)   79

19. The *Vita Eadwardi Regis*, extract from a poem on Harold's Welsh wars.
    (BL, Harley MS 526, f. 52v)   84

20. The Rood, Romsey Abbey. (RCHME © Crown Copyright)   86

21. Harold is taken captive. (The Bayeux Tapestry – 11th Century.
    By special permission of the City of Bayeux)   94

22. Harold is handed over to Duke William. (The Bayeux Tapestry –
    11th Century. By special permission of the City of Bayeux)   97

23. Harold is presented with arms by William. (The Bayeux Tapestry –
    11th Century. By special permission of the City of Bayeux)   98

24. Harold swears the oath to William. (The Bayeux Tapestry – 11th Century.
    By special permission of the City of Bayeux)   100

25. The sundial at St Gregory's Church in Kirkdale, North Yorkshire.
    (RCHME © Crown Copyright)   106

26. The Chronicle of John of Worcester, the entry for 1065. (The President
    and Fellows of Corpus Christi College, Oxford)   109

27. The death of King Edward, 1066. (The Bayeux Tapestry – 11th Century.
    By special permission of the City of Bayeux)   115

page

28. The crown is presented to Harold. (The Bayeux Tapestry – 11th Century.
By special permission of the City of Bayeux)   118

29. Harold's 'portrait', as represented on his coinage. (Copyright British Museum) 121

30. The 'Pax' motif on Harold's coinage. (Ashmolean Museum, Oxford)   122

31. Harold rescues two men. (The Bayeux Tapestry – 11th Century.
By special permission of the City of Bayeux)   124

32. The Waltham Chronicle, extract recording Harold's gift of relics.
(BL, Cotton MS Julius D VI, f. 93v)   126

33. Harold rides through the countryside. (The Bayeux Tapestry – 11th Century.
By special permission of the City of Bayeux)   134

34. Harold's coronation, 1066. (The Bayeux Tapestry – 11th Century.
By special permission of the City of Bayeux)   137

35. Writ of King Harold. (Reproduced by permission of the Dean and
Chapter of Wells)   139

36. Silver penny of King Harold. (Ashmolean Museum, Oxford)   141

37. Halley's Comet. (The Bayeux Tapestry – 11th Century. By special
permission of the City of Bayeux)   143

38. Domesday Book, detail of an entry for land in Hampshire. (Reproduced
by kind permission of Alecto Historical Editions)   146

39. Anglo-Saxon Chronicle E, the entry for 1066. (The Bodleian Library,
Oxford, MS Laud Misc. 636, f. 57v)   156

40. An invasion fleet at sea. (The Bayeux Tapestry – 11th Century.
By special permission of the City of Bayeux)   159

41. A scout brings news to King Harold. (The Bayeux Tapestry – 11th Century.
By special permission of the City of Bayeux)   161

42. The traditional English shield wall formation. (The Bayeux Tapestry –
11th Century. By special permission of the City of Bayeux)   163

43. Norman cavalry attack. (The Bayeux Tapestry – 11th Century.
By special permission of the City of Bayeux)   170

44. Englishmen surrounded by Normans. (The Bayeux Tapestry – 11th Century.
By special permission of the City of Bayeux)   175

45. The fall of Gyrth and Leofwine. (The Bayeux Tapestry – 11th Century.
By special permission of the City of Bayeux)   177

46. The death of King Harold. (The Bayeux Tapestry – 11th Century.
By special permission of the City of Bayeux)   179

47. The English flee the field. (The Bayeux Tapestry – 11th Century.
By special permission of the City of Bayeux)   180

page

48. The Normans burn down a house. (The Bayeux Tapestry – 11th Century. By special permission of the City of Bayeux)   184

49. A Norman castle. (The Bayeux Tapestry – 11th Century. By special permission of the City of Bayeux)   185

50. Norman soldiers of the occupation. (The Burrell Collection, Glasgow Museums)   186

51. Norman cavalry. (The Bayeux Tapestry – 11th Century. By special permission of the City of Bayeux)   189

MAPS

1. Map of England, *c.* 1060. (© Ian W. Walker)   xvii
2. Map of north-west Europe, *c.* 1060. (© Ian W. Walker)   xviii
3. Map of Europe, *c.* 1060. (© Ian W. Walker)   xix
4. The earldoms, 1045. (© Ian W. Walker)   210
5. The earldoms, 1050. (© Ian W. Walker)   210
6. The earldoms, late 1051. (© Ian W. Walker)   210
7. The earldoms, late 1052. (© Ian W. Walker)   210
8. The earldoms, 1056. (© Ian W. Walker)   211
9. The earldoms, 1060. (© Ian W. Walker)   211
10. The earldoms, end 1065. (© Ian W. Walker)   211

ACKNOWLEDGEMENTS

I would like to thank a number of people for their assistance during the writing of this book. I would like in particular to thank Sheila. She inspired and encouraged me to write this book in the first place. I would like to pay tribute to my tutors at the University of Glasgow, who fostered my interest in history and provided me with the investigative skills necessary to study the subject. I would like to express my appreciation to Denis Butler, whose admittedly somewhat romantic account of Harold Godwineson in *1066 The Story of a Year* (London, 1966) nevertheless first attracted my attention to this fascinating character, and provided a starting point for many years of interesting research thereafter. I would like to express my gratitude to the staffs at Glasgow University Library, Edinburgh University Library, the Library of the University of Wales, Cardiff, and East Kilbride Public Library, who provided access to many of the sources consulted, and to the staffs of all those various organizations which supplied illustrations and provided the necessary permissions to reproduce them herein. I would like to express my warm appreciation to Jane and Clare and the rest of the staff at Sutton Publishing, who succeeded in making the process of publication almost entirely painless. I would also like to thank Dr Bill Aird of the University of Wales, Cardiff, who read this work at an earlier stage and offered encouraging advice and helpful suggestions. This improved the final text immensely and saved me from a number of errors and omissions. I must accept full blame for any mistakes which remain in the finished book. Finally, I would like to thank my father and mother, without whose assistance on the word processor and in type-checking this book could not have been completed.

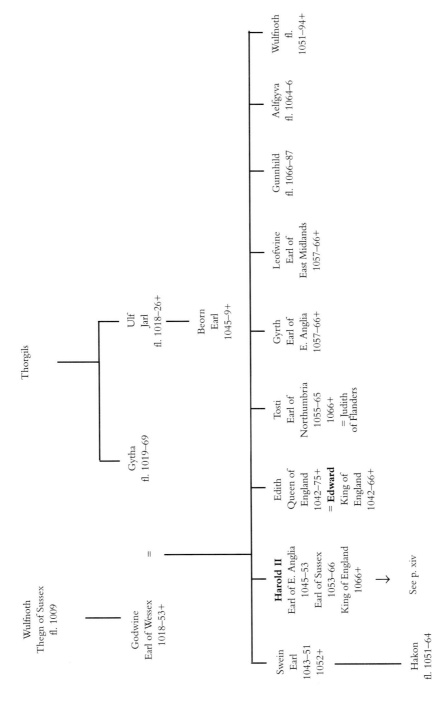

The Godwine Family

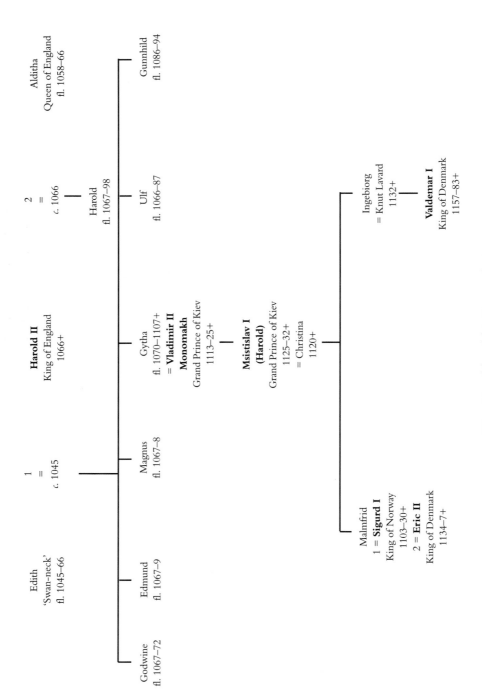

King Harold and his Descendants

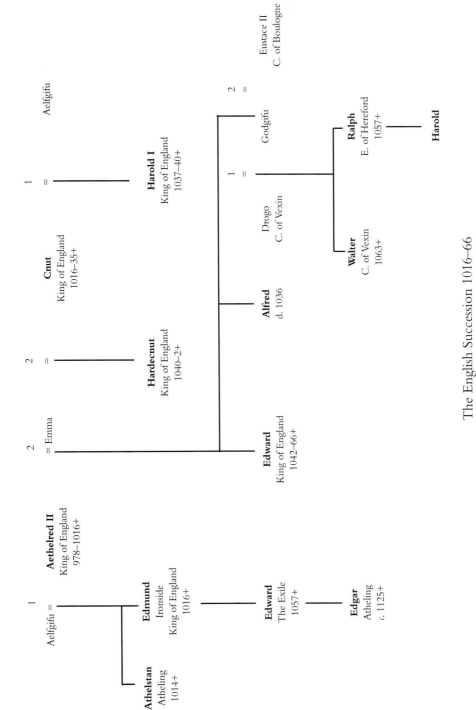

The English Succession 1016–66
(Names in bold signify a claim to the throne)

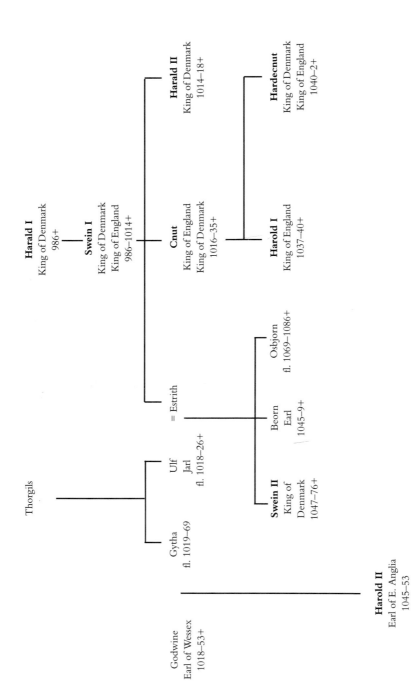

King Harold and his Scandinavian Connections

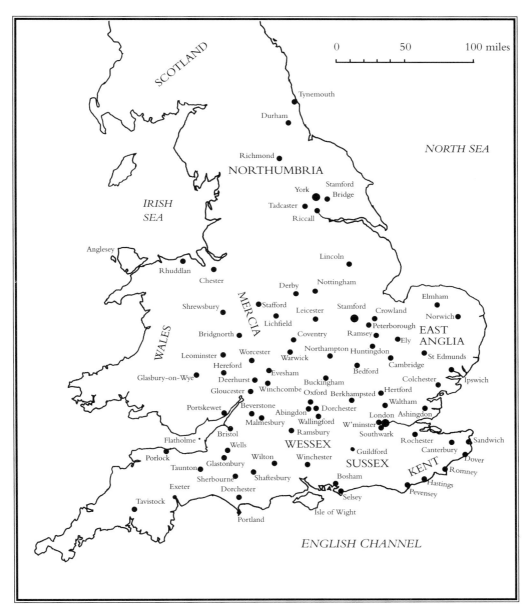

Map of England, *c.* 1060. (© Ian W. Walker)

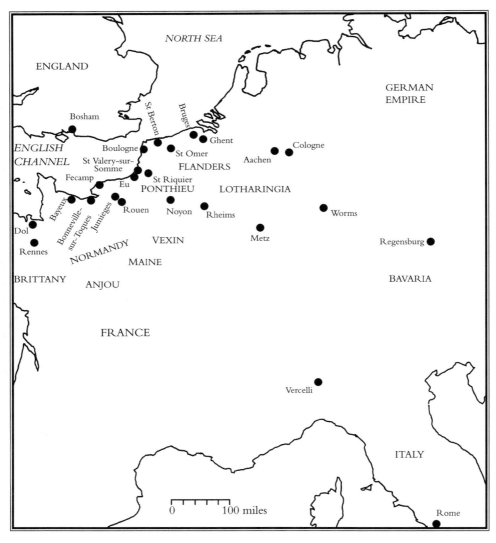

Map of north–west Europe, *c.* 1060. (© Ian W. Walker)

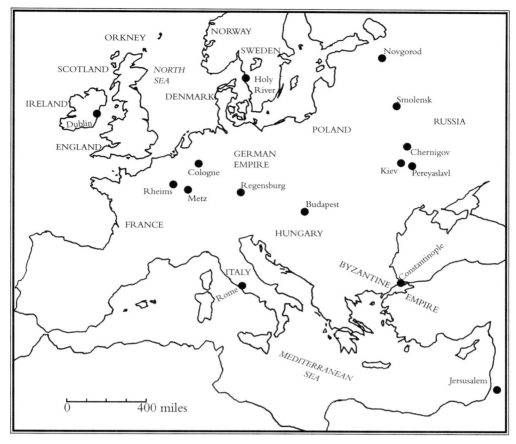

Map of Europe, *c.* 1060. (© Ian W. Walker)

INTRODUCTION

King Harold Godwineson is one of history's shadowy figures, almost unknown to the public at large. The few who are familiar with his name at all, usually know little more than that he lost the battle of Hastings and was killed by an arrow in the eye. Many general histories of England begin with the Norman Conquest and those which look back, beyond it, to the Anglo-Saxon period usually pass over Harold as a minor interruption between the long reigns of Edward the Confessor and William the Conqueror. This obscurity is partly, it is certain, a result of King Harold's brief reign of only nine months and nine days, almost the shortest in English history. Nevertheless, he reigned at a crucial turning-point in that history and played a vital role in the events of the memorable year 1066. As a result one would expect him to have received rather more attention than he has received.[1]

Only two modern works have dealt with Harold's career in any detail: a biography of 1961, and a commemorative lecture of 1966. Only the latter sought to examine Harold's career in a critical fashion. Otherwise, discussion of Harold has been largely confined to a number of academic essays on specific aspects of his career, or on his role as a supporting character in the careers of others. The former, by their nature, cannot consider his career in its entirety. The latter naturally tend to place him in an historical framework constructed with reference to the careers of others and as a result his own image is somewhat distorted. He has been portrayed as an over-mighty noble, who ruthlessly manipulated a weak King Edward the Confessor in order to oust his rivals, overshadow the king and ultimately seize the kingdom itself. He has also been seen as a man who rashly opposed Duke William of Normandy, Edward's designated successor, only to find himself outmatched as a statesman, as a general and as a propagandist, and paying the ultimate price for his folly.[2]

There is a need to consider Harold and his career in its proper context and to review his actions in this light. A full understanding of Harold's actions and their historical context in the years leading up to 1066 is a prerequisite for developing a complete perspective on his role in the events of that year. A number of recent historians have made a start but this book is intended to do so fully by focusing directly on Harold.[3]

BACKGROUND

In eleventh-century England, the monarchy was the focus of all political authority and the cornerstone of society. The king reigned by the Grace of God and his power over the people was divinely sanctioned. He provided leadership and protection for his people in time of war and dispensed justice and preserved order in time of peace. In order to perform these functions, he drew on tribute and taxation from his subjects. In practice, although royal power could ultimately be imposed by coercion this did not make it absolute. In fact, no king could successfully rule for long by force alone, especially if his subjects were united in their opposition to him. In most cases a significant degree of cooperation between ruler and subjects was usually required. A king could not be physically present throughout the kingdom and in order to operate beyond his immediate environs he required the cooperation of subordinates in each local area to act as his deputies, perform his duties, impose his authority, and collect his dues. These subordinates, who included both clergy and laymen, were royal civil servants, who gained rewards in return for their loyal service.

The clergy, the archbishops, bishops and abbots, whose appointments were subject to royal approval, supplied the king with both a religious sanction for his authority and administrative skills to support it. There did exist an alternative source of Church authority to that of the king in the Roman Papacy. However, until King Edward's reign this had fallen into the habit of merely endorsing the choice of clergy appointed by the monarch. The secular officials, the earls, sheriffs and others, provided services which included collecting royal taxes, supplying provisions to the royal household, and providing men for the royal armies. All of these royal officials in turn appointed their own deputies, deans and priests, *thegns* and reeves, who served them in similar ways.

Many of these men, clerical and lay, wielded great power and influence but ultimately all remained subject to royal authority. They formed a nobility founded on service to the king. They were men from families of local lords with local lands and supporters, who were recruited by the king in order to harness their local power to support his kingship. In return they were endowed by the king with a share of royal lands and wealth, which assisted them in their performance of delegated royal functions. If they performed their duties well these men would be further rewarded by personal gifts of lands and wealth, which in turn reinforced their position and their family's local power. These lords had similar relationships with their own followers, who provided them with services in return for reward. In each case this symbiotic relationship brought benefits to both sides and provided a strong bond for society as a whole.[4]

It is true that there were tensions and divisions between the local lords and the king, including between King Edward the Confessor and his great earls, and these often distract attention away from the cooperative side of the relationship. However, when we look closely at King Edward's reign what should strike us are the long periods of cooperation and harmony rather than the relatively few instances of dispute. The earls, in fact, most often operated with the king to impose justice, to collect taxes and to defend the kingdom. It was only on a few occasions that one or more of these men found themselves in dispute with the king – there were only four cases of exile or rebellion during Edward's entire reign of twenty-four years. Such upheavals were common in other kingdoms too, and Normandy under Duke William witnessed a number of similar rebellions. They did not necessarily mean that a ruler was weak and his subjects too powerful, but simply that in a cooperative relationship it was inevitable that tensions would sometimes arise.

In general, the relationship between a king and his great lords was essential to effective rule. It was this relationship of lordship and service that provided the key to the rise of Harold and of his family. It was only when this relationship was disrupted that they encountered problems, as occurred during Godwine's exile in the period 1051–2. It was the ability of Harold's father, Godwine, and later of Harold himself to foster and occasionally to manipulate this vital relationship both upwards and downwards that allowed them to advance in power and influence. By 1066 Harold would prove himself so effective in his role as first deputy for the king that he was able to make the final transition to the kingship itself. Thereafter, the performance of his royal duties was to encounter a series of threats, not least from William of Normandy.[5]

SOURCES

It is by no means an easy task to review Harold's career, since even in contemporary sources we are given conflicting and contrasting views of Harold himself and his role in events. He is described in often insulting terms by the Norman writer William of Poitiers, but is referred to affectionately in the Anglo-Saxon Chronicle. King Harold's central role in the controversial events of 1066 was responsible for these contrasting views. The strenuous opposition he offered to the Normans earned him the hatred of his conquerors. Indeed, as the Normans gradually established their rule, they commenced a process which sought to undermine Harold's reputation and deny his royal status. Although immediately after William's coronation English royal documents continued to refer to his predecessor as King Harold, thereafter he would gradually be downgraded to earl and King Edward would appear as William's direct predecessor. This process was to reach its apogee in 1086, in Domesday Book where Harold is consistently termed *comes* or earl, and land holding is recorded as it stood in the time of King Edward. The reader must be aware of the background to this process in order to make an accurate assessment of the information contained in the sources for Harold's reign.

The main contemporary English source for Harold's career is the Anglo-Saxon Chronicle. During the period under consideration this was being compiled on a near contemporary basis in three different recensions. This work has been discussed in detail elsewhere (as indicated in the notes) but there is one thing which should perhaps be added here. Each of the different recensions of the Chronicle is often represented as holding a consistent political viewpoint over this period. Thus Chronicle C is stated to be anti-Godwine or royalist, Chronicle E is pro-Godwine, and Chronicle D neutral. However, when they are examined in more detail they appear to be much less straightforward. Chronicle C, compiled at Abingdon, is usually judged to be either royalist or at least hostile to the Godwine family. However, it includes events which appear sympathetic or favourable to the family, like Harold's burial of his murdered cousin Beorn in 1049, and the tender account of Earl Godwine's demise in 1053. It turns down a golden opportunity to criticize Godwine and his family by treating their rebellion in 1051 in a brief summary only, while providing a very full account of their triumphal return in 1052. These entries do not appear hostile to the family at all. Chronicle E, compiled at Canterbury, is widely considered to be a source favourable to Earl Godwine. It is certainly fascinated by the great crisis of 1051–2 and Godwine's role in these events. However, it should be noted that many of the events of this crisis occurred close to the compiler – in Canterbury, in Dover, along the south coast, at Sandwich, and in London. It may be that the proximity of these events to his base rather than sympathy for Godwine explains the detailed knowledge of the compiler of Chronicle E. For example, Eustace of Boulogne's men passed through Canterbury on their way to Dover and this would naturally be likely to feature prominently in the local Chronicle. Indeed, the impact of this crisis on the Archbishopric of Canterbury itself is perhaps enough to explain the prominence of its events in this text. The crisis, after all, began with a disputed election to the archbishopric and ended with the expulsion of one archbishop and his replacement by another. In contrast, other successes of the Godwine family, which might be expected to feature prominently in Chronicle E, like Harold's invasion of Wales in 1063, are in fact treated rather briefly. The text is not, in fact, always favourable to the family. Lastly, Chronicle D is described as neutral but it alone refers rather affectionately to Harold in 1066 as 'our king'. Thus the differences which occur in the various recensions of the Chronicle appear to reflect local or personal viewpoints of individual chroniclers, rather than any consistent political view.[6]

The chronicle now attributed to John of Worcester in a sense represents yet another recension of the Anglo-Saxon Chronicle. It was started perhaps in the late eleventh century and completed around 1140 but includes annals drawn from an earlier version of the Anglo-Saxon Chronicle. This was probably related to the extant Chronicle D, but in John's text these annals incorporate additions and variations, in some cases possibly added after reference to another existing version of the Anglo-Saxon Chronicle but in others more probably added by John himself. John's own additions often represent his own clarifications of the existing Chronicle texts, but he sometimes adds further details, perhaps culled from other textual sources available to him at the time but subsequently lost.[7]

The other major contemporary English source is the *Vita Eadwardi Regis*, attributed to Goscelin of St Bertin, which was written for Queen Edith, Harold's sister. The original purpose behind its composition appears to have been to glorify the Godwine family and Queen Edith, and the latter's marriage to the king in particular. It emphasizes the role of her family in the events of Edward's reign and sometimes tends to exaggerate their importance and this must be kept in mind when using it. However, it is by no means entirely eulogistic in tone, as might be expected by its purpose, and both Godwine and Harold are subjected to some unfavourable associations by its author. He speaks of right being on the side of Archbishop Robert of Canterbury in his land dispute with Godwine in 1051 and refers to the earl's involvement in the death of *Atheling* Alfred in 1036. He also records an accusation made by Tosti that his brother Harold instigated the Northumbrian rebellion in 1065. Aside from King Edward and Queen Edith, the main focus of Goscelin's attention is not solely Harold but rather Harold and his brother Tosti, who appears to have been their sister Edith's favourite. As a result, Harold is not the sole or even main focus of devotion of this work as is the case with William of Normandy in the work of William of Poitiers. In addition, although the original intention of Goscelin's work may have been to enhance the prestige of the Godwine family, the contemporary events of 1066 and the death of all the Godwine brothers left this plan in ruins and the author asks plaintively 'for whom shall I write now? This murderous page will hardly please the queen their sister . . .'. All of this means that this work is not simply a straightforward eulogy of Earl Harold and provided one is wary of accepting all of its views uncritically much can be learned from the facts it relates.[8]

In contrast to the English sources, which are all based on contemporary or near contemporary accounts, both of the main Norman sources which deal with the events of Harold's career postdate the Norman Conquest of England. They also clearly set out to legitimize the succession of William of Normandy to the English throne. They are therefore partisan to a greater or lesser extent, and this must be kept in mind when using them. This does not necessarily mean that we need to doubt the basic facts of their narratives, but rather that we should consider carefully both their interpretation of these facts and the context in which they place them. The fact that these Norman accounts were compiled with the benefit of hindsight is also significant, as this puts them in a position to assemble their facts into an apparently natural and consistent account. This account comprises three principal elements: King Edward's designation of William as his heir; Harold's journey to Normandy to confirm this by oath; and, following Harold's breach of his oath and seizure of the English throne, William's successful campaign to claim his rightful inheritance.

The first of these Norman sources, the *Gesta Normannorum Ducum* of William of Jumieges, was written with the explicit purpose of recounting the way in which Duke William succeeded in becoming the 'orthodox' king of the English. William wrote that part of this work dealing with the Norman claim to the English throne around

1070. He therefore had the benefit of hindsight in organizing his material and directing it to his purpose. He placed great emphasis on the Norman claim that Harold was a perjured usurper, mentioning the latter's oath some four times in his otherwise very spare narrative of these events. The very sparseness of his account, which largely sticks to relating the unembroidered facts, may indicate that it is basically reliable. In addition, William was able to use Robert of Jumieges, the exiled Archbishop of Canterbury and a central character in these events, as a direct source of information for his narrative. Indeed, it would appear that William's account was accepted by subsequent generations as the fundamental record of the events of the Conquest, since almost fifty surviving manuscripts of his work are recorded.[9]

In contrast, William of Poitiers adds a great deal of elaborate detail to his own very polished and highly literate version of the events of the Conquest. William of Poitiers probably wrote his *Gesta Guillelmi ducis Normannorum et regis Anglorum* around 1077. According to R. Allen Brown, it is 'very much a planned literary work . . . steeped in the classics' whose theme is 'the deliberate justification' of Duke William's conquest of England. In it, William of Poitiers provides a much more elaborate account of the Norman claim to the English throne than William of Jumieges, but in doing so raises a significant number of inconsistencies which tend to detract from his trustworthiness. This trustworthiness is also rather undermined by his very clear bias in favour of Duke William and against Harold. It appears that this is also how subsequent generations viewed his work since it only survived into the modern period in a single unique and incomplete manuscript, which was itself subsequently lost during the seventeenth century. William of Poitier's work is Norman propaganda and therefore must be treated with considerable caution, his evidence sifted very carefully for possible additions and omissions, and his views or interpretations closely questioned. In spite of these problems, William does provide some support for the basic account of William of Jumieges and, in addition, offers plausible information on some events, which is found nowhere else. For example, his account of the Battle of Hastings is unique and convincing in most of its aspects.[10]

The last 'Norman' source for Harold's life is certainly the most unique and also the most tantalizing. This is the great pictorial representation of Harold's downfall and William's triumph contained in the Bayeux Tapestry. This work is, clearly, part of the Norman propaganda offensive, along with the works of William of Jumieges and William of Poitiers, since it was made for Bishop Odo, William's half-brother, perhaps around 1077. However, the allusive nature of the medium in which it is composed and the brevity of the accompanying text have often left it open to differing interpretation. Indeed, this may have been the intention of its makers since, although the Tapestry appears on the surface to repeat the Norman version of events, the accompanying text sometimes hints at other possibilities. The fact that the Tapestry was created by English hands makes divergent meanings a fascinating prospect and perhaps indicates an alternative English version of the events of the Conquest. Indeed there may be evidence in the later account by the monk Eadmer of Canterbury to support such a version of these events. Despite its difficulties, the Tapestry remains a very important source for Harold's career.[11]

An important factor to bear in mind when examining these three Norman sources is the fact that although they are interrelated they do not appear to be derivative. They all incorporate accounts of the same basic events, but occasionally present some of them in a different sequence while omitting others altogether. William of Jumieges emphasizes Edward's promise and Harold's oath but provides little information on the actual conquest. William of Poitiers provides an elaborate account of all the events from Edward's promise to the Battle of Hastings. The Tapestry omits Edward's promise of 1051 altogether and concentrates instead on Harold's visit to Normandy and the subsequent conquest. The differences and similarities between these sources can sometimes be useful in attempting to interpret events.[12]

The construction of all these Norman accounts of the events of 1066 may have been inspired by concerns expressed around 1070 by the Pope about the nature of the Norman Conquest. The Papacy became concerned about the aggression and brutality involved in the conquest of England and, perhaps in particular, the recent and notorious Harrying of the North. This concern is clearly evidenced by the Penitential Ordinance of Bishop Erminfrid, issued around 1070. This placed a penance on all those who had participated in the Conquest. The purpose of these Norman texts may have been as attempts to justify the Conquest under Papal scrutiny, and hence their emphasis throughout on the legitimacy of William's cause. The substantial additions of William of Poitiers are perhaps best interpreted in this light. Thus the latter's introduction of the English earls as guarantors was intended to reinforce the bare promise of the crown, which was all that William of Jumieges recorded. Similarly, the elaborate oath sworn by Harold, according to William of Poitiers, was intended to reinforce the impact of his subsequent perjury. It is difficult to see for whom such additions were intended if not the Papacy, and if this is the case then it too should be borne in mind.[13]

There are other sources for Harold's career besides these narrative texts. Domesday Book records unique details of Harold's landholding in England, without which we would have a very limited idea of the extent of his power. However, this source has a number of practical drawbacks. It was compiled in 1086, chiefly as a record of who held specific lands and rights and therefore who owed particular services or dues at that date, and it provides clear documentary evidence for this later period. However, it also attempts to record who held the equivalent lands and rights and owed equivalent services or dues in the time of King Edward some twenty or more years earlier. For this earlier period, rather than offering strict documentary evidence, it represents a record of local memory and this has resulted in a number of apparent errors or inconsistencies. In addition, the text, even as regards 1086, does not provide consistent information for all areas of the country and omits some northern areas altogether. It has also suffered a certain amount of Norman interpretation so that Harold is neither referred to by his royal title nor shown as holding the royal lands, which are instead listed as King Edward's. Nevertheless, it remains a vital text without which our information about Harold would be much poorer indeed.[14]

The few other, principally documentary, contemporary sources which still exist have been used wherever possible. By their nature, these can cast only oblique, if invaluable, shafts of light on Harold's story. However, the small number of surviving diplomas and writs from this period is a major barrier to any study of Harold or other contemporary figures. An exception to this pattern of poor survival is provided by the royal coinage, which casts considerable light on the effectiveness of Harold's government.[15]

A number of later sources remain to be considered. These must be viewed with some caution as they are more distant in time from Harold's day and may have been subjected to later interpretation. The main examples of such sources are later accounts of the period by a number of Anglo-Norman historians, including Orderic Vitalis, Eadmer of Canterbury, William of Malmesbury, Guy of Amiens and Geffrei Gaimar. In addition, there exist the records of a number of religious houses, which have preserved local traditions concerning their house and its lands and patrons. These include, in particular, the Waltham Chronicle, of Harold's own foundation, which although compiled in around 1177 has much to relate about its patron. These sources have in general only been used where they appear to offer reliable locally preserved traditions which do not survive in more contemporary sources.[16]

It is on the basis of these different sources of variable value that we must attempt to reconstruct an account and an assessment of Harold's life, character and actions. In doing so, we must try to consider and assess all of these sources against what we know of the contemporary scene. Only in this way can we seek to avoid the influence of hindsight, which is the bane of all historical writing but weighs perhaps particularly heavily on Harold.

The decisiveness of the Norman Conquest itself and the undoubted impact of the event on subsequent English history, however it may be assessed, has resulted in a very natural tendency to see it as the logical consequence of the events of King Edward's reign. As a result the Norman sources, which were compiled to provide just such a logical pattern and sequence to these events, have received less critical assessment than they perhaps deserve. Although it is the task of the historian to assess the credibility of all his sources, in the case of the Norman records few have made a realistic evaluation of their account of William's claim to the throne. The fact that William succeeded in enforcing this claim sometimes leads rather easily to a judgement about its validity, but any such judgement must be made against an assessment of the contemporary scene.

Similarly, any view of the significance of Normandy in English policy during this period needs to be made against contemporary events. The great danger to England at this time was Scandinavia, whence Swein and Cnut had conquered the country within living memory. In a similar way, the decisive outcome of the Battle of Hastings itself has led to a tendency to assume that the Norman army or its leadership were somehow naturally superior. The immense gamble involved in any medieval battle should warn us against such assumptions. If the Normans had been defeated at Hastings, would we consider William as an incompetent general and the Norman troops as poorly trained? In these instances and others, knowledge of the outcome must be separated from consideration of the events themselves in their contemporary setting. Only this will permit a realistic assessment of King Harold and of his rival William of Normandy and so enhance our view of both.[17]

It is as well to remember that true biography is not really possible for any early medieval figure as a result of the paucity of surviving evidence. Nevertheless, in spite of the difficulties and pitfalls outlined above, there does remain enough evidence to permit a fairly detailed account of Harold's career to be compiled. There remain obscure matters and gaps in our knowledge where we can do no more than make the best assumption possible on the evidence which we have. The effort should be made in order to restore to King Harold that which he deserves: a rightful place among the eleventh-century kings of England and a central role in the events of 1066.

CHAPTER ONE

FAMILY ORIGINS

*In the reign of this King Cnut Godwin flourished in the royal palace, having the first place
among the highest nobles in the kingdom. . . .*[1]

The family of Harold Godwineson first came to notice during the final years of the
troubled reign of King Aethelred II 'the Unready' when the Kingdom of England was
facing a grave threat from Viking raids. These had been almost an annual event since
997 and had increased in extent and ferocity each year. Following the latest of these
raids in 1006, when a great fleet 'harried' every shire of Wessex, the raiders were paid
off in the following year with £36,000 of silver, in order to provide a respite for the
overstretched defences.[2]

However, this respite could only be temporary, and so during 1008 an immense fleet
was constructed to defend England against future raids. Larger than any prior to that
time, this fleet was brought to Sandwich in Kent, ready to intercept the Vikings at sea;
among its commanders were two men who would bring to naught all the efforts
involved in its preparation.[3]

The first was Brihtric, brother of one of the most notorious figures in Anglo-Saxon
history – Eadric of Mercia. This Eadric, named *Streona* or 'The Grasper', was a
Shropshire *thegn* who gained royal favour in 1006 by murdering *Ealdorman* Aelfhelm of
York, on King Aethelred's orders. The king also had Aelfhelm's sons blinded at this
time and the removal of these prominent Mercian nobles paved the way for Eadric's
rise to power in the region. He was rewarded with the post of *Ealdorman* of Mercia in
1007 and also received the hand in marriage of Edith, the king's daughter. Eadric was
thus a man who had benefited from royal favour at the expense of other nobles, and his
brother Brihtric probably sought the opportunity to do likewise.[4]

The second fleet commander in 1008 was a Sussex *thegn* called Wulfnoth *Cild*, father
of Earl Godwine and grandfather of the future King Harold. This man was possibly the
same as the Wulfnoth who witnessed four extant diplomas of King Aethelred between
986 and 1005. Wulfnoth is an unusual enough name for this to be possible, and his
position near the bottom of the lists of *ministri* or *thegns* in these diplomas indicates a
relatively minor figure who attended court only infrequently. The reason for
Wulfnoth's presence with the fleet probably relates to his Sussex origins, as this county
often provided ships and men for English fleets. Apart from his part in supplying ships
and seamen, Wulfnoth probably had personal reasons for opposing the Danes as they
had ravaged Sussex in 994, 998 and 1006.[5]

Anglo-Saxon Chronicle E, the entry for 1009.

The Anglo-Saxon Chronicle relates quite clearly what happened to the great fleet in 1009:

It happened at this time. . . that Brihtric, *Ealdorman* Eadric's brother, accused Wulfnoth *Cild* to the king, and he went away and enticed ships to him until he had 20 and then he ravaged everywhere along the south coast, doing all manner of damage. Then the naval force was informed that they (Wulfnoth's party) could easily be surrounded if people were to set about it. Then the aforesaid Brihtric took with him 80 ships,intending to make a big reputation for himself and to capture Wulfnoth alive or dead. When they were on their way thither, such a wind blew against them that no man remembered its like, and did beat and dash to pieces all the ships, and cast them ashore, and at once Wulfnoth came and burnt the ships. When it became known to the other ships, where the king was (at Sandwich), how the others had fared, it was as if everything was in confusion, and the king betook himself home, as did the *ealdormen* and chief counsellors, and deserted the ships thus lightly. And the people who were on the ships took [the ships] back to London, and let the toil of all the nation thus lightly come to naught; and no better than this was the victory which all the English people had expected. When this ship-levy had ended thus, there came at once after Lammas the immense raiding army, which we called Thorkel's army, to Sandwich. . . .[6]

We do not know why Brihtric made accusations against Wulfnoth. Perhaps it was a personal rivalry; perhaps Brihtric resented Wulfnoth's influence with the fleet as an experienced sailor, compared with his own inexperience – a notion ironically borne out when he lost eighty ships in the storm while Wulfnoth's twenty escaped unscathed. John of Worcester claims the accusations were 'unjust'. Whatever caused the dispute, Wulfnoth fled to avoid being taken into custody – the fate of *Ealdorman* Aelfhelm and his sons in 1006 had demonstrated clearly what became of those who crossed King Aethelred and *Ealdorman* Eadric. Wulfnoth was subsequently sentenced to exile, as is confirmed by the loss of his lands at Compton, although these were restored in 1014 to his son, Godwine. As the Chronicle entry cites, the former responded to his expulsion by taking twenty ships and raiding along the south coast, perhaps seizing provisions from his own confiscated lands in Sussex. Brihtric pursued him, eager for glory and rewards to match those of his brother, but instead was caught in the storm and his ships lost.

The loss of a total of 100 ships in this incident meant the English fleet could no longer oppose the Danes at sea and indeed the latter subsequently landed unopposed at Sandwich. This disaster is clearly laid at the door of Brihtric by the chronicler. It was he who caused the initial dissension and, whether by poor seamanship or bad fortune, lost eighty ships of the fleet. Indeed, King Aethelred may have endorsed this view himself as Brihtric disappears from the record in this same year.[7]

The will of Atheling Athelstan, 1014.

Wulfnoth also disappears at this time. It is possible that he raided independently or even joined the Danes, but whatever happened it appears that he was dead by 1014. Although Wulfnoth was exiled and his lands forfeited, his son, Godwine, seems to have remained in England perhaps in an attempt to salvage the family fortune. In this he seems to have done well as, by 25 June 1014, he was a sufficiently valued member of the entourage of *Atheling* Athelstan, the king's eldest son, to feature prominently in his will alongside such important persons as Athelstan's younger brothers and foster mother.[8]

In his will, Athelstan made the following bequest: 'I grant to Godwine, Wulfnoth's son, the estate at Compton which his father possessed'. It was very unusual for a son not to inherit land once held by his father, and Athelstan's statement confirms that Wulfnoth must have been dispossessed of his land. There are a number of Comptons in England, but given Wulfnoth's Sussex origins the one referred to is probably one of the two in that county and most likely that in Westbourne Hundred, still listed as held by Godwine in Domesday Book. This bequest shows that despite Wulfnoth's exile his son had, within five years, established himself among the close followers of the king's eldest son and begun the recovery of his patrimony.[9]

If Godwine was to maintain this recovery of fortune after Athelstan's death in 1014 it would be necessary for him to seek the patronage of another great lord. Fortunately for Godwine such an alternative patron was available in the person of Edmund, the elder of Athelstan's two full brothers. It would appear that Athelstan and Edmund were close. This is supported by the fact that Edmund is named as the second lay beneficiary after the king in his brother's will, receiving both lands and treasures, including a valuable sword which once belonged to King Offa, and acting as executor for some of the bequests. In contrast, Athelstan's younger full brother, Eadwig, receives only a sword.[10]

In addition to this personal closeness, the two brothers also shared a similar political outlook which may have facilitated Godwine's transfer of allegiance. Thus Athelstan and Edmund, the sons of Aethelred's first marriage, had a common interest in ensuring that they were not superceded in the royal succession by the sons of his second marriage. This was a fairly common phenomenon, the sons of Cnut in England and of Louis the Pious in the Carolingian Empire providing the most notable examples. In this context it may be significant that Athelstan's will includes bequests to both of his full brothers, Edmund and Eadwig, but nothing for his half-brothers, Edward and Alfred. Edward, the elder of these, was now reaching maturity and being shown considerable favour by his father. Indeed, the later *Vita Eadwardi* even suggests that the English swore an oath he should succeed his father, although the context it presents for this is unlikely. Therefore Athelstan, and Edmund after him, may have been recruiting supporters for the day when they might have to enforce a claim to the throne against their half-brother Edward.[11]

On the evidence of the bequests in Athelstan's will these supporters included, apart from Godwine himself, Sigeferth, Morcar, and Thurbrand, three leading *thegns* of the

Danelaw. The brothers Sigeferth and Morcar were related to that *Ealdorman* Aelfhelm of York murdered by Eadric *Streona* on Aethelred's orders in 1006, and Thurbrand was a rival of Uhtred, whom Aethelred had chosen to replace Aelfhelm. Thus we can see Athelstan building up supporters among those *thegns* under threat from or out of favour with the king and his party. When Athelstan died in 1014, it seems probable, although largely unproven, that Edmund provided all these disaffected men with an alternative rallying point. Indeed, as regards Sigeferth and Morcar the family's link to Edmund is further confirmed by the latter's eventual marriage to Sigeferth's widow, and his occupation of both of the brothers' lands. The link to Thurbrand is not similarly established and must certainly have been severed by 1016 when Edmund sought support from the former's rival, Uhtred. If we accept Edmund as leader of a party opposed to the policies of Eadric and the king, then we should consider the likelihood that in summer 1014 Godwine, son of Wulfnoth and rival of Eadric, also joined his following. One piece of evidence for this link may be the later naming of Harold Godwineson's second son (that is, Godwine's grandson) as Edmund, probably in honour of the *Atheling* and possibly in memory of his support for Harold's father.[12]

In 1015 King Aethelred reacted to the build-up of this party by having its chief representatives, Sigeferth and Morcar, murdered by Eadric *Streona* and their lands seized. The king also seized Sigeferth's widow, no doubt intending to prevent her marriage to anyone who could then claim the brothers' inheritance through her. The king, it is likely, felt threatened by this rival power base and decided to eliminate it. There exists the alternative possibility that Sigeferth and Morcar were killed for submitting to the Danish raider Cnut in 1013. The Chronicle in that year relates the submission of the *thegns* of the Five Boroughs to Cnut, although Sigeferth and Morcar are not specifically named. (At some time during this period also, Cnut married Aelfgifu of Northampton, daughter of *Ealdorman* Aelfhelm of York, the relative of Sigeferth and Morcar slain in 1006.) Whatever the true version of events, the fact remains that King Aethelred's actions, however motivated, effectively removed two of Edmund's main supporters.[13]

Atheling Edmund's response to this was decisive. He freed Sigeferth's widow, Ealdgyth, from royal custody at Malmesbury and in direct defiance of his father, married her and seized control of the lands of her late husband and his brother. Edmund was now effectively in rebellion against his father and all the men of the Five Boroughs submitted to him. This may have been an attempt by Edmund to force his father to recognize him as heir, or an attempt to seize the throne as his father may already have been suffering from what was to prove a fatal illness, leaving Eadric *Streona* in command of the royal army. In the midst of this crisis, and indeed while the king was lying sick at Cosham, the Danes under Cnut invaded, and the two rival camps in England each raised an army to oppose them. Unfortunately, the two English groups proved unable to put aside their differences and combine against the Danes.

The climate of suspicion between Edmund and Eadric was too great and as a result both armies disbanded. It seems likely that throughout this period Godwine supported Edmund against Eadric and the king.[14]

As King Aethelred's illness became more serious, Eadric's position became perilous for if the king died he would be left unprotected from Edmund's vengeance. In anticipation of this, Eadric attempted to save himself by deserting to Cnut with forty ships of Aethelred's fleet, probably those of Earl Thorkell. This volte-face effectively deprived the West Saxons of leadership, since Aethelred was now lying gravely ill in London, and hence they submitted to Cnut and his army. This left England divided into three contesting zones: Cnut and Eadric controlled Wessex and Western Mercia; Edmund held the Five Boroughs and East Anglia; and the much weakened King Aethelred clung on to London. Cnut may have ravaged Warwickshire at Christmas 1015 because its *thegns* were considering defecting to Edmund. Although Edmund gathered an army in 1015 from 'the north' it is unlikely that this included the Northumbrians, who only appear to have joined him in the following year when he sought *Ealdorman* Uhtred's support. This situation must have posed problems for Godwine, as a West Saxon landowner. However, it is likely that he remained with Edmund, although probably temporarily losing control of his Sussex lands. The alternatives for Godwine were, after all, not very attractive. King Aethelred was a dying man who could offer him little hope, while Cnut was now supported by Eadric *Streona*, Godwine's enemy.[15]

Godwine probably participated in *Atheling* Edmund's joint raid with *Ealdorman* Uhtred of Northumbria against Eadric's lands in West Mercia during 1016. The chance to avenge the loss of his own lands by raiding Eadric's must have been a pleasant prospect. When Cnut responded by attacking York and executing Uhtred, Edmund moved on London to secure the succession, and Godwine probably accompanied him. There Edmund succeeded to the kingship following his father's death on 23 April 1016 and, escaping Cnut's besieging forces, regained control of Wessex, including perhaps Godwine's own lands in Sussex. It was possibly during the many battles between Edmund and Cnut, which took place in the summer and autumn of 1016, that Godwine gained his later reputation for being 'most active in war'. The submission of his enemy Eadric *Streona* to King Edmund in the autumn of that year, although all too temporary as it turned out, must have posed a dilemma for Godwine, which only his loyalty to Edmund could have overcome. At the Battle of Ashingdon soon afterwards, this difficulty was resolved when Eadric *Streona* betrayed King Edmund, who was defeated with the loss of many of his greatest supporters. King Edmund himself escaped the disaster and Godwine, if present, must also have done so. The king was now forced to come to terms with Cnut and divide the kingdom with him. Edmund retained Wessex, where Godwine's lands lay, while Cnut took control of Northumbria and Mercia, including London. This political arrangement ended soon afterwards with King Edmund's death on 30 November 1016, perhaps as a result of wounds received at Ashingdon.[16]

Godwine now found himself bereft of his royal lord and protector and was compelled like the rest of the English nobility to submit to Cnut, Edmund's great rival. This might have been expected to be the end of his career, if not in death at least in disgrace. This was indeed the case for the majority of the late King Aethelred's senior nobles between 1016 and 1020, when Cnut carried out what amounted to a purge of the English nobility. During this period, Cnut removed all of the surviving *ealdormen* appointed by King Aethelred, even including those who had switched allegiance to him during the struggle for the kingdom, most notably Eadric *Streona* of Mercia. In the period 1016–17 *Ealdormen* Uhtred, Northman and Eadric *Streona* were executed, as were the sons of *Ealdormen* Aethelmaer and Aelfheah. In 1020 *Ealdorman* Aethelweard was outlawed, while an *Ealdorman* Godric also disappeared at about this time. Indeed, Eadric *Streona* and Aethelweard were both removed despite retaining their posts initially at Cnut's accession. In fact, only *Ealdorman* Leofwine is known to have survived the purge. In place of these men, Cnut appointed Scandinavians who were either related to him or among his close followers: Earls Erik and Eilaf were Cnut's brothers-in-law; Earl Hakon was a son of Erik; Earl Thorkell may have been Cnut's foster-father; and Earl Hrani was among his followers. The object of this policy was undoubtedly to place in power men the new king felt he could trust and who owed their positions directly to him.[17]

Perhaps surprisingly, Godwine also appears among these favoured Scandinavians, as the *Vita Eadwardi* says, as one of the 'new nobles . . . attached to the king's side', in spite of the lack of any known link between him and Cnut. He is recorded as an earl in the witness list of a diploma of King Cnut dated to 1018. At first sight, it is difficult to explain this sudden acceptance and elevation of Godwine. However, a source composed for Cnut's widow, Queen Emma, perhaps provides the key. There it is stated that Cnut 'loved those whom he had heard to have fought previously for Eadmund faithfully without deceit, and . . . hated those whom he knew to have been deceitful, and to have hesitated between the two sides'. Thus Godwine's steadfast loyalty to Edmund through many vicissitudes may have proved to Cnut that he was a man to be trusted in contrast to the treacherous Eadric, who had been executed in 1017 lest he betray Cnut as he had done Edmund. Indeed the execution of Eadric itself must have eased Godwine's transfer of allegiance.[18]

Nevertheless, it seems likely that Cnut must have required some concrete evidence of Godwine's loyalty and indeed ability, before raising him to the rank of earl by 1018. The occasion for this may have been Cnut's collection of an immense tax during 1018, with which to pay off most of his Scandinavian mercenary troops. The cooperation of English administrators in the collection of such a large tax would have been essential and perhaps Godwine was one such cooperative agent, rewarded for his contribution

Diploma of King Cnut in favour of Lyfing,
Archbishop of Canterbury.

when Cnut appointed him earl over the area of central Wessex. This position had fallen vacant with the death of the previous incumbent, *Ealdorman* Aelfric, at Ashingdon in 1016 and it was an apt appointment given Godwine's lands in nearby Sussex. This office also must have brought with it an increase in his lands in the central Wessex shires of Hampshire and Wiltshire. This promotion was probably intended by Cnut to secure Godwine's loyalty to him personally and at the same time provide him with a trustworthy subordinate to control this area. If so, it was a successful move, and Godwine responded to Cnut's trust by providing him with loyal service thereafter. Indeed, Godwine's first appearance as earl in a diploma of 1018 appears to seal his transfer of allegiance, as he witnesses Cnut's confirmation of a grant made to Bishop Burhwold of Cornwall by his previous lord, King Edmund.[19]

An opportunity to test Godwine's new loyalty soon presented itself. In the autumn of 1019, and again in 1022–3, Cnut returned to Denmark – on the first occasion, to secure that kingdom for himself, and on the second probably to stifle a potential rebellion by the recently exiled Earl Thorkell. According to the author of the *Vita Eadwardi*, on one or perhaps both of these occasions Godwine accompanied him. This source is close to the earl's family and can probably be relied on for his presence on such an expedition, but unfortunately it provides no date. As fitting reward for his services on one or other of these expeditions, Godwine's authority appears to have been extended to the western shires of Wessex also, either in 1020 or 1023, and he was given Cnut's sister-in-law, Gytha, for his wife. The exile of *Ealdorman* Aethelweard on 17 April 1020, probably for fomenting a rebellion in favour of *Atheling* Eadwig, made possible this promotion of Godwine to control all of Wessex. The important marriage to Gytha further tied Godwine to Cnut and drew him into the circle of Scandinavian earls related to the king. Godwine was now brother-in-law of Earl Eilaf of Gloucestershire and *Jarl* Ulf of Denmark, the latter of whom was himself married to Cnut's sister, Estrith.[20]

Later legends in England and Denmark explained the rise of Godwine, Wulfnoth's son, by romantic tales of a farmer's son providing refuge and assistance either to King Aethelred, lost in the forest while hunting, or to the Danish *Jarl* Ulf, lost in the hostile English countryside. As a result, in the former case King Aethelred raised Godwine to an earldom, and in the latter Ulf is said to have given him his sister, Gytha, in marriage and to have advised Cnut to reward him with an earldom. These romantic tales in widely separated traditions add little to our knowledge but reflect a common perception of the spectacular nature of Godwine's rise.[21]

Whatever the background to his rise and whatever its exact dating, by 1023 at the latest Earl Godwine held what was a unique position in Cnut's kingdom. He was an Englishman appointed to one of the highest offices in the land by the Danish king himself, and closely related to him and his Scandinavian followers by marriage. The only other English survivor, *Ealdorman* Leofwine, had originally been appointed by King Aethelred in 994 and was not related to Cnut, as far as is known. In these circumstances Leofwine's survival and appointment to succeed Eadric of Mercia in 1017 are a mystery. It is possible that Cnut's execution of his son, Northman, in the same year was sufficient to ward off any threat of treachery on the part of his father. Earl Godwine was to retain and develop his own unique position amidst occasionally very difficult circumstances until his death in 1053, and his success in doing so shows that Cnut was justified in placing his trust in him and was in turn repaid with loyalty.[22]

Cnut's trust in Godwine is reflected in his swift rise to first place among the lay witnesses to the king's diplomas. This appears to have occurred as a result of Cnut's exile of Earl Thorkell in November 1021 and of the death of Earl Erik around 1023. The dearth of surviving diplomas for Cnut's reign makes it difficult to be sure on the latter point but it seems likely. Although Thorkell and Cnut were subsequently reconciled in 1023, the former never returned to England. Previously, Thorkell had been the Danish king's leading supporter, followed in turn by Erik, but they were now succeeded in this role by Earl Godwine, who heads the lay witnesses of every surviving diploma of Cnut from this point onwards. The brevity of Chronicle entries at this time means that the reason for Thorkell's exile is unrecorded but it may have been another symptom of Cnut's distrust. After all, Thorkell had previously deserted the Danes to serve King Aethelred, only returning to Cnut's allegiance after the former's death. A further augmentation of Godwine's power came probably sometime after 1023, though when exactly is unclear; at this time the little known Earl Sired disappears from the witness lists of Cnut's diplomas and Godwine appears to succeed to his authority over Kent.[23]

After 1023, Earl Godwine solidly maintained his allegiance to King Cnut and even his new family ties in Scandinavia failed to draw him from this. Even when his brothers-in-law, *Jarl* Ulf and Eilaf, rebelled against King Cnut in 1025, joining the Norwegians and Swedes, perhaps in an attempt to place his infant son Hardecnut on the Danish throne, Godwine remained loyal. When Cnut sailed to fight the combined forces of these opponents in 1025 or 1026, at a battle on the Holy River on the borders of Denmark and Sweden, Godwine probably supported Cnut and he may even have provided men for him as the Chronicle refers to Englishmen who fell there.[24]

Although, according to the Chronicle, Cnut appears to have been defeated in this battle, the huge resources of England allowed him to recover and strike back against his enemies. Cnut's letter of 1027 to the English tells of his returning from Rome by way of Denmark, 'to conclude . . . peace . . . with those nations . . . who wished to deprive [him] of the kingdom and of life, but could not since God . . . destroyed their strength'. Cnut struck back at his opponents by executing *Jarl* Ulf around 1026, and then invading Norway in 1028 and expelling King Olaf Haraldsson, assisted by his English wealth. On this occasion, Earl Godwine may again have accompanied him since the Chronicle refers to fifty ships of 'English *thegns*'. It is possible that these were supplied by Godwine, just as his father Wulfnoth had supplied twenty ships for Aethelred's fleet in 1008. However, there exists no early evidence for Godwine's personal presence on either of Cnut's later expeditions, only that of unnamed Englishmen,[25] and it is possible that rather than accompanying Cnut, Godwine instead fulfilled an even more essential role. This was that of Regent of England during Cnut's absence in Scandinavia, the post held by Earl Thorkell before his downfall. The *Vita Eadwardi* perhaps suggests this possibility, with its references to Godwine's 'first place among the nobles of the kingdom' and the fact that 'he throve mightily in the seat of authority'. Godwine had after all replaced Thorkell as Cnut's leading supporter around 1023 and was the obvious man to assume his mantle as regent during Cnut's later absences. However, this cannot be proven as Cnut's regent in England is unfortunately unnamed in his letter of 1027 to the English.[26]

The rewards of Godwine's service whether at home or abroad, were lands and office, and he received both in large measure. Thus he had been made Earl of Wessex, which after 1023 incorporated all England south of the Thames, and he probably gained many of his later lands in connection with this office. Others may have arisen from royal grants – a single diploma of Cnut to Godwine survives granting him land at Polhampton in Hampshire but others have undoubtedly been lost. Whether private grants or related to his office the bulk of Godwine's lands probably came from his great patron Cnut.[27]

Godwine's great debt to Cnut is reflected by the names he gave the children born to him and his Danish wife Gytha during these years. Thus Swein, his eldest son, was probably named after Cnut's father; Harold, his second son and the future king, after either Cnut's grandfather or brother; Tosti, his third son, probably after a famous war captain commemorated on Swedish rune stones who perhaps served Cnut; and lastly Gunnhild, his younger daughter, was probably named after Cnut's own daughter. Gyrth, his fourth son, also had a Danish name, though not apparently connected with Cnut. This left only Leofwine and Wulfnoth, his youngest sons, and Edith and Aelfgyva, his other daughters, with English names. Leofwine was perhaps named after Godwine's surviving English colleague and Wulfnoth was undoubtedly named after his grandfather. The origin of Edith's name is unknown but may have previously occurred in the family.[28]

The most significant aspect of Godwine's career during Cnut's reign, apart from his sudden rise to the summit of power, was his survival there; by the end of the reign, apart from the obscure Earl Hrani, Godwine alone remained from all of Cnut's original appointees. We have seen above that Thorkell was exiled in 1021 and that Eilaf went into rebellion in 1025 or 1026 and appears to have vanished thereafter. Earls Erik, Sired and Leofwine probably died around 1023, as this is the date of their last attestations of royal diplomas, and Earl Hakon died in 1030. This left only Earl Hrani of Herefordshire and Godwine himself.[29]

Cnut's reign was a time for survivors and Godwine was the greatest of these, perhaps as a result of lessons learnt during the upheavals of Aethelred's reign. This instinct for survival was soon to stand Godwine in good stead. Meanwhile, he was foremost among the three great earls of Cnut's later years, each of whom were in charge of large areas of England, the others being Leofric and Siward. The former was the son of the Leofwine retained by Cnut from Aethelred's reign and the latter a Dane of unknown origin. The king relied heavily on the support of these men while he concentrated on ruling his North Sea empire.[30]

This relatively stable period of Godwine's life came to an abrupt end on 12 November 1035 when King Cnut died at Shaftesbury. The situation on his death brought a severe crisis which Godwine was only to survive at considerable cost. The essential elements of this crisis were that Cnut was survived by two sons of different mothers, who became rivals in their attempts to succeed to his empire. Hardecnut, Cnut's son by Emma of Normandy, was at this time ruling in Denmark having been installed there by his father, while Harold 'Harefoot', his son by Aelfgifu of Northampton, was in England probably with his mother's relatives in the Midlands.[31]

At an assembly or *witan* held in Oxford soon after Cnut's death, the English nobles were divided over who to support as his successor. Harold 'Harefoot', Cnut's eldest son, locally based in England and strongly supported by his mother's relatives, was chosen as king by Earl Leofric and the Mercians and by Cnut's Danish mercenary fleet stationed in London. Godwine, along with Archbishop Aethelnoth and the men of Wessex, supported Hardecnut, and is described by the Chronicle as his 'most loyal man'. Cnut may have intended Hardecnut to succeed him in both England and Denmark, although our main evidence for this comes from sources favourable to Queen Emma and Hardecnut. The fact that Cnut's loyal subordinate Godwine supported Hardecnut even when it would perhaps have been easier not to do so perhaps supports this suggestion. Alternatively, Godwine may simply have felt his position would be more secure under Hardecnut who, like his father, had no links in England and would therefore have to depend on him. In contrast, Harold 'Harefoot's' strong family ties in the Midlands would make him less dependent on Godwine.[32]

Whatever the reasons, Godwine gave his support to Queen Emma and her son, and held Wessex on their behalf. In the meantime, Leofric and Siward held Mercia and Northumbria for King Harold 'Harefoot'. This division is reflected in the coinage of the time: coins in Hardecnut's name were struck throughout Wessex from dies produced in Winchester, Emma's base, while coins in Harold's name were struck north of the Thames. Hardecnut was expected to arrive from Denmark in the near future and claim his share of the now effectively divided kingdom. However, this proved impossible as Magnus of Norway, who had recently expelled Danish influence from his country, was now threatening to invade Denmark. Hardecnut, therefore, was forced to remain in Denmark and Godwine consequently found himself out on a limb. From the start he had been unable to oppose Harold's control in the north. Now it seems that he could do nothing but watch helplessly as Harold, probably in 1036, seized much of his father's treasure from Queen Emma at Winchester within Godwine's own earldom.[33]

Thereafter, Harold began to win support south of the Thames as reflected by his taking control of the minting of the coinage there. Earl Godwine was now in danger of losing influence altogether since Hardecnut was still unable to leave Denmark. To save himself he would have to make some form of accommodation with Harold, perhaps on a temporary basis, in the hope that Hardecnut's arrival might restore the situation. This action by Earl Godwine appears to clash with the pattern of his loyalty to Edmund and then Cnut, but the contemporary circumstances were particularly difficult. We should recognize also that Godwine now had a great deal more to lose if he backed the wrong side, and the future prosperity of his large family to consider.[34]

It was probably at this point also that Queen Emma herself, increasingly insecure at Winchester, decided to abandon Hardecnut and seek help from her sons by her previous marriage, to King Aethelred, who were currently in exile on the Continent. This scenario seems more likely than her biographer's suggestion that Harold 'Harefoot' set a trap for his half-brothers, which is a clear attempt to deflect blame away from Emma for what subsequently occurred. As a result of her plea, the *Athelings*

Edward and Alfred crossed to England, partly to support their mother but also it would seem with the intention of rallying support to take the kingdom. This latter possibility seems validated by Alfred's attempt to reach London, in contrast to Edward's more direct attempt to join his mother at Winchester. If this was the case, the brothers were badly misled as to the reception they might expect.[35]

Edward, the elder brother, landed near Southampton but, in the face of what was probably local opposition, he returned to Normandy without reaching his mother in Winchester. The Norman accounts of Edward's invasion speak of a force of '40 ships filled with armed men' which was victorious over 'a great host of English' but which was nevertheless forced to retreat without achieving its aim. The size of the fleet could well be an exaggeration by the Norman sources; John of Worcester, in contrast, mentions only a few ships. In 1042 Hardecnut intended to conquer England with only sixty ships while Cnut had earlier maintained a fleet of forty to defend it. It seems feasible to believe, therefore, that had Edward indeed possessed forty ships he should have been able to achieve more. It seems likely that he had a much smaller force, similar to that of his brother, Alfred, and meeting local resistance, perhaps from the Hampshire *fyrd,* he was forced to abandon the attempt. [36]

Meanwhile, Edward's brother, Alfred, sailing from Wissant, landed at Dover at a time when the Chronicle says 'feeling was veering much towards Harold'. The Chronicle reference to Alfred's intention being to join Queen Emma may be a confused echo of his brother Edward's expedition. Instead, Alfred's route as recorded in the *Encomium Emmae* indicates him moving against Harold's base in London. John of Worcester's suggestion that Alfred wished simply to confer with Harold is possible but seems belied by subsequent events indicating either that he is wrong or that Alfred's reading of events was poor. The author of the *Encomium Emmae* speaks of Alfred being accompanied 'by only a few men of Boulogne' in addition to his own company, implying a small force. This is confirmed by the *Vita Eadwardi*, which speaks of 'a few armed Frenchmen'. These references should warn us against the exaggeration of the Norman role in this event by the later Norman writers William of Jumieges and William of Poitiers. The earlier records suggest instead that the exiled *athelings* probably drew their support from Boulogne, where their sister Godgifu had just married Count Eustace, or possibly from the Vexin, where their nephew was count, rather than from Normandy. Indeed, at this time William of Normandy was having difficulty holding his own duchy and could probably have spared little to assist the *athelings*. What happened to Alfred after his arrival in England was to overshadow Godwine's subsequent career and ultimately that of his son, the future King Harold.[37]

The sources are confused and contradictory but all agree that Alfred's return was opposed by those in power. This is not surprising since everyone except Queen Emma must have viewed his arrival as an unnecessary complication to an already confused situation. Almost all the sources name Godwine as the man who arrested Alfred and dispersed or killed his followers at Guildford and this makes sense as the town lay in his earldom. The author of the *Encomium Emmae* does say that Godwine only detained them under his protection and that King Harold 'Harefoot's' men actually arrested Alfred and slew his followers, but this source was influenced by a desire to blacken Harold's name and can probably be discounted. This action by Godwine was in all probability prompted by the pressing need to curry favour with King Harold, to whose authority he had now decided to submit. This motivation is suggested by the fact that Godwine almost immediately handed over the captive Alfred to Harold. Godwine's previous support for Hardecnut had made the performance of some important service to Harold a necessity to gain his favour. The seizure of *Atheling* Alfred, to whom Godwine had no feelings of loyalty, suited this purpose admirably. A curious statement by John of Worcester, that Godwine was especially devoted to Harold, perhaps arises from this occasion. This had certainly not been the case in late 1035 or early 1036 when Godwine had solidly supported Hardecnut, but it may reflect what he now wished Harold to think.[38]

Captivity and the ruin of his hopes were not all that befell the unfortunate *Atheling* Alfred for he was cruelly blinded at Ely, and he died shortly afterwards. This murder was to be laid at Godwine's door in later years, although the sources closest to the event fail to identify him as the culprit, implicating Harold 'Harefoot' instead. That the crime took place at Ely, an area under Harold's control at this time, seems to reinforce this. Important confirmation is provided by the later Norman writers William of Jumieges and William of Poitiers, who despite other conscious efforts to blacken Godwine's reputation, both clearly identify Harold 'Harefoot' as the man responsible for Alfred's murder. Godwine therefore appears to have been guilty essentially of Alfred's capture and of handing him over to Harold 'Harefoot'. Nevertheless, he was unable to escape being tarnished by association, and that Edward, Alfred's brother, harboured ill-feeling towards Earl Godwine as a result, was later to become clear.[39]

One of the immediate results of these events was to reconcile King Harold 'Harefoot' and Earl Godwine, and in 1037 the former was 'chosen as king everywhere' and became 'full king over all England' while Godwine remained Earl of Wessex. As part of this process, Queen Emma, Hardecnut's mother, was finally driven from Winchester and fled into exile at Bruges in Flanders, whence she tried unsuccessfully to persuade her son Edward to come to her aid once more.[40]

Thus Godwine managed to survive what was a major crisis in his career, though at considerable cost to his reputation. However, within two years of this settlement being achieved and before it could be put to the test of time, another crisis loomed. Hardecnut had somehow temporarily resolved his problems with Magnus of Norway and in 1039 sailed with a fleet to join his mother at Bruges with the intention of invading England to enforce his claim to the throne in the summer of 1040. Before he could do so, his half-brother King Harold 'Harefoot' died on 17 March 1040 leaving Hardecnut to take control of the kingdom unopposed.[41]

Harold 'Harefoot's' death saved Godwine from making a further choice between the two rivals but left him with the problem of excusing his actions in support of Harold to Hardecnut. This would be no easy task, for Hardecnut appears to have been an angry man unlikely to give Godwine a sympathetic hearing, as demonstrated by his first actions: the new king had his half-brother's body dug up from Westminster and thrown into a nearby fen, and then punished the English nobility for supporting Harold by taxing them to pay off his invasion fleet of sixty ships. To make matters worse for Godwine personally, John of Worcester adds that Aelfric, Archbishop of York, and others accused Godwine and Bishop Lyfing of complicity in the murder of *Atheling* Alfred. No other source records this episode but it may reflect rivalries among those who had formerly supported King Harold. Archbishop Aelfric may possibly have crowned Harold in 1036 since at that time Archbishop Aethelnoth of Canterbury had been in Hardecnut's party and is unlikely to have done so. Hardecnut's command that Earl Godwine and Archbishop Aelfric take part in the desecration of Harold's grave may have been a punishment for their earlier actions in support of the latter. In an attempt to regain royal favour, Aelfric may have chosen to accuse Godwine and Lyfing in the hope of saving himself at their expense. He may have accused Lyfing largely in order to acquire his see of Worcester, of which he certainly appears to have gained temporary control in 1040. Indeed, Lyfing's supposed role in Alfred's death is otherwise unknown and since he soon regained his see it appears to have had no basis in fact. In contrast, Godwine's role in Alfred's death was well known and the accusation a serious threat to his position, especially if Hardecnut's subsequent action in recalling his half-brother Edward to England was an indication of strong family ties between the half-brothers.

In response to these charges, Godwine is said to have cleared himself of guilt by swearing on oath that it was not by his counsel that Alfred was blinded but that Harold 'Harefoot' had ordered it. In addition and to make doubly sure, Godwine presented Hardecnut with a magnificent ship as a peace offering. This gift was very expensive and reflected both Godwine's wealth and his maritime connections as Earl of Wessex. As a result of these actions Godwine weathered the storm and assuaged the new king's anger, at least for the present.[42]

The following year, 1041, in obedience to Hardecnut's command, Godwine and the other earls ravaged Worcester and its shire in punishment for the killing, by the townsmen, of two royal *huscarls* who had been involved in collecting the tax to pay off his fleet. Hardecnut's earlier arbitrary actions and now his huge tax demands probably weakened his support in England. As a result, according to a number of sources, he invited *Atheling* Edward, brother of the murdered Alfred, to England to share the rule of the kingdom and perhaps foster English support. This appears to have been a common practice in Scandinavia, designed to avoid dangerous strife between kinsmen.[43]

King Edward. (The Bayeux Tapestry – 11th Century. By special permission of the City of Bayeux)

However, before this arrangement had time to settle, fate again intervened when Hardecnut died on 8 June 1042 at a wedding feast in Lambeth and Edward became king. The *Vita Eadwardi* and John of Worcester speak of Earl Godwine leading the calls for Edward's accession but this looks like special pleading as no alternative candidate existed. The *Vita Eadwardi* also records Godwine's gift of a ship to Edward, apparently as magnificent as that presented to Hardecnut, and this suggests some trepidation on his part about Edward's intentions towards him, no doubt based on fear of further accusations about Alfred's death. Nevertheless, it is likely that Godwine, by virtue of his power and position, played a pivotal role in this kingmaking as he had already done in those of Harold and Hardecnut. Edward was very much a new arrival, with little local support, lacking even the support of a foreign fleet like Hardecnut, and hence dependent for his succession on the support of the three great earls, Godwine, Leofric and Siward. And of this triumvirate Godwine was the most important because he controlled ancestral Wessex, the land south of the Thames, where English kings spent most of their time and where most royal lands lay.[44]

Initally, therefore, King Edward had to rely on his earls, and Godwine in particular, to secure and preserve his throne and he was enough of a realist to recognize this. Thus on 16 November 1043 he used their support to deprive his mother, Queen Emma, of her lands and of her treasure, which would no doubt help to restore a royal treasury diminished by Hardecnut's expenditure on his fleet. This action has been viewed as a demonstration of Edward's disapproval of his mother's lack of support for him in the preceding years, or even for her supposed provocation of Magnus of Norway to invade. However, it seems unlikely that Emma should wish Magnus to invade as she would then lose her influence as Queen Mother, unless she proposed to marry him and so become queen again! It is more likely that Edward's action was prompted by his desire to take a wife, who would usurp Emma's position of influence as Queen Mother, a position she had resolutely sought to maintain through the previous seven years.[45]

Another indication of the growing links between the king and Earl Godwine in this period came in 1044 when Eadsige, Archbishop of Canterbury, resigned his post due to infirmity. The latter sought permission to consecrate Siward, Abbot of Abingdon, as suffragan in his place, not only from King Edward, as was customary, but also from Earl Godwine. We should beware of reading more into this than is necessary. Some have seen it as evidence of Godwine's interference in Church appointments but, with the exception of the events of 1051, there is otherwise little sign of this. Instead, it was probably an attempt to gain strong secular support for the archbishopric in what was likely to be a difficult period. The sickly Archbishop Eadsige would no longer be in a position to personally maintain the Church's rights to its lands and properties. He would therefore require the active assistance and protection of powerful secular authorities including the king and, in the local context, Earl Godwine, providing another example of king and earl acting in concert. In return for his agreement to fulfil this protective role by supporting Siward in the shire courts, Godwine probably received grants of Church lands. These grants, although no doubt judged by Eadsige as a worthwhile investment at this time, would be perceived rather differently by his successor and were to cause considerable difficulties for Godwine. However, such problems lay in the future, and for the moment king and earl worked together.[46]

In return for such backing by the three earls, and by Godwine in particular, King Edward issued rewards of land and authority and many of these naturally fell to Godwine's family. Among these were earldoms for two of Earl Godwine's sons, Swein and Harold, the future king, and for his nephew, Beorn. The seal was set on this alliance between the king and his great earl when King Edward married Earl Godwine's eldest daughter, Edith, on 23 January 1045. In this year Earl Godwine was at the height of his power and influence. He was father-in-law of the king, he was Earl of Wessex, the richest earldom in England, and members of his family held a further three small earldoms.[47]

CHAPTER TWO

HAROLD,
SON OF GODWINE

His eldest – and also his wisest – son Harold, . . . wielded his father's powers even more actively, and walked in his ways.[1]

Earl Godwine had survived this crisis period between 1035 and 1042 and emerged, as a result of his new alliance with King Edward, with enhanced power and influence. As part of this triumph his elder sons, royal brothers-in-law, entered public affairs, including his second son, Harold, the later king, who became Earl of East Anglia. Harold witnessed several royal diplomas, dated to 1044 and 1045, as *nobilis* or *ministri* but he first appears as earl at the head of the Norfolk witnesses in the will of Thurstan, son of Wine, which has been dated to 1044. This apparent confusion may arise from differing dates for the start of the year, but what is clear is that from 1045 onwards, Harold is styled *dux* or earl in all surviving royal diplomas.[2]

There had been no earl in East Anglia since Cnut removed Earl Thorkell in 1021. The main reason for Harold's appointment here and at this time probably lay in the renewed threat from Scandinavia at the start of King Edward's reign. Cnut had needed no earl to defend this region after 1021, when he himself had controlled Denmark and dominated Norway thereby neutralizing any potential Viking threat. In contrast, King Edward was faced with an active threat from Magnus of Norway, who now also controlled Denmark, and he needed a trustworthy subordinate in this area. Indeed, Harold may have led ships from his earldom to Sandwich that same year of 1045 to defend the country against the threat of Magnus of Norway.[3]

The appointment brought Harold, still a young man of around twenty-five years and a younger son at that, into the mainstream of English administration. He was now the local representative of the king addressed in royal writs, with wide powers to act on his behalf in witnessing wills and land transactions, making legal judgements in local courts and leading the men of his earldom in war or emergency. The royal office of earl also carried with it wide lands in Norfolk, Suffolk and Essex. Harold succeeded to the authority and perhaps some of the lands of his predecessors, Ulfkell *Snilling* and Thorkell the Tall in East Anglia, and *Ealdorman* Byrthnoth in Essex. He may have gained lands from Gunnhild, the widow of Earl Thorkell's son Harald, when she was exiled in 1044. By 1066, he was certainly in possession of estates at Colne in Essex previously held by Byrthnoth's wife. These and other grants of lands provided Harold with a local power base and allowed him to dispense patronage and wield influence in the area. He quickly began to receive bequests, including half a mark of gold in the will of Thurstan, son of Wine, and land at Fritton in Norfolk in the will of Lady Wulfgyth, intended to secure his support for the bequeathers' other provisions.[4]

Harold's elevation to an earldom also introduced him to a by now rather exclusive group of royal officials. In 1042 King Edward inherited a kingdom with only three great earls, Godwine, Leofric and Siward, each of whom controlled large areas, namely Wessex, Mercia and Northumbria respectively. These men had wielded power in these regions under four different kings and so had become, in a real sense, representatives of these ancient regions and former kingdoms, and in particular of the political views of their nobility before the king. Harold and his brother, Swein, were inserted into this existing framework as relatives of the king and Earl Godwine. They would need to work hard to consolidate their own authority and forge a similar relationship with the men of their new earldoms and with the king.

A useful short cut in securing local support was to form links with those families already wielding power in the area. It was probably for this reason that Harold appears to have married Edith 'Swan-neck' around this time. She was apparently the heiress to extensive lands and influence in Cambridgeshire, Suffolk and Essex, and these provided a solid support for Harold's new position in the area. Further details concerning Harold's marriage and the lands he gained at this period will be found in Chapters Eight and Four respectively.

As earl, Harold would have divided his time between attendance on the king at the royal court and undertaking duties as the king required in the wider realm, and performing his duties as earl in East Anglia. Typically, Harold would have attended on the king on a regular basis, particularly at the major Christian festivals of Easter and Christmas, where he would witness royal diplomas. He would have performed royal services as required, for example, military service with the fleet as he did in 1049. He would have attended shire courts in East Anglia, and in this role, would have been the recipient of royal writs ordering him, for example, to supervise the transfer of lands between landholders.[5]

During the early years of Harold's new appointment, King Edward began to oust many Danes of Cnut's following, perhaps fearing they might support Magnus of Norway or perhaps simply to replace them with his own supporters. Thus Gunnhild, niece of Cnut and wife of Harald, son of Thorkell the Tall, and her sons were banished in 1044 and the prominent local *thegn* Osgod *Clapa* followed in 1046. This policy was not opposed by Godwine and his fellow earls, since it did not directly affect them and may have removed significant local rivals. Gunnhild's sons were grandsons of Earl Thorkell, and might have sought similar honours in competition with the sons of Godwine and the other earls. Indeed, their father, Harald, who had been slain by order of Magnus of Norway on 13 November 1042, is called earl by John of Worcester. Osgod *Clapa* was a prominent East Anglian magnate and royal servant under Cnut, who also witnessed many of Edward's early diplomas, often in a leading position among the *ministri*. Harold was not responsible for either of these exiles, although he may have gained from their downfall. In 1066 his mother, Gytha, held an estate at Wroxall on the Isle of Wight, which Osgod may once have held. Certainly Earl Harold, as part of his official duties, would have supervised the seizure of the lands and goods of such exiles.[6]

At the same time as removing Cnut's men, King Edward sought to promote men who had entered his service during his period of exile on the Continent. These included the priests Robert of Jumieges (Bishop of London from 1044), Hereman (Bishop of Ramsbury from 1045), and Ulf (Bishop of Dorchester from 1049), as well as laymen like Earl Ralph and the *stallers* Robert Fitzwimarch and Ralph. This policy was one which ultimately proved less acceptable to Godwine but for reasons which have been obscured by the suggestion that Edward pursued a policy of promoting Normans as a sort of fifth column, intended to help secure the later succession of William of Normandy.[7]

If we leave aside the question of the Norman succession, from which this suggestion seems largely to derive, it is in fact far from clear that King Edward had such a policy. For a start, the number of foreigners introduced by Edward was actually fairly small and, secondly, it has still to be proved that many of them were 'Normans' at all. Proven Normans represent only three out of Edward's seven foreign bishops, and none of Edward's four or five foreign nobles. In addition, the Frenchmen of the Herefordshire castles, Osbern 'Pentecost', and Hugh and Richard Fitzscrob, would appear, as followers of Earl Ralph, much more likely to have come from the latter's native county of the Vexin than Normandy proper.

A further factor in undermining the theory of a 'Norman' fifth column arises from the location of the landholdings provided to them by King Edward. The strategic significance of Earl Ralph's lands in Hereford and the East Midlands, and the lands provided for the Bretons Ralph and Robert in Lincolnshire and East Anglia can hardly be sustained in terms of securing a Norman invasion or landing. It would surely have been more important to have such potential infiltrators based in Kent, Sussex or Hampshire where any Norman invasion would be likely to attempt to land, and indeed where such an invasion eventually occurred. Although the Norman Robert of Jumieges eventually succeeded to the archbishopric of Canterbury, the Norman William held the bishopric of London, the Norman priest Osbern held the church at Bosham, and the Norman Abbey of Fecamp received land at Steyning in Sussex none of these were warriors with their own military followings. They could hardly be expected to provide armed support for any Norman landing or occupation. The main role of all these Frenchmen in the relations between the king and Earl Godwine was to be that of potential and actual rivals for power and influence in England rather than as a 'Norman' fifth column. In the absence of a 'Norman' policy on the part of the king, the situation, for the moment, appeared very favourable for Harold and his family, but within a year a shadow was to fall over their good fortune.[8]

In 1046 Harold's elder brother, Earl Swein, was raiding in South Wales in alliance with Gruffydd of North Wales, probably in order to prevent Welsh raids on Herefordshire, which was part of his earldom. This successful raid was part of his normal duties as an earl on the Welsh border and even the alliance with Gruffydd was just an example of the customary policy of playing the Welsh princes off against each other. However, what Swein did on on the way home with his victorious forces was beyond the pale. As the Chronicle relates, 'he ordered the abbess of Leominster to be brought to him and kept her as long as it suited him'. John of Worcester names the lady concerned as Edith, and states that Swein actually wished to marry her. This suggests that her abduction may not have resulted from a simple infatuation but perhaps had a deeper cause. It should be noted that abbesses were commonly noblewomen and Swein may, like Harold, have been seeking an alliance or lands by his action but if so he chose the wrong lady. Even though he was the eldest son of Godwine, and whatever his intentions, Swein's behaviour could not be tolerated. Eventually, almost a year later, he was persuaded to release the woman, possibly under threat of excommunication. Thereafter he went into exile, initially to Bruges in Flanders over the winter, and then to Denmark the following summer (1048). Even Earl Godwine could not save his son from this fate, despite his power and influence, though he may have delayed it for a year and tempered its severity.[9]

This episode is important for several reasons. First, it provided Earl Harold with an unexpected extension to his power, as he and his cousin, Beorn, were apparently each given a share of Swein's forfeited earldom. This arrangement was perhaps intended to mollify Godwine for the expulsion of his eldest son. More importantly, it revealed not only that there were limits to Godwine's apparently wide powers, but also that his own wishes could be overruled by the consensus of opinion among the English nobility. This requirement for consensus was to have a bearing on subsequent events in the careers of both Godwine and his son Harold, and would also reveal important differences between them. Meantime, Swein's outrage also set in motion the erosion of Godwine's personal alliance with King Edward. Godwine had undoubtedly supported his eldest son in spite of his behaviour, and this interference with the royal enforcement of justice must have annoyed the king. It was to be the first of a number of incidents which would lead to an estrangement between the two men, and over them all would gradually loom the spectre of Edward's childless marriage to Edith.[10]

Another dispute arose in 1047, when Swein Ulfson of Denmark, Godwine's nephew, sent ambassadors to England to seek help to defend his kingdom against Magnus of Norway. Godwine advised King Edward to provide his nephew with fifty ships, but he was opposed by Earl Leofric of Mercia and others, and the king decided in the end to refuse him help. This might appear unusual since Edward had an interest in distracting Magnus from plans for an invasion of England, but he may have feared retaliation if Swein was defeated. Indeed, perhaps as a result of Edward's failure to assist

Harold at Bosham Church in Sussex. (The Bayeux Tapestry – 11th Century. By special permission of the City of Bayeux)

him, Swein of Denmark swiftly lost his kingdom to Magnus of Norway. This failure to help his nephew may have rankled with Godwine, coming as it did after the expulsion of his own son Swein, and probably further undermined his relationship with Edward. Indeed Godwine may have decided to aid his nephew on his own account since his exiled son subsequently journeyed to Denmark in 1048 and may have taken a force of ships with him. Certainly Swein Godwineson would return from his exile in Denmark with seven or eight ships in 1049, which suggests that he may have been sent with a military force to aid his Danish cousin but, if so, his assistance was not appreciated.[11]

Meanwhile, Godwine's second son, Earl Harold, was busy defending his own earldom and was probably among those who sailed with the English fleet from Sandwich against some German raiders in 1048. He is not specifically mentioned on this occasion but he is known to have commanded a ship in the fleet the following year. The fact that the German pirates were able to ravage Essex unopposed, seizing booty and prisoners, suggests the earl's absence, probably with the fleet. The policy of Baldwin V of Flanders, to harbour such pirates and English exiles and supply them with vessels and crews with which to raid the English coast, had become a significant problem for Edward. He had been freed from the Scandinavian threat by the recent death of King Magnus in 1047 and the subsequent outbreak of war between Swein of Denmark and Harald of Norway, and he was now in a position to act against Baldwin. His opportunity came in 1049 when the German Emperor Henry III sought the aid of an English fleet against Baldwin, who was in rebellion against him, and Edward duly brought the English fleet to Sandwich, including a ship or ships commanded by Harold, and remained there until Baldwin accepted terms from the Emperor.[12]

It was in the midst of this campaign that Godwine's prodigal son Swein returned from Denmark, where he had apparently managed to outstay his welcome having 'ruined himself with the Danes'. He came seeking to make peace with Edward in return for the restoration of his lands and earldom, only to be opposed by his own brother, Harold, and cousin, Beorn. They refused to surrender anything that the king had granted to them, probably including their shares of Swein's former earldom. Here we see Harold for the first time acting independently of his father. Godwine probably wanted his eldest son reinstated, judging by his past and future actions, but Harold opposed his father's wishes and those of his brother, in order to safeguard his own position. Under these circumstances of division within the Godwine family, King Edward felt safe in rejecting Swein's overtures. He gave him only four days' safe conduct in which to leave England again, and Swein, temporarily blocked, withdrew to his ships at Bosham.[13]

At this point, King Edward received news of enemy shipping movements and ordered Godwine to move westward into the Channel to counter this threat. Godwine accordingly sailed with forty-two ships, including one commanded by Earl Beorn and others commanded by Earl Harold and his younger brother, Tosti, to Pevensey, where they became weather-bound. Soon afterwards Swein arrived there; perhaps his ships were weather-bound at nearby Bosham, but it seems more likely that he had refused to leave the country without a last attempt at reinstatement. He persuaded his cousin, Beorn, to change his mind and accompany him to intercede with the king on his behalf. They rode together to Bosham, presumably in order to travel thence by sea to King Edward at Sandwich. However, once there Swein had Beorn, who had taken only three men with him, bound and taken aboard his ship. He then sailed away, perhaps initially intending to use Beorn as a hostage in further negotiations. Instead, for some unknown reason, Swein killed his captive and defenceless cousin at Dartmouth and buried him in an unmarked grave. Perhaps Beorn had refused to speak to the king on Swein's behalf or to return him his lands – this would hardly be surprising after Swein's ill-treatment of him.[14]

Again, Swein had breached the bounds of acceptable behaviour, and this heinous betrayal and killing of a kinsman outraged both the king and the men of the fleet. They declared Swein *nithing* in the Viking manner, indicating someone utterly and irreparably disgraced. Swein's own sailors perhaps felt the same, as immediately afterwards six of his eight ships deserted him, forcing him to flee to Bruges. He could hardly return to Denmark after his behaviour there the previous summer. Meanwhile, Harold recovered the body of his murdered cousin and had it buried at Winchester beside his uncle, Cnut. Once again Swein's erratic behaviour, in sharp contrast to that of his brother, Harold, had brought him to exile in Flanders and damaged the prestige of his family. Godwine's somewhat ambivalent attitude during this affair further weakened his position with King Edward. He appeared to sympathize with his son, but as opinion was already against him he was unable to stand by him openly either. On the other hand, Harold probably emerged with his personal relationship to the king enhanced because of his opposition to his brother's return. Even if this was initially done for the selfish motive of retaining his share of Swein's forfeited earldom, it had proved amply justified by Swein's subsequent conduct.[15]

Nevertheless, Godwine had still not given up on his eldest son and over the winter he worked on King Edward, attempting to persuade him to permit once more the return of his beloved Swein. He must have exerted considerable pressure to achieve this and Edward cannot have been happy about the situation. Harold himself was perhaps more inclined to accept the proposal because the redistribution of the deceased Beorn's earldom meant that he would not now lose by Swein's return. Similarly, Edward's nephew Ralph, who had gained Herefordshire from Swein's fall, could also be accommodated with some of Beorn's former earldom. In return, Swein must also have made concessions, perhaps undertaking to go on a pilgrimage to Jerusalem in penance for his crime, which he did in 1052. Whatever the specific arrangements, Swein's malign influence returned to England in 1050 under the escort of Ealdred, Bishop of Worcester, who was returning from a synod in Rome. Swein's restoration is confirmed by his appearance among the witnesses to a royal diploma, confirming Papal dispensation for the removal of Bishop Leofric's see to Exeter and dated 1050. It undoubtedly increased the tension in England as Swein and Ralph uneasily disputed control over the lands of the earldom of Hereford, which had just been transferred between them. This would probably be the source of the accusations made by Swein in 1051 against the Frenchmen of the castle. The confusion and scope for contention resulting from Swein's exile, Ralph's appointment, and Swein's reinstatement must have been considerable.[16]

King Edward was by now becoming increasingly stifled in the claustrophobic grip of Earl Godwine. Unlike previous English kings, Edward did not have full control over Wessex but had to share it with Godwine, who controlled much of it through his extensive landholdings there. Despite minor triumphs of independent action, such as

Diploma of King Edward in favour of Leofric, Bishop of Exeter, 1050.

his refusal to aid Swein of Denmark in 1047 and the expulsions of Earl Swein in 1047 and 1049, Edward was still very much under Godwine's tutelage and must increasingly have resented this. Under Godwine's influence Edward had twice been compelled to restore Earl Swein, a criminal who had been declared *nithing* by the fleet and who was described by a writer, commissioned by his own sister, Queen Edith, as a 'gulping monster'.[17]

In addition to these conflicts and pressures, it must, by this time, have been becoming clear to Edward that he and Queen Edith would have no heir, probably because the queen was barren. It is true, but unlikely, that Edward might have chosen to be celibate, the most plausible reason being that he wanted to prevent a grandson of Godwine succeeding to the throne thereby permanently securing the latter's influence. Although later monastic writers were naturally only too happy to encourage the idea of celibacy as evidence of Edward's sainthood, this appears to be refuted by Bishop Leofric's composition of a benediction for a childless king, undoubtedly Edward himself. Whatever the details of the situation, Queen Edith could not provide an heir and as a result she appeared to the king increasingly as little more than a symbol of her father's domination. Certainly from 1046 onwards she had been missing from among the witnesses to royal diplomas, perhaps indicating some disfavour. King Edward now needed an heir to secure the kingdom and this effectively meant divorcing Edith in order to remarry. However, there was a major obstacle to this – Earl Godwine was quite unlikely to permit such an action which would undermine his influence over the king. At this point, therefore, Edward was not in control of his own destiny and was surely seeking a way out. He began by disbanding the mercenary fleet in 1050, which the Godwine family had been prominent in leading, either to deprive them of a source of support in the forthcoming struggle or, more probably, to boost his own popularity by abolishing the burdensome tax associated with it. This was the background to the great crisis of 1051, when Edward attempted both to secure the succession and to shake free of Godwine's control, the two problems being elaborately intertwined.[18]

Edward's frustrations concerning Godwine's influence were no doubt shared by his intimates, including Robert of Jumieges, who had been brought by Edward from Normandy and promoted to the bishopric of London. No doubt he loyally shared his royal master's disapproval of Swein's conduct and Earl Godwine's support for him, and of the earl's power and influence generally, but soon he was to add to this a more personal grudge against him.[19]

On the death of Archbishop Eadsige of Canterbury on 29 October 1050, the monks of Christ Church sought to elect one of their own number named Aethelric to succeed him. This Aethelric was a kinsman of Earl Godwine and the monks quite naturally appealed to him to support their cause. Indeed, Godwine had possibly been supporting Christ Church in its temporal business since 1044 when Archbishop Eadsige became too infirm to do this himself. The earl spoke to the king on Aethelric's

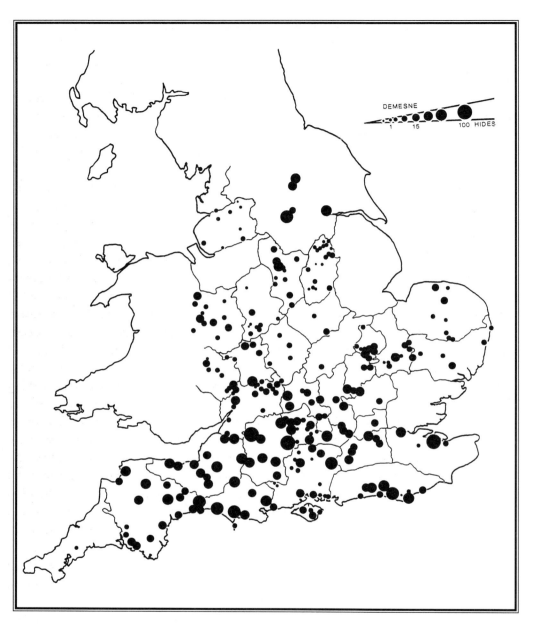

The lands of King Edward, 1066.

behalf, but given the current tensions this probably only made matters worse. Edward had regularly appointed bishops during his reign and had not permitted any free elections, and he was not about to do so as a favour to Godwine. Thus, as the *Vita Eadwardi* states, 'the earl suffered a defeat in pressing his request'. Instead, Edward appointed his favourite, Robert of Jumièges, to the archbishopric at a council held on 1 March 1051, and selected Spearhafoc, Abbot of Abingdon, to replace the latter as Bishop of London. This significant victory over Godwine probably whetted Edward's appetite for further action against him, and his new archbishop was soon to have his own reasons to support such action.[20]

That same Lent, Archbishop Robert left for Rome to receive his pallium from the Pope. He returned apparently imbued with the fire of reform currently burning in Rome, and was installed on 29 June 1051. Following his election in 1049, Pope Leo IX had issued a series of canons against simony and dealt ruthlessly with any clergy accused of this sin. In 1050 at Vercelli Bishop Ulf of Dorchester, another of Edward's appointees, had almost been deposed by Leo on suspicion of this sin. Robert was undoubtedly impressed by this display of the power of the Church, as were many at the time, and at once he seems to have set out on what he probably saw as a personal mission: to reform the English Church, and perhaps enhance his own power and influence in the process. He began by refusing to consecrate Spearhafoc as his successor in the bishopric of London because 'the Pope had forbidden him', probably for the sin of simony. Indeed, this man was Edward's royal goldsmith and may have purchased the position, something the Pope could only have learnt from Robert himself. This action was in direct defiance of the king and in spite of Edward allowing Spearhafoc to occupy the bishopric throughout that summer and autumn. Robert's stance reveals not only his new found zeal for reform, but also a certain amount of arrogance in opposing his mentor, the king himself. It also shows that he was not acting purely as a Norman infiltrator out to harm Godwine and his family. In this situation, Robert was not purposefully showing allegiance to Edward or Godwine, but was following his own agenda. The categorization of all interests as either pro-Norman or Godwinist at this time is not helpful. Men had their own interests, some but not all of which may have coincided with what might be interpreted as pro-Norman or Godwinist. There is no real evidence to suggest that Spearhafoc was associated with Godwine rather than the king, and Robert's action in blocking his promotion was in defiance of the king rather than Godwine.[21]

The new archbishop soon applied a similar rigorous scrutiny to the property of his see and discovered that Earl Godwine had invaded some of the lands of the archbishopric and was keeping them for his own use. It is possible that the estates in question were part of those granted to Godwine by Archbishop Eadsige in return for his assistance in secular affairs during the latter's period of infirmity but it is suspicious that the archbishop's claim is not denied by the author of the *Vita Eadwardi*, a source close to the earl. Robert immediately attempted to recover these lands in the shire courts but met with little success against Godwine's entrenched power. He therefore started a whispering campaign with King Edward, reminding him of Godwine's involvement in the death of his brother, Alfred. This accusation was a particularly sensitive issue with both Edward and Godwine, one which had never really been resolved. King Edward and Archbishop Robert both had their reasons to seek Godwine's downfall as tensions became potentially explosive during the summer of 1051. In need of an heir, Edward contemplated the removal of his wife and her father's possible reaction; Archbishop Robert disputed control of lands with Godwine; and Swein and Ralph contested the control of lands and men in Hereford. It only required a spark to ignite a major crisis between them.[22]

The spark was provided by the visit to England of Edward's former brother-in-law, Count Eustace of Boulogne. Chronicle E, associated with Canterbury and therefore closest to the scene, provides the fullest account of the events which followed. According to its account, Eustace appears to have arrived in England soon after the return of Archbishop Robert to Canterbury, possibly in July 1051. He had talks with his kinsman King Edward and then on his way home was involved in an incident with the citizens of Dover, in Earl Godwine's earldom, in which a number of men were killed. Chronicle D, more distant from the scene, records the incident as having happened on Eustace's initial landing at Dover, and lacks detail. Chronicle C fails to record the event at all despite its obvious potential for showing Godwine in a damaging light. This is an example of the danger of accepting the theory of any general political bias in the text of the various Chronicles. Chronicle C, supposedly anti-Godwine, misses this opportunity to condemn Godwine unless, of course, he was indeed innocent and there were no points to score. The local source, Chronicle E, should probably be preferred and it points to Edward putting Eustace up to the attack, though the latter may have been only too willing to participate. The fact that Eustace and his men put their armour on before entering Dover indicates preparedness for trouble, probably because they planned to cause it. In order to banish Godwine, Edward needed a very good cause if he was to ensure the backing in England necessary to do so effectively. It would seem that he planned this incident with his former brother-in-law hoping, in the charged atmosphere of the time, to provoke Godwine into a reaction which he could exploit. This seems to fit the outline of events better than theories that it was part of an attempt at securing a planned Norman succession. It has been demonstrated that Eustace probably had an interest in securing Edward's support against both William of Normandy and Baldwin of Flanders, who were on the point of concluding a marriage alliance which would directly threaten him. In contrast, he had little interest in helping Edward offer his crown to William of Normandy, as this would result in the possibility of three major powers being ranged against him. Indeed, the proposed alliance between Normandy and Flanders could also be seen as a threat to England itself to be opposed by stronger links with Eustace.[23]

Anglo-Saxon Chronicle E, part of the entry for 1051.

If this interpretation is correct then the plan worked perfectly. Edward was able to feign anger at the conduct of the townsmen of Dover and their treatment of his relative and ally, and consequently to send for Godwine and order him to ravage the town in retaliation. This was too much for the powerful earl, who had personal memories of the ravaging of Worcester by Hardecnut in 1041, and he refused to inflict the same treatment on the people of his own earldom especially when they appeared to have right on their side. Edward therefore summoned a meeting of the royal council to Gloucester on 8 September to deal with the earl. A showdown was now inevitable, as both parties were only too well aware, and they made their preparations.[24]

Until now Godwine had probably considered that he had maintained his position well, in spite of increased tension with the king and a number of set-backs at his hands. Now he appreciated that things were more serious and his own position under threat as Edward resurrected the old accusation of Godwine's complicity in the murder of his brother Alfred. He decided to call out the forces of his earldom to provide him with some leverage at the council meeting, and his loyal sons, Earls Swein and Harold, rallied to his aid by doing likewise. He may also have made arrangements for the marriage of his son Tosti to Judith, sister of Count Baldwin V of Flanders. The wedding is said to have been celebrated just prior to Godwine's exile, probably about this time. This marriage would certainly provide the family with a safe refuge should they require it, but may also have been intended to balance Edward's alliance with Eustace. On the other hand, it may already have been planned, ironically as it would turn out, as part of an attempt to stop Baldwin giving refuge to other English exiles. If so, then the plans for the marriage may have contributed to the crisis by offending Eustace of Boulogne, the prime mover of the events at Dover, who had no wish to see a *rapprochement* between England and Flanders.[25]

Meanwhile, Edward set about rallying his own supporters. These would no doubt have included his loyal followers like Archbishop Robert and other clerics, but more important in subsequent events were the laymen with military followings. These included his relatives Earl Ralph and possibly Count Eustace, who was apparently still in the country, and perhaps other more minor figures including the Herefordshire Frenchmen. However, Edward's most vital supporters were the other great earls Leofric and Siward, who alone could provide the necessary counterweight to Godwine. He probably attempted to win them over by complaints of Godwine's rebellion and by offers of land and offices, or they themselves may have considered that Godwine had now gone too far.[26]

On 1 September, Edward was resident at Gloucester, awaiting the council called for 8 September, when he was surprised by the arrival of Godwine and his sons at nearby Beverstone, a week early and supported by an armed force. Thus Godwine gained the initiative from the king, though briefly in the event. He demanded at least the opportunity to refute the charges being made against him, including complicity in

Alfred's murder, or alternatively the surrender of Count Eustace and the Frenchmen of Herefordshire for trial for offences allegedly committed by them. Godwine undoubtedly hoped his show of force would intimidate Edward, caught unprepared as he was, and bring about his capitulation. This was a grave mistake. It merely made Edward more determined than ever to deal with him once and for all. He summoned armed assistance from his own supporters, particularly the northern earls, while stalling Godwine and his sons. In his summons to the other earls, Edward portrayed Godwine's action as that of a rebel against his lawful king. He highlighted those aspects of events which reflected this, namely Godwine's arrival with an armed force and his demands of the king. Indeed, Chronicle E states that it was claimed that the Godwine family 'meant to come to betray the king'.[27]

This tactic proved effective with the northern earls, who had initially brought south only small retinues of followers. On learning of Godwine's virtually open rebellion and the apparently imminent danger to the king, they called out the full armed forces of their earldoms and prepared to oppose Godwine by force. Godwine's bluff had been called. Edward had not been intimidated and Godwine could only gain his ends by giving battle. Civil war loomed large, and hotheads on both sides were advocating it, but fortunately wiser counsels prevailed.[28]

This is a notable aspect of the whole crisis of the years 1051 and 1052 which is worth comment. Neither party involved, no matter how inflamed tempers became, was prepared to resort to open warfare. Thus when Godwine held the initiative at Beverstone on 1 September, he did not attack the king, despite Edward's rejection of his demands. Similarly, when reinforced by the northern earls, Edward did not crush Godwine by force. This same attitude was to be reflected during the rest of the crisis and it does credit to those involved on both sides. (It probably arose from the nightmare situation towards the end of Aethelred's reign and immediately thereafter, when opposing forces of Englishmen clashed in support of rival kings, a period which Edward, Godwine and Leofric had all witnessed at first hand.)

Since neither side was willing to resort to force, negotiations got underway and it was agreed to exchange hostages and to reconvene at London at the equinox on 21 September. The hostages given at this stage for Godwine's side were probably his own youngest son, Wulfnoth, and Swein's son, Hakon. It is perhaps odd that no mention is made of a hostage for Harold, as might be expected. It seems unlikely that Harold had no sons who might fulfil this role as he was now about thirty years old and had been married since 1044 or 1045. In 1066 he had a total of seven children, three of whom were sons old enough to take part in raids against England. This suggests strongly that at least one of his children, and probably a son, had been born before 1051. If this was the case, it would appear natural for Harold's son also to be taken as a hostage, but the sources which record details of the hostages at this time mention only two. They may omit Harold's son in error but it seems possible that Harold was not required to provide a hostage. King Edward perhaps did not consider him to be untrustworthy in the way that his father and elder brother were. Nothing is said of any hostages given by the king's side, which probably reflects the superiority of his position at this stage, or alternatively they may have been returned in 1052 when Godwine was restored.[29]

On 21 September at London, the opposing sides faced each other again with their armed forces in support. The delay had worked to Edward's advantage and against Godwine. The northern earls, who now accepted that Godwine had gone too far by his armed threat to the king, had since had time to gather larger forces from their earldoms. On the other hand, Godwine's forces had begun to dwindle; although many were prepared to support their earl, as at Gloucester, they were not prepared to oppose their rightful king by force. Indeed, the king may have summoned all royal *thegns* holding land directly of the king to join the royal army and so suborned many of those commended to the Godwine family but holding of the king. Perhaps this is the sense of the curious statement in Chronicle E that 'the king asked for all those *thegns* that the earls had had, and they were all handed over to him'. Desertions gradually sapped Godwine's strength and, in particular, the *thegns* of his son Harold transferred their allegiance to the king. This is perhaps not surprising since Earl Harold had only had some seven years to foster the loyalty of East Anglia, unlike his father's thirty or more in Wessex, and the king's forces north of the Thames lay directly across the road from the homes of Harold's men.[30]

His confidence boosted by knowledge of Godwine's difficulties, Edward now declared Swein an outlaw, without even waiting for the discussions to start. This precipitate action clearly confirms Edward's reluctance to permit his return in 1050. He then commanded Godwine and Harold to appear before the council to answer the charges against them. Godwine now feared for his safety and attempted to obtain additional guarantees of safe conduct with hostages, before coming to the council to clear himself. However, these guarantees were refused as Edward became even more adamant that Godwine must be dealt with. Godwine was now in an impossible position, unable to risk meeting the angry king and unable, with his outnumbered forces, to fight to retain his earldom, even if he had been able to persuade his men to do so. He was beaten and began to make preparations for inevitable exile.[31]

Edward now had Godwine where he wanted him and pushed his advantage, declaring him an outlaw and all his sons with him, around the beginning of October. This message was probably conveyed to Godwine by Bishop Stigand of Winchester, who appears to have acted as an intermediary in these negotiations. He was skilled in diplomacy and trusted by both sides and was to play a similar role in 1052. As a royal bishop he was one of King Edward's servants, and as current Bishop of Winchester and previously Bishop of East Anglia he would be well known to Godwine and Harold. Edward may even have granted the Godwine family five days' safe conduct to leave the country, in order to encourage their flight. The considerable organization involved in the exile of the family is a possible confirmation of this.[32]

Godwine, his wife Gytha and his sons Swein, Tosti and Gyrth all boarded ship at their estate of Bosham in Sussex, taking with them a great hoard of treasure, and crossed to Flanders. They were assured a friendly reception, not just as another group of English refugees like many before, but as a result of Tosti's recent marriage to Count Baldwin's sister, Judith. The store of treasure they had taken would not only provide for their own financial needs, but more importantly would pay for Flemish mercenaries to support an attempt to return to England.[33]

Meanwhile, Godwine's other sons, Harold and Leofwine, went west to Bristol, avoiding interception by the forces of Bishop Ealdred of Worcester. There they took a ship, initially prepared by Swein for his own anticipated exile, and sailed from the river Avon for Ireland. The likely purpose of Harold's journey there was also to recruit mercenaries, this time Norsemen from Dublin, to support an attempt by his family to return to power in England. After a stormy voyage, during which they lost a large number of men, the brothers reached Ireland. There they were received by Diarmait Mac Mael-Na-Mbo King of Leinster, who currently dominated the Viking city of Dublin and was to take possession of it directly in 1052. Here Harold's first efforts at diplomacy were to prove successful. King Diarmait was to provide Harold with aid and treat him well enough for his sons subsequently to seek refuge at his court in the period after Hastings. It was possibly on this occasion that Harold collected the holy relic, the mantle of St Brigit of Kildare, which his sister Gunnhild later donated to St Donation's in Bruges. It was probably also during his Irish sojourn that Harold had an opportunity to review the events of autumn 1051 that had led to the expulsion of his family from England and to learn important lessons that would benefit him in the future. He had seen that it was foolish for an earl, no matter how powerful, to directly challenge the king, that it was important to ensure the loyalty of one's own followers, that the English nobility had a strong aversion to the risk of civil war, and that it was vital to consider the reactions of the other earls to any action. He realized that the ability to negotiate and compromise were essential skills for any great man.[34]

In England King Edward's triumph seemed complete with the family of Godwine exiled. It was a remarkable turn of events, as emphasized by Chronicle D, which states 'it would have seemed remarkable to everyone in England if anybody had told them that it could happen'. Edward was now free to deal out the spoils among his supporters. He probably retained most of Wessex for himself. He rewarded Archbishop Robert by finally expelling Spearhafoc from London in favour of William, a Norman priest. In return for Earl Leofric's support, his son, Aelfgar, received most of Harold's earldom. In return for his support, Earl Siward probably received Huntingdonshire and Cambridgeshire from Harold's earldom. Odda of Deerhurst, a kinsman of Edward, was given an earldom in the south-west with lands taken from Godwine and Swein. Earl Ralph, Edward's nephew, was re-established in his possession of Herefordshire, and other shires taken from Swein. The Frenchmen of Herefordshire were rewarded with the manors of Burghill and Brinsop in Herefordshire worth some £28. The suggestion that these changes were designed to secure or facilitate a Norman succession seems unlikely given the location of the grants made by Edward, which were all away from any direct Norman invasion routes. The list of those rewarded as a result of King Edward's triumph certainly included a number of Frenchmen though not necessarily Normans, and they were not shown any particular favour, compared, for example, to the Englishmen Siward, Aelfgar and Odda.[35]

Freed from Godwine's influence at last, King Edward now turned his attention to one of the main reasons for disposing of him. He repudiated Queen Edith and deprived her of all she owned, placing her in the keeping of the Abbess of Wilton. Then Edward and Archbishop Robert made arrangements for separation and divorce, since their primary concern was to provide Edward with an heir of his own, rather than to secure the succession of William of Normandy. The author of the *Vita Eadwardi* placed responsibility for Edith's expulsion from court on Robert, Archbishop of Canterbury. The archbishop, as head of the English Church, would naturally have an important role to play in any royal divorce. The need for his support was a powerful reason for the king, finally, to concede the bishopric of London to Robert's choice, William, and sacrifice his own nominee, Spearhafoc. It should be recalled here that the *Vita Eadwardi* was written, in part, to celebrate the marriage of Edith and Edward. The author could not therefore portray the king as having himself contemplated a divorce and hence we have the story of the honourable pretext of Edith being sent to Wilton only for her own safety. This circumstance also explains the *Vita Eadwardi's* hostility to Archbishop Robert, since Edith could hardly have liked someone who had participated in an attempt to deprive her of her royal status. In both real life and as recorded in the *Vita Eadwardi* Robert of Jumieges was to fulfil the role of scapegoat for Edward – not only in this attempted divorce but also in the whole episode of the exile of Godwine – when it was in fact the king who had initiated both of these processes himself.[36]

CHAPTER THREE

EXILE AND RETURN

And forthwith Earl Harold came from Ireland with his ships to the mouth of the Severn near the boundary of Somerset and Devon. . . .[1]

Chronicle D states that it was during the exile of the Godwine family late in 1051 that William of Normandy visited King Edward, though his purpose in doing so is not recorded. This visit has been linked, although not by the Chronicle itself, to later Norman accounts of William's claim to the English throne, and it is regarded as the likely occasion when King Edward promised the throne to William. However, a number of factors suggest that this episode may be a later interpolation in the Chronicle, made after the events of 1066. In the first place, William Douglas, the foremost authority on William of Normandy, considers such a visit extremely unlikely given the latter's preoccupations in Normandy at the time. More importantly, the Norman writers William of Jumieges and William of Poitiers fail to record any such visit, in spite of the fact that it could obviously have been employed to reinforce William's claim to the throne. It seems likely therefore that this visit did not in fact occur, and that the Chronicle record here has been adjusted at a later date.[2]

In the absense of any actual visit to England by the duke, the Norman accounts of King Edward's designation of William as his heir stand alone as evidence in placing this event during this same period of eclipse for the Godwine family. A number of post–Conquest English sources relate a similar story, but these all derive from the same original Norman accounts. In the earliest of these, William of Jumieges states that Edward sent Robert, Archbishop of Canterbury, to William to nominate him as heir to his kingdom. This basic outline is enlarged upon by William of Poitiers, who states that this offer was made to William in gratitude for the refuge given to Edward in his early years and came with the assent of the English nobility, specifically earls Godwine, Leofric and Siward, and 'Archbishop' Stigand of Canterbury. William of Poitiers adds that Edward sent to William, by the agency of the same Archbishop Robert and at the same time, the son and grandson of Earl Godwine, Wulfnoth and Hakon, as hostages to guarantee the agreement. Although they give no dates, these sources clearly place the events, by association with Archbishop Robert, in the period between his promotion to this office in March 1051 and his death in exile sometime between 1053 and 1055.[3]

Neither of these Norman sources are contemporary in the way that the Chronicle is, nor can they be described as unbiased. Indeed, both authors explicitly make clear that their purpose in writing was to justify William's conquest of England and his succession to the English throne. No contemporary English sources support their account, which is particularly surprising given that William of Poitiers portrays the designation of William as a widely acknowledged event in England. Nevertheless, it is essential that the evidence they offer is fully considered, as this event was to have important consequences for Harold. The account of William of Jumieges, as we have seen, provides little more than a few basic facts. The account of William of Poitiers elaborates considerably on these facts, but in doing so introduces some inconsistencies, which tend to undermine confidence in the chronicler's reliability. For example, he names 'Archbishop' Stigand among those who assented to William's nomination, when the latter was in fact only Bishop of Winchester at the time.[4]

The problems with the Norman accounts make it very difficult for a clear narrative to be established which is consistent with other sources, although many are prepared to accept their account without such consistency. If we are to establish the full background to William of Normandy's invasion of England in 1066 we must attempt a reconciliation between the Norman and English accounts. This involves a need to establish where they come together and where inconsistencies exist. The accounts then need to be reviewed to see which elements within them can be reconciled. This also involves the need to consider the likelihood of events which are described by the Norman writers alone, emerging from contemporary circumstances in England. If we can establish an account which allows the main events of the two traditions to be reconciled, then this is probably as close to the truth as we are ever likely to get.[5]

The main points of contact between the Norman and English accounts are Robert, Archbishop of Canterbury, and the hostages from Godwine's family. In most accounts of these events the obvious time for Robert, Archbishop of Canterbury, to communicate Edward's designation of William as his heir, as recorded by the Norman accounts, has been seen as during the course of his journey to Rome for his pallium, between his appointment in March 1051 and 29 June 1051 when he was enthroned on his return. This is a period when he is known to have been abroad, and he may have passed through Normandy. However, if this was the case, then he could not have brought Godwine's hostages to William at the same time, as William of Poitiers clearly states. According to the contemporary Anglo-Saxon Chronicle, these hostages were given into King Edward's hands, as a pledge for Godwine's appearance at the London council, in September 1051, long after Robert had returned to England in June. This undermines the perceived sequence of events as established by William of Poitiers' account, but the anachronism concerning the hostages extends beyond one of timing. It would be contrary to custom for King Edward, as donor of the kingdom, to send hostages to William, his suitor, without the latter sending hostages in return. Also, if hostages were expected from the English guarantors – Godwine, Leofric, Siward and 'Archbishop' Stigand, as named by William of Poitiers – then why were they only received from one of these parties? This all serves to undermine the additional details provided by William of Poitiers. In contrast, William of Jumieges provides a much briefer account which shows no such inconsistencies and therefore appears more trustworthy. They must both now be assessed against contemporary events in England to gauge whether they can provide a plausible scenario that fits these events.[6]

The key factor in the events of 1051, which is not dealt with by the Norman accounts, is the background provided by Edward's childless marriage. The succession to the English kingship in the eleventh century rested on a number of factors. The first was a natural right of inheritance usually but not always through primogeniture and based on family relationship with the existing or a previous monarch. In this way, sons or sometimes brothers of the reigning monarch were recognized as potential heirs to the throne, often being given the title *atheling* to signify their throne-worthy status – thus the references to all of King Aethelred's sons, Athelstan, Edmund, Eadwig, Edward and Alfred, as *atheling*. In cases where a king had a number of sons or brothers, the selection of a single heir to the kingdom might be secured by his designation, usually but not always given to the eldest son. Thus Cnut is said to have favoured his younger son Hardecnut before Harold 'Harefoot'. This designation by Cnut was not in fact enforced, as we have seen above, since it was not supported by all the great men in England. The support of these men could often sway a disputed succession, as in Harold 'Harefoot's' case, since royal power usually rested on such support. However, it is important to note that these men could not of themselves choose or elect a king, but only provide support to one of two or more rival candidates. In exceptional circumstances, an outsider could succeed in seizing the kingship by enforcing his authority on the country by conquest. This could usually only be achieved with the support of a foreign army, as under the Danes Swein 'Forkbeard' and Cnut. However, even these conquerors often sought to secure support from a portion of the great men to ease their path to the throne.[7]

In the circumstances of 1051, King Edward had no surviving brothers and no sons by his wife Edith. He therefore required either to find assistance in order to remove Earl Godwine, divorce Edith, and remarry in search of a son of his body, or to find an alternative heir, who satisfied the required criteria. The former might imply assistance from the relatives of a prospective bride. In these circumstances, the question must be whether or not William, Duke of Normandy, was best placed to satisfy either of these requirements in the period 1051–2.

If Edward was seeking an opportunity to remarry in order to have an heir of his own, then he needed a bride and support to remove Godwine, who could not allow Edward to repudiate his daughter Edith unchallenged. Such support would best come from someone with enough power to counter Godwine, and also with an eligible daughter. In 1051, William of Normandy was either unmarried or only recently married and therefore without eligible daughters. He did have a sister, Adelaide, but she was probably already married to Enguerrand of Ponthieu. William therefore had no eligible bride for Edward. Similarly, although he was already a powerful lord in 1051, his energies and military forces were almost entirely engaged in campaigns to ensure his own survival and security as duke. These circumstances would appear to indicate that it is unlikely that Edward sought to form an alliance with William via marriage, which might later be construed as designation of him as his heir.[8]

Of course, the Norman accounts did not claim that William offered any marriage alliance, but rather that he was designated as an alternative heir. We must now consider whether William met the criteria for an alternative heir for Edward in 1051. When we examine the criteria for a royal heir, we come across a number of possibles among Edward's relatives, some with stronger claims than others. Earl Ralph, Edward's nephew by his sister, Godgifu, and her first husband, Drogo, Count of the Vexin, was already present in England and married to an Englishwoman. He was undoubtedly the best heir available, in spite of his French background. Walter, Count of the Vexin, Ralph's elder brother, had an equivalent claim, but was not present in England and had no direct English connections. Strictly speaking, the claim of these brothers through the female line was weak, but still much stronger than any such claim by William. However, the man with the strongest claim was *Atheling* Edward, the son of Edward's older half-brother, King Edmund 'Ironside', although at this stage he was exiled in Europe, his exact whereabouts unknown. As an *atheling* and the son of a former king of England, this Edward's claim was far stronger than those of either of the king's French nephews. The crucial point is that any of these men were more likely as heirs than William of Normandy. William's only tenuous connection to the English dynasty was through his great aunt Emma and he had no English royal blood. It is of course possible that Edward intended to abandon traditional practice altogether and appoint someone unconnected to the dynasty. However, if he chose to do so it would represent a major breach of tradition and as such it seems highly unlikely that it would have received much, if any, support in England. William was not of royal blood, a foreigner, a relatively unknown quantity in England, and still struggling to hold his own duchy at home.[9]

Certainly, King Edward was half-Norman on his mother's side but he spent his formative years, up to the age of fourteen, being raised as an English *atheling*. He does appear to have developed a fairly cosmopolitan outlook, as demonstrated by his promotion of a number of Continental clerics and laymen. However, Edward's cosmopolitan sympathies do not appear to have been focused solely on Normandy but instead extended to other areas including Brittany, Flanders and Lotharingia. Thus Edward's Norman blood would not in itself appear to be enough to explain the designation of William of Normandy as his heir. Indeed, William of Poitiers himself does not seek to rely on this background alone but specifies particular reasons for Edward's action.[10]

If the general circumstances were unfavourable for King Edward's designation of William as his heir, can it be explained instead by the specific reasons provided by the Norman sources? William of Jumieges provides no reasons, but William of Poitiers provides a number of them. He states that Edward designated William as his heir in gratitude, first for providing him with refuge in Normandy in 1016 and then for securing his restoration to England in 1041. However, Edward's gratitude to William seems unlikely for a number of reasons. It is certainly possible that King Edward felt gratitude for his refuge in Normandy under Dukes Richard II and Robert, William's grandfather and father respectively. Indeed, Duke Robert appears to have attempted to invade England in 1033 or 1034 on Edward's behalf, only for the attempt to end in abject failure, as a result of adverse weather conditions, and abandonment in favour of a raid on Brittany. However, any gratitude in this instance, if indeed such a fiasco warranted it, was perhaps due to Robert rather than his son. It is also possible that Edward actually resented his position as an exile, dependent on his Norman relatives, and felt that they had failed to do enough to assist him. This possibility is perhaps suggested by the lack of any major concessions to William or any other prominent Norman laymen in the early part of Edward's reign. Indeed, it appears that Edward and his brother, Alfred, had been forced to rely on forces from outside Normandy to support their own invasion attempt in 1036. Subsequently when Edward had returned to England in 1041, it was at the invitation of his half-brother King Hardecnut. A fact accepted by William of Jumieges and at one point also by William of Poitiers. There is no contemporary evidence that Edward received any Norman aid to secure his return. In all this, therefore, it seems that there are insufficient reasons for Edward to make such a grand gesture as designating William as his heir out of gratitude to him, especially after a period of some ten years during which there appears to have been no contact between them.[11]

The overall impression gained from the Norman sources is that the details they contain are not completely satisfactory. The contemporary chronicles and the general situation in England would seem to offer no support to their accounts. However, something most compelling must surely have prompted such an ambitious scheme as William's eventual invasion of England in 1066. William himself clearly believed that he had been designated as Edward's successor, and therefore it is unlikely that the story is simply a later fabrication. The immense risk William took by invading England and the emphasis in the documents on his rightful succession to King Edward both suggest otherwise. The key to this mystery surely lies with Robert, Archbishop of Canterbury, the man the Norman sources name as bearing Edward's designation to William of Normandy and a central figure in the events of 1051–2. Archbishop Robert is unlikely to have brought word of Edward's designation of William during early 1051, as has been seen, and the only other time he was present in Normandy was following Godwine's return from exile in September 1052, when Robert himself was banished from England and fled overseas. This possibility has the advantage that it would reconcile with William of Poitiers' statement that the archbishop brought Godwine's hostages with him and handed them over to William. Archbishop Robert would have been in a position to do this in 1052, whereas he could not have done so during his previous visit in 1051. However, before this possibility can be considered more fully the restoration of the Godwine family must first be examined.[12]

This dramatic turn of events arose because Godwine and his family, like Osgod *Clapa* before them, were not prepared to accept their exile tamely. Indeed, they had deliberately selected their places of exile in Bruges and Dublin because of their suitability as springboards for a return. Both were within easy sailing distance of

Harold in a foreign palace, perhaps like that of Diarmait of Leinster in 1052. (The Bayeux Tapestry – 11th Century. By special permission of the City of Bayeux)

England, especially Bruges, and both had plenty of mercenaries readily available for hire. Earl Godwine probably set about recruiting Flemish mercenaries with the treasure he had taken with him and with the support of Count Baldwin, but he was also joined by supporters from England. The fact that the family returned with a 'large fleet' does suggest the recruitment of mercenary forces in addition to those who may have followed them into exile.[13]

Meanwhile, in Ireland Earl Harold carried out a similar task of recruiting mercenary forces to support a return to England. He had apparently been well received by King Diarmait of Leinster, who had a reputation for welcoming and helping exiles. A later Welsh text, when recording Diarmait's death, describes him as 'gentle towards pilgrims and strangers', a description attributable to Welshmen who, like Harold, had found refuge at his court. Harold was able to persuade Diarmait to use his influence to assist him in recruiting men and ships, perhaps in return for some of the family treasure or possibly promises of improved trading concessions in important English ports like Bristol or Exeter. At this time, Diarmait gained direct control of Dublin and its mercenaries by expelling its Norse–Irish King Eachmargach and installing his own son, Murchad, as ruler. It is possible that Earl Harold may even have assisted him in this task, although the account of the conquest in the Irish Annals indicates a straightforward campaign to destroy Dublin's hinterland prior to King Eachmargach's flight. At the least, Harold's visit appears to have fostered a sympathy with Diarmait which was to extend, after Harold's death, to his young sons. It is also possible that the raid made on Earl Ralph's earldom early in 1052 by Gruffydd of Wales was encouraged by Harold from his vantage point in Dublin, although it is more likely that this was a simple case of Gruffydd taking advantage of Ralph's absence with the fleet.[14]

As preparations for the family's return made progress in Bruges and Dublin, Godwine may have finally decided to remove a major obstacle to his acceptance back in England, namely his eldest son Swein. It was probably at about this time that he sent his son on pilgrimage to Jerusalem as a penitent for his all too many sins. (It has already been seen how Swein's behaviour had caused him to be exiled, and how King Edward had accepted his return in 1050 only with great reluctance.) The Chronicle says Swein went there from Bruges and that he died on the return journey at Lycia near Constantinople on 29 September 1052. In this case, he must have set out during the family's exile with the intention that when he returned his family would be restored and that he, Swein, might thereafter prove more acceptable as a penitent pilgrim.[15]

The various activities of Godwine and his sons did not go unnoticed by Edward, and he made his own preparations to oppose them. He gathered a fleet of forty ships at Sandwich under the command of Earls Ralph and Odda. This was the customary response to a threat from Flanders and it had proved sufficient to repulse German raiders in 1048 and Osgod *Clapa* a year later. However, the circumstances were now rather different. The professional fleet which had provided the backbone of defence then had been disbanded in 1050. Although the two commanders of the new fleet had gained from the Godwine family's fall, and had an interest in preventing their return, there is no evidence they were experienced naval commanders, in contrast to the men of the Godwine family who had commanded ships in previous fleets. In addition, neither the German pirates nor Osgod *Clapa* had any wide base of support in England. The Godwine family, with its wide lands and influence, was a very different case. Although the *Vita Eadwardi* probably exaggerates support for Godwine, the contemporary Chronicle entries confirm that it was considerable. The men of Dover, whom Godwine had saved from Edward's wrath in 1051, may have been prominent among his supporters.[16]

On 24 June 1052 Godwine, despite his by now advancing age, made a first sortie across the Channel from Bruges, to test the defences and perhaps to communicate with supporters and potential supporters. He landed undetected at Dungeness and proceeded to recruit seamen from nearby Hastings and the Kent ports to join his forces. News of this reached the royal fleet at Sandwich, and Ralph and Odda sailed to oppose him at sea while other forces moved against him on land. However, Godwine was warned, probably by local supporters, and he retreated to Pevensey in his native Sussex, where marshes shielded him to the landward, and he could continue his recruitment unhindered. A violent storm subsequently blew up, which appears to have forced the two earls to return to Sandwich, but which Godwine was able to use to cover his return to Bruges unscathed. He had tested the defences and found them weak, and had also made contact with his partisans in Kent and Sussex. King Edward had also noticed the unsatisfactory, to him at least, performance of the fleet, and ordered it to London where he dismissed the two earls and their crews. Perhaps the latter, if recruited from the Kent ports including Dover, had shown too much sympathy for their exiled earl. The king apparently intended to appoint replacements but seems to have had such difficulties, his previous fleet commanders after all had been Godwine and his sons, that the fleet was abandoned altogether. Godwine's local contacts informed him of this development and he immediately seized his chance. He sailed from Bruges with his enlarged fleet, westwards to the Isle of Wight, and ravaged and collected tribute from the inhabitants for some time. It was probably during this period that Godwine sent word to Harold in Ireland to come and join him. He then proceeded to Portland and ravaged there also. These raiding actions against men of his own earldom seem odd in view of his earlier refusal to punish the men of Dover, but they were perhaps directed against those who had deserted him in 1051 or who refused to aid him now. King Edward, who now lacked a fleet, was unable to respond to these attacks coming as they did in areas most readily reached by sea.[17]

Meanwhile, Harold had received his father's message to join him, and sailed from Ireland with his brother, Leofwine, and nine ships crewed by mercenaries. They entered the Severn, landed at Porlock and ravaged the area, probably as retribution

Harold aboard a ship, as on his return from exile in 1052. (The Bayeux Tapestry – 11th Century. By special permission of the City of Bayeux)

against Earl Odda, in whose new earldom it now lay. A large force of locals gathered to oppose him but he defeated them, killing more than thirty *thegns* and others. This was the first military action of Harold's career and a victory even if on a small scale. Thereafter, he gathered booty and rounded Land's End to join his father off the south coast, either at Portland or at the Isle of Wight.[18]

In spite of the exaggerations of the *Vita Eadwardi*, the activities of the family had until now amounted to little more than piracy similar to that of Osgod *Clapa*. However, their combined fleet now headed eastwards up the Channel towards the heartland of Godwine's patrimony, and their journey became almost a triumphal progress as the family gathered supporters from the towns of the Sussex and Kent coasts. There was little raiding now, but rather a general rallying of support to Earl Godwine. Chronicle C speaks of them not doing 'any great harm', a curious statement in a text often seen as opposed to the family, while it is Chronicle E, supposedly favourable to them, which suggests that some force was used. Again, these variations in reporting probably result from local knowledge on the part of Chronicle E composed in nearby Canterbury.

King Edward, alarmed by this turn of events, sent inland for support to defend London against what was becoming a considerable force. At this point, he seems to have experienced difficulties recruiting support. A close reading of the Chronicle accounts reveals no reference to the northern earls Leofric and Siward. The unnamed earls recorded in Chronicle E appear to be Ralph and Odda, who had been with the fleet and therefore must be those mentioned as pursued to London. They would also seem to be those earls referred to as being with the king and his fifty ships in London. The absence of Leofric and Siward is perhaps confirmed by the reported difficulties Edward had in replacing Ralph and Odda as fleet commanders; in the absence of the Godwine family, only Siward and Leofric would have been able to fill these roles, had they been present. Their absence is notable given their importance in the kingdom, and in contrast to their obvious presence in 1051, when they played a central role in events. Why were they apparently withholding support which they had provided to the king in the previous year?[19]

An important factor was probably the apparently final and complete nature of the exile of Earl Godwine and all his family in 1051. The northern earls had probably expected some compromise to be reached, redefining Godwine's position. When instead he and all his family were banished and deprived of all their lands, Leofric and Siward must have been disturbed. After the relative stability enjoyed by the three great earls for the previous twenty years, the sudden downfall of one of their number must have caused the others to look to their own security. If Edward could destroy the great Earl Godwine in this way, why not them too? The fact that the king appears to have assumed direct control of the bulk of Godwine's earldom of Wessex and so substantially enhanced his own power made this possibility all the more likely. When Godwine returned, therefore, the northern earls apparently held themselves aloof.

Thus when Godwine sailed up the Thames with his fleet, the power of Edward to oppose him was severely weakened, limited in effect to his new appointees, Earls Ralph and Odda, and minor nobles. Godwine arrived at Southwark, his estate on the south bank of the Thames, on 14 September and there awaited the turn of the tide in order to pass London Bridge. During this period, he pressed his advantage by negotiating directly with the Londoners. In this he was successful, persuading most of them to support him, or at least not to oppose him. Then Godwine's fleet moved past London Bridge on the incoming tide and the opposing forces again faced each other across the Thames, as they had the previous year. However, this time Edward's forces were almost certainly weaker and perhaps less resolute; others besides the northern earls may have felt that the king had gone too far in 1051. Bishop Ealdred of Worcester's actions in 1051, when he failed, apparently deliberately, to intercept Harold as he fled to Ireland, reveal his sympathy for the family. Indeed, he may have been passed over as a potential successor to Aelfric, Archbishop of York, in 1051 as a result of this failure. In the event, neither side was any more willing to start a civil war now than in the previous year and negotiations began with Bishop Stigand again the intermediary.

The negotiations resulted in a truce and a meeting of the council called for the next day. The tide of events was clearly also turning in Godwine's favour, and those who had most encouraged his expulsion were themselves now in fear of his vengeance. Notable among these was Archbishop Robert, who read the writing on the wall and decided to flee without waiting for the council to meet. He therefore escaped from London accompanied by his fellow Norman bishops, Ulf and William. He probably took with him the hostages handed over by Godwine in 1051, Wulfnoth and Hakon, as surety for his safety. These may been given to him by Edward as a gesture to his close friend, or the archbishop may have been holding them for the king and have taken them without royal authority. This latter possibility may explain the deaths recorded by the Chronicle during Robert's flight at the east gate of London – perhaps royal *thegns* were attempting to prevent this breach of royal trust. The Frenchmen from Herefordshire also fled, initially to the protection of their castles, but when their exile was confirmed they sought refuge in Scotland. This flight to Scotland surely confirms that the French castelans in Hereford were not part of William of Normandy's supposed fifth column. If the latter case, they would surely have sought to return to Normandy rather than taking up risky mercenary employment in distant Scotland.

When the council finally met on 15 September, including, finally, Earls Leofric and Siward, part of its work had already been done and the rest was settled through the intermediacy of Bishop Stigand. Godwine cleared himself on oath of all charges against him and his family. In return, Edward had Godwine and all his family restored to their lands and positions. This restoration also included the return of Queen Edith to the royal bed and the ending of all divorce plans. One person may not have been included in this general restoration, although with no certainty, and that is Earl Swein. Only John of Worcester explicitly states this, perhaps under the influence of hindsight, but it makes sense. Swein had been a major cause of the crisis of 1051, and a major irritant to Edward even before then, and his return would be particularly problematic. As has been suggested, his pilgrimage to Jerusalem was probably a way of keeping him out of the way until the crisis had passed.

As well as restoring Godwine and his family, the council made judgements of outlawry on those now deemed responsible for the crisis. This could obviously not include the prime mover in the events, King Edward himself, but it could cover those 'bad' counsellors who had already fled and thereby made themselves easy scapegoats. Thus Archbishop Robert, Bishop Ulf of Dorchester and the Frenchmen of Herefordshire were all declared outlaws. Robert and Ulf had already fled and the latter were soon given safe conduct by Earl Leofric to flee north to Scotland. It is important to note that these actions were not simply a general reaction against Normans or Frenchmen. The Chronicle makes the point that not all Frenchmen were exiled but only those who had 'promoted injustices', passed unjust judgements, and 'given bad counsel', while John of Worcester specifies some of those who were not implicated.

The chancel arch in Bosham Church, Sussex.

Thus many of the royal favourites, Norman and French, were left undisturbed and even Bishop William, who had fled with Archbishop Robert, was soon allowed to return and reclaim his bishopric. Although appointed through Archbishop Robert's influence, he was not blamed for recent events.[20]

The other details of the settlement agreed in the council reflect a return to equilibrium rather than further upheaval. Earls Godwine and Harold had been restored, though perhaps with slightly reduced authority. Earl Aelfgar must have had to resign his earldom to Harold, indicating the agreement of Earl Leofric to the settlement. In 1053 Aelfgar was to succeed again to Harold's East Anglian earldom, when the latter moved on to Wessex, and this succession may have been agreed as part of the terms at this council. Earls Ralph and Odda appear to have retained their earldoms. Ralph's earldom appears to have consisted of parts of Swein's former earldom, and the latter's death later that year removed the possibility of his returning to reclaim them. The position of Odda is less clear; either he may have retained Somerset, which Swein had previously held and could not reclaim, or he may have retained his entire earldom under Godwine. In the Church too equilibrium was restored with absent clerics Archbishop Robert and Bishop Ulf of Dorchester replaced by Stigand and Wulfwig respectively. Some have regarded Stigand's appointment as a reward for his support of Godwine, but this seems unlikely as during the crisis period he played a neutral role as negotiator between the factions. The appointment may rather have been his reward from Edward for arranging a peaceful settlement.[21]

A great deal has been written concerning Stigand's uncanonical investiture with the archbishopric of Canterbury when his predecessor was still alive. However, it must be remembered that his appointment was dictated by politics. The Norman Robert was now politically unacceptable in England, and Stigand was seen by Edward as·a suitable successor to the post, both as diplomat and administrator. William of Normandy himself would later recognize this fact by retaining Stigand as archbishop until 1070, and only disposing of him when he was no longer of value. It has been suggested that the appointment of Aethelric, the unsuccessful candidate of 1050, would have been better. In canonical terms, this is certainly true, but he could hardly be an acceptable choice to Edward, as he was not only related to Godwine, but by now identified too closely with his cause. King Edward had always controlled all Church appointments, as he demonstrated in 1051, and even after Godwine's dramatic change of fortune he still retained this control. Stigand had been a royal servant for many years, first under Cnut and later under Edward himself when, in spite of his early links to Queen Emma, he had been successively promoted to the sees of East Anglia, Winchester and now Canterbury in recognition of his abilities and his service to the king. The fact that he retained control of the see of Winchester, after his promotion to Canterbury, was highly unusual and an important factor in his subsequent condemnation, and it is hard to understand what purpose lay behind this.[22]

The canonical irregularity of Stigand's position was clearly recognized in England, both in terms of his occupation of Canterbury and his pluralist retention of Winchester. He would not be called upon to perform the normal duties of his position and hence did not consecrate any bishops or kings except during his brief period of acceptance by Pope Benedict X in 1058. Similarly, he was not called upon to consecrate Harold's church at Waltham in 1060. Nevertheless, he continued to hold his archbishopric and was even able to sit in council with the Papal legates who visited England in 1062 to supervise the pluralist Archbishop Ealdred of York's surrender of the Bishopric of Worcester. It would seem that much of the distaste for Stigand's uncanonical position arose after his political fall from grace, and it certainly did not hinder his retention of his position prior to this.[23]

It is interesting to note that little of the same concern is ever expressed over the similar position of Bishop Wulfwig, who had replaced the Norman Ulf as Bishop of Dorchester in exactly the same circumstances as Stigand had replaced Robert at Canterbury. This may perhaps reflect the relative importance of the two men and the sees concerned. Stigand's additional pluralism in retaining Winchester may also have played a part. However, Ulf's own unsavoury reputation as a simonist, almost deposed by Pope Leo IX in 1050, may be the main reason for the lack of concern about his successor's uncanonical position.[24]

There was one important result of the crisis of 1051–2 which was unknown in England at the time, but which was to have grave consequences for the future. The defeated Archbishop Robert of Jumieges had fled to the Continent fearful for his own safety and taken Godwine's son and grandson with him, probably as a guarantee of this. There, he learned of his banishment by King Edward and his replacement as Archbishop of Canterbury by Stigand, and travelled to Rome to complain of his treatment and to condemn his successor. This action resulted in the condemnation of Archbishop Stigand by successive Popes and the related decline in the reputation of the English Church.[25]

More importantly, it seems likely that it was at this time that Robert visited Duke William of Normandy, probably soon after his return from Rome, to declare that King Edward had nominated him as his heir and to hand over Godwine's son and grandson, supposedly as hostages to secure his claim. This seems to fit the evidence better than those interpretations which place Robert's declaration of William as King Edward's heir as ocurring during 1051. The Norman sources fail to date the event, except to say that Robert was archbishop at the time, but William of Poitiers clearly links it to the handing over of the hostages. In 1052, as has already been mentioned, Robert was in a position to do this. Further, after his exile in 1052, Robert had plenty of time to raise such matters with Duke William, resident as he was in Normandy until his death, sometime between 9 January 1053 and 1055, perhaps closer to the former.[26]

The truth of what Robert of Jumieges said to Duke William concerning the English throne, in what were probably private discussions, will never be known. He must have been a disenchanted and bitter man, deeply resentful of Godwine, who had brought about his fall from power, and disenchanted with the English in general, who had failed to support him. If Earl Godwine had remained an exile, Robert would have been Archbishop of Canterbury, enjoying the power and prestige that went with the post. He may have attempted to gain William's aid for his restoration, and in doing so may have tempted him with an offer of the English crown as an incentive. It should be remembered that the archbishopric of Canterbury carried with it the duty of performing royal consecrations and Robert may have emphasized this in his discussions with William. All of this would explain the Norman accounts of Edward's designation of William as his heir, as well as William's clear belief in this himself. At the same time, the fact that Edward did not make any such designation personally provides an explanation as to why it seemed such an extraordinary move in the first place, and why no such event is found recorded in contemporary English sources.

It should be noted here that it is possible that an alarmed Edward, faced with the imminent return of Godwine in September 1052, might have been ready to grasp at any straw. In such circumstances, Robert may have dangled the idea, however fanciful, of military aid from William, and gained an impromptu promise from Edward in return, which the latter soon forgot in the heat of subsequent events but which Robert passed on to William as a solemn pledge. This is suggested only as an outside possibility. It seems far more likely that the designation was the work of Robert himself.

Whatever the events, Robert of Jumieges clearly left William with the impression that Edward had designated him heir to his kingdom and perhaps that Godwine's hostages were his guarantee of it. This 'designation' then formed the foundation for the Norman justification of William's conquest, and was truthful in these terms. This interpretation accounts for William's subsequent actions in 1064, his invasion in 1066, and for the constant references in later documents to his succession to Edward by rightful inheritance. It also accounts for the lack of any reference to such a designation in the contemporary English sources. We have seen that it is unlikely that such a promise was in fact made by Edward, but that William believed it had been made there can surely be no doubt. The sequence of events posed here would appear to resolve the main contradictions between the English and Norman records and is probably the closest to the truth we are ever likely to get. It also provides an explanation as to why William of Jumieges made no mention of this 'designation' of Duke William when he wrote that part of his work covering the years 1051–2; that part of the work was completed before Duke William had let the news be known to anyone other than his most intimate circle. William of Jumieges only learnt of it as a result of Harold's visit to Normandy in 1064, when Duke William revealed it to his barons, and then inserted it into his account of this later visit.[27]

Harold at a feast, perhaps like that of Easter 1053. (The Bayeux Tapestry – 11th Century. By special permission of the City of Bayeux)

However, in 1052 this dark cloud was still beyond the horizon, and in England, in the meantime, the great crisis was over and the Godwine family, including Earl Harold, busied themselves in restoring their estates and authority. How long this peaceful *rapprochement* would last was unclear. Edward must have been unhappy about Godwine's restoration and the banishment of some of his close friends and supporters. He had also been forced to abandon his plans for remarriage, and instead found himself still married to Edith with no prospect of direct male heirs. There was also the thorny problem of Swein, who could be expected home from his pilgrimage soon and who would, no doubt, again receive the support of his father for the restoration of his earldom. Thus there remained a number of unresolved problems which required to be dealt with before lasting peace could be restored and the kingdom stand united once again behind King Edward.

However, within the space of a year the political situation was transformed, and Earl Harold was catapulted into prominence. Firstly, probably towards the end of 1052, news came that Godwine's eldest son, the ill-starred Swein, had died on 29 September near Constantinople on his way home from Jerusalem. This made Earl Harold the heir to his father, in addition to removing a major obstacle to improved relations with King Edward. Earl Godwine himself had fallen ill soon after his triumphant return, no doubt as a result of his recent exertions on campaign. He was after all probably in his sixties by this time. He rallied again, but on Easter Monday 1053, during the royal feast at

Winchester and with his sons Harold and Tosti present, he collapsed. Three days later, on 15 April, Earl Godwine died. He was buried in the Old Minster, Winchester. Earl Harold was chosen by King Edward to succeed to his father's earldom of Wessex. The king replaced him as earl of East Anglia with Aelfgar, son of Leofric, who had held that earldom during Harold's exile.

Finally, King Edward was free, both of Earl Godwine's control and also of the possibility of the return of the brutal Swein. The deaths of Godwine and Swein removed two major points of dispute between the king and Godwine's family, and paved the way for the possibility of long term reconciliation. This would depend on relations between the king and Harold, who had now been brought to centre stage. Only time would reveal how relations between the new Earl of Wessex and the king would develop, and how much Harold had learnt from the events of 1051–2. To understand his subsequent career, we must first look at the basis of the power that Harold was to wield at this present stage, which would become the foundation for his future rise to the kingship itself.[30]

CHAPTER FOUR

THE LANDS AND
WEALTH OF HAROLD

He abounded in riches whereby powerful kings and princes were brought into his alliance.[1]

The previous chapters have described the rise of Harold's father from relative obscurity as the son of a minor Sussex *thegn* to the heights of Earl of Wessex. Harold himself had now succeeded to this earldom and would continue this upward progression, ultimately ascending the throne itself. He would become the greatest man in England by 1066, more powerful by far than any of the other earls, and in combination with his brothers more powerful even than the king himself. This rise was based to a large part on an immense accession of lands and wealth to Harold and his family.

The basis of power in all agricultural societies was the ownership of land. It was land which ultimately provided for all the needs of every person in eleventh-century England. It supplied food for the table and clothing for the body, and, through the sale of surplus produce, wealth to permit the purchase of manufactured craft and luxury items both local and foreign. In addition to these immediate needs, the ownership of land also provided a source of political power. A man who owned a significant amount of land could not work it all directly but instead would rent it to tenants to work on his behalf. These tenants would support their own family directly from the land and in return would provide services and income to the owner. In this way, the owner would obtain supplies of food, clothing and other goods, a cash income and labour services for his own estates. He would also obtain political and military services from his tenants in return for his protection and support as their lord. The key significance of land is reflected by the existence of Domesday Book itself, which records landholding and the power stemming from it. The compilation of this work was a tremendous task, which involved significant government resources in eleventh-century terms, and it would not have been done had land not been the basis of royal and all other power.[2]

Domesday Book records that in 1066 Earl Harold himself held lands valued for tax purposes at £2,846, while his men held lands valued at a further £836. (The land valuations in Domesday book represent values for tax purposes rather than the actual worth of the land itself or the amount of income arising from it.) The Godwine family as a whole, including Harold, held lands valued for tax at some £5,187, while their men held lands valued at a further £1,428. This compares with the king, who personally held lands valued for tax at £3,840, although adding the value of the land of

Domesday Book and its chest.

the king's men redressed the balance as it included the land of every man in England, and with Earl Leofric's family, who held lands valued for tax at £2,493 and whose men held lands valued at a further £171. The fact that a contemporary source shows that a slave-woman was expected to feed herself through the winter for 3 pennies provides a comparative gauge for this immense wealth. This extensive landholding by Harold was the basis of the wealth which would later permit Harold's generous gifts to his college of Holy Cross at Waltham and which would enable his mother to offer, for the return of his body after Hastings, its weight in gold. It would also provide the basis for Harold's political power in England, which would very firmly place him second only to the king.[3]

How were Harold and his family able to build up this vast wealth in land? This is not an easy question to answer because of the relative paucity of sources for this aspect of Harold's career – there is an unfortunate dearth of surviving secular writs and diplomas from this period. Although Domesday Book gives an overall idea of the extent of Harold's lands, the amount, its value and its location, the entries therein provide little or no indication of how or when all but a few portions of it came into his possession. In addition, Domesday Book was compiled in 1086, from local memories of how the land was held some twenty years earlier. Inevitably, a certain amount of confusion and distortion must have crept in. The most notable example is the record of Earls Godwine, Aelfgar, Leofric and Tosti as landholders in 1066, by which time all of them had either died or been dispossessed some years earlier. There may be some justification for Tosti's appearance, since he was only dispossessed late in 1065 and arrangements for the appropriation and administration of all his lands may not have been fully in place before King Edward's death. No such justification appears possible for the other cases. Aelfgar apparently died in 1062, Leofric in 1057 and Godwine as long ago as 1053. It has been suggested that in these latter cases the estates mentioned were held in 1066 by the widows of these men and this is certainly a possibility, since all of these ladies were certainly still alive in 1066. These limitations mean that the value of Domesday Book in terms of discovering how land was acquired is therefore restricted. In spite of these deficiencies, there exists a number of scattered clues which enable us to construct an outline of how Harold and his family may have come by their lands and wealth.[4]

The most striking fact about the location of Harold's own lands is their concentration in the south of England and in shires where Harold at one time or another held the position of earl. The shires of Harold's enlarged Wessex earldom contained land valued at £1,834, or 64 per cent of the total. The shires of his former earldom of East Anglia contained land valued at a further £406, increasing this to 78 per cent of the total. The remaining £606 worth of land, or 22 per cent, was scattered through the other shires with smaller concentrations in Hertfordshire (£118), Yorkshire (£107), and Lincolnshire (£201). This points to what was undoubtedly an important factor in his accumulation of lands, that is his employment in royal service as an earl. There were four principal sources of lands in this period. The first was family land inherited from relatives. The second was 'bookland' or land granted by diploma, most often by the king or another lord and in return for loyal service. The third was land attached to an office like that of an earl, which was received on appointment as a royal official. The fourth was straightforward purchase. It will be seen that two of these four ways of securing land, and certainly the most significant to Harold's family, depended on royal service. The location of Harold's lands implies strongly that it was through such service that he came by the majority of his property.[5]

The first source of lands for Harold's family, like any other, would most naturally be those lands inherited from their ancestors. As a Sussex *thegn*, Wulfnoth *Cild*, Harold's grandfather, must have held lands in that county, though we are ignorant of the exact location or extent of almost all of these. The sole exception is the estate at Compton, later forfeited to the crown until restored to Godwine by *Atheling* Athelstan. In order to hold the status of *thegn* Wulfnoth would have required at least

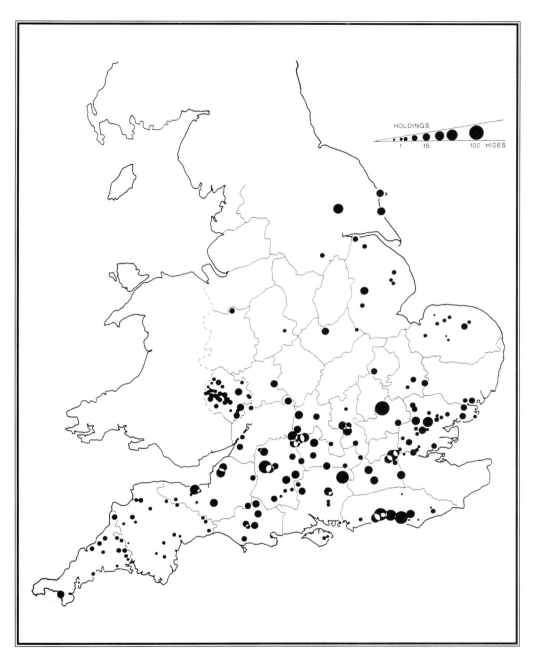

HOLDINGS

1   15   100 HIDES

The lands of Earl Harold, 1066.

five hides of land; his ability to suborn twenty ships of the royal fleet in 1009 suggests considerable influence and more extensive lands in Sussex. The later possession of about a third of this entire shire in 1066 by seven members of Harold's family probably reflects their original strength in their native county. These family lands would, in the normal course of events, have been inherited by Wulfnoth's son, Godwine, but the former's exile and forfeiture for treason in 1009 instead meant their confiscation by King Aethelred.[6]

This placed Godwine in a difficult position as either a completely landless man or one with very little land. In order to restore his position he had no alternative but to seek royal service, which alone could provide him patronage and a source of lands, but as the son of a traitor he obviously could not seek service with the king himself. As we have seen, Godwine was able to solve this problem by entering the service of *Atheling* Athelstan. When the *atheling* died in 1014, the services Godwine had performed were sufficient to result in the recovery of at least part of his patrimony, namely the estate at Compton. Thereafter Godwine probably sought service with Athelstan's brother, Edmund 'Ironside', in order to preserve the lands he had gained or regained and, hopefully, extend them further. The fact that his family were later recorded in Domesday Book as holding almost a third of Sussex suggests that at this stage Godwine concentrated on recovering lands formerly held by his father. Unfortunately, we have no knowledge of the extent of Godwine's landholding at this point, but the fact that Cnut promoted him to earl soon afterwards suggests that he had already made enough progress in royal service to be of use to the king in this office. It seems unlikely, though not impossible, that a very minor *thegn* would have been able to cope with such an important position.[7]

The most crucial period in the growth of the family lands was undoubtedly when King Cnut was seeking loyal servants among the English nobility, following his conquest of England and the death of his rival, Edmund 'Ironside'. Cnut had disposed of a large number of the old English nobility, whom he apparently considered, for one reason or another, untrustworthy. As a result, a great deal of their land fell into his hands for redistribution among men he did trust. One of these trusted men was Godwine. It has been said that Godwine, in Cnut's time, was not 'the colossus' he was to become in Edward's years. Indeed, the Domesday Book indicates that the lands held by his sons in 1066 were vastly extended beyond those he held himself during Cnut's reign. However, if Godwine were not the greatest noble of Cnut's later reign, it is difficult to explain his position at the head of the witness lists of Cnut's diplomas from 1023 onwards, his ability, initially, to hold southern England against Harold 'Harefoot', or his initial attraction as an ally for Edward.[8]

What benefits did Godwine receive, therefore, from Cnut's redistribution of lands? Undoubtedly the main benefit was through his appointment as earl, which brought him lands associated with this office. Thus Godwine appears to have gained lands as a result of his initial appointment as earl over the central shires of Wessex in 1018, perhaps including the comital lands of Aldermaston in Berkshire, Over Wallop in Hampshire and Southwark in Surrey. Similarly, when Earl Godwine's authority was extended in 1020 to include Western Wessex, he thereby gained many lands in the western shires, probably including such estates as Puddleton in Dorset, Moretonhampstead in Devon and Old Cleeve and Brompton Regis in Somerset. Finally, when Godwine succeeded to authority over Kent, perhaps around 1023, he probably gained the associated earldom lands in that county, such as Fordwich and Dover. All these comital lands were probably ultimately acquired as part of Godwine's expanding office of Earl of Wessex and came directly as royal grants from Cnut following their seizure from his predecessors. It was these lands which provided Godwine with the necessary wealth and power to allow him to carry out his duties as earl. They were not lands owned by Godwine and could not be bequeathed to his family but were official lands in the king's gift and would be passed on to the next Earl of Wessex.[9]

In addition to these estates probably associated with the office of earl, Godwine also benefited directly from royal patronage. The Chronicle of Ramsey states that a number of English nobles 'relinquished the hereditary right of posterity and succession . . . to the Danish military followers of the king' and Godwine, through his marriage to Gytha in 1020 or 1023, had joined these Danish followers. Therefore, he probably gained a number of estates, which had been forfeited by disgraced noble families, through private grants from King Cnut as a reward for his loyal service. There are a number of examples of lands once held by old families, which subsequently fell into the hands of Godwine and other new men. In many of these cases the links between the loss by old families and the acquisition by new men are unclear but it should be stressed that this does not mean that any improper appropriation was necessarily involved. Indeed, it is clear in some instances that the way in which such lands came into Godwine's hands was entirely conventional. For example, it has been suggested that, in one case, *Atheling* Athelstan's will was overturned, resulting in an estate at Chalton in Hampshire passing to Godwine. In fact, this estate had been bequeathed to King Aethelred himself and as part of the royal demesne could then be granted to Godwine by a later king, though whether Edmund, Cnut or Edward is unknown. In another instance, *Ealdorman* Aethelweard's sister, Aelfgifu, bequeathed a number of estates, including Haversham and Princes Risborough in Buckinghamshire, to the king and to the Old Minster at Winchester respectively. The former estate was probably then quite properly granted from the royal demesne to Godwine by Cnut. The position of the latter estate is less clear because it came into the hands of the Church. It may have been appropriated by Cnut or even granted to him by the Old Minster and subsequently re-granted to Godwine, either by Cnut himself or possibly by Edward. Alternatively, it may have come into Godwine's control directly through a similar deal with the Old Minster as that which was construed between the earl and Christ Church, Canterbury, and which brought him control of Folkestone in Kent. In the same way, *Ealdorman* Aelfheah bequeathed the estates of Faringdon, Berkshire and Aldbourne, Wiltshire, to his brother, *Ealdorman* Aelfhere, and both of these subsequently passed to Godwine. Aelfhere was succeeded in 983 by his brother-in-law, Aelfric *Cild*, who was then dispossessed by King Aethelred in 985, his lands passing into royal hands to be granted, probably by Cnut, or by Edward, to Godwine. It is important to note that when estates found their way from one family to another we usually have no record at all of how this occurred. However, it seems clear that in the cases we have considered, such evidence as is available usually points to the king as the agent of the transfer.[10]

A few examples of such transfers survive and these provide some confirmation that many of the estates which came into Godwine's hands were granted to him by King Cnut. One such transfer concerns Polhampton in Hampshire, recorded in a rare surviving diploma of 1033. Other lands undoubtedly came as grants from King Edward, who sought to foster Godwine's support early in his reign. Sandford-on-Thames is representative of these, granted to Godwine by a surviving diploma of 1050. Similar royal grants probably lay behind Godwine's possession of estates at Chalton and Catherington in Hampshire and Angmering, Rotherfield and Hastings in Sussex, all of which had formerly been part of the royal demesne. Godwine is also known to have purchased some of his lands, for example Woodchester in Gloucestershire, which he bought from Azur and gave to his wife.[11]

These and similar acquisitions made Godwine a well-established and powerful landholder in southern England, with extensive estates throughout Wessex. As one of Godwine's younger sons, Harold could expect to inherit a portion of his father's lands. Indeed, this may have been the source of many of his Sussex estates, some of which may even have been granted to him by his father during the latter's lifetime. However, that Harold should surpass his father in wealth and power to the extent that he did was unusual and we must now consider how this came about.

Harold probably began to gather a significant landholding of his own only after he had been appointed Earl of East Anglia by King Edward in 1044 or 1045. Harold's appointment to this earldom resulted from his father's alliance with and his sister's marriage to King Edward in January 1045. This appointment to an earldom, and those of his elder brother Swein and cousin Beorn, represented the second great extension of the family's lands. It provided Harold with the opportunity to establish a power base, independent of his father, and to gain directly from the profits of royal service. The appointment made Harold the deputy of the king in East Anglia, collecting taxes, presiding over courts, enforcing royal decisions and grants, and defending the region. In order to carry out this wide range of duties, Harold was granted extensive estates to provide him with the necessary resources. These lands may have included many of those previously held by Thorkell the Tall, when he was the earl of the region under Cnut, but unfortunately we have no direct evidence of this. As earl, Harold received a third of the royal profits from court fines and customs dues, another significant source of income. Harold's extensive powers as earl also meant that many less powerful men and women sought his protection and support, often by way of gifts and bequests such as those presented by Lady Wulfgyth, her son, Ketel, and Thurstan, son of Wine (see p. 63). These people and many others like them sought Harold's protection for themselves and their lands and in return acknowledged him as their lord. Domesday Book records large numbers of men in his former East Anglian earldom who still acknowledged Harold as their lord in 1066 and had probably done so since he was earl there.[12]

The lands granted to Earl Harold through his earldom were not the only lands that he gained, although it is true that they were the basis of his power in eastern England. In 1066, long after he had surrendered the earldom of East Anglia, he still held lands valued for tax at £406 in the counties of Essex, Norfolk, Suffolk, Huntingdon and Cambridge. The Domesday Book entries do not reveal exactly when these lands came into Harold's possession, but it seems likely that the bulk of them passed to him during the period of his rule as earl in this region. It is also probable that most of this land came into Harold's control not because of his position as earl, but through private grants from his new brother-in-law, King Edward. Although there is no specific evidence of this, the subsequent retention of these lands by Harold does indicate that they were not related to his position as earl. They probably represented King Edward's endowment of his new brother-in-law and included former royal properties like Brightlingsea, Writtle, Lexden, Lawford and Newport in Essex, and Necton in Norfolk. The intention behind this fairly widespread alienation of royal demesne was probably to provide Harold with the resources necessary to defend his earldom from the contemporary Scandinavian threat, but perhaps also to win over his loyalty. The strategic location of a number of Harold's estates in Essex strongly suggest that defence was a priority among the reasons for his tenure. It was probably also at some point during his tenure of the East Anglian earldom that Harold was granted a number of estates forfeited by Athelstan, son of Tofi the Proud, including land at Waltham in Essex, Hitchen in Hertfordshire and Lambeth in Surrey, valued at £140 in total. It is also possible that Harold may have purchased some of the lands he held in East Anglia, though we have no specific examples of this.[13]

It was probably as part of the need to foster support in his new earldom that Harold, at around this time, had contracted a marriage with Edith 'Swan-neck', also known as Edith the Fair. She brought wide lands valued for tax at £366 in Hertfordshire, Buckinghamshire, Suffolk, Essex and Cambridgeshire, to her husband's support. This support was undoubtedly of considerable assistance to Harold, particularly the extensive lands held by Edith and the large number of men commended to her in Cambridgeshire, a county where he himself had relatively few of either.[14]

Harold seems to have added to his East Anglian estates following the forfeiture of his brother Swein in 1047, since when Swein sought restoration in 1049, Harold and his cousin Beorn opposed this declaring that 'they would give up to [Swein] nothing that the king had given them'. Although Swein was eventually, temporarily, restored a year later, Harold no longer raised any objection and so may either have retained the lands he had gained from Swein's forfeiture or, more probably, he received compensation from the estates of his murdered cousin Beorn. Unfortunately, we have no direct information about where these estates lay but the fact that Earl Beorn held authority in Hertfordshire, and so perhaps lands as well, may provide a clue. It is possible that it was at this point that Harold began to extend his landholdings into Hertfordshire and the surrounding shires; by 1066 he held extensive lands in this area but never, as far as we know, the authority of earl.[15]

In this way Harold gradually became one of the most powerful landholders in eastern England and, as such, attracted a considerable following. It is fortunate that the Domesday Book entries for the counties of Harold's East Anglian earldom preserve fairly full records of such commended men, who included some forty-five named men and one woman, and many unnamed, with land valued at around £230 in all. These individuals included Wulfric the Priest, who held 14 acres of land valued at 5s at Plunkers Green in Essex; Uhtred, who held 2 estates of 4 carucates valued at £6 in total at Houghton and Newton in Suffolk; Ordgar, who held 2 estates of 6 hides valued at £12 in total at Sawston and Harston in Cambridgeshire; and the single named woman, Aelflaed, who held 3 estates of 6 carucates valued at £14 in total at Wickham Skeith, Stonham and Willisham in Suffolk. In one instance, we are supplied with an example of the kind of circumstances which led such men to seek Harold's support. Stanwine of Peasenhall in Suffolk sought Harold's support during the outlawry of his previous lord, Eadric of Laxfield. Stanwine subsequently returned to Eadric's patronage, presumably after the latter's restoration but with Harold's permission. In addition to these freemen and minor *thegns*, Harold also sought and obtained the adherence of more important men. These included Leofwine of Bacton, who held extensive lands, in Suffolk and Essex from the king. Leofwine, in common with a number of other significant local landowners, although a royal *thegn*, was also commended to Harold for his estate at Bacton and so was, to an extent, Harold's man as well. Another of these prominent local men was Eadric the Steersman, a royal *thegn* and the commander of a royal ship, who held his estate at Blakeney in Norfolk in commendation to Harold.[16]

Other men greater than these also sought Earl Harold's favour, some even presenting him with gifts or bequests to secure this, while he in turn issued rewards for service. Ansgar the *Staller* made a gift to Harold of his estate of Leighs in Essex, 2½ hides valued at £4. Ansgar was a royal *staller* and a very powerful man, holding extensive estates throughout eastern England valued at £447 and with men commended to him holding lands valued at a further £205. Ansgar's gift was perhaps made in return for Harold's support for the retention of his other remaining lands after his father Athelstan's forfeiture, noted above, or for the recovery of some of his father's lost lands. In turn, Harold presented the Leighs estate to Scalpi, his *huscarl*, as a reward for service. A lady named Wulfgyth bequeathed an estate worth 8*s* at Fritton in Norfolk to Harold. In turn, he appears to have passed this land to one of his local supporters, Eadric of Laxfield, who held it in 1066. Harold's link to Eadric seems clear from his fostering of Eadric's men during the latter's exile, as indicated by the example of Stanwine of Peasenhall. Eadric was another powerful local lord with extensive estates in Norfolk and Suffolk valued at £191 and with men commended to him holding lands valued at a further £224. These powerful lords must have provided key supporters for Earl Harold. Similarly, lesser men also sought Harold's favour with gifts; Lady Wulfgyth's son, Ketel, bequeathed a half estate at 'Moran' in Norfolk to Harold, while Thurstan, son of Wine, bequeathed him a half mark of gold.[17]

It was by such grants and bequests that these people and many others hoped to secure the support and protection of Earl Harold. In return, the support of such local men permitted Harold to govern his earldom and to raise forces from it, for example, to join the royal fleet in 1049, and to support his father, initially, during his dispute with King Edward in 1051. In the latter case, however, Harold's authority proved insufficient to hold the loyalty of these men in the face of an open confrontation with the king. This reveals the latent strength of the king's position in disputes with his earls. The king was the lord of all royal *thegns* and could summon them to his aid and although commended to other lords they would normally obey their king, as happened in 1051. The exception came, perhaps, in cases where such men believed that an injustice had been done; when this happened they might well withhold their support as they did in 1052.

It is clear that Earl Harold had already become a wealthy and powerful man as Earl of East Anglia and his forfeiture, along with that of the rest of his family, in 1051–2 was therefore a disaster of unprecedented proportions. It put Harold in much the same position as his father had been back in 1009. Godwine, having already recovered from such a position once, was perhaps more confident about his ability to do so a second time. In contrast, this crisis probably brought home to Harold the need to avoid such a situation arising again, and he resolved to maintain a close relationship with the king. It was fortunate for Harold that his downfall proved transient and that, as the Chronicle makes clear, in 1052 he was restored to 'all that [he] held before'.[18]

Following his restoration, new opportunities to increase his land and influence soon fell to Harold as a result of the deaths, in quick succession, of his elder brother Swein and his father, Earl Godwine. Swein's death made Harold his father's principal heir and as such, on the latter's death in 1053, Harold must have inherited the largest proportion of Godwine's private estates. Unfortunately, there is no direct evidence to

Domesday Book, the opening page of the entries for Sussex.

confirm this. Harold's brothers, Tosti, Gyrth and Leofwine, must also have received a share so that Polhampton in Hampshire, granted to Godwine by Cnut, passed to Tosti. In addition, Harold's mother, Gytha, may have retained a life interest in a number of Godwine's former estates, and this was perhaps the reason for the latter's appearance in Domesday Book. More importantly, Harold also succeeded his father as Earl of Wessex and so came into possession of the extensive lands of this great earldom. Thus he came into possession of such comital estates as Aldermaston in Berkshire, Puddleton in Dorset, Old Cleeve in Somerset and Morehampstead in Devon. It was undoubtedly this dual increase in landholding that made Harold the most powerful man in England after the king, with lands valued at £1,633 in the shires of Wessex. [19]

On succeeding to his new earldom of Wessex, Harold 'resigned the one he had previously held' in East Anglia. Nevertheless, he continued to hold extensive lands in Norfolk, Suffolk, and especially Essex until 1066 and some have seen this as an appropriation of comital estates. There exists no definite proof of this, and, as has been noted above, these lands could have been granted by King Edward to his brother-in-law as private estates, which Harold was therefore entitled to retain after surrendering the lands of the earldom itself. It seems unlikely, too, that Earl Aelfgar, the new Earl of East Anglia, would have accepted a truncated earldom given the sensitivity he appeared to show towards his rights, and which, incidentally, would probably result in his exile in 1055 and 1058. The evidence is rather that clearly established comital lands passed to Harold's successors, so that, for example, his brother Gyrth held the 'third penny' of Ipswich in 1066. In this context it is possible that the distinction between official and private estates may have become blurred during the period following the Danish conquest. It is probable that King Cnut, as a foreigner, was less conscious or less respectful of the niceties of previous distinctions between official and private lands. As a result, he may have granted away lands previously associated with earldoms as private estates. This may be why we find a number of clearly comital estates, those associated with the payment of the 'third penny', in the hands of individuals who had no right to them. It is thus possible that some lands in East Anglia, which appear to show signs of having once been comital estates, came to Harold as private grants. Unfortunately, in view of the limited evidence available, it is unlikely that a final conclusion can be reached in this matter.[20]

One fact that is certain is that, although Harold surrendered his East Anglian earldom, many men of that earldom, including those listed on pp. 62–3, remained supportive of Harold. The reason for this is clearly that Harold was seen as a rising star and it therefore made sense for these men to maintain their links with him. As Harold's power increased as Earl of Wessex, so the protection and patronage he could offer these men increased and they wanted to secure their share of this.

Earl Harold would gain further lands on the death of Earl Ralph in 1057, when part of his former earldom passed to Harold. It was then that Harold probably acquired his extensive lands and rights valued at £201 in Herefordshire and Gloucestershire. A large part of these appear to have been directly associated with the office of earl, including Much Cowarne and Burghill in Herefordshire and the 'third penny' of the burghs of Winchecombe and Hereford. These lands and rights had probably previously been held by Ralph and by Harold's brother Swein, when they governed this area before him. Harold may also have gained from the exile of his brother Tosti in 1065 as he is recorded as holding extensive lands valued at £308 in Yorkshire and Lincolnshire, although he personally never held any authority in these northern shires, but there is nothing to confirm this.[21]

Alongside the direct acquisition of land in southern and western England, Earl Harold also won the support of many men in these areas, as he had done in East Anglia. Unfortunately, the Domesday Book entries for many shires in Harold's Wessex earldom fail to record men commended to Harold and we can only identify a small portion of these individuals. Many of these men no doubt previously supported Earl Godwine. Thus Azur, a royal *thegn* who held lands valued at £271 throughout central Wessex, held lands in Sussex valued at £32 from Godwine and others valued at a further £18 from Harold. Harold's own supporters in Wessex included freemen like Thorkell, who held an estate of 1 virgate valued at 10s at Rotherbridge in Sussex, Thorgils, who held an estate of 9 hides at Ashtead in Surrey valued at £10, and Thorbert, who held an estate of 8 hides at Ashton-under-Hill in Gloucestershire. In addition to these freemen and smaller *thegns*, Harold sought to secure support from more important men, just as he had done in East Anglia. These included Thurkill White, who held lands valued at £68 almost entirely in Herefordshire and largely from Harold himself, and royal *thegns* such as Cypping, who held lands valued at £136 in Hampshire but who also held an estate of 5 hides valued at £5 at Silchester from Harold, and Eadmer *Atre*, who held lands valued at £142 in Wessex and the East Midlands but who held an estate of 13 hides valued at £24 at Berkhampstead in Hertfordshire from Harold. Like those in East Anglia, these men were all to an extent men of Harold.[22]

Harold also sought the support of other great men such as Eadnoth the *Staller*, who held extensive estates in western Wessex valued at £154, and Aethelnoth *Cild*, who held extensive estates in Kent and eastern Wessex valued at £260. In order to win over these men Harold was prepared to offer generous gifts, and his influential backing in legal disputes. He presented Eadnoth with land valued at £1 at Islington in Dorset, which had been taken from a cleric, and Eadnoth also held other lands from him. He provided his support to Aethelnoth *Cild* in holding on to 'Merclesham' and Hawkhurst in Kent, against the claims of St Martin's Church at Dover.

All of these men, however great themselves, contributed their support to Harold in varying degrees and so ensured his firm control of southern England. They would later support his invasion of Wales and his attempt on the throne, and thereafter would fight to defend his kingship.[23]

The dispute between Aethelnoth *Cild* and St Martin's leads us to consider another way in which Harold may have built up his lands – acquisition from the Church. It was a fairly common occurrence throughout this period that churches had to fight hard to retain their lands against encroachment by powerful and unscrupulous laymen. Earl Godwine, certainly, had an unenviable reputation in this respect, having undoubtedly obtained lands at Folkestone in Kent, from Christ Church, Canterbury, which the author of the *Vita Eadwardi* freely admitted rightfully belonged to the archbishopric. It has also been suggested that Godwine may have been involved in the illegal dissolution of Berkeley Abbey and as a result, his wife, Countess Gytha, is said to have refused to consume any produce from its former lands, presumably in fear of God's retribution. In Harold's own case, twenty-three claims of the loss of Church lands are recorded against him in Domesday Book, and a further three are noted elsewhere. This seems rather a large number at first sight. The lands concerned range from one hide in Cornwall, recorded as taken from St Petroc's Church, to some fifty hides in Somerset, claimed by the Bishop of Wells. The accusations appear particularly serious in those cases where the sources tell of lands taken 'wrongfully', and in some instances 'by force' or 'through violence'.[24]

A number of things should be borne in mind when considering the evidence of these cases against Harold. Domesday Book, which contains the majority of these accusations, is a source which is biased against the earl and it seems probable that its compilers took the opportunity to blacken his name by highlighting complaints against him in particular. To some extent this is confirmed by the failure of Domesday Book to record cases against Earl Leofric and members of his family, who are known, from other sources, to have been accused of similar actions. It is also worth noting that in at least eleven out of the twenty-six cases against Harold, Norman laymen subsequently continued to hold the lands concerned, in spite of the clergy's complaints. Thus lands claimed by the Church were later retained by various Normans, including Alfred of Marlborough, Robert of Romney, King William's half-brother, Count Robert of Mortain, the Archbishop of Canterbury, and even King William himself. Indeed, King William kept Melcombe Horsey in Dorset in spite of the existence of a royal writ to the contrary! He did restore Eaton Bishop in Herefordshire to the Bishop of Hereford, but only in exchange for other lands. This suggests that either the Normans were not much different to Harold, or perhaps that in some cases the Church's complaints were considered to have been unsubstantiated.[25]

The difficulty with the majority of the accusations against Harold is that we are unaware of the full background and thus we are unable to confirm or refute them clearly. In effect, we are presented with the case for the prosecution but not with that for the defence, which makes it difficult to reach a valid judgement. The case of Steyning in Sussex may represent the seizure, in 1066, of a coastal estate from a Norman holder to assist the defence of the area and it will be discussed in Chapter Nine. In the case raised by Giso, Bishop of Wells, over the estates at Congresbury and Banwell in Somerset, we are fortunate in having some details of the background. These appear to indicate that his complaint resulted from a legal dispute over the will of his predecessor, Duduc. In this case, Harold may in fact have been fulfilling his duty as head of the shire court by holding the lands until the dispute over the bequest was legally settled. The only surviving writ from Harold's reign as king relates to Wells, and it seems to indicate no major dispute with Bishop Giso. Indeed, King William continued to hold Congresbury in 1086, allowing the bishop to hold only part of it from him, though Banwell had been restored to the bishop by then. In the case where Harold is accused of helping Aethelnoth *Cild* to take 'by violence' land at 'Merclesham' and Hawkhurst in Kent from St Martin's Church at Dover, Domesday itself goes on to tell us that the canons were given 'an unfair exchange'. This perhaps speaks of some astute dealing by Aethelnoth, rather than any actual misappropriation, and Harold's violence may simply have meant the firm hand of the secular law. It should also be noted that these lands were among those the Normans would fail to restore.

A total of nine of the twenty-six cases against Harold concern lands taken from the Bishopric of Hereford, and it seems likely that Harold took control of these lands for reasons of national defence. In June 1056 Gruffydd of Wales slew Bishop Leofgar leaving the bishopric exposed to Welsh attacks, like the one which had resulted in the sack of Hereford the year before. It was probably at this point that Harold took control of these estates of the bishopric, in order to provide him with local resources to assist in the defence of the Border. Earl Harold would not secure authority over the earldom of Hereford until Earl Ralph's death a year later, and so probably held few lands in the shire. Earl Ralph had lands there but had already proved himself incapable of defending the area. Bishop Ealdred, who had assumed temporary control of the bishopric at this point, may have invited Harold's control of these lands. He was probably eager to adopt this arrangement as he already had his hands full administering the two bishoprics of Hereford and Worcester, without also having to look to their defence. However, Harold would subsequently retain these lands despite gaining control of the earldom of Hereford itself after 1057 and despite the final elimination of the Welsh threat in 1063. Therefore, there is a strong possibility that Harold acted dubiously in this case, although this is not certain.

There are no clues to assist us in determining the validity of the remaining twelve cases. The Church's own custom of leasing lands for 1, 2 or 3 lives often resulted in disputes about ownership. There are hints of reasons or causes behind some of the alleged seizures, and the remainder involve rather small amounts of land representing a tiny proportion of Harold's total estates. The recorded cases, excluding that of Steyning in Sussex, involve only some £150 worth of land compared to Harold's total holdings of £2,846. If this does represent misappropriation, it seems rather small scale and not too different from that alleged against many others.[26]

In these various ways, legitimate and possibly unscrupulous, as Earl of Wessex Harold continued to build up a position of landed wealth which was unrivalled by any other noble in England. It was this which provided Harold with the means to make himself King Edward's right-hand man and, ultimately, provided a base for his advance to the kingship itself. How Harold made use of his lands and wealth is another difficult question to answer because of the lack of sources, but again there are some clues.

Most importantly, the ownership of such large tracts of land allowed Harold to reward his own followers and to foster relations with royal *thegns* through gifts and leases of some of his land. Three of Harold's *huscarls*, Scalpi, Gauti and Tofi, who had probably all retired from active service, are recorded as holding land in Domesday Book. Scalpi was provided with 4 hides and 128 acres of land in Essex and Suffolk valued at £7 in total. Gauti was provided with 5 hides of land in Middlesex, Essex and Hertfordshire valued at £8 and 10s in total. Tofi was provided with 4 hides of land at Great Barrington in Gloucestershire valued at £7. In the case of Scalpi's estate at Leighs in Essex, he was certainly granted it by Harold, no doubt in return for his earlier loyal service, and this presumably is also how the others obtained their lands. There were probably many other men who had been endowed by Harold directly, but few are recorded. The exceptions are Beorhtweald of Wokefield in Berkshire and Leofgar of Thames Ditton in Surrey. The former was granted 1½ hides at Wokefield as a gift by Harold, and the latter received 6 hides at Thames Ditton valued at £4 in return for his service. Greater landholders were also propitiated by gifts of land, as in the cases already noted concerning Aethelnoth *Cild* and Eadnoth the *Staller*.[27]

These extensive lands also provided Harold with a cash income. However, although we know the tax valuation placed on Harold's estates, we are unable to calculate the exact income that these lands produced for the earl. There can be no doubt that it was an immense fortune, especially given the favourable tax concessions on a number of Harold's estates, such as that at Pyrford in Surrey, where the assessment had been reduced from 27 hides to 16 hides. In addition to the direct income from his lands, Harold's official position as earl allowed him to reap the profits of the 'third penny' from royal dues associated with it. These peace-time profits could on occasion be boosted by loot from successful warfare, like Harold's later campaigns against the Welsh and the Norwegians.[28]

The wealth thus gathered was put to many and varied uses, but again we have to search carefully for evidence of these. Firstly, a significant proportion would have been required simply to cover the costs arising from Harold's official duties as earl and later royal lieutenant. This would have included the expenses of administration, taxation and justice, the costs of defence of the realm and of attendance at court and on royal embassies. The payment of the 'third penny' and the income from the comital estates was intended to cover the costs of these official duties. Secondly, a large portion would have been required to cover Harold's own daily expenses and those of his immediate family. This included payment of stipends for those of his personal *huscarls* attending on the earl or garrisoning his estates, and not yet endowed with lands, unlike Scalpi, Gauti and Tofi mentioned above. It would also have had to cover the expenses of those reeves who administered Harold's estates, like the unnamed man recorded by Domesday Book as responsible for Harold's estate at Writtle in Essex. This personal income would also have been used to maintain priests, ranging from the unnamed individual, recorded only as Harold's priest, also at Writtle in Essex, to Harold's own chaplain Leofgar, later promoted to the Bishopric of Hereford. These priests ministered to the spiritual needs of Harold and his family. Other private expenses, such as the costs of his future pilgrimage to Rome, of the education of his daughter, Gunnhild, at Wilton, of the purchase of religious relics, of his hunting and hawking, and of commissioning precious books, would also have been met by these resources. [29]

Above and beyond these necessary expenses, a man of Harold's stature was expected to reflect his wealth and power by means of personal display and by the giving of gifts. Harold's personal ostentation is reflected in his banner, which portrayed the image of a warrior worked in pure gold and jewels and was later judged a fittingly expensive gift to be despatched to the Pope in Rome. The gifts Harold presented to his favourite church of Holy Cross at Waltham also give an indication of the ostentatious manner in which he and his family may have lived. If Harold could donate to Waltham vestments made of cloth of gold and adorned with gold and jewels, as well as furnishings of gold and silver, his own household must have been similarly blessed. In the scenes of the Bayeux Tapestry, Harold's lifestyle is illustrated, including the lavish banquets he attended, the grand palaces he frequented, and the fine horses and ships he used for travel. He himself is usually portrayed finely dressed, in a way which indicates a man of rank. The need to display power and wealth would also have extended to Harold's followers, who would have needed to reflect suitably their patron's wealth. There are few examples in the records of gifts by Harold to others and those that do exist relate to gifts to the king. Nevertheless, these may stand as an indication of his ability to reward his followers. Thus Harold presented Edward with the solid gold figure-head from Gruffydd's ship and other treasures from the spoils of his Welsh victory in 1063. He also built and furnished a hunting lodge at Portskewet in conquered Wales for the king's use. In such ways, Harold sought to cement his relationship with the king and would have done the same with his followers, though on a lesser scale.[30]

In addition to the need to foster and encourage support among his lay supporters by gifts of land or money, there was the equally vital need for a great man like Harold to propitiate the Church. There were two reasons for this: firstly, senior churchmen, like great laymen, could provide support in many secular affairs, and Harold would certainly benefit from this on several occasions; and secondly, and far more importantly, the Church alone could intercede with God for a man's immortal soul. The giving of gifts, whether in goods or lands, to the Church played a vital part in medieval life. It may appear from what has been written above about Harold's apparent predation on some Church lands, that his status in this area was not good, but this is not the case. In common with other men of the time, Harold was selective about the churches which received his attention and bounty, and as a result was open to criticism by those which did not benefit. A similar favouritism was shown by King Edward to Westminster, Earl Leofric to Coventry and Earl Odda to Deerhurst.

Harold would be recorded as a benefactor or champion of Malmesbury Abbey, Durham Cathedral, Peterborough Abbey, Abingdon Abbey and in particular, of his own special foundation of Holy Cross at Waltham. Harold and his father, Godwine, apparently interceded with King Edward to prevent Hereman, Bishop of Ramsbury, taking over Malmesbury Abbey as the new seat of his diocese. The clerks of Durham recorded the obit of Harold Godwineson in their *Liber Vitae*. The monks of

The seal of Harold's College of Holy Cross at Waltham.

Peterborough also remembered Harold as their benefactor, despite their Abbot, Leofric, being a member of the supposedly rival family of Leofric. Harold also intervened to assist Abbot Ordric of Abingdon in the enforcement of the abbey's rights to land at Leckhampstead and Kingston Bagpuize. In addition to Harold's own patronage, Edith 'Swan-neck', his wife, was a benefactor of St Benet of Holme, presenting it with an estate at Thurgarton in Norfolk. However, the bulk of Harold's attention was reserved for his own particular foundation at Waltham.[31]

This small church had probably first come to Harold's notice when he received the estate of Waltham, where it stood, as a gift from King Edward, following the forfeiture of Athelstan, son of Tofi the Proud, perhaps in the late 1040s. Tofi's church at Waltham contained a 'Holy Cross' in the form of a carving of the crucifixion with venerable and miraculous associations. Tofi and his wife had made gifts of land and wealth to this church in keeping with their status. When Harold took control of the church he adopted it as his own, motivated, it would appear, by genuine religious devotion. The later *Vita Haroldi* attributed Harold's devotion to a miraculous cure from a paralysis which supposedly affected him after his Welsh campaign of 1063. This story is clearly confused because Harold rebuilt the church in 1060, three years before this. The later Waltham Chronicle reveals Harold's devotion in considerable detail. It includes the story of how he visited there to pray before his last battle at Hastings. He was also later reputed to have used 'Holy Cross' as a battle cry at Hastings. It was at Waltham that Harold instituted the construction and decoration of a new and elaborate stone church, perhaps in emulation of King Edward's Westminster. Unfortunately, no traces of Harold's church remain in the current fabric of the building, all of which is of a later date. We have no idea what form it took or what style of construction was used, although further archaeological investigation may reveal more details. Harold's new building was consecrated to Christ and the Holy Cross at a ceremony held on 3 May 1060, the feast of the Finding of the True Cross, and attended by King Edward, Queen Edith and many others.[32]

Harold staffed his new foundation as a college of canons with a dean, Wulfwine, twelve canons, each of whom would be paid 40s a year, and a Lotharingian schoolmaster called Adelard. He would endow the canons with 13 estates of a total of over 70 hides in Essex, Hertfordshire, Bedfordshire and Berkshire, valued at £43 in total. He also lavished a great deal of treasure on the internal decoration and fittings of the church, including gold and silver church plate, church vestments made of cloth of gold and adorned with jewels, and a magnificent altar of gold and marble, supported by golden lions and decorated with paintings of the apostles. It has been considered that the account, admittedly late, of Harold's gifts to Waltham contains some exaggeration of his generosity, but when compared with King Edward's gifts to Westminster and given the relative wealth of the two men, this seems unlikely. Indeed, an inventory of Waltham's possessions made at the time of the Dissolution in 1540 mentions two Anglo–Saxon Gospel books with ornate silver gilt covers which had earlier featured among Harold's gifts.[33]

Naturally, Harold's generosity made a significant impact on the canons of Waltham. As a result, they performed the final service of burying his body, and thereafter almost alone preserved his memory, despite Norman attempts to discredit or obliterate it. They remembered him as their second founder and greatest benefactor in a later twelfth-century account of their foundation, and subsequently compiled a life of Harold, though this latter was largely pious and legendary. Locally, Harold's name also lived on in the Essex place-names, Harold's Park at Nazeing and Harold's Wood at Romford, both on former Waltham lands.[34]

In spite of the scarcity of the sources and their patchy nature, it has been possible to trace an outline of the way in which Harold built up his huge estates throughout England. The uses to which the wealth arising from this property was put have also been sketched. These ranged from creating a power base for his rise to prominence, through building up political support by gifts to laymen, to expressing devotion to God by gifts to the Church.

CHAPTER FIVE

EARL OF WESSEX

A noble earl who, all the time had loyally followed his lord's commands with words and deeds, and neglected nothing that met the need of the people's king.[1]

In 1053 Harold unexpectedly succeeded to the great earldom of Wessex and to those wide lands of his father discussed in the previous chapter, and he also became head of his large family. He did not succeed to the office of earl by hereditary right but rather as King Edward's choice to replace his father. It was a natural choice since he would in any case have inherited the advantage of extensive family lands and contacts in Wessex from his father. As earl he could use these assets to help him perform his duties for the king more effectively. Most historians give insufficient emphasis to this change, assuming a continuity between father and son which is not entirely justified. Harold was a different man from his father, although he had generally followed his lead until now. He lacked his father's long experience of administration and warfare; his own eight-year tenure of the East Anglian earldom could not compare with Godwine's thirty-three years as Earl of Wessex under four different kings; his military experience largely consisted of small-scale raiding.

However, there were also differences which worked to Harold's advantage. He was free of the stigma associated with his father's implication in the death of *Atheling* Alfred, despite the attempt by later Norman writers to smear him with this. There are indications that Edward liked him personally, when he had disliked or even hated his father. Godwine's dominance and interference in Edward's reign had caused resentment, but the Chronicle refers to his sons as 'the king's favourites'. This cannot refer to the brutal Swein and most probably refers to Harold and Tosti, since Godwine's other sons are rather shadowy figures. Indeed, Edward's feelings for Harold are perhaps shown by his failure to demand hostages from Harold in 1051 and from the ease with which Harold succeeded his father. The latter action might have been made difficult had Edward been determined to destroy the entire family. It will be recalled that Harold had not supported his prodigal brother, Swein, to the extent that his father had. Indeed, in 1049 he had refused to support Swein's return from exile when his father did so. It would seem that much of the tension and bitterness of the past, had now been swept away and Harold and Edward were able to start afresh.[2]

One major difficulty, in the form of Edward's childless marriage to Edith, remained to be resolved. As already shown, this problem had proved a decisive element in the recent crisis. Initially, Edward had been compelled to restore Edith, as

King Edward and Earl Harold. (The Bayeux Tapestry – 11th Century. By special permission of the City of Bayeux)

part of the settlement with Godwine. Now, even with Godwine dead, his sons remained powerful enough for Edward to consider it problematic to repudiate her again. Edward may have hoped for another opportunity in the future, perhaps in the natural course of events, but meanwhile it was probably at this time that serious consideration was given to an alternative solution. This solution was not the designation of William of Normandy as Edward's heir, but the return to England of *Atheling* Edward 'the Exile', son of Edmund 'Ironside'. This solution arose perhaps at the suggestion of Archbishop Stigand, who had been the chief intermediary of the settlement in 1052. He had been Cnut's priest as early as 1020 and so was old enough to remember the exile of *Atheling* Edward and his brother Edmund back in 1017. The fate of the brothers for a period thereafter was unknown, but it was soon discovered that Edward at least was still alive, and after enquiries were made his location was established in Hungary. Subsequently, arrangements were set in motion to establish contact with him. The considerable lapse of time between the restoration of Queen Edith in September 1052 and the first attempt to contact *Atheling* Edward in autumn 1054 arose from the need to establish his exact location and situation, and to prepare the necessary groundwork for the embassy to be sent to secure his return.[3]

The reason for choosing this distant and unknown figure, though he had been born in England, in preference to Edward's other relatives, Earl Ralph and Count Walter of the Vexin, was probably a mixture of his throne-worthy status as a king's son and strong popular sympathy for his father in England. The latter, King Edmund 'Ironside', was still remembered in England as a great hero. It should also be remembered that *Atheling* Edward's mother, Ealdgyth, widow of Sigeferth, was related to the family of Earl Leofric of Mercia. In contrast, Earl Ralph was probably considered less suitable because of his descent through the female line and his French links, but also perhaps because of his poor military showing with the fleet in 1052. Count Walter of the Vexin, lacked his brother Ralph's English connections and was busy ruling his own principality in France. All things considered, the prospect of *Atheling* Edward's return as heir to the kingdom must have been popular generally, while King Edward and his earls no doubt saw the possibility of moulding this stranger to their own designs.[4]

It was in order to settle the succession crisis that, after careful preparation and at the first opportunity, a mission was sent to the Continent under Bishop Ealdred of Worcester in 1054. This skilled diplomat went to Cologne to request the assistance of the German Emperor Henry III in contacting the Hungarian king to seek the return of *Atheling* Edward from his European exile. This was a natural way to progress, since the English knew nothing of this distant land, while it lay on the borders of the Empire and acknowledged its overlordship from time to time. However, the time was not propitious, as the Emperor was currently in dispute with Hungary and despite Ealdred's waiting almost a whole year at Cologne, nothing came of this embassy. The plan was not abandoned though, and following the death of Emperor Henry III in 1056 another attempt would be made.[5]

In the meantime, another of Cnut's great earls, Siward of Northumbria, died at York early in 1055, leaving an infant son, Waltheof, as his heir. Siward had lost Osbeorn, his adult son by his first wife, in battle on 27 July 1054 during his campaign to install Malcolm *Canmore* on the throne of Scotland. A nephew, also named Siward, fell in the same battle, leaving young Waltheof as the earl's only heir. Had it not been for this disastrous event, it is probable that Osbeorn would have succeeded his father in the earldom. Instead, at a council held on 17 March 1055, it was decided that a mere boy could not be expected to control the turbulent northern earldom. A firm hand was required and therefore Edward appointed Tosti, brother of Harold, to the earldom. This choice was Edward's own, as it was for all earldoms, and he certainly seems to have looked on Tosti favourably. The king's choice was undoubtedly supported by both Earl Harold and Queen Edith but it may have dashed the hopes of Earl Aelfgar of East Anglia.

As next in seniority among the earls, Aelfgar had perhaps seen himself as a potential candidate for Siward's earldom. As Harold's replacement as Earl of East Anglia, it must have seemed natural to him that he stood next in line for promotion to a major earldom. He had been loyal to the king in the recent crisis, even when forced to step aside to accommodate the return of Harold. In contrast, the inexperienced Tosti had held no major office and had been involved in the recent rebellion. No doubt Aelfgar, if promoted to Northumbria, would have been prepared to surrender East Anglia to Tosti in turn. It appears that he was not prepared to accept the king's choice of Tosti ahead of him, and he would also have been aware that the promotion of Tosti would result in a significant accession of power to the Godwine family. Aelfgar therefore probably complained to the king, perhaps rather vociferously, and as a result found himself outlawed.[6]

Chronicle E states that Aelfgar was actually charged with treason, the others say he was outlawed without any guilt. The treason involved may have amounted to no more than disputing the king's decision to appoint Tosti as Earl of Northumbria. This may perhaps explain the different assessments in the Chronicle accounts of the extent of Aelfgar's guilt. Some may have considered the disputing of a royal decision as a fairly mild incident not warranting outlawry. There is no suggestion that Aelfgar intended to take any direct action against the king prior to his outlawry; he does not, for example, appear to have made any attempt to call out troops as Godwine had in 1051. It has been suggested that the treason might have arisen from the fact that Aelfgar had forged an alliance with Gruffydd of North Wales. Certainly his daughter, Alditha, was later married to the Welsh prince and the latter was to assist the earl following his exile. Such an alliance with the king's enemy would provide ample justification for outlawry. Against this interpretation is the close link indicated by Chronicle E between Tosti's appointment to Northumbria and Aelfgar's exile, where both decisions were made in the same council. The perceived lack of justification in other versions of the Chronicle for Aelfgar's outlawry would also seem to make an existing alliance with Gruffydd unlikely.[7]

The exile of Earl Aelfgar has been seen as an attempt by Harold and his family to encircle or eliminate their Mercian rivals. This seems unlikely as the decision to outlaw him seems to have received the full backing of King Edward rather than being a Godwine family affair. In addition, Earl Leofric appears to have made no attempt to protect or intercede for his son, as might be expected if this had been an attack on his family directed by the sons of Godwine. No source mentions any action by Earl Leofric in support of his son, although perhaps, after the events of 1051, he knew better than to oppose directly the king's wishes. It has been suggested that Leofric was in failing health and that this was the reason for his inaction, but he was still able to lead his forces against the Welsh in 1056. The sparse details of this event make it difficult to tell what lies behind it. The best suggestion seems to be that Aelfgar was so vehement in his opposition to Tosti's succession that he said something rash which caused Edward to outlaw him. Chronicle E's mention of words of treason slipping out of his mouth against his will perhaps implies this.[8]

Earl Aelfgar followed the way of previous exiles and immediately began to plan his return. Indeed, he followed the path of Harold in 1051 and fled to Ireland, probably to Dublin, to recruit a mercenary fleet, which later went to Chester to await payment. However, he clearly felt this force of eighteen ships to be insufficient, and he decided to seek the assistance of Gruffydd ap Llewellyn of North Wales. The suggestion that the two men had an existing alliance is possible, but it was not without precedent for an exile to arrive in a foreign land with which he had no previous contact, seeking aid. Harold himself had already done this in 1051. Whether they were already allies or not, Earl Aelfgar arrived at Gruffydd's court faced with the need to persuade the latter to aid him. It might seem that Gruffydd would need little excuse to invade England, but at this time he had other priorities. Gruffydd's vital concern at this time was, and indeed had been for the past ten years, his contest with his rival for power in Wales, Gruffydd ap Rhydderch of South Wales. The timely arrival of Earl Aelfgar, with eighteen ships of Irish mercenaries, allowed him to make a raid into South Wales which finally succeeded in disposing of his great adversary. There is no doubt that Aelfgar took his Irish mercenaries to Wales and Welsh sources place Gruffydd's attack on Hereford directly after the slaying of his namesake rival, suggesting that the two are linked. (It should be recalled that Gruffydd had previously sought the aid of Earl Swein in 1046 against his southern rival.) It might be argued that the Welsh sources fail to mention Aelfgar's assistance in the slaying of Gruffydd of South Wales, but they similarly omit all mention of Aelfgar's well-established role in the attack on Hereford. In return for this victory, which brought South Wales into Gruffydd's hands at last, the Welsh king would surely have been only too willing to join Aelfgar and his Irishmen in a raid into England, with the additional prospect of booty to tempt him. The combined forces of Gruffydd and Aelfgar then invaded Herefordshire, where Earl Ralph was in power. The text of Domesday Book records the effects of their devastation in Archenfield. The selection of this target was probably dictated by the need to avoid attacking Mercia, where Aelfgar's father, Leofric, was earl, but this attack on King Edward's nephew may confirm that Aelfgar's dispute was with the king himself.[9]

Earl Ralph gathered the forces of his earldom and met the combined forces of Gruffydd and Aelfgar outside Hereford. Ralph was defeated and the victorious army went on to sack the town itself on 24 October. Chronicle C attributes Earl Ralph's defeat to his attempts to employ English troops in an unnatural role as cavalry, but it appears rather that he was merely unlucky or incompetent, as with the fleet in 1052. After all, English infantry forces had themselves suffered a series of defeats by Gruffydd in 1039, 1049 and 1052, and would be beaten again in the future. Nevertheless, this military disaster forced King Edward to summon assistance, from beyond Ralph's earldom, to defend the border. This force was led by Earl Harold of Wessex, as the senior earl in England and also perhaps because Earl Leofric was not trusted to oppose his own son effectively. Indeed, the wording of the Chronicle that Harold's army consisted of 'a force . . . collected from very nearly all England' may suggest the absence of Mercian troops.[10]

This was Harold's first major campaign as a commander and he moved cautiously. He advanced a short way into Welsh territory, causing Gruffydd to fall back into South Wales to avoid battle with Harold's superior forces. The latter then fortified Hereford against future attacks and opened negotiations with the invaders. This may seem a rather unspectacular start to Harold's military career, but it gained the necessary objective of achieving peace. If he had risked an advance further into Wales, a disaster might have resulted in view of Gruffydd's past successes, especially if Harold's force indeed lacked the active backing of Mercian troops. It should be noted that it is Chronicle C, supposedly anti-Godwinist, which provides details of Earl Harold's successful actions on this campaign.

The terms reached at the meeting between the two sides, held at Billingsley, are only revealed in the sources as they relate to England. Thus Aelfgar was restored to his earldom of East Anglia, but at the price of accepting Tosti's retention of Northumbria. The suggestion that Gyrth had received part of East Anglia during Aelfgar's exile, as

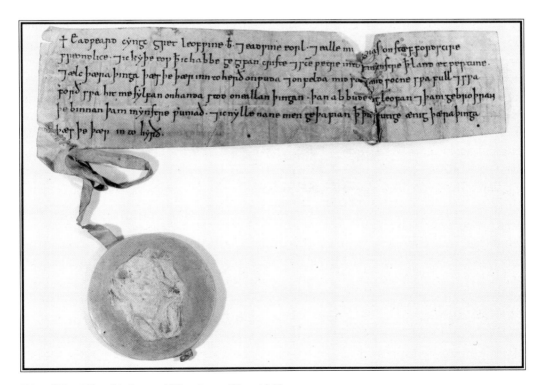

Writ of King Edward in favour of Westminster Abbey, 1065.

stated by the *Vita Eadwardi*, seems unlikely. Presumably, Gruffydd of Wales also gained something, probably some border territory, possibly Archenfield. There are hints in the later Domesday Book of English lands which had fallen into Gruffydd's hands, but, not surprisingly perhaps, nothing is recorded in the contemporary English sources. In return, Gruffydd must have agreed not to raid English territory in the future and to accept Edward's overlordship. This must have seemed a poor return, as the potential threat he presented to England remained undiminished. However, the important thing at this point was to separate him from his dangerous alliance with Aelfgar and this had been achieved, at least for the present. The problem arising from Tosti's succession to Northumbria had been resolved peacefully, and the equilibrium of the kingdom was restored. Such a statesmanlike arrangement achieved with minimal risk sits well with Harold's patient character, as described in the *Vita Eadwardi*.[11]

On 10 February 1056 Athelstan, Bishop of Hereford, died, perhaps as a result of old age, but more likely because of the trauma of the burning of his minster by the Welsh. King Edward took the opportunity to appoint as bishop in his place a man who could bolster the defences of the area against the Welsh threat where Earl Ralph had failed. The man chosen was Leofgar, who had been Harold's personal chaplain, and no doubt Harold advised on the appointment. This should not be seen as an intervention in Church affairs in the same sense as when Earl Godwine intervened in the Canterbury election of 1051, on behalf of his kinsman Aethelric. The reason for the appointment this time was clearly related to the need to select someone to undertake effective border defence. What was required was a bishop trained in worldly arts and able to defend his flock, as Bishop Ealdred of neighbouring Worcester had been called upon to do in 1049. Such a man was unlikely to be found among King Edward's more scholarly clerks, and Leofgar was therefore chosen as a more suitable candidate. He was soon to justify the choice, if not quite as originally desired.[12]

The monks who compiled the Chronicle entries clearly disapproved of Leofgar, but not, it would appear, because of his relationship to Earl Harold or because of any influence the latter may have brought to bear on his appointment. The tone of their accounts clearly reveals their disapproval of the warlike character of a man who was even more militant than Bishop Ealdred or Abbot Aethelwig of Evesham, both of whom led military forces at times. It was clearly felt that Leofgar was unsuitable as a bishop, especially, perhaps, replacing as he did such a saintly old man as Athelstan. In reality, Leofgar's fault lay not in his military outlook, but in the rashness which led him to campaign into Wales against Gruffydd without support. As a result, he was slain at Glasbury-on-Wye on 16 June 1056, along with Sheriff Aelfnoth of Hereford and a large part of their forces. The presence of the sheriff suggests that this had been a local expedition drawn from the shire itself. This was clearly not part of the plan behind his appointment by the king. In view of Harold's reluctance to advance far into Wales even with more men, it seems unlikely he would have wished Bishop Leofgar to do so with only the men of the shire. The raid may have been intended to recover the district of Archenfield, which was probably among the areas lost to Gruffydd the previous year and which had belonged to Leofgar's bishopric, but the result was disastrous. Earls Harold and Leofric and Bishop Ealdred gathered to protect the border in the wake of this defeat, but no attempt was made to advance into Wales, in spite of their much larger forces. Instead, as in the previous year, negotiations were opened which resulted in the English recognizing Gruffydd as King of All Wales in return for his acceptance of Edward as his overlord. Again, Harold fulfilled the role of diplomat rather than warrior, but the threat from Gruffydd, though temporarily stilled, remained.[13]

With the menace of Gruffydd momentarily pacified, affairs of state were once more focused on the succession when news arrived of the death of Emperor Henry III on 5 October 1056. It was at once decided to make another effort to bring about the return of *Atheling* Edward from Hungary. We have seen above how Bishop Ealdred's earlier mission had failed as a result of Henry III's conflict with Hungary. The latter was now removed from the scene, and it was no doubt hoped that the regency council for his young son, Henry IV, might have different priorities. Fortunately, this proved to be the case and the dispute between the Empire and Andrew I of Hungary ended in a compromise treaty soon after. It was felt, therefore, that the time was ripe for another attempt to bring about Edward's return. This time it appears that Earl Harold himself was chosen to perform the vital mission, which it was hoped would finally secure the royal succession.[14]

Although none of the contempory sources refer directly to Harold's involvement in this mission, there are indications which point to it. A *Haroldi Ducis* is found among the witnesses of a diploma issued by Count Baldwin V of Flanders, Harold's brother-in-law, on 13 November 1056 at St Omer. Harold's presence in Flanders so soon after news of the Emperor's death may indicate that he had already set out on the first stage of his mission. From St Omer, Count Baldwin himself proceeded to Cologne, where on 5 December 1056 he arranged peace terms with Agnes of Poitiers, Regent of the Empire, on behalf of her son Henry IV. Harold probably joined Count Baldwin and his party in order to be introduced to the Regent, and to gain an opportunity to explain his mission to her. At Cologne he was probably successful in gaining the support of the Regent and possibly of Pope Victor II, who was also present.

The Imperial party then travelled to Regensburg on the Danube for Christmas, and it was here that Harold probably first opened negotiations with the Hungarian King Andrew I, and then perhaps with *Atheling* Edward himself. However, a great deal required to be discussed and considered before the *atheling* would consent to return to what was, after all, a strange land. He no doubt had to be persuaded of the safety of his person and of his family. King Andrew, likewise, had to be persuaded to release the *atheling*, and was possibly offered gifts or bribes to aid his decision.

While awaiting a response, Harold may have accompanied Pope Victor on his return to Rome for Easter 1057. The *Vita Eadwardi* refers, in a difficult passage, to Harold visiting Rome after conducting business in what is termed 'Frankish' country, and this may reflect a faint echo of this mission. The verity of Harold's visit to Rome has been doubted, but it would be foolish for the author of the *Vita Eadwardi*, a source close to his family, to lie about this. The much later *Vita Haroldi*, in an account which shows much confusion with his brother Tosti's own visit to Rome, refers to Harold collecting relics in Rome and a surviving Waltham Abbey relic list seems to provide some confirmation of this by recording a number of items which may have come from Rome. Thereafter, Harold may have returned by way of Bavaria, where he collected *Atheling* Edward and his family, who had finally made up their mind to return, and from whence he escorted them back to England.[14]

Apart from the fact that Harold was in Flanders in November 1056, and that he is known to have visited Rome, there exists no direct evidence for these events. The record of religious relics donated by Harold to his church at Waltham provides some evidence that he may have visited the regions of Europe covered by a journey like that outlined. He is known to have obtained relics from Ghent, Aachen, Cologne, and Worms, perhaps en route from St Omer to Regensburg, and similarly he collected items from Metz, Rheims, Noyon and St Riquier, which he could have visited on his return journey. It is possible, of course, that Harold merely sent agents to collect these relics, but it is perhaps too much of a coincidence that the pieces all originate from places which could have been on his route. Of course, the relics could have been collected on other journeys and at other times, but if so it is difficult to place these in Harold's busy career.[15]

Aside from this circumstantial evidence, proof of Harold's journey to seek out *Atheling* Edward rests largely on the coincidence of events and probability. What can be said is that Harold is not recorded as being anywhere else between his presence around July/August 1056 on the Welsh border and sometime before September 1057, when *Atheling* Edward probably arrived in England. The *atheling's* return is entered in the Chronicle immediately prior to the death of Earl Leofric which occurred on 30 September 1057. After the failure of Ealdred's earlier mission, it is certain that someone with considerable diplomatic skill and great prestige was required, first to smooth the passage to Hungary, then to persuade the *atheling* to return, and finally to escort him safely back. After his recent diplomatic achievements in Wales and given his position as a trusted servant of King Edward, Harold was surely an obvious choice.

Unfortunately, *Atheling* Edward had not long arrived back in England when he died unexpectedly in London, sometime before September 1057. Chronicle D expresses great dismay at this event, but this should not be read as signifying suspicion of an unnatural death. The many hopes for the future which rested on Edward, only to be dashed when he died so soon after his return, are surely enough to justify this reaction by the chronicler. He had spent some forty years in exile and undertaken a return journey of 800 miles but died before he could even meet his uncle, King Edward.[16]

Although disappointing for those anticipating his return, *Atheling* Edward's death did not unduly disturb the succession as his young son, Edgar, had arrived safely with the family party. Within a decade or so this boy would be old enough to succeed and could, in this time, be prepared for kingship. In the meantime, other candidates, such as Earl Ralph, were still available in case of any further accidents of fate. The succession had finally been secured, as had been required since 1050. Although King Edward and Queen Edith could not have children of their own, the safe arrival of young Edgar and his two sisters provided them with a ready-made family, and the kingdom with an heir. Confirmation of Edgar's position is provided by the designation *atheling* found in all the sources and signifying his status as prospective heir, and by the Chronicle's later reference to the kingship as 'his proper due'.[17]

This same year of 1057 brought other deaths among men of note, and consequent changes in the English polity. On 30 September Earl Leofric, the last of Cnut's great earls, died and his son, Aelfgar, succeeded to his Mercian earldom. This succession was not made by hereditary right but rather as a result of a decision by the king. However, as in the case of Harold's succession to Wessex, the decision was a natural one given Aelfgar's succession to his father's lands and his influence in the region. In turn, it was probably now that Gyrth, brother of Earls Harold and Tosti, gained East Anglia in succession to Aelfgar. On 21 December Earl Ralph, Edward's nephew, also died, leaving an infant son called Harold, who remained a minor in the wardship of Queen Edith until 1066. It was vital for Ralph's earldom to be held by someone who could defend the western part of it from the still present threat of Gruffydd of Wales. Earl Aelfgar was not chosen as it was unlikely that he would have been welcomed by the men of Hereford, whose shire he had ravaged the year before; Harold's younger brothers were not chosen either as they had no military or diplomatic experience. Instead, Earl Harold appears to have absorbed that part of Ralph's earldom which abutted Wales, including Gloucestershire and Herefordshire. It was probably at this time, or perhaps early in 1058, that King Edward appointed Earl Harold's other brother, Leofwine, to an inland earldom free from the threat of invasion carved out of the eastern part of Ralph's earldom. The redistribution of comital authority in this period is complex and the results are discussed in greater detail in Appendix Two.[18]

The main result of these changes was that Earl Aelfgar was left the only earl in England who was not a member of Godwine's family. The dynamics behind this situation should be remembered. Cnut's three great earls left varying progeny to succeed them. Siward had two sons – Osbeorn, who was killed in Scotland before his father's death, and Waltheof, who was too young to hold office before 1066. Leofric apparently had only one son, Aelfgar, who succeeded him in Mercia. Godwine, in contrast, had six sons, of whom five were ready and available for office, the exception

en qd dicesture sane decentia uerba
epperies. arta undiq; septa loco
ictabas pueros regu de stirpe decenter
oribz instructos omne boni specimen
columen regni studio creuisse uirili
lisu quattuor fluminibz similes
t nunc thebaidos sedo sub scemate carmen
oc opus horrenta discipulo retegis
ebar pncipiu lepidu deducere gtum
e nimio caris corde meo dominis
unc hostile nefas infratru uiscera torrens
onfundit lectu carminis historiam
mathnu iuris ciuile peste regressum
eu germana nimis pectora dura tulit
ec paradysiacos uircitu cursibz amnes
nfernale chaos si magis hic memoras
sq; subextremu deuoti codicis unguen
ebatuit scam dicere pgeniem
unc ut prisca canunt fere telluris maluo
erribz inseras prodiit horrida stirps
ata neci subite grauis y proportio dura
obis muisa ph dolor id tamen est
uis canit occiduos modulator in orbe brittannos
entem caucaseis rupibz ingenitam
ndomita forteq; nimis regnante griphino
ec ia contenta finibus occiduis
ltra si sceleris cursu tulit arma syuerrie
imq; ei regnu ptulit angligenum
onec pclari meritis nomine regis
dwardi rissis erubuit sceleris
um uolucres angli sub haroldo preside iuncti
ostini cuneis agminibz; q; scutis
unc usq; inpauido terrore milite multo

The Vita Eadwardi Regis, extract from a poem on Harold's Welsh wars.

being Wulfnoth, who was a hostage in Normandy. Similarly, the new earls appointed by King Edward left no adult successors. Earl Ralph left only his infant son, Harold, held to be a minor until 1066, while Earl Odda appears to have left no heirs at all. As a result, there was a clear imbalance in eligible candidates for earldoms, and thus King Edward was almost bound to appoint more progeny of Godwine to office, regardless of the relative ambitions and merits of the various families involved.

Despite King Edward having, so it would seem, little choice but to promote members of Harold's family, their rapid accession of power seems to have aroused the enmity of Earl Aelfgar. It is possible that he feared encirclement by Harold's family, or simply felt that his eldest son, Edwin, should have received a share of Earl Ralph's earldom, instead of it being shared out among the Godwine brothers. It has been assumed that Edwin was too young for such a position at this time, scarcely an adult even in 1062/3, but there is no direct evidence for this. The apparent lack of activity he would later show may have resulted from inexperience rather than youth. Indeed, the documentary evidence for this period is so thin that we cannot be sure when Edwin first came to prominence. It is likely that he became Earl of Mercia in 1062, but he is not recorded as such until 1065. It was probably a fear of encirclement that led Earl Aelfgar to turn to his previous ally, Gruffydd of Wales, in an attempt to establish some security for himself. This time he sought to form a firm alliance with Gruffydd by arranging the marriage of his daughter, Alditha, to the Welsh king. This alliance would serve two purposes for the earl: it would protect his long border with Wales from attack, and it would provide him with a source of support in England, should he require it. It is not clear whether the threat from the Godwine family was real or imagined, but clearly Earl Aelfgar took it seriously. In turn, this alliance between one of his earls and the chief enemy of his kingdom alarmed King Edward. In 1058, therefore, Earl Aelfgar was banished for a second time, his treasonable alliance with Gruffydd being a much more likely cause than any supposed plots by Harold's family. We can only regret the chroniclers' reluctance to provide further details of the causes of this important crisis.[19]

This time, Aelfgar fled directly to his new ally, King Gruffydd of Wales. The allies received additional assistance from a Norwegian fleet which happened to be cruising in the Irish Sea under Magnus, the son of King Harald of Norway. This powerful backing allowed Aelfgar to attempt to regain his earldom by force. The Norwegians raided the English coast, perhaps north of the Mersey, while Gruffydd presumably raided the borders. None of the accounts of this year (1058) provide information on the areas affected by these raids, but it seems likely that the Norwegian fleet raided the coast of Tosti's earldom. This would certainly help to account for Tosti's decision to participate in the later invasion of Wales, something never before undertaken by a Northumbrian earl. Domesday Book does record Tosti's lands in Amounderness as waste in 1086, though whether as a result of this Norwegian assault or later Norman action is unknown. We have no information on the English response other than that the result was again a negotiated settlement. Aelfgar was once more restored to his earldom, and further concessions were possibly offered to Gruffydd of Wales. It may have been at this point that Gruffydd received the lands beyond the Dee, later recorded by Domesday Book as having been held by him. Aelfgar himself may have gained the addition of Oxfordshire to his earldom[20]

King Gruffydd, who had now devastated the English borders on a number of occasions without retaliation and defeated a series of English forces, clearly presented a serious threat to England, which had to be dealt with. However, Gruffydd's alliance with Earl Aelfgar currently made it impossible to take effective action against him. Nor did there seem any prospect of an immediate end to this alliance – Earl Aelfgar had twice found it invaluable in securing his own position in England and might do so again. However, this situation of stalemate could not last forever, and King Edward and Earl Harold could wait.

The year 1058, therefore, would appear to have been a turbulent one, yet little precise detail is recorded in the sources. Chronicle D remarks that 'It is tedious to relate fully how things went'. Indeed, for the period 1057 to 1065 the sources are somewhat sparse. Although this lack of detail does not necessarily indicate that the kingdom was peaceful, nevertheless it was during this period that Earl Harold was able

The Rood, Romsey Abbey. The design of the Holy Cross at Harold's College at Waltham may have been similar.

to set aside time to supervise the embellishment and attend the dedication of his newly built collegiate church at Waltham in Essex. According to the later Waltham Chronicle, the dedication of the church was performed on 3 May 1060, the feast of the Finding of the True Cross, with Archbishop Cynesige of York officiating. The participation of Cynesige rather than Stigand, in whose jurisdiction the church lay, probably came about because of the latter's doubtful status at this time. In addition to Earl Harold himself, King Edward and Queen Edith were also in attendance at the eight days of feasting and celebration, as were around eleven bishops and eleven abbots, all of the earls and several other prominent laymen. Although there is no official list, the formal confirmation charter of 1062 bears these names on its witness list, with the exception of Cynesige, and it is likely that most of these people did indeed attend the ceremony. Their names were perhaps recorded in an earlier draft charter compiled at the time to be used as the basis for the later formal document. If this is the case, then this was a formidable gathering for the dedication of what was a non-royal church, and it clearly reflected Harold's status in England at this time. This magnificent occasion was probably also the setting for Harold's formal presentation to his new foundation of the holy relics he had collected during his European travels.[21]

Undoubtedly also during this period, Earl Harold and his brothers consolidated their hold on their new earldoms or the extensions to their existing authority. They would have attended shire courts to supervise the administration of justice and in doing so would have met and developed links with many of the influential and powerful men of their new earldoms. In this respect, Harold's existing power base in nearby Wessex and his association with the defence of Herefordshire in 1055 and 1056 must have eased the establishment of his authority in this shire. Earl Gyrth may have been able to better his position in East Anglia by using many of Harold's contacts in the region, formed during his previous tenure of the earldom and through his landholdings in the area. Indeed, in 1061 Earls Tosti and Gyrth felt confident enough of their authority to journey to Rome with Ealdred, the newly appointed Archbishop of York. In their absence occurred the only known disturbance of these years when Malcolm, the new King of Scots, took advantage of the opportunity presented by Tosti's absence to ravage the northern borders of his earldom including Lindisfarne. However, on Tosti's return, Malcolm withdrew and peace was restored in the north.[22]

This period of relative calm ended with the death of Earl Aelfgar of Mercia. This event is not recorded in any of our sources, but Aelfgar disappears sometime between 1058, when he is recorded as regaining his earldom, and 1065, when his son Edwin is recorded in his place as Earl of Mercia. If the later *Vita Wulfstani* can be relied on, Earl Aelfgar was among those who supported Wulfstan's election as Bishop of Worcester, dated before 27 August 1062, and this appears to have been his last recorded act. That his death is likely to have come in 1062, possibly late in that year, is further suggested by the action taken by Harold after Christmas that year. He launched a lightning cavalry raid on King Gruffydd's palace at Rhuddlan in North Wales. It is unlikely that Harold could have taken this action unless Aelfgar, Gruffydd's English ally, had been removed from the scene, and such a surprise attack would achieve best results if news of Aelfgar's death had not yet reached Gruffydd.

It is likely then that Aelfgar died late in 1062, shortly before Christmas, perhaps while attending King Edward's Christmas court at Gloucester. Earl Harold, who was also present, then decided to strike against Gruffydd at once, hoping to catch him unawares and kill him. He gathered a cavalry force and rode swiftly over more than 100 miles to Rhuddlan on the North Wales coast. John of Worcester is the only source to mention Harold's use of cavalry in this raid, but this is undoubtedly the only way such a surprise raid could have been carried out. Harold narrowly missed catching his quarry, who was warned at the last moment and fled by sea. Instead, he had to content himself with burning Gruffydd's palace and ships. The figure-head and ornaments of Gruffydd's ship were probably taken in this raid.[24]

The *Vita Eadwardi* vividly recalls this raid, which must have achieved wide renown at the time:

> The enemy's house is sacked, the girded chests
> Are broached, and royal pomp exposed to loot.
> In blaze of glory, ably led, the men
> Return, and bring back this fine ornament:
> They smashed the fleet – for Welsh control and lore
> Was not the equal of the Ocean's chiefs –
> And take a prow and stern of solid gold,
> Cast by the smith's assiduous skill, and this,
> With looted treasures and the hostages,
> As proof of victory they give their king.[25]

Although ultimately a failure in its chief objective, that of catching Gruffydd, the raid provided an early demonstration of Harold's ability for rapid military manoeuvres over long distances, which would be a feature of his later campaigns in 1066.

King Edward and Earl Harold were determined now to destroy Gruffydd and remove his threat from England's borders once and for all. Therefore, Earl Harold planned a joint expedition with his brother, Tosti, to take place in spring 1063. Under Earl Harold's overall command, this well-coordinated campaign began on 26 May, when Harold sailed with a naval force from Bristol and Tosti invaded with a cavalry force, presumably entering North Wales from the Chester area. Harold sailed round the Welsh coast, laying waste the land and taking hostages, while Tosti did the same by land. The use of a fleet by Harold was the key element of the plan and it was almost certainly employed in the occupation and devastation of Anglesey, the granary of North Wales and the foundation of Gruffydd's power. Indeed, this same strategy was to be followed by King Edward I in his later conquest of Wales. The author of the *Vita Eadwardi* provides some tantalizing hints of the tactics which may have been used to achieve Earl Harold's first great triumph, and confirms Harold's command of the expedition, although he is usually more favourable to Tosti. The writer speaks of swift-moving small units ravaging in Wales and defeating any Welsh opposition encountered. This account is perhaps confirmed by Gerald of Wales, who much later speaks of Harold devastating all Wales with 'lightly clad infantry' forces and erecting inscribed stones, reading *Hic Fuit Victor Haroldus* (Here Harold was victor), to mark his frequent victories. Although writing over 150 years later, Gerald preserved much local Welsh tradition and had himself seen examples of Harold's stone victory markers. The result of these tactics was to subdue the Welsh countryside and force Gruffydd to retreat into the mountains of Snowdonia, from whence he continued to harass the English forces.[26]

This devastating campaign succeeded in isolating Gruffydd from his supporters and forcing the Welsh to submit, give hostages and promise to pay tribute. John of Worcester declares that the Welsh outlawed and renounced their king. Gruffydd himself might have escaped the net yet again, except that the severity of Harold's campaign led his own followers to lose faith in him. As a result, the Chronicle says he was slain by one of his own men 'because of the fight he fought against Earl Harold'. On 5 August 1063 Cynan, son of Iago, killed Gruffydd and brought his head to Earl Harold, who placed it before the king. This has been seen as an indication that Harold had arranged for Gruffydd's assassination, and this was the sign of success. This seems unlikely as Gruffydd had, to a large extent, been rendered harmless by the devastation of his lands and the undermining of his support. In addition, Harold's preference was to treat generously an otherwise broken enemy, as he demonstrated after Stamford Bridge, rather than to fight bloodily to the bitter end. It is possible that the assassin himself may have hoped for some reward from Harold, in which case he was disappointed, or simply that this macabre gift may have been a signal to Harold of the final submission of the Welsh, and that he could now cease his raiding.[27]

This military triumph over the most powerful Welsh leader of the period was crowned by a political settlement which placed the dead king's half-brothers, Bleddyn and Rhiwallon, in power in North Wales. In return, they swore oaths of loyalty both to King Edward and to Earl Harold, they gave hostages, and they agreed to pay tribute. A number of English border territories were now recovered, including the lands beyond the Dee and Archenfield, which Gruffydd had acquired through his recent aggression. In addition, some territorial advances were made into Wales, such as at Portskewet where Earl Harold set out to build a hunting lodge. Meanwhile, in South Wales several native dynasties were left to struggle for control.

In this campaign Earl Harold had revealed himself as an innovative strategist and tactician and as a great commander, and he had greatly enhanced his reputation. Wales had been subdued and a major threat to England removed. He had won a stunning victory over the only king to rule all Wales. The echoes of his victory can be found in sources dating from as late as the thirteenth century. Gerald of Wales quite reasonably attributes the early Norman successes in Wales to the defeat previously inflicted on the country by Harold. John of Salisbury less credibly reports, that so many Welshmen were killed that King Edward gave permission for Welsh women to marry Englishmen, and that Harold enacted a law to punish Welshmen travelling armed into England.[28]

CHAPTER SIX

WILLIAM OF NORMANDY

Where Harold made an oath to Duke William.[1]

In 1064 Harold was at the height of his power and influence. A successful military commander and the leading noble in England, with the demise of Earl Aelfgar he had no real rivals. Three of his brothers were earls and he himself was right-hand man to King Edward. However, an episode occurred about this time which was ultimately to lead to his downfall. This was his visit to Normandy and his memorable encounter with William, Duke of Normandy. No contemporary English source mentions this episode – the Chronicle record is particularly sparse at this point – thus we are dependent largely on Norman sources, although there are hints of an alternative version in one later Anglo-Norman source. The Norman sources, which are closely interrelated, were composed sometime after the event, around 1067–70, and with the specific purpose of justifying William's claim to the English throne. We must bear this in mind when considering both their accounts of this episode and, more importantly, their interpretations of it.[2]

The Norman sources provide no precise date for Harold's visit to Normandy. William of Jumieges places it somewhere between the death of King Henry of France in August 1060, and the death of King Edward in January 1066. William of Poitiers places it a little more precisely, at about the same time as the acquisition of the County of Maine, by Duke William, which had certainly been completed by 1064. This Norman dating of around 1064–5 fits well enough with the lack of any positive English evidence that Harold was anywhere else between the death of Gruffydd of Wales, in August 1063, and his giving orders for the construction of a hunting lodge at Portskewet, in July 1065. Within this period, a visit to Normandy by Harold is probably best placed in 1064, since by then Maine had been conquered. William's expedition against Brittany, on which Harold is said to have accompanied him, probably also occurred in that year.[3]

According to the Norman version of events, Harold was sent to Normandy by King Edward in order to confirm the latter's earlier promise of the succession to Duke William and to swear fealty to him. However, we have seen that it is unlikely that any such promise was given by Edward, but rather that it was probably invented and imparted to William by Robert of Jumieges, Archbishop of Canterbury, following his exile in 1052. If this was the case, could Edward nevertheless have intended to make William his heir at this later date? This is highly unlikely. In 1051 Edward had no clearly established heir, although he did have a number of potential heirs, all with better qualifications than William. Now, he had secured a suitable and established heir in the person of his nephew, *Atheling* Edgar, and a reserve in Harold, the son of his now deceased nephew, Earl Ralph. As a result of this change in circumstances the reasons adduced against the nomination of William as heir in 1051 apply with even greater force to any such nomination in 1064. He remained a man with only distant links to the English dynasty and little or no support in the country, although he was now secure in possession of his duchy and much more widely known and regarded than in 1051. In addition, William's recent conquest of Maine had resulted in the imprisonment and death of Edward's nephew, Count Walter of the Vexin. Count Walter died in suspicious circumstances while in William's custody, allegedly by poison, something unlikely to endear him to Edward. William of Poitiers hints that Edward was close to death and this was why he now sent Harold to pledge his kingdom. There is no support for this in English sources, which show that the king was still healthy enough to go hunting in autumn 1065. The suggestion that Edward intended William as his heir in 1064 seems less credible even than the case for this in 1051.[4]

Since there seems to be little support for the Norman account that Harold came to Normandy to pledge the English throne to William, should we believe that Harold visited Normandy at all? Harold's previous visit to Europe, to Flanders in 1056, also goes unrecorded in the chronicles, yet is clearly evidenced by the albeit chance survival of his name among the witnesses to a Flemish diploma. Unfortunately, there exists no similarly conclusive contemporary evidence for the Norman visit. The reference in the *Vita Eadwardi* to Harold's personal study of the princes of Gaul is a little too unspecific to warrant use as confirmation. However, this lack of evidence and of any reference to the event in the English sources cannot be taken as an indication that a visit did not take place, and although the Norman accounts are clearly biased, they present facts which cannot be entirely dismissed. Thus it seems likely that the basic facts contained in their accounts, Harold's visit to Normandy, and his oath to Duke William, must have a basis in truth, otherwise their authors would lose credibility completely. This does not mean that the causation constructed around these facts and the elaborate details added to them are necessarily accurate. It must be our task to attempt to reconstruct the most plausible sequence of cause and effect which link the main events related by these sources.[5]

If we accept that Harold visited Normandy, but not to pledge support for William's succession, then some other cause must have brought him there. There exist several alternative explanations for such a journey in other sources. As stated above, the contemporary *Vita Eadwardi* speaks in general terms of Harold making visits in order to study the French princes. Although this is a possibility, for Duke William was undoubtedly the most prominent of these princes and a man well worth study at this time, when he was at the summit of his power, it must remain an outside one.[6]

The Bayeux Tapestry provides no direct information on the reason for Harold's visit. It was probably made for William's half-brother, Odo, Bishop of Bayeux, around 1077 and therefore presents the Norman outline of events. However, it was produced by an English workshop, which perhaps wove its own outlook and sympathies into the design. This mixed origin or perhaps the simple brevity of its textual style mean that the text provides little clarity in a number of controversial areas. Nothing specific is recorded in the accompanying text to explain the reason for Harold's journey. He is clearly shown speaking to King Edward before his departure, but the text fails either to state that Edward sent him, or to provide any reason for the journey. There are hints later in the Tapestry of what may be a marriage alliance, but the scene which reflects this unfortunately remains the most inscrutable in the entire work.[7]

The suggestion that the proposal of a marriage alliance was involved is reflected in a number of later sources, usually in a secondary context, although perhaps it was originally more central. It may have been pushed into the background by the need to tie Harold's visit more closely to the Norman claim to the throne. This required a direct sequence of events consisting of a promise of the throne in 1051, the pledge of it by oath in 1064, and the rightful succession in 1066. The suggestion of another purpose behind Harold's visit to Normandy would obviously detract from this sequence, but the possibility certainly exists that Harold went to Normandy to arrange an alliance, including a marriage, with the new power in northern France. After all, his younger brother, Tosti, had married the sister of Baldwin V of Flanders and gained both prestige and a useful ally as a result.[8]

The sources are confused on the details of any proposed marriage probably because it came to nothing in the end. The later English influenced sources appear to indicate some arrangement involving the marriage of Harold's sister, Aelfgyva, to a Norman. Eadmer implies a marriage to William himself, which is clearly absurd since he was already married, but his eldest son, Robert, was then in his early teens and perhaps a suitable match. (Marriage between men and women of widely differing ages was fairly normal at this time.) One of William's major barons may be an alternative candidate, but this would seem an unlikely match for the sister of someone of Harold's importance. The tone of contempt considered by many to be present in the Tapestry's reference to the woman Aelfgyva may possibly reflect a Norman view of this woman – as an unworthy match, and of a lower status. William may have viewed Harold as of vassal status in contrast to an almost sovereign lord like himself, but Harold undoubtedly viewed them as of equal status, great lords under a king. The Tapestry itself merely refers to a mysterious 'Aelfgyva', who may possibly be a sister of Harold. The form of the name in the Tapestry is English but this may be a result of the Tapestry's English origins rather than an accurate representation of the original name. The woman could equally represent an anglicized

Adeliza, William's daughter, who may have been intended as a bride for Harold as part of William's own arrangements for securing the English throne as later related by Orderic Vitalis. The real basis behind these traditions will probably never be established, but it nevertheless represents a possible reason for Harold's journey.[9]

There also exists the possibility that Harold did not intend to visit Normandy at all. A later Anglo-Norman source, William of Malmesbury, suggests that Harold was on a fishing trip when blown to shore by a storm. The Tapestry in one of its scenes may provide some evidence to support this by showing a fishing pole, although this may, in fact, be the origin of William's story. It may simply be an incidental detail of the design, although it is absent from other scenes of sea voyages. Whether the English nobility of this period actually participated in fishing as a sport or pastime like hunting or hawking is unknown but perhaps unlikely.[10]

The view of William of Malmesbury that Harold arrived in Normandy by accident leads us to the general possibility that Harold could have been en route to somewhere else on the Continent, and was caught in a storm and blown off course, ending up in Normandy. It should be remembered that in 1064 Harold made landfall in Ponthieu and not Normandy at all. He may have been travelling to arrange a marriage alliance elsewhere, hence the presence of his sister Aelfgyva, as, perhaps, recorded by the Tapestry. This would resolve the problem of there being no suitable groom in Normandy itself. Whatever the exact case, although it cannot be proved that his arrival in Normandy was purely accidental, this possibility should none the less be kept in mind.[11]

Harold is taken captive by Count Guy of Ponthieu. (The Bayeux Tapestry – 11th Century. By special permission of the City of Bayeux)

Eadmer, whose writing dates to just before the end of the eleventh century, informs us that the reason for Harold's journey was that he wished to secure the release of those members of his family held hostage by William since 1052. Eadmer was an English monk of Christ Church, Canterbury, in the period from before 1067 onwards. He would have been well informed about Harold and his career through the close contacts of that community with its former member and Harold's relative the monk Aethelric, one-time candidate for the archbishopric of Canterbury and later bishop of Sussex. Full details about Aethelric's career and connections will be found in Appendix One. Indeed, it is known that Eadmer consulted this very Bishop Aethelric when writing his Life of St Dunstan and he could therefore also have been in receipt of inside information from him when compiling his account of Harold's journey. The need for Harold to secure the release of his relatives certainly provides a very direct link between Harold and William, which is perhaps lacking in the accounts of possible marriage alliances discussed above. These hostages had, it is true, been held for some twelve years, and Harold seems to have made no attempt to obtain their release until now. The reason for this is most probably that following his Welsh campaign and with England secure and at peace, Harold finally felt able to perform this mission personally, which had been impossible before. Alternatively, perhaps he had already sought their release but had been unsuccessful, and therefore no record remains. Eadmer's account may represent the closest thing we have to an English account of Harold's visit and one based on sources close to his family. It should therefore perhaps be given more credence than its late date would indicate.[12]

If we dismiss confirmation of the Norman claim to the throne as a valid reason there remain three main possible reasons for Harold's visit to Normandy: he arrived there purely by accident; he went there to arrange some form of alliance, possibly involving a marriage; he went there to negotiate the release of the hostages taken to Normandy by Robert of Jumièges in 1052. If Harold's journey to Normandy was intentional, whether to free the hostages or arrange an alliance, it has been viewed as a grave error of judgement. He had by this action placed himself in the hands of Duke William, a ruthless ruler actively pursuing the English throne, who would not waste such an opportunity. However, if we accept that no promise of the succession was made in 1051, apart from the private pledge of Robert of Jumièges, then there was no reason for anyone outside William's closest circle to know that he aimed at the English throne. This is especially the case when everyone in England in 1064 would have understood that *Atheling* Edgar held an unchallengable position as heir to the throne under all the necessary criteria.

It should also be emphasized that at this time a Norman invasion of England in support of such a claim must have seemed unlikely. In the previous hundred years the real threat to England had always come from the north, from whence Scandinavian kings always stood ready to invade England and seize the throne. Earl Tosti understood this and would seek aid from that quarter in 1066. In contrast, in the same period there had been no invasions at all from the Continent and the only previous threat from Normandy came from Scandinavian raiders using the duchy as a temporary base. True, Duke Robert had planned an invasion in 1033 or 1034 but this proved abortive and did not even come to the attention of the English chroniclers. The landings by *Athelings* Edward and Alfred in 1036, as we have seen, were little more than raids and may have originated outside Normandy itself. The natural assumption based on experience at the time was that Scandinavians invaded England, but Frenchmen did not.[13]

This latter point is sometimes forgotten because William's invasion actually succeeded, but at the time itself his invasion plan was very novel and extremely risky. Normandy had no fleet to speak of and in 1066 one had to be constructed from scratch. A naval expedition was considered fraught with danger, as the Norman barons made clear by their initial reluctance to support one in 1066. Although the duchy was currently at its greatest extent, its resources were still small compared to those of England. All this must have made William's ambition appear unrealistic and unusual. In 1064 the possibility of William becoming king of England probably remained little more than a dream for William himself, and therefore Harold probably had no inkling of it. This point must be kept in mind when considering Harold's actions in Normandy.[14]

Whatever the reason for Harold's journey across the Channel, and the wish to rescue his relatives from Norman captivity, recorded by Eadmer using sources close to the family, seems most likely, he undoubtedly went there. The evidence is clear on this point at least. The outline of events in the Norman sources can now be followed. Almost at once, he encountered bad luck and was blown by a storm onto the coast of Ponthieu, a small county neighbouring Normandy. Here he and his companions were seized and imprisoned at Beaurain by Count Guy, probably with the intention of demanding a heavy ransom for their release. Harold thus found himself in a difficult situation as a hostage himself. As a wealthy man, he would undoubtedly have been able to raise any ransom demanded by Count Guy for his release. However, before any negotiations got underway he was apparently freed by a friendly power.[15]

When William of Normandy heard the news of Harold's capture, he probably saw an opportunity to further his long dormant, but not forgotten English claim and he seized it. He sent messengers to Count Guy and demanded Harold's release under a mixture of threats and promises of rewards. Guy was in no position to resist such force as the duke could bring against him, and personally handed Harold over to William at Eu. William now held in his hands the greatest noble in England, second only to the king, and he intended to take full advantage of the situation. Initially he concealed his true intentions behind the guise of welcoming an illustrious guest in friendly terms. He therefore conducted Harold to his capital of Rouen with proper honour and there treated him with great hospitality.[16]

Harold is handed over to Duke William of Normandy. (The Bayeux Tapestry – 11th Century. By special permission of the City of Bayeux)

William then invited Harold to accompany him on a military expedition against the Bretons. This is the sequence of events which is shown in the Bayeux Tapestry and probably supported by William of Jumieges, who says that Harold was with William for 'some time' and swore fealty only before being sent back to England, and by Orderic Vitalis, who retains this sequence despite drawing on the material contained in William of Poitiers. The latter reverses this sequence by having Harold swear the oath before the Breton expedition which perhaps reflects his desire to focus on the matter of the succession to the English kingdom, supposedly the chief purpose of Harold's visit. It seems more likely that the expedition came first and provided William with a chance to assess Harold closely, while further lulling the latter into a false sense of security. William perhaps also intended the Breton expedition to provide a demonstration of his military and political power in order to impress and perhaps to subdue Harold, before seeking to secure his agreement one way or another to his English claim.[17]

The expedition took the form of a mobile cavalry raid into neighbouring Breton territory intended to undermine the authority of Duke Conan II by supporting a rebellion against his authority by one of his vassals, Rhiwallon of Dol. This would effectively enhance William's authority by weakening that of Conan, his neighbour and potential rival. William accompanied by Harold crossed the Breton border at the estuary of the river Couesnon. It was here that Harold apparently rescued two men from the quicksands in a remarkable feat of strength depicted in the Bayeux Tapestry.

Thereafter, the Normans raised Conan's siege of Rhiwallon's castle at Dol by threatening to cut off both his supplies and his retreat. As a result, Conan was forced to fall back towards his own city of Rennes. William, who was well aware of the risks of pursuing the Bretons into their own territory, wisely refused to be drawn after them. Subsequently, he found his army running short of supplies due to a Breton scorched earth policy and so returned home to Normandy. The Tapestry suggests that William went on to raid Rennes and to capture the castle of Dinant from Conan, but none of this is supported by William of Poitiers and it therefore probably never occurred. Indeed, following William's withdrawal Conan joined forces with Count Geoffrey of Anjou and by approaching the Norman border threatened to retaliate by raiding William's own territory. Duke William therefore turned about and re-entered Breton territory. The opposing armies faced each other, maintaining a cautious distance as neither was prepared to accept the risk of battle. Thereafter, the campaign seems to have fizzled out as each side used up its supplies and then withdrew to its own lands.[18]

Harold is presented with arms by William after their joint campaign in Brittany. (The Bayeux Tapestry – 11th Century. By special permission of the City of Bayeux)

1. *Frontispiece of New Minster* Liber Vitae, showing King Cnut and Queen Emma. *(BL, Stowe MS 944, f. 6)*

2. *Seal die of Godwine the thegn, the symbol of authority of a royal servant. (British Museum, MLA 1881, 4-4,1)*

3. Scene depicting shepherds, from an eleventh-century calendar. This and the plate shown opposite demonstrate some of the activities which produced Harold's wealth. (BL, MS Cotton Tiberius B.v, f. 5r)

4. Scene depicting reaping, from an eleventh-century calendar. (BL, MS Cotton Tiberius B.v, f. 6v)

5. An unsuspecting Harold is handed over to William. (The Bayeux Tapestry – 11th Century. By special permission of the City of Bayeux)

6. The coronation of King Harold. (The Bayeux Tapestry – 11th Century. By special permission of the City of Bayeux)

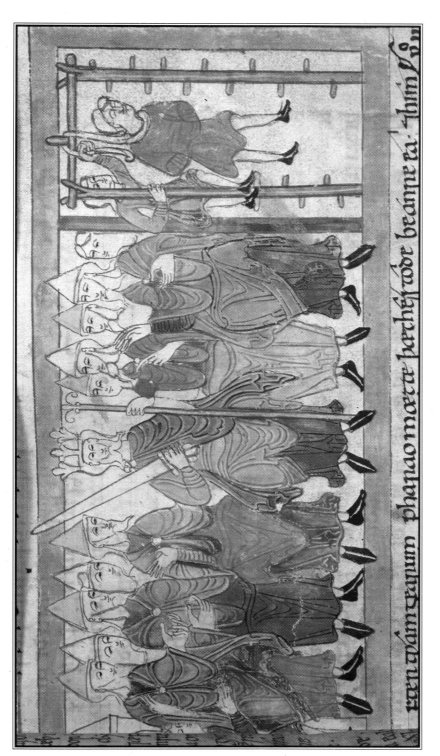

7. *A king and his counsellors. It was in this context that Harold wielded power. (BL, MS Cotton Claudius B.iv, f. 59)*

8. *Anglo-Saxon feast, a typical social setting for Harold. (BL, MS Cotton Claudius B.iv, f. 63v)*

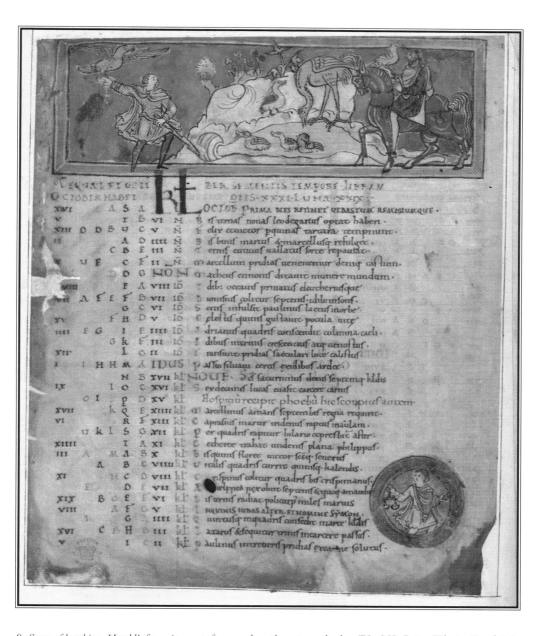

9. Scene of hawking, Harold's favourite sport, from an eleventh-century calendar. (BL, MS Cotton Tiberius B.v, f. 7v)

10. The death of King Harold. (The Bayeux Tapestry –
11th Century. By special permission of the City of Bayeux)

This short and inconclusive campaign must nevertheless have been both fascinating and instructive for these two great men, Duke William and Earl Harold. They must have spent a great deal of the time observing each other and attempting to gauge relative strengths and weaknesses. Both were great warriors and shrewd politicians. William learned about Harold's personal courage and the formidable obstacle he could present to his plans to secure the English throne. He came to appreciate the need to try to neutralize him or weaken his authority in some measure. In turn, Harold learned a great deal about William's military skills and methods of warfare, including his use of the mobility of cavalry and the employment of castles as strongholds, and about how he subdued and undermined his local rivals in France. He was yet to discover William's true intentions, the extent of his ruthlessness, and the scope of his ambitions.

It was when the two men returned to Normandy that William finally revealed his aspirations concerning the English throne and insisted on Harold's pledge to support him. In return, he may have promised to uphold and extend Harold's position in England and perhaps offered him his daughter, Adeliza, in marriage. Harold must have been taken by surprise by this revelation, but equally must soon have appreciated the danger of his position, faced as he was with William's determination for an answer. He was currently William's guest, but if he failed to agree to his demands he can have been in no doubt that he would soon become his prisoner. Harold's own brother and nephew already languished in Norman imprisonment and King Edward's nephew, Count Walter, had died there very recently. This gives a special irony to William of Poitiers' story of William's 'rescue' of Harold from the captivity of Count Guy – a case of out of the frying pan into the fire. Faced with this unattractive prospect, Harold had little alternative but to accept William's terms, which involved the swearing of an oath to work towards his succession to the throne of England. The oath was the corner-stone of medieval judicial procedure and social relations throughout northern Europe and represented in a sense an ordeal before God whose efficacy would be shown by subsequent events. This decision could not have been taken lightly by Harold since the binding nature of oaths on holy relics was clearly recognized in England at this time. The Laws of Cnut set out severe penalties including mutilation or payment of a wergild fine, for the swearing of a false oath on relics. Thereafter, the oathbreakers word could not be accepted unless he atoned very deeply for his offence before God. One wonders if this oath was one of those sins that Harold confessed to Bishop Wulfstan, and whether the holy man absolved him from keeping it.[19]

There has been considerable discussion about the details of the oath but the actual terms sworn by Harold are in a sense academic. The Tapestry is as usual enigmatic, providing no details of the oath sworn. William of Jumieges' account refers only to an oath of fealty to William as claimant to the throne. In contrast, the much more elaborate account of William of Poitiers seems to attempt to cover all eventualities. This may merely reflect the fact that William tried to extract the maximum possible

Harold swears the oath to William. (The Bayeux Tapestry – 11th Century. By special permission of the City of Bayeux)

concessions from the captive Harold. On the other hand, in common with other aspects of his account, it seems more likely that William of Poitiers is here seeking to reinforce his master's case by adding elaborate details, some of which seem rather unconvincing. In particular, the mention of Dover and other castles being handed over to William is rather dubious as the only castles known to exist in England at that time were those constructed by the Frenchmen in Herefordshire. As so often, the account of William of Jumièges is probably to be preferred. Similarly, the exact location of where the oath was taken, whether Bonneville-sur-Toques, Rouen or Bayeux, is almost immaterial, and mention of the latter two sites may perhaps only represent attempts to enhance their prestige by association with this famous event. Thus Orderic Vitalis places the oath at Rouen, with which he himself had connections, while the Tapestry places it at Bayeux in deference to its patron, Bishop Odo. Bonneville-sur-Toques, as stated by William of Poitiers, seems most likely as it has no significance otherwise and is therefore unlikely to have been identified as the location for such an important event unless that event actually took place there. In any case, the form of the oath and the place where it was sworn are unimportant.

What mattered to Duke William was that Harold had sworn to uphold his claim to the English throne before witnesses referred to as 'certain most notable men of utter integrity'.[20]

William calculated that he had now achieved a moral ascendancy over Harold which could be useful later, both to undermine Harold's position and to justify his own. William retained Harold's brother, Wulfnoth, as a hostage in an attempt to guarantee Harold's adherence to his pledge but probably realized that this would not be enough. William could, of course, have kept Harold as his prisoner, so removing an obstacle from his path to the throne. He did not do so probably because the results of such an action were unpredictable and might even bring about a weakening of William's prospects by allowing others to rise to power in Harold's place. It was far better to release him burdened with an oath which he was unlikely to fulfil, and which turned Harold into an oathbreaker. The potential of perjury was perhaps sufficient for William's purposes so that in 1066 he could exploit this to undermine Harold's position and bolster his own. Thus when the more basic attraction of loot proved insufficient to secure the support of all his vassals for his plans in 1066, William could play on their duty to secure his rights against a perjured vassal.[21]

Finally Harold was released to return home with elaborate gifts and accompanied by his nephew, Hakon, one of the hostages taken to Normandy in 1052. Duke William continued to hold Harold's brother, Wulfnoth. If the freedom of these hostages was Harold's original reason for his journey to Normandy, he had failed. In addition, he was now burdened with an oath to aid William's claim to the English throne. The medieval mind viewed Harold's swearing of this oath as a disaster from which his career took an inevitable downward path. This was an argument typical of the period, when disaster and downfall were seen as God's punishment for sin. It was based on the deep-rooted belief that God was responsible for all that happened in the world, and that everything that occurred represented the rewards of virtue or punishment for sin rather than the results of chance or human action. Thus Harold's fall in 1066 clearly produced a need to identify the sin for which this was punishment, and this was conveniently found in his breach of this oath.[22]

In this episode Harold had fallen into William's trap but it was a concealed trap that neither he nor anyone in England could have anticipated. The promise of the succession to William had after all probably been invented by Robert of Jumieges himself, and was thus unknown beyond William's immediate circle. Harold had extricated himself from this trap, in the only way possible, by swearing the oath. As the oath had been extracted under duress, it could be repudiated and he could atone before God for breaching it. Nevertheless, it may have caused him some disquiet and when the author of the *Vita Eadwardi* speaks of Harold's 'generosity with oaths' it may possibly be in relation to this occasion. It is likely that Harold was angered by the outcome of his Norman trip. He was angry with himself for being caught out by

William and at the arrogant presumption of the Norman duke. William of Poitiers indeed refers in a speech which he places in the mouth of Harold to William's 'arrogant temerity' in invading England in 1066, and this is perhaps also an appropriate reaction to William's actions in 1064. After all, William had not only raised an unwarranted claim to the English throne, but had also coerced Harold, his guest and comrade in arms, into promising to support him. He had then offered to reward Harold for this support with his own lands and titles. Duke William had made an implacable enemy. The audacity and arrogance of William's claim is not always apparent today because we know that it did succeed. However, at the time, William's own vassals viewed his plans as 'hazardous and far beyond the resources of Normandy'.[23]

Although an apparently disastrous expedition, Harold may have gained something from it. He was finally fully aware of William's ambitions and the determination that lay behind them. As a result, he could be fully prepared to repel William's invasion, which he knew would come. In 1066 the Chronicle indicates Harold's foreknowledge of William's plans, although this could possibly be as a result of Norman messengers sent to England in that year rather than his earlier visit. He had also been given a demonstration of the Norman methods of warfare, which would allow him to consider countermeasures. It was from this point that Harold must have begun to consider what would happen if King Edward died while *Atheling* Edgar was still too young to succeed him in all royal capacities, but particularly in military leadership. How would England fare against William with a boy king who had no experience as a war leader? In such circumstances, Harold as Earl of Wessex and lieutenant to the king could play a considerable advisory role but it would be much better to have an experienced military campaigner in full control. This may have been the initial germ of the idea which resulted in Harold's succession to the throne in 1066, but at this stage there is no direct evidence for this.[24]

On his return to England Harold probably discussed William's designs on the throne with Edward and with his family. The Tapestry shows Harold reporting to Edward on his return. Otherwise, these matters may not have been discussed more widely at this time. We do not know this, but the lack of any reference to the Norman visit or William's claim in contemporary English sources is suggestive. This may have been to conceal Harold's discomfiture, but more likely it was intended to prevent any undue alarm in England over this new threat. Some sources hint at concern on King Edward's part and this may have resulted from this situation. Indeed, it may have contributed to his deathbed resolution to entrust his kingdom to Harold and to advise others to support Harold's succession.[25]

CHAPTER SEVEN

EARL TOSTI

These two great brothers of a cloud-born land, the kingdom's sacred oaks, two Hercules,
excel all Englishmen when joined in peace.[1]

Harold had been considering the Norman duke's ambitions for a year when a new problem arose which was to split apart his previously close-knit family. The northern earldom of Northumbria, which had been ruled since 1055 by his younger brother Tosti, rose in rebellion against its earl.

It has been suggested that the rebellion was largely the result of the appointment of Tosti, a 'West Saxon' earl, to rule the Anglo-Danish earldom of Northumbria. This conclusion does not fit the facts because although Tosti's father, Godwine, was a West Saxon, his mother, Gytha, was a Dane. Earl Tosti was therefore an Anglo-Dane, raised speaking both languages and steeped in both traditions, very much like the men of his new earldom. He certainly had no local connections but, as far as we know, neither had his predecessor, the Danish Earl Siward, who had ruled Northumbria with considerable success for over twenty years, and nor had the man chosen by the rebels to be his successor, Morcar, younger brother of Earl Edwin of Mercia. Siward had been appointed earl of the southern part of Northumbria by Cnut in 1033 and secured the rest after Earl Eadwulf's murder in 1041. It is true that Siward did subsequently marry into the family of the old Northumbrian earls during his rule, while Tosti could not do so since he was already married to Judith of Flanders. Morcar was equally an intruder. In spite of his Danish name, he had only tenuous connections through his mother, Aelfgifu, with Northumbria. She appears to have been connected to the family of Wulfric *Spott*, which held lands in Lancashire around 1000 and one of whose members, Aelfhelm, was briefly *ealdorman* of York before his murder in 1006.[2] Nevertheless, in spite of his lack of local connections, Tosti successfully ruled the earldom for some ten years before facing rebellion in 1065.[3]

If the cause of the rebellion lay not in Tosti's origins, then it must instead be sought in his actions as earl. He began his rule well by taking full account of local conditions in his new earldom. He appointed as his deputy and advisor a local man called Copsi, who held lands in the North Riding of Yorkshire and Lincolnshire, and who could provide advice on local affairs. In addition, the new earl and his wife lavished veneration and gifts on St Cuthbert's Church in Durham with the intention of propitating the local saint in support of his rule. This generosity appears to have proved effective in securing their good memory in the records of the clerks of Durham, who subsequently remained loyal to the earl. In 1056 Tosti installed Aethelwine, King Edward's choice as Bishop of Durham in succession to the unpopular Aethelric, and he was subsequently to provide solid support for Tosti. The earl also maintained the close relationship that his predecessor Siward had established with Malcolm, King of Scots. The two men are referred to as 'sworn brothers', and in 1059 Earl Tosti escorted Malcolm to make his formal submission to King Edward following the final elimination of his Scottish rivals the year before.[4]

The result of these careful policies was that Tosti ruled the earldom successfully for almost ten years. There are no records of any real dissatisfaction with his rule during this period, indeed there appear to be indications of approval. The earl is widely reported to have enforced law and order in his earldom, something generally approved of by the Church and specifically reflected in a later Durham miracle story. This tells of a certain Barcwith, one of Earl Tosti's men, zealously pursuing a fugitive outlaw called Aldan-Hamal into St Cuthbert's Church. Naturally, Barcwith was struck down by the saint for this violation of sanctuary, but the story nevertheless reflects Tosti's eagerness to enforce justice. The northern earldom was undoubtedly considered more unruly than any others with its blood feuds, the most famous being that involving the family of the Northumbrian earls itself, and with Earl Oswulf falling victim to a robber in 1067. The *Vita Eadwardi* also speaks of Tosti reducing 'the number of robbers . . . by mutilating or killing them'. This enforcement of justice may have produced tensions with local *thegns* by interfering with their local jurisdictions, but these appear to have been not unduly disruptive. Earl Tosti certainly won the approval of some since his name, along with that of his father, Godwine, was entered in gold letters in the *Liber Vitae* of the Durham clerks. The earl's name was also incorporated in the commemorative inscription on the sundial of St Gregory's Church in Kirkdale commissioned by Orm Gamalsson, the father of one of his later opponents. Indeed, the restoration of St Gregory's Church itself, which this inscription commemorates, may imply more settled conditions in the area as a result of Tosti's rule.[5]

The first interruption to Tosti's rule apparently came from outside when a Norse fleet, which had allied itself with Earl Aelfgar, raided England in 1058. This raid probably struck at the Irish Sea coasts of Tosti's earldom, and Domesday Book records of wasted land in Amounderness may be confirmation of this. However, Earl Tosti appears not to have been blamed for failing to counter this 'unexpected' raid. Again in 1061, when Earl Tosti was on a pilgrimage to Rome, Malcolm of Scotland took advantage of his absence to raid the north of England, including Lindisfarne. This incident has been seen as a sign of weakness on Tosti's part because no susequent retaliation is recorded. This may, of course, be a result of the paucity of our sources at this time, but it is also possible that Tosti was able to keep Malcolm in check with diplomacy. The author of the *Vita Eadwardi* hints at this when he speaks of Tosti wearing down the Scots 'as much by cunning as by . . . military campaigns' and indeed no further Scottish attacks are recorded until after the Conquest. It is possible that Tosti's links with Gospatric, son of Maldred, Malcolm's cousin, may have helped him to secure the latter's quiescence.[6]

William Kapelle claims that this Scottish invasion resulted in the loss of Cumbria, and in Earl Tosti's position being undermined by his failure to recover it. However, there is no clear evidence for the loss of Cumbria at this date, and the arguments Kapelle advances in support of this claim are unconvincing. The existence of wasted land in Amounderness proves nothing as it could have been caused by the Norse raids of 1058, or by William's later harrying of the north in 1069. The fact that King Malcolm held Cumbria in 1070 does not necessarily mean that he gained it in 1061, and it seems much more likely that this occurred in the immediate post-Conquest period when Northumbria was in a state of chaos. The suggestion that Earl Tosti was unable to retaliate militarily against Malcolm because of the insecurity of his position in Northumbria, where a force of 200 *huscarls* was needed to hold down the earldom itself, is absurd. In 1063 Earl Tosti's position was sufficiently secure that he was able to lead a major force into North Wales, to participate in his brother's great campaign, with no ill effects in Northumbria. This would have been impossible if he had faced widespread discontent in his own earldom. Indeed, the booty gained on the expedition may have reinforced his popularity there.[7]

If we consider the evidence objectively it is apparent that the discontent against Tosti's rule first arose not in 1055 or 1061 but after the successful Welsh campaign of 1063. This was probably when Tosti began to be drawn into the confused local politics of the Northumbrian nobility. Either late in 1063, after the Welsh campaign, or early in 1064, Tosti had Gamal, son of Orm, and Ulf, son of Dolfin, assassinated in his own chamber at York while they visited him under safe conduct. (The fathers of these men were probably the Orm who commissioned the Kirkdale sundial, and the Dolfin who fell in Siward's battle with Macbeth in 1054.) The date is not clear from John of Worcester, who speaks of these killings taking place 'the year before' the death of Gospatric on 28 December 1064. This Gospatric, the son of Uhtred, was slain by order of Queen Edith while attending King Edward's Christmas court. His murder was reportedly the result of the queen's intervention in a dispute between Gospatric and her brother, Tosti. He was probably the same man who issued the famous writ concerning lands in Allerdale in Cumbria. What were the reasons behind these savage actions carried out by Earl Tosti, or on his behalf? It has been suggested that it was an attempt to stifle opposition by removing its potential leaders and this is certainly possible. Earl Tosti's predecessor, Siward, had acted in a similar manner, killing Earl Eadwulf, who controlled the region beyond the Tees in 1041, in order to seize control of all Northumbria.[8]

However, there is another possibility which could explain these actions by Tosti. When Tosti visited Rome in 1061, among his following was a young man named Gospatric, a kinsman of King Edward. This was almost certainly Gospatric, son of Maldred, a grandson of King Aethelred and cousin of King Malcolm, who was later to become Earl of Northumbria under William. This Gospatric, according to the *Vita Eadwardi*, which was written for Tosti's sister, Queen Edith, showed considerable valour and loyalty in aiding the earl's escape when their party was attacked by robbers on the return journey. The fact that Gospatric accompanied Tosti on this journey indicates that he had probably entered the service of the earl, and the prominence he is given shows that he had become an important member of his entourage. If this was the case, it would not be surprising if Tosti reciprocated by promoting Gospatric's interests in Northumbria.[9]

This would probably involve Tosti in acting against the rival lines of the descendants of *Ealdorman* Waltheof and the murders of Gamal, Ulf and Gospatric would fit such a pattern. Gospatric, son of Uhtred, Lord of Allerdale, was the senior representative of the elder line of Waltheof's descendants. The other two murdered men were closely linked to this Gospatric. Ulf, son of Dolfin, was probably the grandson of the Thorfinn MacThore to whom Gospatric had granted lands in Allerdale in his famous writ, during Earl Siward's rule. Gamal was probably the grandson of his namesake who also appeared in Gospatric's Allerdale writ, and son of the Orm who commissioned the

The sundial at St Gregory's Church in Kirkdale, North Yorkshire.

Kirkdale sundial and who married Gospatric's niece, Aethelthryth. All of these killings may therefore have been arranged to further the career of Tosti's protégé Gospatric, son of Maldred, who came from the junior line of Waltheof's descendants. Whatever the reason behind Earl Tosti's actions, these deaths undoubtedly aroused opposition to his rule among those linked to Gospatric of Allerdale, north of the Tees.[10]

This unrest was not the main cause of the rebellion of 1065, although the rebels did use these slayings as justification for their actions. The identified leaders of the rebellion, Gamelbearn, Dunstan, son of Aethelnoth, and Gluniarn, son of Heardwulf, were *thegns* of Yorkshire with no apparent links to Gospatric. They were unlikely to be interested in the rivalries of Waltheof's descendants. Instead, the interests of the leading rebels were centred on the extensive lands they held in Yorkshire. Domesday Book records these lands, including one estate at Temple Newsham held jointly by Dunstan and Gluniarn, which lay mainly in the West Riding but also included houses in York itself.[11]

It is John of Worcester who indicates the probable reason for the involvement of these men in the rebellion when he speaks of a huge tribute Tosti had 'unjustly levied on the whole of Northumbria'. In addition, the *Vita Eadwardi*, although otherwise sympathetic to Tosti, admits that he had 'repressed [the Northumbrians] with the heavy yolk of his rule', possibly another reference to this tax. It appears that the northern shires may have had a much more favourable tax assessment than the rest of England. Earl Tosti seems to have made the mistake of attempting to redress this anomaly and impose on the northern shires a level of tax closer to that found in the rest of England. The exact change made is unfortunately unknown, but that it may have caused the rebellion is suggested by the widespread participation of minor *thegns* in the revolt, all of whom, naturally, would be affected by such a change. Thus Chronicle C speaks of the participation of 'all the *thegns* of Yorkshire' and notes that 'all Tosti's earldom unanimously deserted him', while Chronicle D adds 'all the *thegns* of . . . Northumberland' as well. The rebellion was also led by fairly minor figures in contrast to the leaders of other revolts, such as Earls Godwine and Aelfgar.[12]

The purpose of such an increase in the tax level was clear. It would result in a substantial increase in revenue for the king, and since the earl took a third of all such revenue, it would enhance his own wealth too. This may have been particularly important since Tosti's participation in Harold's Welsh campaign and his vigorous enforcement of justice must have been draining his coffers. Although he should have realized that such a move would be widely unpopular, he may have considered his position sufficiently secure by 1065 for him to take this chance. He had already secured his government of the Northumbrians through increased enforcement of law and order, which possibly involved intervention in local blood feuds and had probably reduced general unrest in the earldom. This and the elimination of possible threats from Wales and Scotland and from the local nobility may have contributed to what was to prove a false sense of security on Tosti's part.

Whatever the reasons behind it, Tosti's action was to prove a major error of judgement. A proposed increase in taxation naturally aroused a great deal of opposition, far more than his participation in northern feuds or enforcement of royal justice could have done. The reason for this opposition is not difficult to appreciate if we examine the landholdings of the three named leaders of the rebellion, Gamelbearn, Dunstan and Gluniarn, as recorded in Domesday Book. Consider, for example, the effect of an increase in the Northumbrian tax assessment from 2s on every 6 *carucates* to say 2s on every 4. This assessment still represented only a quarter of that of the rest of England, but would in effect increase the annual tax payments of these Yorkshire *thegns* by 50 per cent. Thus Gamelbearn, who held approximately 60 *carucates* of land and paid 20s at the original tax rates, would pay 30s at the new rate. Similarly, Dunstan, who held 48 *carucates* and originally paid 16s, would find this rising to 24s, and Gluniarn, with 39 *carucates* and paying 13s, would find himself liable for 19½s. Such proposed increases would indeed provoke a great deal of opposition, affecting as they did every *thegn* in the earldom. The sources also hint that Tosti was dispensing arbitrary justice, including killings and forfeitures, at this time, which may have been attempts to enforce collection of taxes at the new rate.[13]

In summary, the rigorous imposition of justice by Tosti had probably interfered with traditional jurisdictions and with a local preference for the blood feud, and so aroused resentment from some local nobles. The promotion of the interests of Gospatric, son of Maldred, in preference to those of the senior line of the descendants of *Ealdorman* Waltheof had led to opposition from and the murder of men of this line. However, it was surely the attempted imposition of unaccustomed financial burdens in autumn 1065 which raised the temperature of the whole earldom to boiling point. Taxes may have been collected in the autumn after harvest and this would certainly fit the time-scale of the Northumbrian revolt. It has been suggested that the clerks of Durham had sought to incite the earldom to revolt by translating the relics of St Oswine to Durham and displaying them there in March 1065. However, a later life of St Oswine records Bishop Aethelwine presenting Countess Judith, Tosti's wife, with some hair of St Oswine as a result of this same event. It would therefore seem unlikely that this translation was directed against the earl, but rather was part of Durham's efforts to expand its collection of relics. In fact, it was in the autumn of 1065 that opposition began to form, its objective being the overthrow of Earl Tosti, his representatives and his new taxation. The absence of the earl, who had been called to the south on business at the royal court and had stayed on to hunt with King Edward at Britford in Wiltshire, provided the rebels with their opportunity.[14]

On 3 October 1065 the *thegns* of Yorkshire and the rest of Northumbria descended on York and occupied the city. This accomplished, they proceeded to slaughter Tosti's officials and supporters, including his *huscarls* Amund and Ravenswart, and to sack his

The Chronicle of John of Worcester, the entry for 1065.

treasury. These actions appear to confirm that the primary cause behind the revolt was the new taxes. They emptied the earl's treasury in order to recover those unlawful taxes taken from them earlier, and took revenge on the officials who had sought to enforce that taxation through ruthless measures including forfeiture and killing. They seem to have missed Copsi, Tosti's deputy, indicating perhaps that he too was absent from York, leaving the field clear for the rebels.[15]

Once they had vented their initial anger on the symbols of Tosti's rule, the northern *thegns* met to consider how to seek legitimacy for their rebellion. They did this by declaring Tosti outlawed for his unlawful actions and sending for Morcar, younger brother of Earl Edwin of Mercia, to be their earl. These brothers probably had sufficient reason to participate in Tosti's discomfiture. Despite its sympathetic view of Tosti, the *Vita Eadwardi* admits 'a long-standing rivalry' between him and Aelfgar's sons. This may have originated from Tosti's elevation to the earldom in 1055, which had been considered by their father, Aelfgar, as a usurpation of his seniority. They probably believed that Tosti had deprived their father of a major earldom and probably contributed to his banishment later that year. What made the Northumbrians choose Morcar as Tosti's successor?

The fact that Morcar was, in effect, an intruder has already been discussed, and indicates that he was not chosen for his connections with Northumbria. Neither was he chosen because of a lack of local candidates. There were at least three such men: Oswulf, son of the Eadwulf slain by Siward in 1041; Waltheof, the young son of Earl Siward; and Gospatric, son of Maldred, Tosti's protégé. The last of these was probably unacceptable because of his close links with Tosti, and certainly so to the supporters of his murdered rival, Gospatric of Allerdale. Waltheof may still have been considered too young or was perhaps unacceptable as a son of Earl Siward, who was also remembered for his severe rule. This left Oswulf, a nephew of Gospatric of Allerdale, who would later be appointed to rule part of Northumbria under Earl Morcar and who became Earl of Northumbria soon after the Conquest. However, he was overlooked on this occasion, possibly because backing him would have aligned the partisans of his rival, Gospatric, son of Maldred, against the rebels. The latter Gospatric may have retained sufficient local support, even without his patron Tosti, to effectively bar Oswulf's appointment. The fact that he had not been completely eclipsed by Tosti's fall seems proven by his ability to take control of Northumbria in 1068. In a sense, therefore, the northern *thegns* had to look beyond their own region, and chose Morcar as the most senior nobleman currently available who lacked an earldom.[16]

There were other, more positive reasons for the choice of Morcar. The rebels were fully aware that the deposition of Tosti was bound to arouse strong opposition, for not only was he a favourite of King Edward but his brothers ruled much of England and the eldest, Harold, was second only to the king. In these circumstances, the wise course for the rebels was to ally themselves with the other major family in England, in the person of Morcar. This alliance would bring them the assistance of his brother, Earl Edwin of Mercia. Such major outside support, which could be vital to the success of their revolt, would not be forthcoming for any local Northumbrian leader. The *Vita Eadwardi* confirms this point when it says that they chose Morcar 'to give them authority' for their actions. This was a rebellion against Earl Tosti, rather than a rebellion against southern government in general.[17]

The northern rebels, accompanied by their new 'Earl' Morcar, marched south to press their case with King Edward. They were joined at Northampton by Earl Edwin with the forces of his earldom and some Welsh allies. They had ravaged the countryside on the way south, targeting Tosti's lands and followers in Nottinghamshire, Lincolnshire and Northamptonshire, all of which were part of his earldom. They were met at Northampton by Earl Harold, who it should be noted clearly came to negotiate as he was without an armed following. He had been sent by King Edward, possibly at the suggestion of Earl Tosti, to open negotiations with the rebels. The intention was that he should restore peace to the kingdom and his brother to his earldom.[18]

Harold was now faced with the most difficult negotiations of his entire career, between two sides equally determined not to give an inch. These negotiations were undoubtedly made more difficult because of the passions aroused on both sides and because they reached into the heart of the kingdom and the heart of Harold's own family. In comparison, Harold's earlier negotiations with Earl Aelfgar and Gruffydd of Wales, must have seemed relatively straightforward. On the one hand, Earl Tosti, his own brother, was determined to recover his earldom, even if that meant civil war and the crushing of the rebellion by force. Initially, it appears Tosti was supported in this by King Edward and his sister, Queen Edith. On the other hand, the rebels, consisting of the northern *thegns* from Yorkshire and the rest of the earldom and led by Morcar, wanted Tosti removed. They were supported by Morcar's brother, Earl Edwin of Mercia, and the men of his earldom. The initial positions adopted by Earl Harold himself, and by his brothers Gyrth and Leofwine, are unknown, but were presumably supportive of their brother Tosti. Harold's attitude may be hinted at in Chronicle C, which states that he 'wanted to bring about an agreement between them if he could', including presumably Tosti's restoration. The fact that Tosti may have requested his brother's mediation and the latter's later reaction to Harold's failure to support his restoration may indicate the same.[19]

However, after Harold had spoken with the rebels at Northampton towards the end of October, he realized that it would be impossible for Tosti to retain Northumbria. The latter had completely lost the consensus of support which an earl required to rule. He had succeeded in alienating the majority of the local *thegns* rather than simply one faction or another. As a result, the feelings of hatred and distrust now stirred up against him were too deep to be assuaged, and the opposition was now too well organized and supported to be overcome without a civil war. The spectre of civil war was something which Earl Harold drew back from, just as his father and King Edward had done during the earlier crisis of 1051–2. Therefore, by the time he returned to Oxford where the royal council was to meet on 28 October to consider the crisis, he had probably already made an important decision.[20]

At the Oxford council, Harold announced that the rebels could not be persuaded to withdraw or reduce their demands for Tosti's removal and that they could only be compelled to do so by the use of military force. He advised against this and instead suggested their demands should be met. The *Vita Eadwardi* recounts the arguments raised against military action including the fear of civil war and the imminent onset of winter weather. The fear of civil war, as in the crisis of 1051–2, certainly loomed large in men's minds. Harold himself was also now aware of William's ambition to invade, an ambition which would more easily have become a reality if there had been civil war in England. Nevertheless, Harold's statement must have caused shock and consternation for the king, for Earl Tosti, and for the rest of the Godwine family. The king demanded that troops be called out to restore Earl Tosti by force. It seems that Tosti was so stunned and furious that he actually accused his brother of inciting the whole rebellion, with the aim of expelling him from the kingdom. Indeed, so emphatic was Tosti with this accusation that Harold had to purge himself of this charge by swearing an oath.[21]

Is it possible that any truth lay behind Tosti's accusation? As we have seen, the rebellion had resulted from local causes in the north which Harold could not have created. It is possible that Harold took advantage of the fact of the rebellion to rid himself of a rival or potential rival, but there are no contemporary indications that the brothers were considered as rivals. On the contrary, the brothers had always worked very closely together, particularly during their recent Welsh campaign. In addition, the *Vita Eadwardi*, written for Queen Edith, is clearly confused by this sudden rift between the brothers, and the whole scheme of the work, based on the brothers working together with a common aim, is disrupted and transformed by it. Similarly, Queen Edith herself is stated to have been confounded by the quarrel between her brothers and there is no reason to doubt this. Therefore, there appear to be no grounds for suspecting any important rivalry between the brothers before 1065.[22]

It has been suggested that Harold now saw Tosti as a potential threat to his designs on the English throne and used the rebellion to achieve his replacement with Morcar. This assumes that Harold already intended to take the throne and forestall the rightful claims of *Atheling* Edgar, which is by no means certain. It also requires that Tosti would be opposed to such an action by Harold, and that the latter had already prepared an alliance with Edwin and Morcar to secure a possible future move for the throne. In such circumstances he might have sought to win the support of the brothers Edwin and Morcar by supporting Morcar in his claim to Northumbria. However, there are problems with such a scenario. Firstly, there is no evidence one way or the other to indicate when Harold forged his alliance with Edwin and Morcar, and second, it seems unlikely that Tosti would in fact have opposed any move by Harold to take the throne. There is little evidence, for example, that he was a supporter of the rightful heir, *Atheling* Edgar. The latter is never linked to the earl, although they must have had regular contact at court. The possibility of Tosti himself as a rival candidate for the throne also seems unlikely since as the younger brother, less powerful than Harold and more isolated in the north from the centres of power, his claim could only be weaker than Harold's. All the evidence seems to point to Tosti as Harold's potential supporter in such a venture, as in all previous actions.[23]

The timing of the Northumbrian rebellion itself also causes difficulties. In the autumn of 1065 King Edward was around sixty-three years old but had as yet shown no signs of imminent demise. If Harold was making arrangements to occupy the throne already, his actions could have been premature. He might have had to wait for several years for King Edward's death, by which time *Atheling* Edgar would have reached maturity and perhaps been in a more secure position to succeed in opposition to Harold. In such an interval, any alliance between Harold and the brothers Edwin and Morcar might decay and the latter be tempted to support Edgar instead. This would also appear to make the suggestion that Harold took advantage of the Northumbrian rebellion to remove Tosti seem unlikely, although it cannot be entirely ruled out. It is impossible to establish the truth of this unless we consider the reactions of the rest of the Godwine family and of King Edward to the rebellion against Tosti.

The sympathy of King Edward and Queen Edith for Tosti is clearly recorded. The positions of Gyrth and Leofwine are unknown but it is possible that Gyrth was close to his brother Tosti as he is frequently associated with him in the sources. Thus he was in Tosti's company during the family's exile in 1051–2, and again on the visit to Rome in 1061. In an obscure reference in the *Vita Eadwardi*, Tosti's mother, Gytha, would be described as sorrowing over his exile. In spite of this sympathy for Tosti from the king and members of his family, all these individuals were eventually persuaded, probably in part by Harold but largely by the stark facts of the situation, that Tosti could not remain as Earl of Northumbria. Indeed, they were also persuaded that since he refused to accept his deposition he should be exiled. Gyrth and Leofwine appear to have accepted Tosti's downfall without a murmur, and thereafter supported Harold with complete loyalty until they fell together at Hastings. There are no indications in any sources that either brother considered supporting Tosti instead of Harold and this strongly suggests there existed no suspicion concerning Harold's actions on their part. King Edward is recorded in Chronicle D as finally agreeing to the terms of the northern rebels. Although the *Vita Eadwardi* shows that both he and Queen Edith were deeply upset by Tosti's fall, it nevertheless makes clear that they accepted it, however reluctantly. All of this would seem to indicate that Harold was not purposefully using the rebellion to rid himself of Tosti, but was forced to act as he did as a result of it.[24]

Eventually, King Edward had to accept the northern rebels' terms. The alternative was civil war, which no one was prepared to countenance. Tosti was deposed and replaced by Morcar, the rebels were pardoned and the laws of Cnut renewed, the latter point no doubt signifying the withdrawal of the additional tax demands. Harold returned to Northampton soon after the council of 28 October to give the rebels surety for this settlement, and the immediate crisis was resolved. Tosti appears to have been outlawed a short time later, possibly early in November, apparently because he refused to accept his deposition as commanded by Edward. This seems clear from his accusations against his brother and his subsequent attempts to restore his fortunes by any means possible. Domesday Book preserves notices of land forfeited by Tosti at this time at Bayford in Hertfordshire and Chalton in Bedfordshire. Thereafter, Tosti took ship with his wife and family and some loyal *thegns* and sailed for Flanders and refuge with his brother-in-law, Count Baldwin V.[25]

It was now, in November 1065, that King Edward's health began to fail and he fell into his final decline. Domesday Book records a legal judgement made late in 1065 which was due to be implemented by the king at the imminent Christmas court but which was left unenforced by his rapid decline and demise. As a result, Harold, who is described by John of Worcester as *sub regulus* and by William of Poitiers as second to the king, probably took more and more direct control of the government into his own hands. As he did so, he found himself faced with a dilemma. *Atheling* Edgar, the natural heir to the kingdom, was still too young and inexperienced to take charge of a kingdom, especially one under direct military threat. William of Normandy was at this time free of any rivals or entanglements in northern France and ready to press his claims by force, as Harold was only too well aware from his recent visit. Harold's own brother Tosti was in exile in Flanders, from where he was already planning, like his father before him, to launch a bid to restore his fortunes in England. The *Vita Eadwardi* mentions Flemish knights being placed in his service by Count Baldwin. In addition, Harold was possibly unsure of how much he could rely on Earls Edwin and Morcar under these looming threats. These were the problems which faced Harold as time passed on towards the new year of 1066 and King Edward's strength ebbed slowly away.[26]

It was probably these circumstances which finally convinced Harold of the need to consider what was a radical solution to the difficulties facing both him and the kingdom. In order to safeguard the kingdom and his own power he needed to control the throne itself as the centre of power, wealth and influence in England. He could achieve this by becoming the power behind a new King Edgar, as he had done with Edward, but this would still leave room for rival voices to counsel the immature young king. Harold must have had time to study this young man since his arrival in 1057, and he may already have seen signs of what seems to have been a weak character. Certainly, Edgar was to spend much of his later career being buffeted by events though this may

The death of King Edward, 1066. (The Bayeux Tapestry – 11th Century. By special permission of the City of Bayeux)

simply be a feature of what were very troubled times. If Harold was absent on campaign with the army, as seemed likely to be the case, others might undermine his position with the young king. It must have seemed obvious that the solution was for Harold to become king himself and control the centre of power directly. It cannot be doubted that this was a radical proposal. Harold was the first and only member of the English nobility known to have attempted to gain the throne. Indeed, apart from the Danes Swein and Cnut, no one outside Alfred's dynasty had ever held the kingship.

It was probably now that Harold began to make serious preparations for the possibility of his own succession to the throne. Naturally, there were many things to be done before this would be possible. If Harold wished to ascend the throne he would have to convince others that he was a preferable choice to the rightful heir, *Atheling* Edgar. The continued backing of his brothers Gyrth and Leofwine even after Tosti's fall proved that their loyalty was secure. This meant that only the two northern earls, Edwin and Morcar, possessed the necessary military power required to enforce the young *atheling*'s claims against Harold. If the northern earls opposed him, this could result in a civil war between Harold's supporters and those of Edgar, with the added threat of William of Normandy poised to intervene and seize the throne for himself. We have already seen that no one in England wished for such a result, and so Harold must now have begun discreetly to secure his own support and to persuade the northern earls to join him and abandon any thoughts of supporting *Atheling* Edgar. The obvious occasion to do this was during the Christmas court of 1065 in London.

The court held at this major Christian festival was usually attended by a large number of English nobles and churchmen. Attendance was probably swollen on this occasion by news of Edward's declining health and the need to consider the succession. Fortunately, there are two later Westminster diplomas which appear to reflect genuine contemporary witness lists of 28 December 1065. These indicate that besides the king and queen, both archbishops, eight bishops, eight abbots, all five earls and the usual nobles of the court were all present. This list derives some confirmation from the fact that it includes those later in attendance at Edward's deathbed and who were at the Christmas court just prior to this. It is clear that no representative of Duke William arrived to push his claim to the throne at this time. This may be a result of the swiftness of Edward's decline from being stricken with illness in November 1065 to his death on 5 January 1066. William of Poitiers speaks of the report of Edward's death coming 'unexpectedly' to Normandy, which rather casts doubt on his earlier statement that Edward was severely ill in 1064 and so sent Harold to Normandy to confirm William's succession to the throne. If Edward had been ill then surely William would have expected his death at any time thereafter, and would have had a representative in attendance at court at this time.[27]

Harold worked hard to canvass support among those gathered at this court, employing his great diplomatic skills to win them over. He could rely on his remaining brothers Gyrth and Leofwine. Queen Edith, his sister, had previously favoured Tosti, as is clearly reflected in the *Vita Eadwardi* and confirmed by William of Poitiers, who transforms this into a hatred of Harold. However, Queen Edith would soon find herself entirely dependent on Harold's favour as a childless royal widow and could not therefore afford to act openly against him. The real necessity for Harold was to win Earls Edwin and Morcar over to his side, and he already had some advantage in this. There is no evidence of any ill-will between Harold and the earls, such as existed between them and Tosti. It was Harold who had persuaded the king to accept Morcar as Earl of Northumbria thereby adding immensely to his family's power and prestige. The two earls may have been persuaded by Harold's arguments about the problems of the succession of the youthful *Atheling* Edgar; they showed a reluctance to support the latter even after Harold's death. However, the crucial factor in winning them over was probably a pledge by Harold not to restore Tosti to influence in England. This would secure the brothers' new-found power and influence. The discussions must also have involved the proposal of a marriage alliance to bind the earls and Harold together. The marriage of Harold to Alditha, sister of the two earls, is undated but must have taken place between the death of Gruffydd of

Wales on 5 August 1063 and Harold's own death on 14 October 1066. This period of negotiation seems the most likely time for such a marriage to be discussed.[28]

The success of Harold in winning the support of the earls was the vital part of his diplomatic offensive, but it was not the only element. He had also to persuade the senior churchmen, the bishops and archbishops, whose support would provide the necessary religious sanction for his succession. In particular, he needed to win over the two archbishops, who alone could perform the coronation ceremony. They could not oppose him by force, but could either secure or undermine his legitimacy by granting or withholding God's grace at his coronation. Harold clearly must have brought his diplomatic skills to bear on these men and managed to overcome any objections they may have had to this setting aside of the established succession of *Atheling* Edgar. Archbishop Stigand, a practical man of the world, whose great personal wealth was based on royal service, would be anxious to secure his own position and therefore may have accepted the practicalities of Harold's proposal. The *Vita Eadwardi* later shows him urging Harold to dismiss as mere ravings Edward's deathbed concerns about the kingdom. Archbishop Ealdred appears to have been very close to Harold and his support may have been secure. The other churchmen were perhaps content to follow the lead of these two great men as they were also equally dependent on royal favour. They may have been persuaded by arguments about the *atheling*'s youth but it seems likely that it was an undertaking by Harold to secure King Edward's agreement to this change in the succession that secured their consent.[29]

The securing of the support of these great men, clerical and lay, meant that Harold's objective was in sight. Where the great men led, the lesser nobles and clergy, many of whom were their dependents, would usually follow. This had normally been the case except where opposition had a very widespread basis as in Northumbria in 1065, and even in these circumstances the lesser nobles usually felt the need for support from one or other of the earls. There was to be no such widespread opposition to Harold's succession in 1066 and many of these lesser nobles were later to follow him to Stamford Bridge and Hastings.

In contrast to Harold's wide influence and support, built up over twenty-one years of prominent royal service, at both local and national level, and boosted by success in military command, *Atheling* Edgar could offer little. He was a young boy who had been in England for only eight years. He may have only recently learnt the language as *Atheling* Edward, his father, was a small child when taken to far-off Hungary in 1016. He had few supporters other than his mother, Agatha, and two sisters, who were strangers like himself. He held no land in England and hence had no dependants or supporters. He was probably still in the wardship of his great uncle, King Edward. He held one great trump card in that he remained the king's rightful heir, an important factor in eleventh-century succession disputes. It still remained for Harold to convince King Edward that he, rather than Edgar, should actually be designated as heir.[30]

The crown is presented to Harold. (The Bayeux Tapestry – 11th Century. By special permission of the City of Bayeux)

On 5 January 1066 Edward finally succumbed to his illness and on his deathbed bequeathed his kingdom to Earl Harold. This bequest of the throne is evidenced by a number of sources and cannot be doubted. The *Vita Eadwardi* portrays an elaborate deathbed scene during which Edward commends his kingdom and his queen to Harold's protection. This wording has been interpreted as signifying the passing on to Harold of a regency only until William could claim the throne, but the subsequent references to taking oaths of fealty from Edward's foreign servants surely implies kingship. This scene is closely reflected in the Bayeux Tapestry although, typically for this source, any statement of what is shown is lacking. Thus Edward points to Harold but the text says only that he 'addresses his vassals' and nothing concerning what he may have said. Unusually, all three versions of the Chronicle agree in testifying to Edward's designation of Harold. Even William of Poitiers accepts that Harold was granted the throne by Edward. Although often seen as such, King Edward's designation of Harold should not be surprising when the circumstances of 1066 are considered, with the threat of Norman invasion and the consequent need for strong military leadership. Harold had been Edward's right-hand man since 1053 and had served his interests and those of the kingdom loyally, even in some difficult circumstances. Thus Harold's actions in 1065 although against Edward's wishes were undoubtedly in his interests by preventing a civil war in his kingdom. This crucial designation by the dying king probably swayed any who had doubts about the validity of Harold's succession in place of *Atheling* Edgar.[31]

In addition to the evidence of the sources, the actions of the people of England in response to Harold's succession indicate a broad acceptance. There exists no evidence of rebellion against his kingship, either in favour of *Atheling* Edgar or as we shall see in support of either of the foreign invaders of 1066. There are no significant recorded depositions or exiles by Harold, even of Norman vassals of King Edward, and no indication of major changes of personnel in positions of national or local importance. There was unease in some quarters about his succession in place of *Atheling* Edgar, but this never resulted in any overt opposition to his rule. Thus a source close to Abbot Baldwin of Bury St Edmunds speaks of Harold 'succeeding to the kingdom by craft', probably indicating a natural preference for Edgar as Edward's successor felt by the latter's former physician. However, in spite of this, Abbot Baldwin did not fail in his duty during 1066 to supply troops for the new King Harold's armies. There can really be no doubt that Harold's succession to the kingdom was accepted by the majority of the population.[32]

Before moving on to Harold's coronation, we must pause to look in more detail at the character of the man who was about to ascend to the throne of England.

CHAPTER EIGHT

HAROLD THE MAN

A true friend of his race and country.[1]

We have seen Harold as Earl of East Anglia, as an exile driven from the land, as the powerful Earl of Wessex, and now on the threshold of kingship, but what can be said about him personally? To identify him as an individual, we need to have answers to some of the following questions. What did he look like? What can we tell about his character? What were his relations with his family like? Who were his friends and supporters? To answer these questions for any early medieval figure is difficult. The dearth of sources of the kind necessary to consider these matters is always a problem, and given King Harold's brief fame, this is particularly the case. In addition, the few sources which do survive for Harold tend to suffer from bias, whether in favour or against him, as a result of his central role in the controversial events of 1066. In spite of this, the few available sources are sufficient to permit us at least to attempt to sketch him in outline.

What can we say about Harold's physical appearance? This is always the most difficult aspect to determine of a medieval figure, because at that time symbol and allegory were more prized in art than realism. The few 'portraits' which survive of figures from this period tend therefore to be representations rather than true likenesses. This means effectively that we cannot know what people actually looked like but only how they themselves or others wished them to be represented. We are fortunate in possessing two probably independent representations of Harold's face. The first can be found in the scenes of the later Bayeux Tapestry, and the other on the coinage which he would issue as king. These sources are both very much representational but they share sufficient common features to allow us to consider that they provide a general likeness of Harold. They show him with long hair and a moustache in the style of an Anglo-Saxon noble, which later so intrigued the Normans. The significance of the moustache as representational of a warrior will be recalled from the Chronicle account of Harold's chaplain Leofgar, who retained his moustache as a bishop. The coins add a neatly trimmed beard, perhaps grown after he became king or perhaps considered to represent the gravitas of his new position. In this context, it should be noted that King Edward is shown with a beard in the Bayeux Tapestry, as are a number of English kings elsewhere, although this may be as equally representational of age as of status. The actual 'portrait' of Harold on his coins shows strong influence from earlier Roman Imperial designs, particularly in the construction of the neck muscles. It is not therefore a true portrait of

Harold's 'portrait', as represented on his coinage.

Harold himself, but rather represents how he wished to be shown. It was the king who finally authorised the design to be used on the coinage, even in cases where archbishops may have inspired their choice as with the *Agnus Dei* coinage of King Aethelred II. The fact that Harold's face on the coins has the rugged and determined look of a warrior was ultimately a result of his endorsement of this image.[2]

This face was placed on a body described as handsome, graceful and strong by the author of the *Vita Eadwardi*, who either gained his information from Harold's sister, Queen Edith, or perhaps from direct observation. This is not exactly a detailed description but he was apparently taller than his brother Tosti, and 'well practised in endless fatigues'. Although rather conventional, this account does not seem to be solely panegyric. Harold's strength is witnessed by the famous scene in the Bayeux Tapestry, where he pulls two men from quicksand while crossing the river Couesnon. Harold's endurance would also be amply evidenced in the year 1066, by his ability to undertake two journeys of 190 miles each and fight a tough battle at the end of each of them, all within the space of a month.[3]

So, we know only a little about Harold's actual appearance. What can we say about his character? The author of the *Vita Eadwardi* describes him as wise, patient, merciful, courageous, temperate, and prudent but ruthless with opponents. This portrayal seems to lean rather heavily in Harold's favour, and we need to test it against what we know of Harold's character from his actions as earl and later as king.[4]

The essential dual nature of Harold's character is perhaps best summed up by two very important symbols from his career. The first of these is the device on his personal banner, which is described in the sources as consisting of the image of a warrior or armed man, worked in pure gold and jewels. This perhaps represented the essential Harold, a warrior, steeped in the military traditions of his English and Danish forebears. This may be confirmed by the names given to two of his sons, Edmund and

Magnus, which were not family names. These almost certainly commemorate Edmund 'Ironside', the warrior king who stoutly defended England against Cnut, and Magnus of Norway, the conqueror of Denmark, both of whom were probably heroic figures to Harold. The probable personal association of Harold's father, Godwine, with Edmund 'Ironside' makes the former likely, while the latter is almost certain since Magnus of Norway was first to bear this name in imitation of Charlemagne. Also Leofgar, Harold's personal chaplain, was seen as a very military figure, who, when appointed Bishop of Hereford in 1056, continued to wear a warrior's moustache and took the field against the Welsh. Harold's own military skills and abilities are indisputable from his record in 1063 and later in 1066. They are indirectly confirmed by William of Poitiers, who described him as warlike, courageous and eager for renown and highlighted his great victory over Harald of Norway.[5]

In contrast to this military aspect of Harold's character was a second, represented by the legend found on the coinage which would be issued on his accession to the throne. This coinage bears, on the reverse, opposite the king's head, the single Latin word *pax* or peace. This has been seen as a rather ironic coincidence, but the iconography of coinage was important to English kings in this period. Harold's active choice of this design is evidenced by the complete change of coin dies on his accession. King Edward himself had adopted a *pax* coin type on his own accession, perhaps in hope of peace after the upheavals of the previous reigns, and Harold may have intended this legend as a symbol of his lawful succession to Edward. However, the symbolism of this word as an appeal for peace and an invocation to Christ probably also represented a desire of his heart. The confirmation of this can perhaps be seen in several cases where Harold sought the path of peace in preference to war, even when this path was not necessarily directly of benefit to himself. On several occasions, he chose to secure peace with Gruffydd of Wales and Earl Aelfgar, and so prevented open war, even though his family might have gained from Aelfgar's permanent exile. Similarly, in 1065 he agreed to Tosti's exile in order to avoid civil war in England, even though this was undoubtedly a major blow to his family.[6]

The 'Pax' motif on Harold's coinage.

It was a blend of these two qualities, an aptitude for war with a desire for peace, which probably brought about the qualities highlighted by the *Vita Eadwardi*. Can we find supporting evidence of these specific qualities? Harold's wisdom and courage are acknowledged by the otherwise hostile Norman sources as well as being shown by his actions. Patience and temperance reveal themselves in his initial dealings with the exiled Earl Aelfgar and Gruffydd of Wales and with the Northumbrian rebels in 1065, when he held talks rather than open hostilities. Mercy was to be shown to Olaf Haraldsson, after Harold's resounding victory at Stamford Bridge. Prudence would reveal itself in his preparations to meet William's invasion and in his cultivation of the northern earls, after Tosti's exile. He was also ruthless when necessary, for example in the way he finally dealt with Gruffydd of Wales, in his refusal to restore Tosti in 1065, and in the way he would deal with Harald of Norway in 1066.[7]

There is thus some evidence to support the description of Harold's character given by the author of the *Vita Eadwardi* and to suggest that it was more than panegyric. Indeed, the account of Harold in this text is not entirely positive and the author mentions also that Harold had two faults. These were a tendency not to share his plans with others and an overindulgence in swearing oaths. These references are possibly related to Harold's Normandy visit, though this is not clear. If so, they may be tinged by hindsight and so be less valuable, but nevertheless we should consider them. If, as Eadmer suggests, Harold visited Normandy as part of a private visit to free his family hostages, that he did not reveal this plan to others who might have dissuaded him may be what is referred to here. This may be confirmed perhaps by the absence of any reference to Harold's Norman visit in the English sources. However, this interpretation depends on Harold's Norman visit being viewed as the entry of an unwary man into what was clearly a trap, which has already been refuted. Therefore, it is unlikely that anyone could in fact have advised against it. Nevertheless, the reference may reflect an early version of Eadmer's later story that Edward warned against the visit. Similarly, the statement that Harold was 'rather too generous with oaths' may be a reference to his Norman oath. Although it has been shown that this was probably a case of an oath taken under duress, it may have caused considerable unease in some quarters close to Harold. The breach of an oath was something which struck at the fabric of early medieval society. However, these references are difficult to judge, and it is perhaps unwise to try and infer more from them.[8]

What of the Norman views of Harold; can anything be discovered about his character from them? The most obvious aspect of these views is their hostility, which in the case of William of Poitiers often verges on the hysterical. Thus he describes Harold variously as 'the basest of men', 'insane', 'defiled by luxury', 'a cruel murderer' and 'the enemy of justice and good'. In contrast to this general vilification, there are relatively few positive comments about Harold in the Norman accounts, chiefly general comments concerning his courage and wisdom. The extreme tone of William of Poitiers' account makes it very difficult to accept much of what he says. The charge

Harold rescues two men from quicksand in Normandy. (The Bayeux Tapestry – 11th Century. By special permission of the City of Bayeux)

of murderer laid against Harold is blatantly false. It refers to the death of *Atheling* Alfred in 1036, which could not be laid at Harold's door. If Harold was as bad as William of Poitiers claimed, why did the English support him to the extent that 'he caused the whole English people also to be faithless to the duke'? Indeed, the negative slant of the Norman sources appears to be based on one charge against Harold, from which the rest follows – his breaking of the sacred oath sworn in Normandy.[9]

The fact that Harold swore an oath on holy relics to William in Normandy and then broke it has been seen as evidence of a weakness in his character – if he was customarily an oathbreaker, then he must be a liar and deceiver and someone not to be trusted. The breaking of an oath was a serious breach of secular law, of one of the most important political and social bonds, and of faith before God. However, if, as we have seen, Harold found himself in a position where swearing this oath was the only way to extricate himself from William's custody, then it is likely that he regarded his actions as fully justified. His subsequent actions show that he clearly regarded the oath as not binding. It is possible that he sought absolution from the Church and was given it. In support of this, there is no evidence that he broke oaths on other occasions but rather the opposite. He was entrusted with delicate negotiations which would involve solemn oaths as security for agreements reached in 1055, 1058 and 1065. Indeed, William of Poitiers describes Harold, before his journey to Normandy as 'greatest in . . . honour' among

Edward's earls. In 1065, when Tosti charged him with inciting the Northumbrian revolt and Harold cleared it by oath, the author of the *Vita Eadwardi*, despite his obvious sympathy for Tosti, seems to have believed him. This suggests his perjury in Normandy was out of character and enforced by circumstances.[10]

This discussion of Harold's sacred oath leads us to consideration of his religious views, which would naturally colour his interpretation of such an oath. Although his own chaplain, Leofgar, was a rather militant figure, Harold appears nevertheless to have shown a personal devotion and veneration for the saintly Bishop Wulfstan. Harold revealed this not only through his support for Wulfstan's election as Bishop of Worcester in 1062, but also by often seeking out his counsel. Harold is said to have made the pilgrimage to Rome, dispensing 'bounty' there, probably in 1056–7. He is shown in the Bayeux Tapestry entering the church at Bosham to pray for a safe voyage to Normandy, and he also stopped to pray at the church of Holy Cross at Waltham on his journey south to Hastings in 1066. As we have already seen, when considering Harold's landholdings, he was looked upon as a benefactor and supporter by a number of religious houses, including Worcester, Malmesbury, Peterborough and Abingdon. However, like many other major figures in England at this time, Harold chose to focus his devotional energies on a particular foundation with a correspondingly significant result.[11]

In Chapter Four we touched on how Harold lavished immense gifts of land and wealth on his foundation of Holy Cross at Waltham. He rebuilt the church there in 1060, on land granted him by King Edward. He donated some 70 hides of land to the church, which supported twelve regular canons, under a dean named Wulfwine and a schoolmaster named Adelard. In addition, he donated gifts of costly gold and silver church furnishings and vestments, including some of Byzantine workmanship. He also gathered a large collection of fifty-nine religious relics from a wide area of England and the Continent, including Rome, for his foundation. Indeed, so grateful were the canons of Waltham that they would preserve Harold's memory in their records and later compose a life of their illustrious founder and benefactor. In this respect, Harold was very much a man of his time; King Edward had demonstrated a similar focus in devotion towards Westminster, Earl Leofric to Coventry and Earl Odda to Deerhurst.[12]

However, in contrast to these expressions of piety, Harold is also accused of acting against God by taking lands from several religious houses, principally in the text of Domesday Book. Indeed, examples of this have already been examined in Chapter Four during consideration of Harold's landholding. It is important to place these actions in context and in this respect Harold was no different from every other layman of the time. King Cnut, Earl Leofric and his family, William of Normandy, many other leading Normans, and even King Edward himself are all known to have faced similar accusations at one time or another. In the cases raised against Harold the lands are small, and the background to Harold's possession of them is often unclear. It should

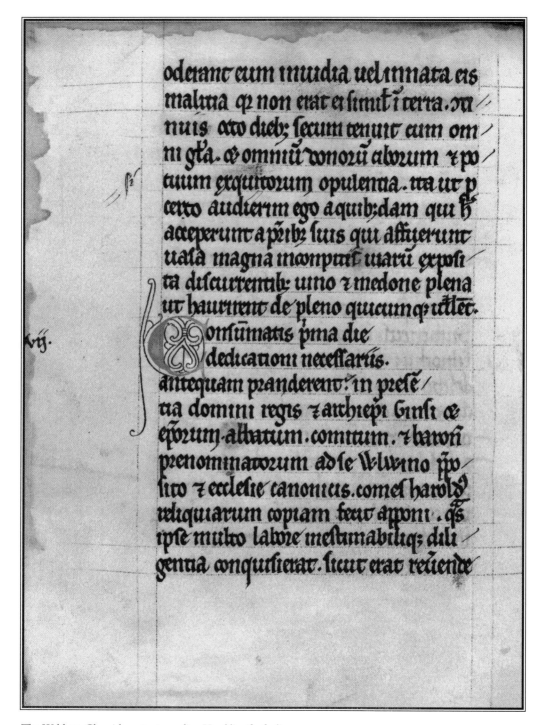

The Waltham Chronicle, extract recording Harold's gift of relics.

also be remembered that by the time most of these accusations were made in Domesday Book Harold was long dead. He had no surviving relatives or supporters to plead his case and was therefore an easy target.[13]

There have been a number of criticisms of the condition of the English Church during this period; what can we say about Harold's attitude to this? It should be remembered that King Edward was actually the man in a position to reform the faults in the Church. He chose not to do so to any significant extent largely for political reasons. Whether Harold was in the same mould we cannot establish, as his reign was too brief to provide any real indication of his attitude to this problem. The only Church appointments that Harold made as king were neither controversial nor particularly notable. William himself, despite his widely supposed intentions to cleanse the English Church, only began to do this in 1070 under Papal pressure. There is nothing in all this to indicate that Harold was any more or less religious than his contemporaries.[14]

In this respect, Harold is also condemned in Norman sources for his association with Archbishop Stigand. It is by no means clear that Stigand was a close associate of Harold and their relationship was at best equivocal. He was sufficiently powerful in terms of independent landholding not to require Harold's support, unlike other clerics such as Ealdred and Wulfstan. In religious terms, Stigand was considered unsuitable due to his uncanonical election to the archbishopric in 1052. Harold had probably known Stigand since the time when he was Earl of East Anglia, and Stigand was bishop there. The two men must have worked together in the administration of that province and its courts. They are jointly addressed in royal writs concerning the lands of Bury St Edmunds and both are bequeathed property in the will of Ketel, son of Wulfgyth. At this point in time Stigand's position was not controversial. It was only later, as a result of King Edward's need for political stability and good administrative ability in the archbishopric of Canterbury, that Stigand found himself in the position of an uncanonical archbishop holding 2 sees in plurality. Stigand's mediating position in the 1051–2 crisis makes it seem most likely that he was linked to both King Edward and the Godwine family and so acceptable to both, rather than a partisan of one or the other. Thereafter, Stigand remained associated not just with Harold but with the king and the rest of the English establishment. He was neither removed nor even spurned by the Papal legates who visited England in 1062. Even William, who was later said to have made Stigand's deposition part of his case to the Pope in favour of his invasion, would retain him as archbishop until 1070. Harold's retention of Archbishop Stigand during his own brief reign does not appear in the least out of place in this setting[15]

A similar conclusion can be reached about what has been seen as Harold's unusual family life. For some twenty years Harold was married *more Danico*, or in the Danish manner, to a certain Edith, *Swanneshals* or 'Swan-neck', and had at least six children by her. In England in the next century such a marriage would be considered unlawful and its offspring illegitimate, but in the eleventh century it was still relatively common, particularly among those of Scandinavian descent. Indeed, King Cnut and Aelfgifu of Northampton had just such a marriage and their children were regarded as legitimate by the laity. In the absence of a Church blessing, such a liaison was frowned on by the clergy, and Edith is always described by clerical authors as Harold's mistress or concubine, but the marriage was widely accepted by the laity. It should be remembered that Harold's mother, Gytha, was Danish, and it is perhaps not surprising that he should follow this Scandinavian custom. Such marriages were contracted by the two parties in the knowledge they could later be repudiated without the need for complex Church divorce, should the needs of family or state require. In contrast, the contemporary position on the Continent was different as William of Normandy, the illegitimate offspring of Robert of Normandy and his mistress, Herleve, had learned. These stricter Continental views on illegitimacy meant that William had been fortunate to inherit the duchy in 1035 and thereafter hold on to it.[16]

Relatively little information is recorded about Edith 'Swan-neck', and we have already touched on some of it in Chapter Four. Harold must have married her fairly early in his career, for three of the sons born to the couple were old enough to campaign in 1068. This implies the eldest of them, Godwine, was perhaps about twenty, dating his birth to the mid-1040s. This places Harold's marriage to Edith around the same time as the former became Earl of East Anglia in 1044, and this circumstance probably provides us with a clue to the identity of his wife. As the newly appointed earl, and a stranger to the area, Harold needed local supporters and, as previously suggested, one way to secure these quickly was by marriage. There exist many examples of such marriage alliances: Cnut to Aelfgifu of Northampton; Edmund 'Ironside' to Ealdgyth, widow of Sigeferth of the Five Boroughs; Earl Leofric and his son, Earl Aelfgar, to, respectively, Godgifu and Aelfgifu of the East Midlands. Therefore, Harold probably sought a wife with local connections and found her in that Edith variously described in Domesday Book as 'the Fair', 'the Beautiful' or 'the Rich'. As we have already seen in Chapter Four, this woman held wide lands in Cambridgeshire, Suffolk, Essex, Buckinghamshire and Hertfordshire. In the mid-1040s she may already have been heiress to these lands, and, as such, represented a very good catch for young Harold. He in turn provided Edith with protection for herself and for her property.[17]

Doubt has been expressed that Edith 'Swan-neck', wife of Harold, is the same woman as the Edith of Domesday Book. Although the neat proximity of her lands to Harold's new earldom, as indicated in the account of Harold's lands, is insufficient proof that the two women are the same, other evidence does indeed suggest it. Edith's nick-name, 'Swan-neck', probably represents a later elaboration of the earlier 'Fair' or 'Beautiful' of Domesday record, arising from the white swan-like skin of her neck which was considered a sign of beauty among English noblewomen. The poetic term *blachleor*, literally 'white cheeked' and meaning 'fair', is found extensively in Old English poetry, representing an ideal of noble feminine beauty in contrast to the countrywoman's sunburnt skin resulting from fieldwork. In one Domesday Book reference an Edith is termed 'countess', perhaps indicating the wife of Earl Harold. However, this woman's name, 'Aedgeva', is not in the usual spelling 'Ediva', found elsewhere for Edith 'the Fair'. It is also unlikely to refer either to the wife of Earl Aelfgar, who is otherwise found as 'Aelveva', or to Harold's later queen, who is found as 'Aldgid'. It may therefore refer to some unknown woman. The crucial factor in the identification of Edith 'Swan-neck' with Edith 'the Fair' is the later abduction by Count Alan of Richmond, of Harold's daughter, Gunnhild, from the nunnery at Wilton in 1093. This episode only really makes sense if it is seen as an attempt by Alan to secure his lands, which had formerly belonged to Edith 'the Fair', by an association with her surviving heiress, Gunnhild.[18]

If we accept the two women are one and the same, what can we say about Harold's first wife? Apart from her beauty, which appears to have been particularly notable judging from the many references to it, she was also undoubtedly rich in terms of her alternative nick-name, *Dives*. In 1066 she held, directly or through men commended to her, nearly 280 hides and 450 acres of land mostly in eastern England worth over £520. She was a power in the land with some twenty-nine men and three women commended to her directly. One of these men was Grimbald, Edith's own personal goldsmith; a gospel book of Thorney Abbey, which was decorated by a certain Wulfwine, also described as Edith's goldsmith, may perhaps once have belonged to Harold's wife. She held four dwellings in Canterbury, and one of her children who died in infancy was buried in Canterbury Cathedral, near St Dunstan's tomb. In addition, she is recorded as a benefactress of the abbey of St Benet of Holme. Later, Gunnhild, her daughter by Harold, was educated at the royal convent of Wilton, an expensive privilege reserved for noble ladies. All this indicates that Edith was a woman of status and prestige, like Aelfgifu of Northampton, Cnut's first wife, rather than simply a mistress or concubine, as clerical sources imply.[19]

The marriage of Edith and Harold was to prove long and fruitful, and apart from its obvious material benefits, there are suggestions that it may have been based on love. Thus the *Vita Haroldi*, though late, portrays her as one who 'had known him well and loved him much'. It was said that it was she who identified Harold's body on the field at Hastings, so that the clerks of Waltham might remove it for burial in their church. In spite of this, Harold was faced with the need, for reasons of state, to marry Alditha, sister of the northern earls, early in 1066. Such political marriages were common at that time, as witnessed by Cnut's parallel marriage to Emma in 1017. The knowledge that an arranged marriage might later be required may explain Harold's failure to seek the blessing of the Church for his earlier marriage to Edith. The Church would of course refuse to permit a second wedding while the first wife still lived. However, if the first 'marriage' had not been recognized by the Church, then a 'second' marriage could proceed. Whether Harold actually repudiated Edith following his sanctified marriage to Alditha is unknown. It would appear that Cnut did not repudiate his first wife, Aelfgifu, even after his second marriage, to Emma, and in fact Harold 'Harefoot', his son by Aelfgifu, was able to make good his claim to the kingdom after Cnut's death. Perhaps Harold followed this example, since after his death in 1066 his sons by Edith also made an attempt to secure the throne. The similarity between the marriage arrangements of Cnut and Harold is close and probably reflects the influence of their Danish background. As far as we can tell, Harold and Edith seem to have accepted the necessity of his subsequent political marriage to Alditha, though whether their sons were content with the arrangement is another matter. Indeed, if Harold had been victorious at Hastings and had died at a later date, there may well have been a dispute over the succession, similar to that between Cnut's sons Harold and Hardecnut, between Harold's sons by Edith and his son by Alditha.[20]

Harold's second marriage was blessed by the Church, and his second wife, Alditha, found herself, for reasons of state, married to the man responsible for the downfall of her previous husband, Gruffydd of Wales. Whether this mattered to her is unknown but perhaps it may not have done because that marriage too was a political one, arranged by her father, Earl Aelfgar, to cement his alliance with the Welsh king. It would probably have been part of the new marriage agreement that Alditha would be recognized as Harold's queen, and her brothers no doubt intended that her offspring by Harold would have prior rights of succession to the throne. Doubts have been expressed about whether Harold ever actually married Alditha on the basis of her lack of any significant landholding as recorded in Domesday Book. This fails to account for the clear reference to 'Queen' Alditha in John of Worcester, or to a son later born to Harold by her. The marriage probably took place in early 1066 and there was therefore little time for any endowments for Alditha to be recorded in local memory before the Conquest. There are many discrepancies in the text of Domesday Book concerning much earlier changes in landholding and these alone should not be allowed to cast doubt on the marriage. Although cut short by Harold's death, this marriage alliance would seem to have been fruitful both in drawing the two families closer together and in providing an heir in the form of young Harold, who was born probably early in 1067, in Chester.[21]

Both of Harold's marriages, different as they were, equally served their purpose in his life and career. The first to Edith initially provided him with allies and a local power base in East Anglia, and later with heirs and perhaps with love. At the same time, it still allowed for the possibility of a future political marriage later in his career. This second marriage provided Harold with important allies to secure his new kingship and with an heir both he and the northern earls had a vested interest in supporting. In this context, Harold's marriages, although not entirely conventional, were by no means unusual for the time, particularly in an England influenced by Scandinavian tradition. As we have seen, Cnut was able to rule England while in effect married to two women, although, like Harold, only one of his marriages was recognized by the Church.[22]

The Scandinavian influence reflected in Harold's relationship with Edith was part of the heritage which Harold passed on to his children. Five of them received Scandinavian names – Magnus, Gytha, Ulf, Gunnhild and Harold – and only two English ones – Godwine and Edmund. What can we discover about Harold's relationship with his children? Harold's namesake son by Alditha was born after his father's death and can therefore be left aside. On the other hand, some of his children by Edith were approaching maturity in 1066, and hence emerging into public life. If Harold's marriage to Edith took place in the mid-1040s, this would make his eldest son, Godwine, perhaps about twenty in 1066, and the others approaching this at intervals. This Godwine is recorded as holding lands in Somerset in 1066, which had probably been given to him by his father and this would seem to indicate that he was the eldest. John of Worcester also lists Godwine first among Harold's sons, indicating his seniority.[23]

We know only a little about Harold's children, but can still glean some details of the upbringing their father provided for them. The sons probably received diplomatic and military training, as befitted sons of a great earl, and as Harold himself had received. Certainly Godwine, Edmund and Magnus, although too young to fight at Hastings, demonstrated this training to good, if ultimately unsuccessful effect during their attempt to restore the family fortunes after the Conquest. They proved well able to negotiate with King Diarmait of Leinster for assistance and to lead mercenary forces in military raids on the south-west of England. Although ultimately these attacks were unsuccessful, the fierceness of some of the fighting involved suggests that the brothers had some talent for military enterprises. They may also have participated in the stubborn eighteen-day defence of Exeter, although their contribution in this instance may have been less effective. Meanwhile, Harold's daughters also received an appropriate education. Gunnhild, as already noted, was perhaps educated at Wilton, as her aunt, Queen Edith, had been before her. It was later considered that she had in fact taken the veil, but this probably occurred after the Conquest, either as a protection against seizure by the Normans or to prevent her becoming a threat to William. This evidence, such as it is, represents a normal pattern for the period and reveals that Harold was concerned to provide for the future of his children. Further evidence of paternal feelings is shown in the record of the burial of another of Harold's children, who died in infancy unbaptised, near St Dunstan's tomb in Christ Church, Canterbury. This action was found offensive by later monks but surely reflects genuine paternal concern for this dead infant, probably another child of Edith.[24]

In this period a man's family provided an important resource in terms of extending and maintaining his lands, power and influence. He inherited these from his parents, developed them with the help of his brothers and sisters, and passed them on to his children. Harold's relations with his family were an essential element in his life and career. We have already learnt much about Harold's relations with his parents and siblings through the events of his career, and will learn more hereafter. Harold loyally stood by his father in the crisis of 1051–2, although he himself appears to have had no personal dispute with the king. He did so in spite of the fact that Godwine apparently favoured his erratic eldest son, Swein, as witnessed by his repeated interventions on the latter's behalf. It was Harold who was at his father's side when the latter died, and his loyalty was finally rewarded by the succession to his father's lands and position. In contrast, Harold's mother, Gytha, appears to have favoured him among all her children. This is suggested by her later apparent desire to recover, at any cost, Harold's body after Hastings, rather than those of his brothers. It may also be suggested by her support for Harold in his dispute with Tosti in 1065, although the *Vita Eadwardi* notes that she wept at Tosti's exile. This attitude may of course reflect her need as a widow for Harold's support to allow her to retain control of her wide lands. Domesday Book records the deceased Earl Godwine as landholder in some eight counties in 1066 when in fact these lands were most probably held by his widow.

Harold seems generally to have attempted to support and assist the members of his family. He had initally supported Tosti's appointment to the Earldom of Northumbria, and similarly supported the appointments of Leofwine and Gyrth. He would later maintain his sister, Queen Edith, in her widowhood. It was he who attended to the proper burial of his cousin, Beorn, in 1049. The exception to this pattern can be seen in Harold's refusal to assist the return of the wayward Swein. That this was an exception can be seen from his attempt to free Swein's son, Hakon, from Norman captivity in 1064. All this demonstrates that Harold was well aware that the support of a united family could greatly enhance a man's power. The decision to support Tosti's deposition in 1065 must therefore have been a very hard decision for him to take.[25]

Second only to family ties during this period were those of friendship and alliance. A great man like Harold with a long career in public life must have acquired many friends and allies. Unfortunately, the surviving sources make it impossible to establish the full extent of Harold's affinity. Instead, we are restricted to establishing the fairly limited number of Harold's connections for which sufficient evidence survives in the sources, but even this knowledge can reveal information about Harold. Harold's lesser supporters have already been discussed when considering his landholdings and here we will consider his major friends and allies.

In terms of Harold's friends among the clerics there was one man with whom he appears to have had a particularly close relationship. This was Ealdred, who initially as Bishop of Worcester and later as Archbishop of York was to play a significant role in Harold's career as his friend and perhaps his mentor. The first evidence of their relationship comes in 1051 when the Chronicle records that Ealdred, who had been sent to intercept Harold as he fled to Bristol, 'could not, or would not' do so, clearly suggesting that he wanted him to escape. It is likely that Ealdred's donation of a large number of relics to Harold's own foundation of Holy Cross at Waltham also represents a token of their close friendship. It is possible though not certain that it was King Edward's suspicion of Ealdred's links to Harold and his family that caused him to be overlooked when the king sought a successor to Archbishop Aelfric of York in 1051. If so, he recovered his position in the king's favour by assiduous royal service thereafter, particularly on the embassy of 1054 to negotiate the return of *Atheling* Edward, and when Cynesige of York died in 1060 he finally gained the archbishopric.

In 1056 Ealdred took over the administration of the diocese of Hereford after the death of its bishop, Leofgar, Harold's former chaplain. In 1062 Harold supported the promotion of Ealdred's acolyte, Wulfstan, to the see of Worcester. It might have been expected that after his appointment as Archbishop of York, Ealdred would have lost contact with Harold but this was not the case. Indeed, perhaps the most significant indication of Harold's trust in Ealdred is that the latter consecrated Harold as king in 1066. The fact that he was chosen for this duty was a result of Stigand's equivocal position, but that he employed an entirely new consecration *ordo* in the service seems to indicate a great deal of trust in him on Harold's part. Unlike Stigand, Ealdred did not possess great personal wealth and he needed the assistance of a man like Harold to maintain the lands of his diocese against predation by other secular lords, including the Mercian earls. In return, he offered Harold his immense administrative skills and his deep knowledge of religious ritual.[26]

In a sense, Harold's close relationship to Bishop Wulfstan of Worcester perhaps arose from a similar circumstance to that with Ealdred. Wulfstan also required Harold's protection and support but in return he offered spiritual advice rather than administrative skill. Wulfstan's holiness was widely recognized and he was later canonized because of it. It is perhaps not surprising then that Harold appears to have turned to him for spiritual guidance. In this period all men, no matter how powerful, considered themselves subject to God's power. It was therefore natural for Harold to ascertain Wulfstan's views and to seek his friendship in order to maintain contact with God through one of his most notable servants. It was the holy Wulfstan that Harold chose to accompany him when he sought to persuade the Northumbrians to accept his rule in 1066.[27]

In terms of Harold's friends and allies among the laymen, we have already recorded his relations with his fellow earls where he perhaps held a somewhat equivocal record. He may initially have favoured the promotion of his brothers over Earl Aelfgar, but he later revised this view by accepting Tosti's inevitable downfall and seeking actively to court Aelfgar's sons. In the case of Earl Ralph, King Edward's French nephew, Harold appears to have been friendly towards him and it is perhaps significant that Ralph had a son named Harold. It is possible that this boy was named after the earl himself, perhaps

Harold rides through the countryside accompanied by hawk and hounds.. (The Bayeux Tapestry – 11th Century. By special permission of the City of Bayeux)

in gratitude for his support against the Welsh in 1055. The age of Harold, son of Ralph, in 1066 when he was a ward of Queen Edith makes it possible that he was named in these circumstances. However, this Harold's mother had the Danish name Gytha and he may therefore have been named after one of her kin. Harold's relations with other more minor laymen, usually as supporters, have already been discussed more fully in connection with his landholdings. These few details are all that can be recovered about Harold's relations with his family and his friends and allies.[28]

We also know something of Harold's personal interests beyond those required to wield authority, administer lands, enforce the law and lead men in war. As was common in this period Harold was keenly involved in sports of the chase, especially hunting and falconry. Harold's interest in hunting is confirmed by his construction of a hunting lodge on conquered land at Portskewet in South Wales, to which he intended to invite King Edward. It is also shown by several scenes in the Bayeux Tapestry, where he is accompanied by his hawk and hounds. Indeed, in one particular scene these clearly valuable animals are carefully carried aboard his ship for the crossing to Normandy. In addition, Domesday Book records the presence of 'a large wood for hunting' on land owned by Harold at Ailey in Herefordshire. Harold's interest in falconry is spectacularly demonstrated by the later attribution to Harold of the possession of a number of important books on hawks and the art of falconry. It is confirmed by Domesday Book, which records that Harold's estate at Limpsfield in Surrey had three hawk's nests, which no doubt provided him with a source of birds.[29]

The reference to Harold's possession of books on falconry raises the interesting possibility that he may have been literate. The *Vita Eadwardi* speaks of his sister, Queen Edith, as immersed in the study of letters and it is therefore possible that Harold was also literate. It was more common at this time for education to be lavished on male children than female. Such a skill would certainly have been of considerable benefit to an earl or king in the fairly sophisticated administrative kingdom which England was at this time. It is possible that Harold did not read his books himself but simply that he had others read them to him, but the possession of literacy by a layman, while unusual for the time, is not impossible. However, this must remain no more than conjecture.[30]

From the little we know of him, Harold appears to have been, in many ways, a man of his time. Thus he was a warrior and military commander, but also a diplomat and administrator. He was a pious man, in terms of his personal devotion, though not a saint. He appears to have been equally at home in English Sussex, Anglo-Danish York, Norse-Irish Dublin, and on the Continent. He was in general strongly supportive of his family, but not at the expense of his own wider interests. He had a small but varied and powerful group of friends and allies able to support him in a number of different capacities. This was the man who now stood on the threshold of the kingship. He had many of the qualities and abilities needed for this high position, but it remained to be seen how he would employ these.

CHAPTER NINE

KING HAROLD

*Earl Harold was now consecrated king and met little quiet in it
as long as he ruled the realm.*[1]

Following King Edward's death, Harold, *sub regulus* and now designated heir of the king, succeeded to the kingdom and was crowned on 6 January 1066, the same day as the old king was buried. This has been seen as unseemly haste but is probably the result of Harold's thorough canvassing of support over the Christmas period. Also, with the danger of invasion by William of Normandy hanging over the land, as noted in the Chronicle, it was important to act decisively to forestall other claims, including William's but more importantly that of *Atheling* Edgar. Indeed, William received news of Edward's death and Harold's succession at the same time and was unable to take advantage of any period of confusion to intervene.[2]

Harold's coronation, which is illustrated in the Bayeux Tapestry, was unusual in a number of respects, as perhaps befits the coronation of the first English king not descended from Alfred's line. First of all, it probably took place in King Edward's newly consecrated Westminster Abbey, the first of many coronations to be performed there. The fact that it directly followed Edward's burial in that church makes this very likely. If Harold's coronation had occurred in St Paul's instead, this would have meant a rather complex transfer of people from Westminster to St Paul's, which in addition to the two services seems a lot to cram into one short winter day. There would also be a natural desire on Harold's part to associate his kingship with that of his predecessor, as William would also do later that year. Secondly, the ceremony itself probably followed a new coronation *ordo* adapted by Archbishop Ealdred from that of the German Empire, rather than that followed at Edward's own coronation in March 1043. This innovation was probably a result of the unusual circumstances of that year when the ceremony was performed by Ealdred, Archbishop of York, rather than the Archbishop of Canterbury. The former was suddenly faced with the need to deliver a coronation *ordo* and as a result chose one he had to hand. This new *ordo* was subsequently to be followed by William, again under the direction of Archbishop Ealdred.[3]

The ceremony was not only novel, but also became the subject of controversy as a result of William's rival claim. The Norman sources claim that Harold was consecrated by the controversial Stigand, Archbishop of Canterbury. In contrast, the English sources claim the rite was performed by Ealdred, Archbishop of York. The roots of this confusion lie in the Norman requirement after the Conquest to undermine Harold's

Harold's coronation, 1066 – an image from his lost seal? (The Bayeux Tapestry – 11th Century. By special permission of the City of Bayeux)

legitimate reign and present it as a usurpation. The association of Harold's kingship with 'unholy' consecration by Stigand, a man who had gained his archbishopric uncanonically and who held no valid pallium, was part of this process. It is more likely that Archbishop Ealdred performed the ceremony, for although it was customary for the Archbishop of Canterbury to do so, the English were just as aware as the Normans of Stigand's uncanonical position. Thus Stigand had consecrated no bishops during his term of office, with the exception of Aethelric of Sussex and Siward of Rochester, who were only consecrated because at that point Stigand held a pallium, received from Pope Benedict X before the latter's expulsion from office. In all other cases Ealdred of

York had performed Stigand's duties of consecration and he was to do so after the Conquest as well. It is therefore almost certain that Harold received consecration from Ealdred as stated by John of Worcester, who was in a position to know. In view of the need to legitimize his kingship as a king not of Alfred's line, Harold would have wished no doubt to be cast on his legitimacy by Stigand's involvement. It should be recalled that Harold showed similar concern about the consecration of his church of Holy Cross at Waltham in 1060, when he sought the services of Archbishop Cynesige of York rather than Stigand. In similar circumstances, William sought consecration from Ealdred later the same year and there is no reason to think that Harold did otherwise.[4]

One of the first actions of the new King Harold was probably to receive messengers from Normandy demanding that the throne be surrendered to Duke William as Edward's rightful heir. Harold made clear to them that the oaths extracted from him under duress were worthless and that he had no intention of accepting William's demands. Thus William was faced with the daunting prospect of actually turning his claim into a reality, and he set about this with his customary determination. Well aware of William's ruthless ambition, Harold in turn set about organizing his kingdom and its defences against this danger.[5]

As we saw in Chapter Seven, support for Harold's succession seems to have been fairly widespread, but there was one source of restlessness, the Earldom of Northumbria. This unrest is only recorded in the later *Vita Wulfstani*, but it is not unlikely in view of recent events in the earldom. It is perhaps confirmed by two coin hoards deposited at around this time at Harewood and Bishophill near York. The disinclination of the Northumbrians to welcome King Harold's accession probably reflects a fear that he would restore Tosti to favour, rather than simple dislike for a West Saxon on the throne. They probably considered that the settlement of 1065 had been made by King Edward, and now that he was dead they feared that Harold would overturn it and allow Tosti's return.[6]

King Harold had to settle this anxiety and did so by travelling north, not with an army to ravage the land but with a small party, including Bishop Wulfstan of Worcester, a man widely renowned and respected for his holiness. Harold's conciliatory approach and powers of persuasion were successful and the Northumbrians swore allegiance to him. In return, Harold must have confirmed that Tosti would not be permitted to return. It was perhaps to reinforce this pledge that at this point Harold probably completed a marriage alliance by marrying Alditha, the sister of Earls Edwin and Morcar. This marriage must have taken place some time between the death in August 1063 of Gruffydd of Wales, Alditha's first husband, and October 1066, when she is recorded as Harold's queen, and it is unlikely that it took place before autumn 1065, when the Northumbrian revolt and the exile of Tosti made a *rapprochement* with Edwin and Morcar essential. Negotiations on such an important matter would have taken some time and thus early 1066 is perhaps the most likely time for the marriage.

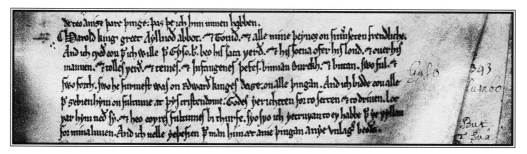

Writ of King Harold in favour of Wells.

This date seems confirmed by the fact that not only was Alditha Harold's queen by the end of the year, but that she bore a son to him, named Harold after his father and probably born after his death. In addition to removing any concern on the part of the Northumbrians at the possibility of Tosti's return, this marriage also further bound the northern earls to Harold. They now had a direct stake in the success of their brother-in-law's kingship. Unfortunately, Chronicle accounts mention nothing of this and record only Harold's return from York, in time to spend the Easter festival on 16 April at Westminster.[7]

King Harold's position was now securely established and we can examine what is recorded, albeit very little, about the government of England during his reign. Few documentary records remain of his actions as king. The single writ, in Latin and English versions, which survives relates to the rights of Giso, Bishop of Wells. This is in the regular form for such documents, addressed by King Harold to Abbot Aethelnoth of Glastonbury, Tofi Sheriff of Somerset and all the thegns there. There are no surviving diplomas from his reign. Such documents would have been endorsed by Harold's great seal, but this has also been lost although it may perhaps be suggested that its form is preserved in the arrangement of the Bayeux Tapestry scene of Harold's coronation. A number of Tapestry scenes appear to have been derived from existing models in manuscript sources and there is a general similarity between the portrayal of King Edward on his great seal and that of Harold in the Tapestry.[8]

The reasons for this scarcity of documents include the brevity of the reign itself, and the emphasis which was placed by William on his position as Edward's rightful heir and on Harold as a usurper. Thus if we compare the ninety-nine genuine writs and diplomas which have survived from King Edward's twenty-four-year reign (that is, four per annum) with the single genuine writ surviving from Harold's nine-month reign, the latter equation appears not unusual. However, many such documents must have been issued by Harold since it was customary for men to seek confirmation of their lands from new rulers, but following the Conquest their value would, of course, have been limited. William could not afford to acknowledge Harold's kingship by accepting them as legal documents, and there can be no doubt that the Norman insistence on William as Edward's direct successor meant that those who did possess writs or diplomas from the 'usurper' King Harold later found them worthless. Most were therefore probably lost, or where possible swiftly replaced by new grants under William's name. Thus Regenbald the Chancellor, Abbot Wulfwold of Bath, and the City of London all sought early confirmations of their rights from the new King William in 1067. This process began in William's written acts soon after the Conquest. Some very early acts represent a transitional period when William had to recognize the existence of Harold's reign in order to smooth the operation of English government but thereafter King Edward is consistently referred to as William's immediate predecessor. This process reached its culmination in Domesday Book in 1086, where Harold is referred to throughout as *comes* and all land is listed as it was held *Tempore Regis Edwardi* and not when William conquered the kingdom.[9]

In spite of this, a few sources do give some indication of King Harold's activities. John of Worcester, though writing later, says he 'began to abolish unjust laws and make good ones' and 'to imprison robbers and disturbers of the kingdom'. This may be merely conventional praise of a new king, but it is perhaps surprising, given the general treatment of Harold's reputation at Norman hands. We also know from Domesday Book of at least five instances of men, admittedly minor, who were deprived of their lands by King Harold: Leofman and Godwine lost their lands at Hayling Island and Soberton in Hampshire, and Eadmer, Wiflet and Aelfric their lands at Haresfield, Down Hatherley and Sandhurst, and Harescombe and Brookethorpe respectively, all in Gloucestershire.[10]

However, the major evidence for the regular functioning of King Harold's administration comes from his coinage. Not unnaturally, this has survived much better than the written documents. During his short reign his government replaced Edward's last coinage with a fine new design which survives in issues from some forty-six mints throughout England. There he appears as *Rex Anglorum*, or King of the English. Many of Edward's moneyers continued to strike coins under Harold and would subsequently do so for William also.[11]

Another indication of the actions of King Harold's government are appointments made during his reign. An English king normally made appointments to a number of official positions, including those of earls, sheriffs, and court officials such as *stallers* and those of archbishops, bishops and abbots in the Church. At least two abbacies fell vacant during Harold's reign, and Harold played his part in the appointment of successors. On 22 January 1066 Abbot Ordric of Abingdon died and Ealdred the provost, in charge of the abbey's external property, was appointed by Harold to replace him. Abbot Wulfric of Ely appears to have died on 19 August 1066 and his successor, Thurstan, was also appointed by Harold. Neither of these appointments was in any way

Silver penny of King Harold.

unusual and were continued after the Conquest at least until the abbots concerned became involved in rebellion.[12]

There exist two other appointments which may possibly have been made by Harold, although these are very much conjectural. The first is that of Waltheof, son of Siward, to an earldom. Sometime between the expulsion of Tosti, in October 1065, and the return of King William to Normandy in spring 1067, Waltheof had been appointed to an earldom in a part of the East Midlands previously ruled by Tosti. It is generally assumed that Waltheof succeeded to this Midland portion of Tosti's earldom at the same time as Morcar obtained Northumbria in October 1065. This assumption rests partly on the basis of a reference in Domesday Book, which appears to imply that some lands transferred direct from Tosti to Waltheof, although this is not certain. However, there exist other references in Domesday Book where King Edward is recorded holding Tosti's former lands before they passed to Earl Waltheof. Thus estates at Potton and Chalton in Bedfordshire were transferred from Tosti to King Edward and only thence to Waltheof. In spite of these latter references, most commentators believe that Waltheof was made earl of Northamptonshire and Huntingdonshire some time between October and December 1065. The resultant attempt to squeeze Tosti's expulsion, Edward's forfeiture of his lands, and Waltheof's appointment and succession to the lands into the period between 1 November 1065 and 5 January 1066, during which time Edward was seriously ill, seems rather inconceivable. The possibility has been overlooked that King Harold may have promoted Waltheof to this earldom created out of Tosti's forfeited lands. The reason for this appointment would then be found in its value as a further gesture intended to reassure the Northumbrians that Tosti would not return. This would probably place it between 6 January and 16 April 1066, when Harold was active in the north.[13]

The second appointment which may have been made by King Harold is possibly that of Marleswein Sheriff of Lincolnshire as a *staller*. However, the only evidence which might suggest this is very late and imprecise. A twelfth-century source, which may draw on local traditions and which knew much about Marleswein, suggests that in the aftermath of the battle of Stamford Bridge, King Harold placed Marleswein in some sort of official position in the north. This is sometimes seen as Harold replacing Earl Morcar, but it may in fact have been a move intended to provide assistance to the earl by appointing a royal *staller* to bolster his position in the north. Such a man, a sort of royal troubleshooter, provided a direct royal influence in local government such as might be required to raise further troops for the king's war with William of Normandy after the losses at Fulford.[14]

Other than these few new appointments, King Harold largely continued to employ the same personnel as served Edward during his last years, many of whom went on to serve William after him. The majority of Edward's clerics also continued in post under Harold and then William, including Regenbald the Chancellor. The same thing occured among laymen, so that the *stallers* Ansgar, Robert Fitzwimarch, Ralph Aelfstan, Bondi, and Eadnoth appear to have remained in their posts under Harold. In a time of uncertainty, both Harold and William initially considered it best to retain the same personnel in post rather than create disturbance by making changes. In Harold's case, he was never given the time to make changes but had he been victorious at Hastings he may have done so. Alternatively, it is possible that as Harold had already worked closely with many of these men for a number of years, their loyalty to him was simply not in question. The period of over twenty years that he had spent as earl, first of East Anglia then of Wessex, and more recently as *sub regulus* must have allowed Harold to foster widespread ties with men in all areas of government.[15]

In all this, King Harold's government appears to have functioned normally and without any significant opposition. Indeed, Norman sources admit that he was growing daily in strength. This was remarkable for a new king not from the traditional dynasty, and surely reflects the confidence felt in this man who had been Earl of Wessex since 1053 and *sub regulus* probably since the death of the last of the old earls in 1057. The Chronicle in 1063 speaks of Harold himself appointing Welsh princes, and William of Poitiers the following year calls him 'second only to the king'. It was still admittedly early in Harold's reign and perhaps this lack of unrest was merely acquiescence. If so, men's loyalty to Harold was soon to be put severely to the test. The fact that his support was subsequently to prove solid, even in the face of major threats, surely indicates that it was genuine.[16]

With his position established, King Harold had returned from York probably accompanied by his new bride to celebrate the Easter festivities at Westminster on 16 April. This festival presented King Harold with his first major opportunity to demonstrate his new status and splendour to his subjects. As King Edward had done before him, Harold presided over a period of feasting, worship, receptions and royal business attended by many of the nobles of England, and probably wore his crown and royal robes. This would have reinforced the message that he was their king and lord, and he would have dispensed gifts and received their pledges of loyalty in return. He probably chose Westminster for this occasion because of the need to remain close to the centre of communications at London in the face of the threat of a Norman invasion.[17]

Shortly after, on 24 April, Halley's Comet made its regular appearance in the skies above the earth. It came fairly close on this occasion and, from observations recorded throughout Europe and the Far East, appeared at the time to be unusually bright. This is confirmed by English records which state that it was seen all over England and describe it as a sign such as no one had ever seen before. John of Worcester speaks of it shining with 'exceeding brightness'. The artist of the Bayeux Tapestry also shows it as large and impressive. It remained visible in England for a full week and provoked wonder and fear at what it might portend. Such heavenly apparitions commonly presaged disaster, although its connection in later sources with the fall of King Harold was, of course, a product of hindsight.[18]

Halley's Comet. (The Bayeux Tapestry – 11th Century. By special permission of the City of Bayeux)

In the short term, it was merely a prelude to the return of Harold's exiled brother from Flanders. Tosti had been provided with a large Flemish fleet by his brother-in-law, Count Baldwin V. In May he landed in the Isle of Wight, and collected money and provisions from the inhabitants as his father had done in 1052. He may also have collected supporters from his own estates there. He then raided along the south coast until he reached Sandwich, possibly in an attempt to repeat his father's successful campaign of 1052. However, Tosti does not seem to have encountered the welcome that Earl Godwiné received then, as the damage he inflicted on his brother's estates implies. In this connection, it should be recalled that Tosti's lands in the south were smaller and more scattered than those of his brothers, and that he had spent some ten years ruling in the north. In the end all he achieved was the recruitment of some sailors at Sandwich, partly under the threat of force.[19]

King Harold was in London, possibly recovering from the celebration of the feast of the finding of the True Cross on 3 May, when news of his brother's attacks on the south coast was received. In response he called out land and naval forces to deal with him. News that these forces, led by King Harold himself, were heading for Sandwich quickly caused Tosti to retreat. He had failed to win any significant support in the south and therefore could not hope to face the royal forces of his brother. Therefore, he turned north, hoping perhaps to rally support from his more extensive former landholdings there. Some versions of the Chronicle confuse this call-out of troops to deal with Tosti at Sandwich with Harold's assembling of 'a naval and a land force larger than any king had assembled before in this country' to face the Norman threat. The reason for this is probably that the two events did indeed follow on closely. It seems though that King Harold, forewarned by Tosti's actions that conditions were now favourable for a Channel crossing and aware of William's intentions, and after ensuring that Tosti was no longer an immediate threat, called out more forces to deal with the likelihood of Norman invasion.[20]

The force gathered by King Harold to face William was clearly of extraordinary size, and this surely confirms his secure grasp on the machinery of royal government. It also reflects the unprecedented concentration of wealth in King Harold's hands. This is sometimes overlooked, perhaps as a result of Domesday Book's record of the situation in the time of King Edward. Domesday Book only records the lands held by Harold as Earl of Wessex and lists the royal lands under King Edward. In reality, of course, Harold now held not only all those lands listed as held by 'Earl Harold', but also those listed as held by 'King Edward'. Such a concentration of lands had not fallen to an English king since at least the days of King Aethelred II, if even then. It is likely that a fleet was also collected in the Thames, which then proceeded to join Harold at Sandwich. The collection of this fleet took some time, not surprisingly when it is remembered that the last time a large fleet was summoned was in 1052 to oppose the return of Godwine. The fleet called by Harold for his campaign against Wales was probably a smaller local fleet from Bristol. At the same time, the largest land force in living memory was summoned and stationed all along the Channel coast. Such an effort speaks more than any number of lost documents about Harold's power and control over his kingdom.[21]

While Harold gathered forces to repel a Norman invasion, Tosti moved northwards. He made a brief attempt to entice his brother, Earl Gyrth, to support him but this was apparently rebuffed and instead he raided near the mouth of the Burnham river in Norfolk. He entered the Humber estuary with sixty ships, and ravaged and slew many men in Lincolnshire, probably on lands now held by Morcar but formerly his own. King Harold had left the defence of the north to his new brothers-in-law, Earls Edwin and Morcar, and they undertook the task with vigour. They were no doubt fired by their previous rivalry with Tosti and mindful of their vested interest in retaining Northumbria. The two earls led a land force into Lincolnshire which expelled Tosti decisively and, deserted by his men, the latter fled with only twelve ships to the protection of his sworn brother, Malcolm King of Scots. Thereafter, Tosti remained impotently in Scotland throughout the summer. He had made his threatened move and had been dealt with decisively by King Harold and his new allies, the northern earls, and without outside help he could not return.[22]

King Harold had dealt with the first threat to his position and was now free to concentrate on what he undoubtedly considered a much more serious one, that from William of Normandy. He did this by basing himself and his newly recruited fleet on the Isle of Wight, ready to move against any invasion fleet which crossed the Channel. The fleet was probably commanded by Eadric the Steersman, described in Domesday Book as *rector navis* or commander of the king's ship, and organized by Abbot Aelfwold of St Benet of Holme. Indeed, both these men would later suffer exile under William because of their role in the defence of the coast under King Harold. In case this interception plan failed, Harold had stationed land forces at vital points all along the Channel coast. It may have been at this time that Harold appropriated the estate of Steyning in Sussex from Fecamp Abbey. This estate was situated near the coast and Harold perhaps feared that it would become a landing point or centre of intelligence for the Normans. About June 1066 William confirmed that Steyning would be restored to Fecamp if he was victorious, which may reflect some truth in this story. However, other lands held by Fecamp Abbey, notably Rye, show no evidence of seizure by Harold. Harold himself sent spies across the Channel in an attempt to gather information on the extent of William's preparations and in particular on the timing of any crossing. All these actions were sensible precautions against the anticipated Norman invasion and prove Harold's sound judgement.[23]

King Harold's spies probably brought word that across the Channel William of Normandy was indeed making his own preparations. Initially, William encountered great difficulty in persuading his nobles to participate in his plan for invading England to claim the throne. William claimed the English throne as his rightful inheritance and

Domesday Book, detail of an entry for land in Hampshire which includes a unique acknowledgement of Harold's reign.

many of the Norman nobles had probably been present when Harold swore to support this claim. They were fully aware of his breach of fealty and of his oath before God. In spite of this, William's barons were also aware that, with Harold securely installed as king, the only hope of William achieving his aim was to undertake a risky invasion. They knew this would involve the expensive construction of a large fleet, a risky sea crossing, and an opposed landing in a largely hostile country. A Norman diploma of the period speaks of the time when William 'was about to cross the sea to wage war against the English', a sign that they understood that Harold was not lacking in support. William of Poitiers reflects this opinion by portraying the English at Hastings fighting, some out of 'love for Harold' but 'all out of love for their country which . . . they wished to defend against aliens'. The Norman lords were naturally concerned that such an enterprise would be hazardous in the extreme and were therefore reluctant to take part. That William nevertheless convinced many of them to participate says a great deal for his determination and strength of will, which in the end overcame their opposition. Another important factor in persuading many of them was the lure of the riches of England which, not for the first time, attracted men who were hungry for wealth to prey on her. Therefore, William was able to set about the construction of a fleet and the collection of an army as a first stage in achieving his ambition to rule England.[24]

In the first of a number of examples of good fortune the diplomatic situation was favourable to William's enterprise at precisely this time. King Philip of France was a minor under the tutelage of Baldwin V of Flanders, who was not only a relation of William but had recently provided aid to Tosti in his attempt to invade England. The other principalities of northern France were either vassal states of William or, like Anjou, were absorbed in their own internal troubles. If William had faced opposition in northern France it is unlikely he could ever have undertaken his invasion at all.[25]

However, on the wider European scene William of Poitiers' picture of William's diplomatic successes seems a little unrealistic. It is highly unlikely, for example, that Swein of Denmark gave his backing to William's enterprise. He would be more likely to welcome Harold's accession since the latter might favour aiding his Danish cousin against his Norwegian enemies, as had his father, Earl Godwine. It should be noted here that Swein had just emerged from a long and bloody war with Norway and was fearful of further trouble. In this context, William of Poitiers contradicts himself when he later speaks of the Danes sending troops to assist Harold against the Normans. This contradiction somewhat undermines our confidence in the further claim made by Poitiers that the Emperor Henry IV provided his own endorsement for William's claim. This seems unlikely. Henry IV or his regents, since he was still in his minority, had many other concerns and the contemporary Annals of Corvey compiled at that royal monastery in Saxony were to describe William in 1066 as removing the 'legitimate' King of England (Harold) and seizing his kingdom. What these diplomatic 'successes' described by Poitiers seem to represent is nothing more than the fact that neither Swein nor Henry IV were in a position to interfere directly in William's plans.[26]

There remains one important aspect of the later Norman account of William's diplomatic preparations which needs to be considered. William of Poitiers states that Duke William received the approval of Pope Alexander II for his invasion of England and that he was presented with a Papal banner in confirmation of this. It is usually assumed that this action on the part of the Pope was influenced by his desire to bring about the reform of the English Church and its principal archbishop in particular, and that William portrayed himself as the man who would achieve this. In addition, some have presented the influence of the Normans of southern Italy as important in convincing the Pope to support William's plans, since they had after all brought him to power in Rome and could expect to have some influence on him. This interpretation is based solely on the evidence of Poitiers, but given his unreliability in a number of areas it is in need of reassessment.[27]

Such a reassessment has in fact already been undertaken by Catherine Morton and the main thrust of her arguments are as follows. In regard to the state of the English Church in terms of the existence of pluralism, concubinage, simony and worldly prelates she points out that the position of the Norman Church under William was not dissimilar. Indeed, William's own half-brother, Odo of Bayeux, was perhaps in some ways a worse example of an unreformed prelate than Stigand. The irregular position of Archbishop Stigand was well known, but Pope Alexander II's own legates had sat in council with him in 1062 without demur. In addition, William's immediate actions after the Conquest cast doubt on any idea that he already had a Papal commission to depose Stigand, since he in fact maintained the archbishop in power until 1070. It is possible that William simply allowed Stigand to retain power for reasons of political expediency. However, he also permitted him to consecrate Remigius as Bishop of Dorchester in 1067, an odd action for someone holding a Papal commission to depose him. The Normans of southern Italy were in fact as much a threat to the Pope's position as a support, and he would therefore need to be wary of any action which might increase their power. In addition, the different Norman groups were as often at each others' throats as they were allied, and there is no evidence of any alliance between the Normans in Italy and their former duke back in France at this time. The southern Italian Normans who later joined William's expedition were clearly individual fortune hunters. William of Poitiers' account of the Papal banner supposedly presented to Duke William is based on a misunderstanding of the purpose of such banners at this time. They were issued only to endorse war either against Muslims or rebels against papal authority and not to endorse aggression against fellow Christians. They were also associated with the remission of sins and not with penances like those later imposed on the Normans by the Papal legate Erminfrid of Sion in 1070. Indeed, the improbability of Pope Alexander risking the enmity of the powerful and wealthy King of England in order to support the ambitious and risky plans of the Duke of Normandy needs to be considered. It is difficult to understand why the Papacy should have supported William's plans which were directed against a kingdom which had been a major European power for over a century and a half and which provided a significant source of support for the Papacy. Particularly important in this respect was Peter's Pence, a substantial subsidy which had been paid to the Papacy by the English kings intermittently since the time of Alfred. Indeed, the Papal desire not to offend King Edward is evident from the fact that the Papal legates, who visited England in 1062, took no action against Stigand.[28]

A realistic assessment of the probabilities would appear to indicate that no Papal support was in fact provided for William's expedition. Indeed, William of Jumieges makes no mention of any such support for William, a curious omission if it had in fact existed. Instead it would seem that what William of Poitiers reflects in his account is a later retrospective sanction by the Papal court for the *fait accompli* represented by William's conquest. In particular, the imposition of a penance on the Norman troops, who participated in the expedition, suggests that it was not seen as a 'just' war but rather as one of aggression. This would also explain the curious lack of any diplomatic response from Harold to William's claims at the Papal court since there were in fact no such claims at this time. William of Malmesbury's later account of Harold's failure to counter William at the Papal court is clearly inspired by the need to respond to the Norman texts. The story of Papal support for William probably arose after the Conquest, when few men had an interest in proving otherwise. After 1066 and particularly after 1070, the Papacy was unlikely to support dispossessed English exiles against the by now securely installed King William. By then, William's victory had made the judgement of God clear and the Pope still had to avoid offending the King of England, who was now William himself.[29]

It is likely therefore that Duke William prepared his expedition in a favourable political climate but without the almost universal backing indicated by William of Poitiers. William's fleet was ready in the mouth of the river Dives sometime after 18 June, when the dedication of his wife Mathilda's abbey at Caen may have represented a preliminary to the great venture. It was probably ready to set sail in July, but contrary winds confined it to harbour for around a month. Subsequently the fleet moved from the Dives to St Valery-Sur-Somme at some point between mid-July and 27 September, most possibly late August or early September. This event has been seen as a prepared move to secure a shorter crossing. However, the evidence of Poitiers is rather that once it had set out for somewhere else (surely England), it was 'blown by westerlies' into the roadstead of St Valery. This surely indicates an unintentional arrival at St Valery and losses by drowning suffered on the voyage are also suggestive of this. The most likely explanation of this evidence is that the invasion actually set out from the Dives at this time but that the wind changed and perhaps rose also, driving the fleet to seek shelter in St Valery. There, contrary winds prevented any further invasion attempts. William of Poitiers' eloquent pleas in favour of William's strength in adversity at this point speak of this being a reverse rather than a planned move.[30]

Meanwhile, on the other side of the Channel Harold had maintained his watch against invasion all summer and autumn with his fleet on the Isle of Wight and his land forces along the coast. No invasion arrived because of the contrary winds noted above. The English sources agree that Harold was then forced to disband his land and sea forces on 8 September. The reason for this was that all their provisions had been consumed and that they could not be kept any longer. This is hardly surprising, following four months on standby, by the largest forces ever assembled in England. This date probably marked the end of the two-month service period of the second of two hosts called out one after another that summer, an immense and complex feat of organization. This has been seen as a failure of Harold's organization, in comparison with William's success in maintaining his invasion forces, even though Poitiers admits that the latter also faced scarcity. It is unclear how long the Norman forces were actually maintained. It may have been as little as two months, and it seems likely that the invasion force was smaller than that required to garrison the long Channel coastline. It would seem that both men in fact had excellent logistical support.[31]

As Harold's forces disbanded on 8 September and he rode inland, probably towards London, the fleet sailed back up to London apparently losing many men on route. This statement in the Chronicle is not elaborated on and may represent no more than drownings due to bad weather, possibly even the same as that which struck the Normans during their pre-emptive invasion and led them to St Valery around this time. However, there are some hints at the possibility of more than a coincidence of bad weather linking the two naval forces. Chronicle E states that Harold 'went out with a naval force against William'. Unfortunately, this particular text is extremely brief at this point and since Chronicle C shows Harold not present with the fleet at this time, it may in fact refer merely to his earlier sailing from Sandwich to the Isle of Wight against William's possible invasion. More interesting is the reference in Domesday Book to Aethelric, who 'went away to a naval battle against King William'. This appears to suggest a clash actually occurred between the fleets since otherwise no such naval conflict is known. If this interpretation is correct, it places William's initial sortie from the Dives around 8 September when Harold's fleet returned to London, and the forces may have met in mid-Channel. It would also help explain William's retreat to St Valery and the losses suffered on both sides, but this must remain speculative.[32]

In any case, by the middle of September Harold was back in London perhaps preparing for the feast of the exaltation of the True Cross on 20 September, and the large forces he had gathered back in May had been stood down. William had failed to arrive because of the unfavourable weather, and the prospect of invasion must have appeared to have been receding. The season of autumn storms was now approaching fast and no invasion was likely to come after that. In 1014 a great tide (no doubt a combination of gales and high autumn tides), which flooded many parts of the country, is recorded for 28 September – the very day of William's subsequent landing at Pevensey in 1066. Also, if Harold was informed by his spies of William's failed attempt to cross the Channel and his losses, it may have appeared to him that the invasion had already failed. This latter possibility would be reinforced if a fleet encounter had taken place and Harold's men had reported back on losses in the Norman fleet and its subsequent withdrawal.[33]

CHAPTER TEN

HARALD OF NORWAY

Then Harold our king came upon the Norwegians by surprise and met them beyond York at Stamford Bridge with a large force of English people.[1]

In September 1066 King Harold may have considered that his major problems were behind him. He had beaten off the attacks of Tosti and had apparently faced down William of Normandy's projected invasion, if not defeated it. However, both these threats were about to revive in even more formidable form and would eventually overwhelm him.

The new threat inspired by Tosti emerged from Scandinavia, an area very familiar to the people of eleventh-century England. The population of large areas of northern and eastern England included significant numbers of descendants of earlier Viking settlers, whose culture had significantly effected that of their new home. It was also from this region that a series of Viking attacks and raids had been launched which had culminated in Cnut's conquest of England in 1016. In 1066 the region was made up of the three relatively new kingdoms of Denmark, Norway and Sweden. The last of these does not concern us here but the others had strong links with England during the late tenth and early eleventh century. The rulers and potential rulers of these new kingdoms – men like Swein 'Forkbeard' and Olaf Tryggvason – had launched raids against England in order to secure wealth, which in turn enabled them to employ troops and reward followers, and hence rule more effectively at home. This process reached its apogee when Cnut actually conquered England in 1016, securing not just a share of England's wealth but all of it. It was this wealth which enabled him subsequently to build up a North Sea empire incorporating England, Denmark and Norway. He also used it to employ troops to enforce his rule in Scandinavia and to bribe men to support him and desert his rivals.[2]

The death of Cnut in 1035, quickly followed by those of all his sons by 1042, not only brought about King Edward's succession to the throne of England, but also left Denmark and Norway to their own devices. In Denmark Swein Ulfsson, Cnut's nephew, secured the kingship. In Norway Magnus Olafsson returned from exile in Russia, where he may have secured the wealthy backing of Prince Iaroslav of Novgorod, to seize control and expel the Danes. He went on to invade and conquer Denmark, forcing Swein Ulfsson into exile in 1043 and, as we have seen, to seek English aid in 1047. In 1043 Magnus's control of both Denmark and Norway presented a threat to England which, it will be recalled, King Edward took very seriously.[3]

It was into this arena that Harald *Hardradi*, who was known as the 'Thunderbolt of the North', returned in 1045. Harald's career is recounted only briefly and rather inaccurately in Adam of Bremen's contemporary account. A much fuller account is included among the later sagas of the Norwegian kings composed by Snorri Sturluson in the thirteenth century. These sagas, including that of Harald, were written down anything up to 200 years or more after the events which they describe, and are therefore not very reliable. However, the saga narrative does incorporate a number of short verse stanzas, composed by contemporary skalds or court-poets, which although also orally transmitted are so constructed as to make the introduction of significant errors or changes somewhat more difficult than in the prose. On the other hand, although normally less easily changed, the very complexity of these skaldic poems sometimes makes them difficult to interpret. In general terms, the poems do tend to be more reliable than the prose, but can only be considered useful where other more contemporary sources provide support for them.[4]

Harald *Hardradi* was uncle of King Magnus Olafsson, who now ruled both Norway and Denmark. Earlier, both men had been chased into exile at the court of Prince Iaroslav of Novgorod, when Cnut completed his conquest of Norway in 1030. There Magnus remained, awaiting an opportunity to return, which duly presented itself on Cnut's death in 1035. In contrast, Harald took service as a mercenary with the famous Varangian regiment of the Eastern Emperors between 1034 and 1043. Fortunately, his career as a mercenary is recorded in a contemporary Byzantine source called 'Advice for the Emperor', which shows that he served in Sicily and Bulgaria and was rewarded with titles of rank. As a result of this service, Harald gained great experience of all kinds of warfare, and accumulated immense wealth in mercenary wages and captured booty. He used this wealth to secure an advantageous marriage with Elizabeth, the daughter of Iaroslav of Novgorod, probably in 1044, and to finance his return to Norway in the following year.[5]

On his return Harald also used his wealth to purchase, or extort, from his nephew Magnus a share of his kingdom, and following Magnus's death in 1047, Harald took the whole of Norway for himself. The Byzantine influence on Scandinavian coin design at this time, resulting from the dispersal of Harald's treasure, has been noted. Almost immediately, Harald attempted also to seize Denmark, which Magnus had ruled and which Harald no doubt considered part of his inheritance. In the confusion following Magnus's death, that kingdom had been re-occupied by Swein Ulfsson, and thereafter Harald engaged in a bitter sixteen-year struggle with Swein for possession of it. In this long contest, Harald seems to have won most of the battles, burning the Danish trading centre of Hedeby in 1050 and the churches of Aarhus and Schleswig. However, he failed either to eliminate Swein or to gain full control of Denmark. Meantime, the wealth he had brought back from the east, and whatever he had collected from successful raids on Denmark, was gradually dissipated. Thus the early skaldic poems in

Harald's Saga often refer to his riches on his return from Constantinople, but seldom do so after the end of the long war with Swein. Indeed, some confirmation of this can be seen in the coinage struck in Harald's later years, which was much more crude and debased than that of his early reign. Perhaps Adam of Bremen's claim that Harald despoiled the tomb of his own half-brother, St Olaf, at Trondheim, and Pope Alexander's letter of admonishment to Harald concerning the selling of bishoprics are also evidence of his increasing need for cash. Thus when the long war with Swein ended in a rather inconclusive treaty in 1064, Harald stood in need of a new source of wealth to support his rule and one was soon to be offered to him.[6]

The exiled Tosti spent the summer of 1066 in Scotland, smarting from the failure of his single-handed attempt at restoration in May. He now sought potential allies powerful enough to assist him in restoring his fortunes. King Malcolm of Scotland was still consolidating his hold over his own kingdom and, in any case, was not capable of opposing Harold of England. Tosti may have sought assistance from his cousin, King Swein of Denmark, as the later *Harald's Saga* states. If he did so, he must have been disappointed. King Swein was also Harold's cousin, and, in any case, was unable to leave his kingdom for fear of a resumption of Norwegian attacks. Although Swein had ended his long war with Harald of Norway in 1064, the latter remained a potent threat. In these circumstances, Tosti's thoughts must have turned quite naturally to Norway and to King Harald.[7]

Harald of Norway certainly had more than enough experience and the necessary temperament to undertake an invasion of England. He had a battle-hardened army and fleet at his command, which despite their recent failures in Denmark had just spent two years restoring its fighting strength and its morale in a series of local campaigns in Norway. Tosti would have had little difficulty in contacting Harald from his base in Scotland and there can be little doubt that he did so. It is unlikely that Tosti actually visited Norway, but not impossible. A late source speaks of Tosti's Northumbrian ally Copsi visiting the Orkney's to recruit troops for Tosti, and perhaps he also acted as his ambassador to King Harald in Norway. Certainly in some form or other, contact was made, as Chronicle C and John of Worcester make it clear that Tosti had a prior agreement with King Harald of Norway to join him in an invasion of England.[8]

It has been suggested that Harald of Norway's invasion was a long-term plan of his which Harold of England should have foreseen, and that Tosti only attached himself to it. Indeed, the attack on England in 1058 by Magnus, son of King Harald, has been seen as a forerunner of his father's 1066 invasion, but there is no direct evidence for this. The Irish Annals of Tigernach do say that Magnus intended to take the kingdom, but this probably reflects the fact that although primarily an Irish Sea expedition, it had actually been directed against England rather than the Celtic lands. It is unlikely that Harald would have sent a boy to do a man's job. In addition, no other recent Viking expedition of conquest against England came from this isolated quarter, which provided no direct access to the centres of English power. Moreover, the contemporary English sources make it clear that Harald's invasion was very much a surprise. Therefore, it seems unlikely that it could have been a long-term plan, as such would inevitably have been the subject of rumour on the trade routes, as was Magnus's planned invasion of 1045. It is more likely that Tosti's plea for aid acted as a spur to Harald, and indeed William of Poitiers seems to confirm this when he states that Tosti brought alien arms against Harold. Harald probably saw the invasion of England as a fitting substitute for his failure to take Denmark. England was a very wealthy kingdom, which could provide him with gold in plenty to replenish his treasury. For a man like Harald, this was reason enough to invade. He required no elaborate legal justification such as William of Normandy had adopted. The later saga story that, as successor to King Magnus, Harald had inherited a claim to England that was supposedly derived from a treaty King Magnus had made with Hardecnut, was, to Harald, simply irrelevant.[9]

The reasons for Harald joining up with Tosti are perhaps less obvious; with their trading links to Northumbria, the Norwegians must have been well aware of the former earl's unpopularity there. Certainly, Tosti had local knowledge, which would be useful, and in spite of his fall he may have retained some local supporters. He had ruled the area for ten years, after all, and, for example, the young Gospatric, to whom he had shown favour, may still have been sympathetic to him. In addition, Harald of Norway may have intended to use Tosti as a figurehead in opposition to his brother, King Harold. He perhaps hoped that Tosti could help rally support in southern England against his brother and so assist the Norwegian campaign. Indeed, Tosti may have played up his influence over his younger brothers and other English nobles in order to persuade Harald to support him. In Harald's mind, once the expedition had succeeded Tosti could be suitably rewarded or disposed of, as the situation required.[10]

An alliance was made, with Tosti very much the subordinate according to the English sources, and in the late autumn of 1066 King Harald summoned a large army and crossed the North Sea in 300 ships. The Norwegian fleet sailed down the east coast of Scotland, using the same northerly winds which confined William of Normandy to port. The fleet joined up with Tosti's small force, either off the Scottish coast or at the mouth of the Tyne. The two allies then sailed down the coast and up the Rivers Humber and Ouse, before landing at Riccall. John of Worcester alone names this as the landing place, but it fits with the location of the subsequent battle at Fulford. After disembarking, Harald led his forces north directly towards York but just outside the city he encountered opposition from Earls Edwin and Morcar on the left bank of the Ouse at Fulford. Via reports of the Norwegian progress down the east coast, the northern earls had been given just enough time to gather as large a force as they could from their earldoms and bring it to York. The speed of these events is emphasized by Chronicle C, which contains the fullest account.[11]

Anglo-Saxon Chronicle E, the entry for 1066.

The statement in Chronicles D and E that Harald's army 'went up the Humber until they reached York. And there Earl Edwin and Morcar his brother fought against him', has been seen as implying that the Norwegians took York without opposition and then fought against the earls. However, this seems to be simply the result of the brevity and compression of these accounts and the fact that the battle took place just outside York, at a location not named until later. This is confirmed by the fuller account in Chronicle C, which makes it clear that the Norwegians were forced to fight for the city. More importantly, if the Norwegians were already in occupation of York when the army of the earls came against them, the location of the battle at Fulford is confusing. If they had needed to do so, the army of the earls could only have advanced against an occupied York from the right bank of the Ouse, and hence the battle could not have taken place near Fulford. Instead, the battle took place because the northern earls sought with their forces to prevent the Norwegian army from taking the city.[12]

This decision by the inexperienced earls to accept battle at Fulford, before King Harold could join them, has been seen by some as an act of folly. However, we must remember the initial confusion resulting from Harald of Norway's surprise assault. The northern earls reacted to this in a natural way by calling up their own forces and perhaps those of Earl Waltheof also. A Norwegian poem suggests that Earl Waltheof was present at the battle and, although he is not referred to by the English sources, this is not impossible. The earls had sent word to King Harold of this new menace, but until he could arrive with support, obviously they had to act on their own. If the Norwegians had entered York unopposed they would have been able to consolidate their position, while at the same time undermining the morale of the Northumbrians. Consequently, the earls chose to make a stand outside York. They selected Fulford, an estate owned by Earl Morcar, where they could bar both the road and the river, and marshes provided protection for their flanks. They appear to have taken all possible precautions to give themselves the best chance of success.[13]

The battle of Fulford took place on Wednesday 20 September, and appears to have been long and bloody. It may not have been as one-sided as the final result implies, as Chronicle C speaks of the battle causing 'heavy casualties' among the invaders as well as the English. John of Worcester expands on this, claiming that the English had some initial success before finally succumbing to the Norwegians. The heavy losses among the English are reflected in the poems contained in the later Harald's Saga, which record that 'warriors lay thickly fallen around the young Earl Morcar'. In the end, the Norwegians' greater experience appears to have given them the edge and the earls were defeated and their army put to flight. Earls Edwin and Morcar had had no previous experience of war and while some of their Northumbrian and Mercian troops had probably fought in earlier campaigns in Scotland and Wales, this could not compare with the Norwegian army's sixteen years of experience in the wars against Denmark. The earls themselves managed to escape the carnage, but many of the English troops were slain or drowned in the nearby marshes.[14]

The victorious Norwegians now entered York 'with as large a force as suited them, and they were given hostages from the city and also helped with provisions'. This statement has been interpreted as evidence of a willingness by the men of York, and Northumbria in general, to submit to the Norwegians. However, few, if any, citizens faced with a foreign army at their gates, having just lost their defenders and with no help immediately to hand, would dare to oppose that army openly. In this situation, the Northumbrians bowed to the inevitable and accepted Harald of Norway's terms for peace. Besides calling for provisions and hostages, the latter perhaps selected by Tosti, these terms also provided for the citizens to assist the Norwegians to conquer the kingdom. It seems doubtful that the Northumbrians would actually have provided such help without compulsion. The hated Tosti was Harald's ally, and few could contemplate his restoration without fear. In addition, there is evidence to show that the Northumbrians at this time considered themselves very much a part of the English kingdom, and the contemporary scribe of a text called the Law of the Northumbrian Priests ends it with a prayer that the land might have 'one royal authority forever'. In the event, the Northumbrians were never put to the test, as King Harold of England came north to their aid.[15]

The northern earls had probably sent word of the Norwegian invasion to King Harold sometime before 20 September, as soon as the Norwegian fleet was first sighted off the north-east coast of England. Chronicle C suggests that Harold received the news not long after he returned from his watch on the Channel coast about mid-September. At once, the king began to gather troops in what was probably the third summons of that hectic year. That he found them at all reflects both his firm grip on the reins of power and a willingness among the English to support their king. Men came to join his 'very great' army from many areas of England. Evidence of only a few of these men survives, but it is sufficient to provide an indication of the wide reach of Harold's power. According to Domesday Book, an uncle of Abbot Aethelwig of Evesham came from an estate at Witton in Worcestershire 'to die in Harold's war against the Norse', and his presence may signify that Harold was attended by the men of Evesham Abbey on this campaign. This man presumably fell at the battle of Stamford Bridge on 25 September because the same entry goes on to say that his death occurred 'before William came to England' on 27 September. An unnamed *thegn*, with land at Paglesham in Essex, gifted it to St Peter's at Westminster before 'he went to battle in Yorkshire with Harold'. In addition, a later source speaks of Harold being cheered on his march north by Abbot Aelfwine of Ramsey, who informed him of a vision he had had of the late King Edward, who prophesied Harold's victory. Beneath the hagiographical elements in this story may lie the possibility that men of Ramsey Abbey were also present in Harold's army. Indeed, it is not impossible that Abbot Aelfwine himself accompanied the army as Abbots Leofric and Aelfwig did later at Hastings.[16]

An invasion fleet at sea. (The Bayeux Tapestry – 11th Century. By special permission of the City of Bayeux)

Unfortunately, there exists only a little evidence as to how Harold was able to raise large forces and move them rapidly to York. The army that Harold collected, in common with that which later faced the Normans at Hastings, would have consisted of two main elements. The first of these was the force of *huscarls*, which on this occasion probably included those who served Harold himself, those royal *huscarls* who had previously served King Edward, and perhaps those of Earl Gyrth, who is said in one late source to have accompanied Harold on this campaign. These men were household troops who served a lord in war and peace and received pay in return. They fought for their lord in war and at other times performed the duties of garrison, tax collection and law enforcement. The second element of Harold's army was the *fyrd*, which consisted of a select levy of men summoned from the population of the shires. This was not a summons to all men to defend the land but a call to relatively well-equipped representative troops who had been nominated by their communities to serve. It also included men who represented religious houses, whose monks were naturally not able to serve in person. It also seems likely that a single summons did not command all *fyrd* men to appear but rather that they were called up in relays. This was surely not beyond the power of the English kings of this period, and it is difficult otherwise to see how Harold could have called up four such levies in 1066.[17]

It seems likely that most of Harold's forces were mounted for the advance north, otherwise it is difficult to account for them reaching York so quickly. There is certainly sufficient evidence that the English used horses in this way, though not that they were used in battle itself. The rates of travel offered for mounted troops of this period, of around 25 miles per day, would bring Harold's forces to Tadcaster by 24 September and to Stamford Bridge by the afternoon of 25 September, if they left London early on 16 September. It is certainly possible that Harold received word of the Norwegian fleet by this last date, and Chronicle C confirms that he began his march north before the battle of Fulford had taken place. If this is correct, then the journey would have been completed by riding during the day and resting overnight. It is known from the Laws of Cnut that earls, *thegns* and their followers were each expected to attend for military service with an extra horse. This would have allowed for one horse to be rested on alternate days during the journey. The comparable rates of travel for infantry of around 15 miles per day would make the journey almost impossible in the time allowed.[18]

If Harold had set out on 16 September, this would not have allowed sufficient time to collect any forces, apart from his attendant *huscarls*, before leaving London. Therefore, he must have collected the *fyrd* as he went north, although we cannot prove this. It is known that Domesday Book records the existence of royal messengers, who could have ridden on fast horses to summon the necessary troops from the shires and arrange for them to ride to named points on the route north. If these troops travelled at similar rates to Harold's own force they could have joined him en route to York, from Essex, Ramsey Abbey and even Worcestershire. It was during his journey north that Harold learnt of the disaster at Fulford on 20 September. This news must have come as a severe blow as he would now have to face the victorious Norwegian's without the help of the forces of the northern earls. Nevertheless, he continued his progress northward undaunted, trusting in his own abilities and those of his men.[19]

Harold's plan in undertaking this rapid journey seems clear; he intended to reach York as soon as possible in order to prevent the Norwegians from consolidating their hold on the north. The consequent plan, to catch them unawares when they thought they were safe after their recent victory, probably only arose after Harold's arrival at Tadcaster on Sunday 24 September. There, he stopped briefly to marshal his troops and gather information. He learned that the Norwegians were 8 miles beyond York at Stamford Bridge and some 13 miles from the safe refuge of their ships at Riccall. They were ideally positioned to be caught and destroyed, and it was probably at this point that Harold decided to attempt to surprise them. This plan depended, of course, on no word of his arrival reaching the Norwegians and, according to the sources, this appears to have been the case, even though King Harold's army passed through York itself, en route to meet the Norwegians at Stamford Bridge. This surely refutes suggestions that the Northumbrians were only too eager to throw off Harold's yoke and accept the

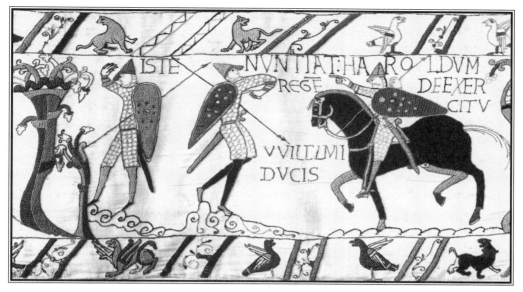

A scout brings news of the enemy to King Harold. (The Bayeux Tapestry – 11th Century. By special permission of the City of Bayeux)

Norwegian king in his place. It seems rather that, in common with the rest of the English, they recognized Harold as their king, so that Chronicle D speaks fondly of Harold as 'our king', and Chronicle E of him 'valiantly' overcoming 'all invaders'.[20]

On Monday 25 September, with his army rested and regrouped, Harold advanced through York to meet the Norwegians at Stamford Bridge. The latter had moved to this small village on the river Derwent to await the arrival of further hostages from the rest of Yorkshire. This need to collect hostages from the shire would appear to indicate that the Norwegians did not trust their Northumbrian hosts. The location also offered the Norwegians the opportunity to live off King Harold's own nearby estate at Catton, which would avoid the possibility of their troops, or more probably Tosti's, plundering York itself. There is no direct evidence for this last threat, but it would not be surprising if Tosti had scores to settle with the local *thegns* as a result of his expulsion in 1065. Following their recent victory, it appears that the Norwegians considered themselves safe from any immediate reprisal; at Stamford Bridge they could easily find themselves cut off from their ships at Riccall. If they had been aware of Harold's approach they would surely have sought to oppose him at York, where they could bar the river Ouse against him. Perhaps they considered that King Harold would remain in the south to face the threatened Norman invasion, or perhaps they felt he would not risk attacking them after the defeat suffered by his earls at Fulford. Most probably they were surprised by the speed of his reactions and did not expect his arrival yet. Whatever the reason, they were completely unprepared for Harold's sudden arrival at Stamford Bridge on 25 September.[21]

The battle which took place at Stamford Bridge was King Harold's greatest victory. It was one of the decisive battles of the Middle Ages, and the one which finally ended the Viking Age. It was important in terms of Harold's own immediate future for another reason. The losses suffered in this battle had an impact on the outcome of the subsequent battle at Hastings. Therefore, it must be considered in some detail, in order to allow an assessment both of Harold's military abilities and of its impact on subsequent events.[22]

The numbers involved in the battle are not recorded but an estimate can be made for the Norwegians based on the Chronicle record of their 300 ships. Assuming a figure of 25 fighting men per ship, this would give them a total of 7,500 men when they first landed in Northumbria. It has been estimated that the later Viking longships could carry between 50 or 60 men; allowing for some exaggeration in the number of ships and the fact they may not all have been large ships, this appears a not unreasonable figure. They suffered heavy losses at Fulford, perhaps around a third seems feasible, leaving them perhaps about 5,000 men. They are known to have left men to guard their ships, and so maybe about 4,000 were actually at Stamford Bridge. Though there is no direct evidence for the numbers on the English side, King Harold perhaps had an equivalent number of men. His forces must have been of a sufficiently manageable size to allow for their rapid collection on the advance to York. They would also have needed supplies on this journey, and more than this number would probably have been too large. The closeness of the fighting itself, Chronicle C speaks of the opposing sides 'fighting strenuously till late in the day', suggests that the opposing forces were fairly evenly matched.[23]

The Norwegians at Stamford Bridge appear to have been completely unprepared for battle. They had even left their mailcoats at their ships, according to the poems incorporated in the later Harald's Saga. That this story is not simply a later excuse for their defeat is perhaps confirmed by its appearance in the contemporary Chronicle of Marianus Scotus. The Norwegians 'had been promised for certain that hostages would be brought to them' and therefore expected the arrival of small groups of local *thegns*, but certainly not an English army under King Harold. A poem preserved in the later saga declares bitterly that 'the army has been duped'. The terrain itself may have worked in favour of the English; Harold may have known this as it lay so close to his own estate at Catton. The Norwegians, encamped in the river valley, truly may not have been aware of Harold's army until it was nearly upon them. In contrast, King Harold knew exactly where the Norwegians were, and advanced with his forces to engage them in battle with a clear advantage.[24]

As King Harold's army approached, the Norwegians appear to have fallen back across the river Derwent. The surprise and shock of the sudden English attack probably meant that the Norwegians were unable to hold them at the river, where defence would have been much easier had they been ready. The account at the end of Chronicle C of a lone Norwegian holding the bridge against the English is a much later addition to the text. It was perhaps drawn from a later English saga about the battle and probably has no basis in fact. Harald of Norway as likely as not rallied his troops in the area later known as Battle Flats, to the east of the river. The battle which then began probably took the customary form for an all infantry battle – two opposing masses slugging it out at close quarters. The account in the prose sections of the much later Harald's Saga speaks of the English use of cavalry in the battle. This does not fit with what we know of English warfare from more contemporary sources, where horses were not used in battle itself, and must be disregarded. Although the English had the initial advantage of surprise, they probably suffered from fatigue later in the day as a result of their 15 mile advance from Tadcaster that morning. Consequently, the battle was long and bloody, but the Norwegian lack of body armour must eventually have reduced their power of resistance.[25]

The traditional English shield wall formation. (The Bayeux Tapestry – 11th Century. By special permission of the City of Bayeux)

The crisis of the battle apparently came late in the day, after many had fallen on both sides, when both Tosti and King Harald of Norway were slain. As the Norse poet Arnor recounts it;

> It was an evil moment
> When Norway's king lay fallen
> Gold-inlaid weapons
> Brought death to Norway's leader.
> All King Harald's warriors
> Preferred to die beside him.
> Sharing their brave king's fate,
> Rather than beg for mercy.[26]

Despite the sentiments expressed in the poem, the fall of their great leader probably broke the morale of the remaining Norwegian troops and the survivors attempted to flee. This is certainly the sequence of events found in the Chronicle accounts and it reflects the usual fate of armies whose leaders were slain. The English army pursued the survivors vigorously, all the way to their ships. The retreat became a rout, and Norwegian losses were so heavy that only twenty-four ships were required to carry the survivors home. This suggests that perhaps only about 500 to 1,000 men survived the battle and rout that followed. The shattered remnant of the Norwegian army was brought to bay by the English at Riccall, but instead of destroying them King Harold gave them quarter. The Norwegians had invaded his kingdom and slaughtered many of his countrymen, but in spite of this Harold was generous in victory. He did not seize or imprison the survivors, although they included Olaf, the son of the dead king, and Earl Paul of Orkney. Instead, King Harold allowed them to return home after obtaining their oaths to maintain peace and friendship with him thereafter. Certainly no further invasions were attempted by young Olaf, who would later be known as 'the Peaceful'.[27]

King Harold was now at the summit of his career. He had earlier driven off Tosti's raids, and outfaced the threat of a Norman invasion across the Channel. Now he had defeated and slain one of the most renowned warriors of the day, in open and decisive battle. We can perhaps see traces of what was originally intended as a celebratory poem dedicated to Harold in the *Vita Eadwardi*:

> And who will write that Humber, vast and swollen
> With raging seas, where namesake kings had fought,
> Has dyed the ocean waves for miles around
> With Viking gore. . . .[28]

This campaign also demonstrated further the continued effectiveness of the English military system. Thus Earls Edwin and Morcar were able to recruit a force substantial enough to oppose the large Norwegian army in what must have been a period of only a few days from the time that the alien fleet was first sighted. Although this force was defeated and York taken, it may have inflicted sufficient casualties on the Norwegians to delay their plans to move south. Thereafter, King Harold himself recruited a substantial army from places as widely scattered as Essex and Worcestershire, brought it to York in only ten days, and totally defeated the still considerable Norwegian army in a difficult battle. This cannot suggest that the English army of Harold's reign represented an obsolescent force.[29]

This achievement was undoubtedly Harold's greatest, and his crown now must have seemed secure. The battle had not only removed the Norwegian threat and finally disposed of the problem presented by Tosti, but such a thorough victory would cause other challengers to pause for thought. Surely William of Normandy would think twice before making another invasion attempt when he heard the news. Everything seemed set fair for King Harold, but then the north wind, which had blown Harald of Norway to his doom, veered to the south.

CHAPTER ELEVEN

THE LAST CAMPAIGN

Here King Harold was killed.[1]

While King Harold celebrated his great victory in Yorkshire, and perhaps mourned and buried Tosti, Duke William's fleet lay trapped at St Valery by the same northerly winds which had brought Harald of Norway to England. William's position was rapidly becoming untenable as supplies ran short, and he resorted to desperate prayers to stem the contrary winds. Then finally, as if in answer, the wind veered round to the south on 27 September and William seized the opportunity for which he had waited so long. The Norman army embarked in its ships, crossed the Channel overnight and made landfall at Pevensey, on 28 September.[2]

One of the most dangerous parts of William's risky enterprise, the Channel crossing and landing in England, had now been completed successfully. His plan had succeeded thus far partly because of the unusually favourable weather conditions this late in the season, but more importantly because of King Harold's absence in the north. This latter fact meant that William's landing was unopposed, which would not have been the case before 8 September, when Harold was still maintaining his coast watch. It has been suggested that William knew of the disbandment of Harold's coastal defence forces and that he chose to set sail at this time in order to exploit this circumstance. However, it is likely that King Harold would have remained in London even after the disbandment of the coastal garrisons, and that he could have moved rapidly against William's forces before they became established. It was Harold's absence in the north that enabled William to secure seventeen clear days in which to disembark his army and consolidate his position in England, the distraction of the Norwegian invasion proving the vital factor in his unopposed landing. It has also been suggested that William knew about the Norwegian invasion and arranged his crossing to exploit Harold's absence. This is very unlikely; William of Poitiers makes it quite clear that the change in wind direction was the crucial factor in William's actions at this point rather than any knowledge of Harold's circumstances. In addition, he shows that William only learned of Harald of Norway's invasion after his own landing in England. There is no reason to doubt William of Poitiers' account on these points, and it fits with English reports of surprise at the Norwegian invasion.[3]

Soon after his landing, Duke William began to construct a castle at Pevensey in order to consolidate his foothold. However, the unsuitability of his landing place as a base of operations quickly persuaded him to move along the coast to the nearby port of Hastings. The security afforded by Harold's absence in the north, and his knowledge of it, allowed him to carry out this move successfully on 29 September. There, based on the narrow peninsula on which the town of Hastings stood, William was in a position to protect the escape route to his ships anchored in the harbour. If the need arose, he could defend the base of the peninsula with a rearguard while the bulk of his army re-embarked safely. Here William ordered another castle to be built, while his forces combined scouting with raiding the surrounding countryside. This raiding was necessary because the Norman army was now short of supplies, but it may also have been intended to provoke an English response.[4]

The measures William took in the first few days after his landing were sensible precautions to adopt in a strange land when he was still unsure of the situation. However, he remained in this same position at Hastings for a total of seventeen days, which seems rather a long time. This has been seen as a prudent policy of remaining near to the coast and his line of retreat. Although a certain amount of caution had undoubtedly been an important element of William's previous campaigns, his present invasion of England had, so far, been anything but prudent. He may simply have returned to his more familiar policy of wariness, but if so it seems an odd time to have done so. William was in a restricted position at Hastings, where he would have found availability of supplies gradually reduced as his troops denuded the surrounding area. It is difficult to see how he hoped to win the kingdom by remaining near his line of retreat until he ran out of supplies. It would surely have been preferable for his cavalry to move out into more open country, where he could make full use of the advantage conferred by their mobility both to secure provisions and to conquer the kingdom. Indeed, he could probably have taken advantage of Harold's absence in the north to advance on Dover, Canterbury or Winchester. So why did William fail to adopt a more active course of action? The answer probably lies in the news he received soon after his landing.[5]

The news that Duke William received, probably on the day after his landing, was that King Harold had secured a crushing victory at Stamford Bridge. The news was provided by Robert, son of Guimara, who was most likely a local man known as Robert of Hastings, recorded in Domesday Book as holding land in Sussex from the Abbey of Fecamp. It must have given William considerable food for thought, and indeed he did not follow the bold words attributed to him by William of Poitiers: 'I will not hide behind ditches or palisades . . . but will engage Harold's army as soon as possible'. In fact, William did not seek to engage Harold at all, but on the contrary remained in his defensive position. He clearly realized that if the Normans advanced inland then they might well be caught by King Harold's victorious forces returning from the north. At this point, William may even have momentarily considered abandoning the invasion, and some of his followers probably did so. Although there exists no direct evidence for this, the tone of William of Poitiers' account makes clear the significance of Harold's victory. This news and the previous reluctance of the Norman nobles to invade in the first place, make second thoughts about the feasibility of the invasion a distinct possibility. However, this would involve William abandoning the dream for which he had now risked everything. He could only continue, but probably decided to adopt his static defensive posture in response to the new situation. As a result, the Norman army remained close to its ships and escape routes, and made no effort to advance inland and use its mobility, which were the usual tactics. This would certainly explain William's relative inactivity during the period leading up to the battle of Hastings.[6]

News of the Norman landing probably reached King Harold while he was still in York, perhaps two or three days later on 29 or 30 September. According to John of Worcester, he was in the midst of restoring the strength of his tired and depleted forces and tending to the wounded. Once again, King Harold received an extremely unpleasant surprise, and once again he set about dealing with it in the same purposeful manner. He is said to have assembled a large army, in effect the fourth to be summoned during this astonishing year – the first two summoned for two months each to garrison the coast, and the third to deal with Harald of Norway. This was a remarkable feat for a supposedly moribund military system. It seems likely that this new army was once again formed around the surviving core of the force of *huscarls* which had just destroyed the Norwegians. In order to restore its losses, additional troops were drawn from a wide area of the country, stretching from East Anglia to Hampshire. Some of these reinforcements may have joined Harold's army as it journeyed south, but the bulk of them probably gathered in London to await his arrival. They may have been collected under the auspices of one of his brothers. A late source speaks of Earl Gyrth accompanying the king to Stamford Bridge, so perhaps Earl Leofwine had been left in charge in the south.[7]

Unfortunately, as in the case of the earlier campaign against the Norwegians, we have only fragments of information on the men who answered Harold's summons. Again, the men of the English abbeys appear to have been well represented, although this seeming preponderance may simply be a result of the greater survival rate of monastic sources. Two abbots are known to have died during the Hastings campaign, presumably while accompanying their men: Abbot Aelfwig of the New Minster at Winchester, who fell apparently in the battle itself, and Abbot Leofric of Peterborough, who died of an illness contracted during the campaign. In addition, men holding land of the abbeys of Abingdon, St Benet of Holme, Bury St Edmunds, and St Augustine's, Canterbury, appear to have fought in this campaign. A number of other men came to serve their king, including Godric, Sheriff of Berkshire, Eadric the Deacon, an unnamed freeman of Harold from Cavendish in Suffolk, Breme from Suffolk, a freeman of King Edward and, presumably therefore, of his successor Harold, and two unnamed freemen from Tytherley in Hampshire. It may simply be a coincidence but it is nevertheless interesting that those abbeys and counties noted as sending forces to join Harold at Hastings are different from those who had sent forces to join him at York. This may possibly reflect a sophisticated form of selective summons, whereby different abbeys and counties provided troops on different occasions. Unfortunately, there is insufficient evidence to prove this.[8]

The absence of the northern earls from King Harold's army at Hastings has been seen as evidence of dissension between Harold and his 'rivals'. In fact, Orderic Vitalis describes the earls as Harold's 'close friends and adherents' and we must remember that the earls' sister, Alditha, was Harold's queen, and therefore they had a stake in his success. A late source claims that Harold replaced Earl Morcar with Marleswein, Sheriff of Lincolnshire, and possibly a newly appointed *staller*. This seems unlikely as Morcar is still named earl, later in the year, and was probably taken hostage to Normandy early in 1067 as Earl of Northumbria. It is more probable that the crushing defeat at Fulford had resulted in such disastrous losses among the forces of Edwin and Morcar, and particularly among their *huscarls,* that they required time to rebuild them. The reference to Marleswein's activities in the north might then be part of his function as a royal *staller* to assist them in this process. This delay meant that the earls were unable to march south with King Harold but followed him when they were ready, arriving in London not long after the battle of Hastings.[9]

Meantime, King Harold moved rapidly southwards with the core of his northern army, the remnants of his own and perhaps Earl Gyrth's *huscarls.* This was the second great journey of this year, and brought Harold to London possibly around 8–9 October. This assumes a roughly comparable speed for this southward journey, based on the same rates of progress for mounted troops, as for the recent journey to Stamford Bridge. It is probable that Harold again made use of mounted royal messengers to carry his latest summons to the shires. In this way, he could have ensured that another substantial army was already collected in London on his return. The period of time involved would easily allow for such a possibility, and this would mean the bulk of Harold's forces would be reasonably rested and ready for him to collect on his way south. He halted briefly in London, perhaps for a day or two, to rest those troops he had brought back from the north and to allow reinforcements to join him. Chronicle D speaks of another large army being raised, and the probable size of the English force at Hastings also indicates that Harold received substantial reinforcements. It was only when suitably reinforced that Harold then marched his army the 60 miles or so southwards into Sussex. This final march perhaps took some three days, allowing for slower progress of 20 miles a day through the more difficult country of the Sussex Weald to where the Norman army remained at Hastings.[10]

The rapidity of King Harold's reaction to William's landing is undoubtedly impressive, but some have seen weakness in the haste attending his journey to Sussex. It is important here to distinguish between Harold's rapid journey south to London and his

Norman cavalry attack the English shield wall at Hastings.. (The Bayeux Tapestry – 11th Century. By special permission of the City of Bayeux)

subsequent advance into Sussex. The former served to bring him swiftly to the scene of action in southern England, but should not be given undue weight in consideration of the subsequent battle. As discussed above, it is probable that Harold spent one or two days in London collecting reinforcements, resting those troops brought back from York and considering what course of action to adopt. According to the recorded dates, he was then left with three days for the onward movement to Hastings, and it is this short period, the time that Harold spent in London and his subsequent march to Hastings, that should be examined when considering the claim that he acted rashly. It has been suggested, on the basis of the Chronicle texts, that Harold went into battle with less than his full forces, even though time had been on his side, and that he should have waited for his full strength before engaging the Normans. In this context, Chronicle E is rather ambiguous, stating only that Harold 'fought with him [William] before all the army had come', which could mean that the battle began before all Harold's army had arrived on the field, but that reinforcements joined him as the day progressed. This suggestion may receive support from Chronicle D, which states that the battle was joined 'before his [Harold's] army was drawn up in battle array'. John of Worcester, writing later, elaborates on these statements but whether on the basis of additional knowledge or in an attempt to clarify the earlier texts is unknown. He states that 'although he [Harold] knew that all the more powerful men from the whole of England had already fallen in two battles, and that half of his army had not yet assembled, yet he did not fear go to meet his enemies in Sussex, with all possible speed'. John's account clearly intends to imply that Harold left London without all the troops he had summoned, but its author goes on to complain that the narrowness of Harold's position at Hastings prevented a full deployment of his army, rather than there being a depleted number of men in the first place. This is confusing and contradictory. The sources are not entirely conclusive and either interpretation is possible; the balance of the contemporary accounts perhaps favours Harold having sufficient forces available, but that not all were deployed at the start of the battle. The length and intensity of the battle itself seems to confirm that there was no lack of English troops.[11]

If Harold did in fact arrive in Sussex before the full force he had gathered could be deployed, what was the reason for this? The contemporary Chronicles provide no explanations for Harold's motives. John of Worcester is not specific, but perhaps suggests an element of recklessness in his account of Harold's great haste and insufficient forces. However, recklessness does not appear to have been one of Harold's normal character traits. He had previously showed considerable caution in his dealings with Gruffydd of Wales, and only mounted his surprise attack on Rhuddlan after careful calculations as to the chances of success. Similarly, he had only attacked the Norwegian army at Stamford Bridge after first collecting intelligence at Tadcaster, and therefore being confident of success. William of Poitiers suggests the reason as a desire to curb, as soon as possible, the Norman devastation of his family lands in Sussex. This almost certainly played a part in King Harold's reasoning, but it is unlikely to have been more than an incidental factor. A man who had previously sacrificed his brother, when the larger interest required, was unlikely to be distracted from his purpose by the ravaging of his lands. Also, as king, Harold held vast lands all over England and the temporary wasting of a small portion is unlikely to have affected him very deeply.[12]

The Norman accounts suggest Harold intended to repeat the tactics used to such effect against Harald of Norway and to catch William by surprise at Hastings. Initially, this seems a more plausible reason for Harold's actions, but it must be considered that now the circumstances were very different. In September the Norwegians had just won a major victory against local forces and had taken York with ease. They were off guard and not expecting the swift arrival of a southern army when Harold attacked. Even then, Harold had first confirmed that the Norwegians were unprepared and isolated from their fleet before launching his attack. In contrast, the Normans were still anxiously awaiting an English response to their landing, in what must have seemed a rather exposed position, and were fully prepared for flight. Therefore, they would be alert and prepared to respond to any attack. Any supposed plan for a surprise attack is further called into doubt by William of Poitiers' account of Harold's messenger and his talks with Duke William. Of course, this may be merely a conventional elaboration added to his story to enable him to set out Duke William's case, but equally it may be true and if so, effectively removes surprise as a possible reason for Harold's haste.[13]

A more important factor in Harold's actions may have been the personal knowledge of William and of Norman tactics that he gained during his visit to Normandy in 1064. There he had witnessed at first hand the mobile tactics of the Norman knights, when he accompanied Duke William on his Breton expedition. He had seen how William could rapidly move his cavalry from place to place, ravage wide areas of territory, and swiftly pursue enemies. He had also seen castles used as refuges, from whence raids could be sent out to subdue the surrounding countryside. If the Normans were able to advance inland from Hastings to more open country in Kent or Hampshire, they would become a major threat. They could exploit the mobility of their cavalry to plunder widely and live off the land, easily outmanoeuvring the less mobile English infantry and throwing up castles to preserve their communications and provide fortified refuges behind them. This last point was a particular threat because by these means the Normans could establish footholds in a territory rather than merely raiding it and moving on like the Vikings had done. Indeed, these were the very tactics pursued by the Normans later in their march on London and during their subsequent subjugation of England.[14]

It was probably this knowledge, rather than a desire to catch William unawares or to preserve the family lands, which persuaded Harold of the need for haste in advancing into Sussex. He had to contain the Normans in Sussex and in the peninsula on which Hastings stood, in order to prevent them taking full advantage of their mobility. Once he had the Normans bottled up there, he could build up his forces against them, while simultaneously cutting off their supplies and preventing their raids on Sussex. Thus he moved the forces he had gathered rapidly in order to block a Norman break-out and at the same time summoned a fleet to destroy their ships and cut off their retreat. Harold intended to deal with William as thoroughly as he had Harald of Norway and his actions were directed to that end.[15]

King Harold ordered his army to meet at the 'hoary apple tree', a local Sussex landmark obviously well known to the English. Indeed it may have lain on the boundary of Harold's own estate at Whatlington, just over a mile from the battle site. If Harold did intend to trap William's forces then this would explain why he apparently sent a messenger to treat with William. The intention behind this would be to stall William at Hastings until Harold's army and fleet arrived to trap him. We need not believe the exact words put into the mouth of the messenger by William of Poitiers, although interestingly the emphasis he places on the gift of the kingdom to Harold by the dying Edward, reflects English traditional practice. The gist of Harold's message, that William should leave England before he was destroyed, is probably accurate enough. Duke William could not back out now without a loss of prestige of incalculable consequence, and he therefore rejected Harold's ultimatum. According to William of Poitiers, Duke William is supposed to have made a challenge to single combat, which was ignored by Harold. This challenge probably represents a literary device which has no foundation in truth, although Harold's refusal of such a challenge would reflect English tradition, which found trial by combat an alien concept. In a sense, William's rejection of Harold's ultimatum reflected the fact that his position was improving in that he would soon be trapped with no alternative but to fight. Therefore, he was able to set aside the earlier doubts, which had plagued him after Harold's victory over the Norwegians.[16]

King Harold's army emerged from its march through the Sussex Weald probably in the late afternoon of 13 October. Harold had achieved his primary purpose by interposing his army between the Normans and the more open country beyond the peninsula on which Hastings stood. He could now build up his own forces and watch the Normans become weaker before attacking at the time of his choosing. Warned by their scouts, the Normans withdrew their foragers back to their camp near Hastings. William was obviously more wary of Harold's military reputation than later historians, or the result of the battle, would appear to admit. He clearly feared a sudden attack by Harold, possibly during the hours of darkness, and had his troops armed and stood to throughout the night, expecting an assault which never came as Harold did not yet intend to attack.[17]

As dawn of 14 October approached, the situation was close to crisis point, and we must establish the intentions of the two commanders. King Harold, as we have seen, probably intended to contain the Normans until he could destroy their fleet and bring superior force to bear on them. This may seem rather cautious but it is likely that he had lost a large number of his most seasoned troops at Stamford Bridge and, additionally perhaps, not all his troops had yet arrived on the field. He could afford to wait before he sought battle until he was confident of victory, or until the Normans were starved into surrender. On the other hand, William could not afford to wait at all. He was now trapped at Hastings, unable to forage for supplies and faced with the prospect of his line of retreat and reinforcement being cut, either by an English fleet or by bad weather, which was increasingly likely at this time of year. Therefore, he had to attack Harold soon. If he did not, he would certainly be defeated. It was a simple matter of survival. This is reflected in the exhortatory speech placed in William's mouth by his biographer William of Poitiers, which emphasizes that there was no way of escape. The situation effectively resolved any doubts he or his followers had about their expedition.

At this stage, King Harold must have been aware that his cornered opponent would be likely to strike back, and he would have accepted this risk to his plans, yet the Chronicle states that William came against him by 'surprise'.[18] The reason for this seems fairly clear. William had maintained his troops on stand-by throughout the night in preparation for a possible night assault by Harold. Therefore, when dawn broke, at around 5.30 a.m., it was a relatively easy task for William to assemble them in battle array and advance on King Harold's force soon afterwards. On the other hand, the English had arrived late the previous day, after a three-day march from London through the Weald. They were tired and in need of rest, so they probably camped round the 'hoary apple tree' on Caldbec Hill and slept soundly through the night. Later fanciful Anglo-Norman accounts of the English army's overnight celebrations can safely be dismissed as the excuses of hindsight.

Consequently, at daybreak, when warned of the Norman army's approach, some time was needed to draw up the English army in battle formation. As a result, King Harold's force was surprised in the sense that his army was not drawn up in battle array, as recorded in Chronicle D. This scenario could also explain the statement in Chronicle E that not all the army had arrived, since the activity of an army being drawn up might appear, to an observer, to be the arrival of reinforcements.[19]

In spite of his surprise, Harold apparently still had sufficient time to assemble the bulk of his troops and move them forward to take up position on Senlac Ridge half a mile in front of Caldbec Hill. There they arrayed themselves on foot, around Harold's personal standard of a warrior embroidered in gold thread, in the traditional English defensive formation known as the shield wall. The position on Senlac Ridge was undoubtedly the best defensive position in the area, as Harold was probably aware either from reconnaissance the previous evening, or more likely from his own local knowledge. It should be remembered that Sussex was Harold's native county, that he owned estates at nearby Whatlington and Crowhurst, and that the army had been ordered to meet at the well-known 'hoary apple tree' on Caldbec Hill. All this suggests that Harold had detailed local knowledge of the area, or at least that someone in his following had such knowledge. It is unlikely that Harold had made no plans to deal with a Norman attack, as his strategy of containment would eventually have provoked such. Therefore, he had probably always intended to occupy Senlac Ridge in such circumstances, although this situation arose much earlier than he anticipated.[20]

The swift Norman advance failed to prevent the English army from manning a good defensive position, although it may have resulted in their not being drawn up entirely as Harold wished. In particular, the stationing of the more highly trained and experienced *huscarls* to bolster the less experienced *fyrd* men may not have been completed at points along the ridge. This would certainly help to explain events during the battle. The *huscarls* of the king and earls were trained and disciplined household warriors ready to serve at short notice. The *fyrd* was a select call-up of less well-trained and disciplined 'reservists', although these were still well-equipped *thegns* and freemen rather than peasants or rustics. Another important fact was that the English had already fought a very bloody battle in which they had lost many of their best men. The details of English losses at Stamford Bridge are unknown, but are likely to have fallen more heavily on the élite *huscarls*, who would probably have spearheaded the attack. However, these deficiencies in the English army were compensated for by the strength of their position and the resolution in defence of King Harold. Another positive factor for the English was that morale must have been high, given their recent resounding victory over Harald of Norway, and King Harold's reputation for success. In terms of numbers, the English army probably numbered around 7,000 men. If we accept that not all Harold's troops had arrived, then there is the possibility that the number was initially lower than this but that it increased during the day as others arrived.[21]

The Normans had the disadvantage of facing an enemy in a very strong position, which they had to attack uphill and over heavy ground and which they could not outflank. This negated the effect of their cavalry which would lose its customary momentum and mobility in such circumstances. Although Norman morale was probably not as high as that of the English, they were emboldened by the iron determination of Duke William, and the firm knowledge that only victory could save them. William's reported address to his troops includes both a stirring call to arms and a stark portrayal of their fate should they fail to win. They also had the advantage of a more balanced force, consisting of infantry, cavalry and archers, with a more consistent level of training and experience. Their strength was probably also around 7,000 men.[22]

An isolated group of Englishmen are surrounded by Normans. (The Bayeux Tapestry – 11th Century. By special permission of the City of Bayeux)

As a result of these various factors, the opposing armies were fairly evenly matched when the battle commenced at 9.00 a.m. It began with the Normans launching missiles against the English position and following this up with an infantry attack, which was met by a shower of English missiles. These caused losses among the Norman infantry and their attack quickly faltered. Next, the Norman knights advanced against the English line, engaging them at close quarters. The English infantry maintained their position and, in turn, inflicted considerable casualties on the Normans, particularly with their battle-axes. William of Poitiers places great emphasis on these 'murderous axes . . . which could easily find a way through the shields and other defences'. This close-quarter fight raged furiously until gradually the ferocity of the English defence took its toll. The Breton troops on the Norman left wing panicked and broke under the English assault. The collapse of its left wing caused confusion and fear to spread through the whole Norman army, fanned by a rumour that Duke William himself had fallen. William of Poitiers' statement that 'almost the whole ducal army falls away' makes it clear that this was a major disaster for the Normans.[23]

As the Normans fell back a part of the English forces advanced from their hilltop position in pursuit of what appeared to be the routed enemy. Unfortunately, we have no account of this incident from the English side and cannot establish the full background to it. It may have been a breach of discipline by members of the *fyrd*, who broke ranks without orders to pursue what appeared to be a defeated enemy. Alternatively, it may have been an official counter-attack, ordered by King Harold in an attempt to finish the battle. If we accept that Harold had been forced to array his troops in haste, then the former is a strong possibility. A large group of *fyrd* men on the English right, with perhaps too few of the more disciplined *huscarls* in support, could have broken ranks in this way. On the other hand, if the Bayeux Tapestry is correct in showing the deaths of Harold's brothers, Gyrth and Leofwine, in what looks like an isolated group, possibly at this stage of the battle, then perhaps it was a major counter-attack intended to finish off the Normans. However, William of Poitiers' statement that Harold's brothers 'were found lying beside him' at the end of the battle must cast doubt on the validity of any judgements based solely on the positioning of this particular scene in the Tapestry. The Bayeux Tapestry is known to rearrange scenes out of sequence for convenience or dramatic effect – the scene depicting King Edward's funeral procession, for example, is placed before that of his death. Although we will probably never know for sure what was the cause of this English attack – and the balance of probability favours an undisciplined charge – the consequences of the action are clear.[24]

The initial impact of this English advance, whether planned or not, fell on the Breton contingent on the Norman left flank, which was severely handled and may indeed have been knocked out of the battle for a time. However, Duke William was

The fall of King Harold's brothers, Gyrth and Leofwine. (The Bayeux Tapestry – 11th Century. By special permission of the City of Bayeux)

able to intervene, and managed to halt the retreat of his 'own troops', the Norman cavalry of the centre. They turned and wheeled round, cutting off those English who had routed their left wing. The latter were surrounded and overwhelmed by the recovered Normans, and are probably shown in the Tapestry as the small group of Englishmen isolated on a hill.[25]

Although this crisis has been seen as the decisive point of the battle, the fighting did not end here but continued until late in the afternoon, suggesting that it cannot have been so conclusive. Instead, the damage inflicted on William's left wing and the losses from Harold's forces appear, in effect, to have cancelled each other out. In other circumstances, of course, it could well have been the decisive point for Harold and the English: if William had failed to rally his own knights, the whole Norman army might have collapsed as William of Poitiers himself admits; if Harold had undertaken a full counter-attack, he could possibly have gained the victory. King Harold has been censured for this failure but it should be remembered that the army he now commanded was not the same force which had destroyed Harald of Norway. It had been weakened by its losses in that earlier battle, particularly among the élite *huscarls*, and it may also have been understrength.

This was the crucial legacy of the hard-won victory of Stamford Bridge. It meant that Harold could not afford to take the risks involved in leaving his prepared defensive position to mount a counter-attack. Instead, he wisely held the bulk of his men back on their ridge rather than risk an encounter with William's cavalry in the open. The fate of those English who did break ranks suggests that Harold was correct in not taking this risk. The usual intention in medieval warfare was to avoid risk unless the odds were very much in favour, and this was probably not how Harold saw things at this point.[26]

After this confused episode, which may have occurred about midday, both sides would have required time to rest and reform. The English appear to have regrouped successfully, perhaps drawing in their flanks to fill the gaps left in the right of their line. William of Poitiers confirms that, in spite of its losses, the English army 'seemed no less' and remained 'densely massed'. The Normans also probably regrouped and rebuilt their left wing, perhaps taking the opportunity to underpin it with Norman knights. Thereafter, the contest was resumed. The Normans returned to the assault and again the opposing forces fought each other furiously, but the Frenchmen gained little in comparison to their mounting losses. William of Poitiers speaks of the Normans 'realising . . . they could not overcome an enemy . . . standing so firm'.[27]

In an attempt to repeat the earlier unintentional breach in English ranks, caused by the rush of some in pursuit of fleeing Normans, William now ordered a series of feigned retreats. This part of the Norman account has been disputed by many, but such a tactic, in which a group retreats to draw the enemy out of position then turns to catch them unawares in the open, appears to have been performed quite often during this period. It was most likely carried out by small units of highly trained knights, who had the skills to perform such a complex manoeuvre. This strategem did succeed in drawing forward further small groups of the less disciplined English *fyrd*, who were surrounded and killed, but it still failed to make any significant impact on the English main body, which remained 'a formidable force'.[28]

It must by now have been late afternoon. King Harold's forces still held their position on Senlac Ridge, 'as though rooted to the soil', and the Normans were still trapped. If this deadlock remained until nightfall, then William was beaten – Harold could expect reinforcements, William could not, and the next day would surely bring Norman defeat and destruction, or ignominious surrender. The northern earls were marching south with reinforcements and the English fleet was preparing to cut off William's escape route. William was now desperate and threw everything he had left into one final throw, combining archers, infantry and cavalry. The archers perhaps fired into the English army from the flanks, as illustrated by their appearance in the Bayeux Tapestry's borders. This last assault had all the ferocity of Norman desperation, as they literally fought for their lives, and the language used by William of Poitiers reflects this increasing tempo, as they 'shot, smote and peirced'. As a result, there first appears, according to Poitiers, a weakening on the English side, which he attributes to nothing more than fortune's favour. A curious hiatus appears in his narrative at this point, as he digresses to write about the deeds of William during the fight and omits entirely what was the crux of the whole battle – the death of King Harold. This is an uncharacteristic lapse in Poitiers' otherwise fulsome account, and deserves fuller consideration than it has received.[29]

Fortunately, the gap in William of Poitiers' account is filled for us by the Bayeux Tapestry, and there we find the reason for the sudden weakening of the English army after such a long and hard struggle. It is not merely cruel fortune, for there on the Tapestry, amidst the final assault by knights and archers, can be seen King Harold, clearly depicted, stationed under his standard, with an arrow piercing his eye. Here surely is the reason for the sudden and unexplained weakening of the English defence. King Harold is struck in the eye by a stray arrow and is fatally wounded. The reliability of this part of the Tapestry account has been doubted, but there is a great deal of circumstantial confirmation for it. William of Jumieges says that Harold 'fell . . . pierced with lethal wounds', and later local tradition, recorded in the Chronicle of Battle Abbey, speaks of him being 'laid low by a chance blow'. William of Poitiers himself speaks later of Harold's body being 'recognised not by his face', implying such disfigurement as an arrow might produce. This news would have at once sent shock waves through the English army, as had happened earlier within the Norman ranks, when rumour of William's death had spread. At confirmation of the news, the English army wavered and broke, and only then was the Norman cavalry finally able to penetrate their ranks. Both William of Jumieges and the Bayeux Tapestry make clear the direct link between Harold's death and the break-up and flight of the English army.[30]

The death of King Harold. (The Bayeux Tapestry – 11th Century. By special permission of the City of Bayeux)

Thereafter, the broken English army was cut down by Norman knights. It was probably at this point that Harold's banner fell into Norman hands and that Gyrth and Leofwine were killed, since their bodies were found near that of Harold. Although already mortally wounded, there is a possibility that Harold himself was not struck down until now. We have seen that William of Poitiers curiously makes no mention of Harold's death. It is unlikely that he knew nothing of it, after all, he had detailed information on all other aspects of the battle. It seems more probable that he deliberately chose to omit this episode from his account. It may be that he did not wish to detract from William's victory by attributing it directly to Harold's fall. It is also possible that he did not record the moment when the already dying Harold was struck down because he did not want it to be remembered – there was little glory for the Normans in the felling of a dying man. The royal *huscarls* may have died with their king, but the remaining English, confused and demoralized, decided to make their escape into the gathering dusk. A few turned at bay to inflict a final severe blow at the pursuing Normans. However, King Harold's death had removed the spirit which had held the English 'rooted to the ground' for almost the entire day against all that the Normans could throw against them.[31]

Thus the battle reached its fatal climax for King Harold, but as we have seen, it had been a very close run thing. The fact that King Harold did not seize the opportunity offered by the collapse of the Norman left wing and the rumour of William's death has

The English flee the field after Harold's fall. (The Bayeux Tapestry – 11th Century. By special permission of the City of Bayeux)

puzzled many. However, we should remember the condition of his army. A basically cautious man like Harold would be unlikely to take unnecessary risks by advancing from his position when all he really needed to do was stand his ground and force William into submission. If he had held the field at the end of the day, William would have been finished, and he almost succeeded in this, falling just before nightfall. That he ultimately failed was largely because of the fortune of war, and the evidence suggests that it was King Harold's fall to a chance arrow which finally broke English resistance and left the field to the Normans. We must remember that what in hindsight was to prove such a decisive defeat for the English, was in fact balanced on a knife edge throughout the day.

As dusk fell on that autumn day, Harold lay dead, his face unrecognizable, surrounded by the bodies of his loyal brothers and many of his *huscarls*. Also among the fallen were Aelfric of Yelling, Aelfwig, abbot of the New Minster, Eadric the Deacon and many other unnamed English *thegns*. The king's body was finally identified, perhaps by distinctive armour or marks on his body, and brought to William's camp. William apparently refused the request of Countess Gytha, Harold's mother, to allow her to remove her son's body for burial, even when she offered its weight in gold. He may have feared that Harold would become a martyr to the English and his body a source of unwanted devotion. This stands in contrast to Harold's magnanimous actions after Stamford Bridge, and perhaps indicates an unease behind William's claims. Instead, William turned the body over to William Malet, ordering him to bury Harold on the sea shore. It would not have been inappropriate for Harold's body to remain in this resting place in his native Sussex, but local tradition at Waltham later recorded that it was in fact removed and reburied in his own foundation there. This may be true, as the author of the Waltham Chronicle claimed to remember, as a boy, the translation of Harold's body into the new Norman church around 1120, and the supposed site of Harold's grave is still marked there. Alternatively, this story may simply reflect the desire of the canons of Harold's foundation to remain associated with their distinguished patron.[32]

William's concern that Harold would become a focus for English devotion was indeed fulfilled. Thus a cult developed around Harold's grave which naturally caused the canons considerable embarrassment under Norman rule. As a result, they sought to minimize Harold's cult by developing a cult of the Holy Cross itself, to redirect the devotion of pilgrims. In 1120 they transferred Harold's body to a less attractive location in their church where it was less likely to be such a focus of devotion. The Augustinian canons who later assumed control of the church also sought to deflect this devotion to Harold into a form which did not threaten the Normans. Thus they fostered existing legends which reported that Harold had in fact escaped death in the battle and was not buried at Waltham at all. He was said to have travelled to Denmark and Germany, seeking allies to restore his throne. Unsuccessful in this, he then humbly accepted his fate, became a pilgrim in expiation of his broken oath to William, and lived as a hermit either in Chester or Canterbury. The association of Harold with Chester may dimly reflect that of his own son, also called Harold, with this city, where Queen Alditha sought refuge after Hastings and where young Harold was born after his father's death. These legends reflect Harold's other role as an English folk hero, but were also successful in their purpose of neutralizing any potential cult of Harold the martyr.[33]

CHAPTER TWELVE

END OF A DYNASTY

Harold's sons came unexpectedly from Ireland with a naval force.[1]

King Harold lay buried by the sea shore near the battlefield where he had fallen, with his loyal brothers Earls Gyrth and Leofwine and his *huscarls* at his side. The victorious Norman invaders now began a rampage through Kent, taking Dover and Canterbury almost unopposed. The shock of the defeat at Hastings, the loss of King Harold and his brothers, and the severe losses of fighting men in the battles of 1066 go far to explain William's largely unimpeded march towards London. In spite of their desperate situation, the remaining English leaders did not consider submission. Indeed, William had already waited at Hastings in vain for this. This indicates the lack of reality behind William's claim as portrayed by William of Poitiers. If this claim had been widely agreed by the English in 1051 and Harold had usurped the throne, why did the English not accept William as king immediately after Harold's death at Hastings? Instead, the principal surviving English leaders, including Archbishops Stigand and Ealdred, Earls Edwin and Morcar, and the men of London, coalesced around *Atheling* Edgar in London. This was almost a reflex reaction in that they rallied to him as the familiar symbol of their ancient dynasty, but it reflected their desire to fight on. Indeed, Edgar's supporters, who probably also included Ansgar the *Staller*, successfully held the Thames bridges against Norman attack. They clearly possessed sufficient forces to defend London against William's now reinforced army and to compel him to attempt to cross the Thames further west at Wallingford.[2]

As William's army moved cautiously through Wessex, ravaging the countryside, the English discussed their options. The Chronicle states that they wanted to have *Atheling* Edgar as king, and that the northern earls intended to fight for him. But, in the absence of Harold, there was clearly a lack of political and military direction. The two northern earls were relatively young and inexperienced, and Harold's remaining family were currently leaderless. As William of Poitiers suggests, it seems likely that it was actually the experienced Archbishops Stigand and Ealdred who were behind the *Atheling's* candidacy. They perhaps feared that Harold's fall had been God's judgement and sought to reverse this by invoking the traditional and legitimate dynasty. No doubt they also sought in this way to secure their own positions. However, the *Atheling* was not crowned and there was no fighting. On the contrary, English resistance now began swiftly to collapse.[3]

The Normans burn down a house. (The Bayeux Tapestry – 11th Century. By special permission of the City of Bayeux)

The reason for this was principally military. The English now lacked a successful war leader. Earls Edwin and Morcar, with their depleted forces, appear to have been unprepared to face a now reinforced Norman army under William. This is hardly surprising following King Harold's recent defeat and their own earlier experience at Fulford. The English had been able to defend the Thames crossing at London, but were less willing to face William's cavalry in the open. In addition to this, there was the political confusion which resulted from the lack of a satisfactory successor to King Harold. None of the surviving male members of Harold's family, chiefly his young sons, carried enough political weight to be considered at this point. The preferred choice, *Atheling* Edgar, still laboured under the handicap of his youth and inexperience as he had in January, when he had been passed over in favour of Harold. Indeed, he had only his descent to recommend him and under the pressure of the relentless Norman advance this was not enough. The fact that Edgar was not crowned as he could have been makes it clear that the English were reluctant to endorse him whole-heartedly and that some were having second thoughts about their choice.

The initially powerful group supporting *Atheling* Edgar, which controlled most of the remaining English military resources, began to break up. The loss of the royal treasure, when the widowed Queen Edith surrendered Winchester to the Normans, was undoubtedly a blow to the hopes of Edgar's supporters, depriving them of significant resources with which to finance opposition to William. According to John

A Norman castle, a symbol of occupation. (The Bayeux Tapestry – 11th Century. By special permission of the City of Bayeux)

of Worcester, Edwin and Morcar were the first to abandon Edgar. It is likely that they were acting out of self-interest in doing so. It is surely no coincidence that just before abandoning Edgar, they had sent their sister, Queen Alditha, Harold's wife and probably heavily pregnant with his child, north to Chester for safety. These actions were probably part of a long-term plan of their own, to await the birth of Harold's heir by their sister and then push his or her claims to the throne. In the meantime they would bow to the inevitable and submit to William.[4]

The withdrawal of the support of the earls with their forces was probably decisive in leaving *Atheling* Edgar at the mercy of William's victorious army. Thereafter, Archbishop Stigand, who astutely saw the writing on the wall, hastened to submit to William at Wallingford. Subsequently, the other main English leaders submitted to William 'out of necessity' at Berkhampstead. After this, William entered London unopposed and was crowned king at Westminster on Christmas Day. The new king then received further submissions, constructed castles to provide security for his garrisons in occupied south-east England, and appointed lieutenants to govern this conquered area on his behalf. With the country apparently subdued, William returned to Normandy in March 1067, loaded with looted treasures and accompanied by those English leaders who might serve as rallying points for any opposition, including the *Atheling* himself, Earls Edwin and Morcar, and Archbishops Stigand and Ealdred.[5]

We must not underestimate the impact of the Norman invasion because of its distance from us. This impact went beyond the killing, raping and looting normally associated with warfare at this time, and certainly committed by the Normans as recorded in the penance imposed on them by the Papal Ordinance of 1070. This was not a conquest by Danes or Norwegians, whose speech was understood and whose manners were familiar throughout England. The new invaders spoke a language which few Englishmen could comprehend, and had some strange and unfamiliar customs. They had already devastated a swathe of the heartlands of England, from Kent to Hampshire. They now began to rob churches, to seize large areas of land, and to demolish houses to make way for their castles. In modern Britain, perhaps only the inhabitants of the Channel Islands can fully understand what 1066 must have been like.[6]

The activities of the Normans aroused frustration, resentment and hatred among the English, which gradually grew into opposition. This gathered strength during William's absence in 1067, and rebellions were planned in a number of regions. In a sense, the ground was fertile for such activities as the Normans had as yet, secured only the southeast corner of England. The English had been temporarily stunned by the sudden and complete nature of their defeat. They had lost most of their natural leaders and best men on the bloody battlefields of that year – Fulford, Stamford Bridge and Hastings. However, their opposition to the invaders had been stilled only temporarily. They soon recovered from their shock, and their opposition grew into open resistance.[7]

Norman soldiers of the occupation.

The remnants of Harold's family had been particularly affected by the defeat at Hastings. With the fall of the king and both his brothers, they had been deprived of their senior representatives. Harold's sons and heirs were as young and untried as *Atheling* Edgar. Faced with a stark choice between these boys, the majority of the leading Englishmen had returned not unnaturally to their familiar loyalty to Alfred's dynasty. Deprived of political influence and military support, Harold's family were forced to retreat before William's advance, and seek refuge in their lands in south-west England. All the bright hopes of the beginning of the year had been dashed before its end, but the family were Harold's heirs and fully intended to make every attempt to restore their fortunes. They also had the resources to do this. Countess Gytha's offer for the return of Harold's body provides an indication of the wealth still available to the family.

The family began to construct a basis for their planned return to power in the south-west, beyond William's reach, probably under the direction of the redoubtable Countess Gytha. They chose Exeter, the fourth largest town in England, as their base. It was a wise choice as a city with direct links by sea to sources of possible support in Ireland and Denmark. In addition, the family held wide lands in the surrounding counties of Devon, Somerset and Cornwall. There they began repairing the town fortifications and securing support among the *thegns* of the region. They were apparently supported by a remnant of Harold's *huscarls*, perhaps those occupied on other duties during the Hastings campaign or survivors of the battle, and these men provided a nucleus of trained soldiers for a new army. The intention of the family was to make a bid for the throne based on the right of an *atheling*, or king's son, to succeed his father on the throne. King Harold's sons, Godwine, the eldest, Edmund and Magnus, were all eligible for the throne on this basis. It has been held that their mother Edith's marriage *more Danico* to the then Earl Harold disqualified them from the kingship. However, the succession of Harold 'Harefoot', son of Cnut and Aelfgifu of Northampton, in 1035 shows that such descent was not necessarily a disqualification. Not surprisingly, they appear to have had no intention of supporting *Atheling* Edgar, who had already been put aside by Harold and who had now passed into Norman captivity.[8]

The evidence for a revival by Harold's family is scarce but not entirely lacking. Countess Gytha seems to have granted land at Warrington in Devon to Abbot Sihtric of Tavistock at this time, perhaps in return for his support. This appears to have been effective, as William of Malmesbury tells us that Sihtric later became a pirate, probably indicating that he joined the raiding fleet of King Harold's sons. Abbot Ealdred of Abingdon was another supporter of Harold's family, in breach of an oath of allegiance to King William, and he later travelled abroad with them. The fact that Ealdred supported Harold's family is confirmed by the abbey's own chronicle, which connects his opposition to William specifically with that of Countess Gytha. It is even possible that it was Gytha's advice that the abbey's *thegns* listened to when they went armed to join what is termed a gathering of William's enemies. The Abingdon Chronicle places this latter event with Bishop Aethelwine's rebellion in 1071, but there is no strict chronological sequence in this source and thus no reason to place it in 1071 rather than 1067 or 1068. Indeed, it is possible that the men of the abbey's forces were on their way to Exeter when they were intercepted by Norman forces during William's offensive of winter 1068. Another of the family's supporters may have been Abbot Saewold of Bath, who fled to Flanders at the same time as they did, taking his valuable library with him. The family must also have rallied others to their cause and recruited support locally from their own lands and possibly former royal estates. It is possible that this scenario provided an occasion for the appropriation by Queen Mathilda of the wide estates of Brihtric, son of Aelfgar, which were situated in the region. If Brihtric had been among Gytha's supporters at Exeter, William may have ordered the forfeiture of his estates and presented them as a gift to his wife when he met her at Winchester in Easter 1068 for her coronation, just after his campaign against Harold's family. In addition, Orderic Vitalis records that envoys were sent from Exeter to urge other cities to join its stand and this may have been part of the family's process of rallying support. They may also have sought aid from Swein of Denmark, but, if so, none was apparently forthcoming.[9]

The opposition to William developed and fostered in this way by Harold's family during this period was not a national movement. At this stage, the prospect of Godwine, Harold's son, as king of England did not receive much support outside Harold's former earldom. Godwine was young, unproven and little known in comparison with his father. The family could probably rely on old loyalties in Wessex to provide them with support, but could not count on such support beyond its borders. Nevertheless, the rebellion in the south-west inspired by Harold's family was one of the most significant of those which occurred in William's absence.

The situation in England was very tense and confused by the end of 1067, with widespread unrest but no recognized central authority among the English. King William's control was limited largely to the south-east, and his soldiers were probably little in evidence outside an area from Kent to Hampshire and from the Channel coast to East Anglia. He himself had been absent since March 1067 and his forces had been left without his direct oversight. This situation allowed many separate rebellions to develop under their own leaders and with differing aims. By the time William returned to England in December 1067, many areas of the country were in open revolt, including Dover, the Welsh Borders and much of Northumbria, as well as the south-west. In most of these areas the uprisings were locally inspired and led by fairly minor local figures and until the return of the captive English leaders from Normandy, it was the rebellion in the south-west which provided the principal rallying point.[10]

Norman cavalry ride out to quell English unrest. (The Bayeux Tapestry – 11th Century. By special permission of the City of Bayeux)

The significance of Harold's family's stand is made clear by the fact that, despite the wide extent of these rebellions, William on his return chose to strike first against Exeter. He did so almost immediately, undertaking a difficult winter campaign early in 1068. This haste was undoubtedly because William considered this to be the greatest threat to his position. It is likely that William reached this conclusion not simply because it was indeed the most substantial threat he faced, but also because it involved the sons of his dead rival, King Harold. Although Godwine, Edmund and Magnus were still young, they were old enough to lead military forces later in 1068 and therefore already represented a potential menace to William's still insecure throne. They had refused to submit to William in 1066, unlike *Atheling* Edgar, and were obviously dangerous threats to the legitimacy of his kingship. Taking these things into account, the reason that William directed his entire army against Exeter in the depth of winter immediately on his return is readily understandable.[11]

Correspondingly, the strength of Exeter's resistance to William surely indicates something more than Orderic's statement that it arose from a desire to preserve the laws and customs of the town. This purpose would surely be much better served by a speedy submission and a request for a writ from the new king securing these customs, as in the case of London. The real reason may have been loyalty to King Harold's family; Countess Gytha was certainly present, if not also his sons, in the town during the siege. The attempts of the citizens to recruit wider support certainly speak of more serious reasons. Whatever the reason, William spent some eighteen days laying siege to the town, and a large part of his army perished in the process. The eighteen-day defence put up by the citizens demonstrates that the English *burh* was still a very effective defensive structure when properly garrisoned, despite the fashion among some for considering the Norman castle superior. Nevertheless, William's persistence paid off and the city was forced to submit, according to the Chronicle, 'because the *thegns* had betrayed them'. This may indicate that the citizens expected relief or aid from the local *thegns* which did not come. Alternatively, it may mean that some of the *thegns* who made up the garrison deserted. John of Worcester portrays the garrison as consisting of the citizens and only some *thegns*. In either case, this failure probably reflects the political and military inexperience of those directing the defence, possibly Harold's sons.[12]

Whether King Harold's sons were actually present in Exeter during the siege, escaping before the surrender as his mother did, or whether they were perhaps among those who failed to bring relief is unknown. John of Worcester mentions Gytha's escape with 'many others', and perhaps this included Harold's sons and other family, and Abbot Sihtric of Tavistock. Escape by ship down the river Exe seems most likely given the siege conditions on land and Gytha's subsequent move to Flatholme. William's swift and decisive action against Exeter had severely undermined the family's position in the south-west, and his subsequent pursuit into Cornwall compelled them to take flight overseas. Countess Gytha and other ladies, probably including Harold's daughter, Gytha, and his sister, Gunnhild, went out to the island of Flatholme in the Bristol Channel where they were relatively safe but prepared for a quick return. Despite the set-back at Exeter, King Harold's sons were not yet ready to give up and, perhaps recalling stories of their father's previous exile, they sailed to Dublin with their *huscarls* to seek aid from King Diarmait. He still ruled Dublin and commanded its mercenaries, and he welcomed them as he had their father. He and 'his princes', perhaps a reference to his son, Murchad, provided them with support, possibly in memory of their father but more likely in return for some of the family treasure. Indeed, part of this treasure, 'the battle standard of the King of the Saxons', was presented by King Diarmait to his ally Toirdelbach, King of Munster, that same year. This may have been the standard of the deceased King Edward, perhaps the Dragon of Wessex shown in the Bayeux Tapestry, as King Harold's own personal banner undoubtedly fell into Norman hands after Hastings.[13]

With Diarmait's assistance, King Harold's sons returned unexpectedly from Ireland in the summer of 1068. Their naval force, recruited in Dublin, landed at the mouth of the river Avon and ravaged the surrounding district. They then attempted to take the town of Bristol, perhaps to replace their lost base at Exeter with one closer to their new supporters in Ireland. The citizens of Bristol proved unsympathetic and they were forced to attempt to take it by storm, which suggests that they had a considerable force under their command. The citizens resisted them fiercely, perhaps fearing the same fate as Exeter when William retaliated or simply distrustful of the brothers' Hiberno-Norse mercenaries. Their assault unsuccessful, the brothers were forced to take what booty they had gathered and move down the coast to Somerset, perhaps near the mouth of the river Parret. There, Godwine held lands at nearby Nettlecombe and Langford Budville, and the Taunton mint could be raided. Again the brothers met with resistance, this time led by Eadnoth the *Staller*, who had previously served their father but had now submitted to William. In the battle which resulted, many fell on both sides, including Eadnoth and probably one of the king's sons as only two appear to have returned a year later. The brothers were apparently victorious in this battle but it did not provide the swift breakthrough or accession of support they hoped. William's decisive action at Exeter had been too effective in cowing English resistance. The surviving brothers, Godwine and perhaps Edmund, though the latter's name is nowhere recorded, returned to Ireland with their remaining forces and a considerable amount of loot. The reference to spoils in John of Worcester may reflect these events, or perhaps those of the following year as he mentions raids in Devon and Cornwall and Harold's sons were to raid that area in 1069.[14]

King Harold's sons were still not prepared to give up their attempts at the restoration of their fortunes in England. In the next year, 1069, at midsummer they secured another large fleet from Dublin, consisting of over sixty ships this time. Orderic says 'they landed first at Exeter', and if this is correct and not a confused reference to their possible earlier sojourn there this probably represents an attempt to revive their earlier success. However, the new Norman castle in the town effectively prevented any further rebellion on the part of the citizens. In addition, William's relatively lenient treatment of their rebellion in 1068 encouraged them not to risk these terms by further insurrection. The brothers then appear to have turned to raid the south coasts of Devon and Cornwall, perhaps in frustration at their failure to rouse Exeter. Domesday Book records lands laid waste there by the Irishmen of their fleet between Kingsbridge Estuary and Bigbury Bay. Similarly, waste recorded in the Lizard peninsula may also be attributable to their activities.[15]

The brothers then rounded Lands End and came ashore in the mouth of the river Taw in north Devon. They laid waste the countryside around Barnstable and moved inland, perhaps again heading for Godwine's estates at Nettlecombe and Langford Budville near Milverton in Somerset. However, the lack of any opposition so far on this trip appears to have made the brothers incautious, and they were caught out by a large Norman force under Count Brian. In the battle or series of encounters that followed, most of the brothers' best men were slain, as many as 1,700 according to William of Jumieges and including a number of *thegns*, and only a small force escaped at nightfall to return to Ireland.[16]

This disaster finally put an end to the immediate attempts by King Harold's sons to reclaim the English throne. They were unable to recruit further mercenary forces, perhaps because their resources of treasure were running out, but principally because of their lack of success to date, and especially in 1069. It was probably at this time that Countess Gytha and her ladies finally abandoned their refuge on Flatholme and sought refuge at St Omer in Flanders. King Harold's dynasty had abandoned its hopes of regaining the throne directly and, as circumstances were to prove, finally.[17]

Many have seen the family's hopes as foolish, and the actions of King Harold's sons as irrelevant. However, England during the period 1067–9 was in chaos and the whole country seethed with rebellion. During this time, several claimants to the throne competed for support, including *Atheling* Edgar, Earls Edwin and Morcar, using Harold's son by Aldithat, Swein of Denmark, and William himself. Therefore, it was not unreasonable for King Harold's sons also to enter this contest, and to feel that they had as good a chance as any of success. The failure even to come near to achieving their aim was due in the main to William's decisive reaction to the very real threat they posed. His campaign in the south-west decisively nipped their schemes in the bud. Subsequently, they were forced to base themselves abroad and use mercenary troops, making it difficult for them to win any real support in England. Another significant factor was their failure to win the support of their cousin, Swein of Denmark, who was clearly intent on pursuing his own claim to the throne rather than supporting that of his cousins. The fact that many of Harold's key supporters had fallen at Hastings and that the Normans controlled a large part of the family lands in the south-east severely handicapped them. The brothers inexperience in warfare was also a contributory factor to their failure, although the long defence of Exeter and their victory over Eadnoth suggest this was not decisive. Perhaps if either Gyrth or Leofwine, with their greater authority and experience, had survived the battle at Hastings things might have been different.[18]

The brothers' bid for the throne was over, but this was not the end of the story. A considerable amount is known about the fate of the remnants of King Harold's family after their final withdrawal from England in 1069. The elderly Countess Gytha, with Harold's sister, Gunnhild, probably settled in quiet retirement at St Omer in Flanders, where Count Baldwin VI apparently received them charitably as relatives of his aunt Judith and in spite of their rivalry with his brother-in-law, William of Normandy. Countess Gytha's remaining treasure may have helped to persuade Baldwin to provide them with refuge. Thereafter, the royal ladies performed good works, and the death of the king's sister, Gunnhild, was recorded at Bruges in 1087. She bequeathed a psalter with Anglo-Saxon glosses to St Donation's in Bruges and this book, known as 'Gunnhild's Psalter', was still there in the sixteenth century. She also donated a collection of religious relics to St Donation's, most notably the mantle of St Bridget. A copy of Aelfric's works donated to St Bertin's may, perhaps, have been a legacy of Countess Gytha.[19]

It seems likely that King Harold's sons escorted these ladies to Flanders, as it would have been rather risky for them to navigate the Norman controlled Channel alone. Although Baldwin's hospitality was undoubtedly extended to the ladies of Harold's family, it might seem unlikely that he would also provide refuge for Harold's sons. After all, he had close ties with King William, and Harold had also been responsible for the death of his aunt Judith's husband. It is possible that Baldwin intended to use them as a form of insurance should his alliance with William fail. It should be recalled that the Flemish counts had a long history of hostile relations with England, and William, of course, was now King of England. If this assumption is accurate, then the presence of these exiles must have caused King William considerable unease. Indeed, the arrival of this group in Flanders, perhaps in late 1069 or early 1070, may have prompted William to depose Bishop Aethelric of Sussex on 24 May 1070, in case he became a fifth column in support of their return. He was, after all, a relative of the family and based in the ancient family heartland just across the Channel from them. Therefore, it became imperative to remove him for political reasons. It seems likely that this was the reason for Papal concern about this particular deposition, as expressed in a number of later Papal letters. On 16 July 1070 Baldwin VI died and a succession dispute broke out between his infant sons, supported by King William, and his brother, Robert the Frisian. This dispute ended on 22 February 1071 at the battle of Cassel, the victory falling to William's enemy, Robert, who became the uncontested Count of Flanders. The threat of a descent by Harold's sons on Sussex from a hostile Flanders may have contributed to the unusual organization of the Norman castellanries in the Sussex rapes.[20]

It was probably from Flanders, where they had accompanied or followed the ladies of the family, that King Harold's sons, Godwine and Edmund, journeyed to the court of their cousin, Swein of Denmark, accompanied by their sister, Gytha. This is recorded by Saxo Grammaticus, who, although writing much later, seems to portray a not improbable situation and whose account is perhaps confirmed by two independent sources. The latter record an embassy to Denmark by Godwine the younger, mistakenly identified as Harold's brother rather than his son, which sought King Swein's aid against William. The brothers may have hoped that their arrival in Denmark would finally secure Swein's backing for their restoration. If so, they were swiftly disillusioned, as Swein's own recent invasions of England had proved fairly disastrous and he was in no hurry to repeat them. Thereafter, Swein's death in 1074 or

1076 ushered in a period of confusion, which was not fully resolved until well into the next century. The final fate of Godwine and Edmund is unknown, but Gytha, according to later Scandinavian sources, was sent by Swein to marry the Russian Prince of Smolensk, Vladimir *Monomakh*. The date of this event is unclear but it probably occurred in 1074 or 1075. It has been objected that no Russian source records the name of Vladimir's first wife and Vladimir's own testament records her only as the mother of his son, George. However, this is not unusual and many women are unnamed in Russian sources, including Vladimir's own Byzantine mother, and the fact of the marriage appears to be generally accepted.[21]

Prince Vladimir was then around twenty-one years old and ruler of the city of Smolensk in western Russia. He held an important but not key position in the complex hierarchy of Russian princes. At this time, Russia consisted of a series of principalities each based on a major city and each ruled by a member of the dynasty of St Vladimir. The principalities were arranged in a rough hierarchy with Kiev at the summit, usually ruled by the senior prince. Vladimir probably welcomed his marriage as providing him with a royal connection. It also brought with it an alliance with the Danes, which might prove very useful in dissuading the neighbouring Poles from invading Russia.[22]

The marriage proved fruitful and in 1076 Msistislav, the first of a number of sons, was born to Gytha in Novgorod. Two years later, Vladimir was promoted to the position of Prince of Chernigov, following the expulsion of his cousin, Oleg, from that city. He successfully ruled this, the second city in Russia and an important bastion, for some sixteen years, defending it against a series of attacks by the steppe nomads. Finally, in 1094, he was expelled by Oleg with the aid of nomad allies and he moved to his father's city of Pereyaslavl. It is likely that Gytha accompanied her husband throughout this period and shared his successes and failures. She appears to have provided him with a large number of children, perhaps as many as eight sons and three daughters. In this respect, Gytha appears to have been as fruitful as her mother, Edith 'Swan-neck', and her grandmother and namesake, Gytha.[23]

Gytha's life as a Russian princess may have been relatively pleasant. Although Russia was in many ways a strange land and very different from her own England, some things were familiar. A testament written by Vladimir himself records a great deal about the family. This relates that Vladimir's father understood five languages, one of which must have been Norse, since Vladimir's grandmother was a Swedish princess. This implies that Gytha and her husband both spoke Norse and so were able to converse with ease. In addition, Vladimir was a great warrior and hunter very much in the mould of Harold, Gytha's own father. He was a devout Christian and a founder of churches in a number of Russian cities. He ruled in a similar fashion to an English king through councils, courts and military force. He was very wealthy even by English standards, and Gytha would have lived in some style. He appears to have had very strong feelings for his family, although these are usually only expressed towards his brothers and sons. Thus he records Gytha's death, though not her name, and among the advice he offers to his sons is 'Love your wives, but grant them no power over you'. This perhaps sums up their relationship.[24]

Sadly, Gytha died on 7 May 1107 before her husband attained the pinnacle of his career by becoming Grand Prince of Kiev in 1113. The eldest of her sons, Msistislav, born in Novgorod in 1076, was widely known in the Norse world by her father's name, Harold. He went on to succeed his father as Grand Prince of Kiev in 1125, ruling the city until his own death in 1132. This Russian Harold, according to Norse sources, had a daughter called Ingibiorg, who later married Cnut *Lavard* of Denmark and bore him a son who became King Valdemar I of Denmark, from whom the current queens of both Denmark and Great Britain are ultimately descended. In this way, the blood of King Harold Godwineson, runs again in the veins of the rulers of England.[25]

Other members of King Harold's family also survived the Conquest. Harold, his son by Queen Alditha, born early in 1067 at Chester, and named after his dead father, probably became a pawn in the political struggles against William after 1066. This young Harold was probably used by his uncles, Earls Edwin and Morcar, as a threat to King William in their attempts to secure their own position in England. Although this is not stated in any of the sources, it is probable that when Edwin and Morcar, disappointed with William's treatment of them, rebelled in 1068 and again in 1069, they used the potent threat of young Harold's claim to the kingdom against William. This was also probably the reason for the failure of Edwin and Morcar to join the other English rebels until 1071, when it was too late. The others supported *Atheling* Edgar as king, but the northern earls wanted their young nephew Harold on the throne. The response to this threat was William's dramatic winter march across the Pennines in 1069–70 to occupy Chester, and finally to crush the two earls in a battle near Stafford. As a result, Harold and his mother fled, probably to Dublin, with which, as a former wife of Gruffydd of Wales, she would have been familiar. Ultimately, the young Harold apparently journeyed to Norway, where William of Malmesbury plausibly suggests that he was well received by Olaf Haraldsson, in return for the merciful treatment he himself had earlier received from King Harold, after Stamford Bridge. Young Harold is next found among the followers of King Magnus Olafsson off the Isle of Anglesey in 1098 when a battle was fought against the Norman earls of Shrewsbury and Chester, during which, by one of history's ironies, Earl Hugh of Shrewsbury was struck from a distance with a fatal arrow. Thereafter, young Harold disappears from the records.[26]

King Harold's remaining daughter, Gunnhild, seems to have been stranded in England at the time of the Conquest and she is first recorded in the *Vita Wulfstani* as a nun at Wilton. She was perhaps already there in 1066, as part of her education, like her aunt Queen Edith. Initially, she remained there as a refugee from the Normans, using the protection afforded to those who had taken the veil as her safeguard. She shared her comfortable confinement there with another royal lady, Edith, the daughter of Malcolm and St Margaret of Scotland and the niece of *Atheling* Edgar. Subsequently, she was probably virtually imprisoned there in order to prevent her posing a threat to King William by marrying a rival and thus transmitting a claim to the throne. Indeed, she became the centre of just such a controversy after King William's death. In August 1093, in the reign of William *Rufus*, in her late thirties or forties, Gunnhild was abducted by Alan the Red, Earl of Richmond. She lived with Earl Alan, sinfully according to Anselm, until his death soon after, perhaps in late 1093 or early 1094. Perhaps in an attempt to preserve her freedom, she then sought to marry the dead earl's brother and successor, Alan the Black.[27]

The main evidence for this episode comes from two letters written to Gunnhild by Anselm, Archbishop of Canterbury, at some time after his consecration on 4 December 1093. According to the first of these, Gunnhild, who was now living with Alan the Red, claimed she was not bound to her position as a nun because she had never made a formal profession before a bishop, and that a promise made to her of an abbacy had not been honoured. This argument would have been accepted by Archbishop Lanfranc, Anselm's predecessor, and perhaps provides confirmation of her status as a refugee later forced to remain at Wilton rather than a nun. Anselm accepted these facts, but because of his stricter views he urged her to return to the cloister, although she was no longer a virgin. He suggested that Alan the Red would repudiate her. In spite of its stern message, his letter is written in tenderness to an errant princess and in it Anselm refers to Gunnhild as his 'dearest and most longed for daughter'. He had already met her, probably when he visited England in 1086, and developed a close platonic relationship with her. In a subsequent letter following Alan the Red's death, when Gunnhild had taken up with Alan the Black, Anselm predicted that his death also would follow if she remained with him. Anselm was now aware that Gunnhild had worn the veil willingly and, as a result, his second letter is much colder in tone, as he attempts to disgust Gunnhild with the world and compel her to return to the cloister, but it nevertheless remains respectful.[28]

This episode indicates Gunnhild's continued status and importance despite the passage of nearly thirty years since King Harold's death and the long campaign of villification directed against the latter. The Breton earls desired links with her, probably to legitimize their usurpation of her mother's lands in the Midlands. The Norman kings attempted to keep her in seclusion for fear of her potential threat as an heiress, not merely of these lands, but of a kingdom. The head of the English Church behaved with the respect due to her nobility and royal lineage even when offended by her conduct.[29]

Two other relatives of King Harold remain to be considered, both of whom spent most of their lives in prison. Wulfnoth, his younger brother, had been taken hostage as a boy aged around fifteen, and imprisoned in Normandy. He was to suffer greatly, spending the rest of his life in prison. Harold had failed in his attempt to have him released in 1064, and although his release was ordered by a dying King William in 1087, he was instead taken to England by King William II *Rufus* and imprisoned in Winchester. The latter probably considered his own hold on the English throne too weak to permit Wulfnoth, brother of the last Anglo-Saxon king, to be released to provide a focus of dissent. Therefore, Wulfnoth languished in captivity, produced on occasion for inspection, until his death, an old man of fifty-eight, in 1094 at Winchester. The prior of the cathedral there, Godfrey of Cambrai, wrote a flattering but rather sad epitaph for him. He refers to him as 'Earl', reflecting the dignity of his lineage rather than his actual status:

> The nobility of his forebears, his simple manners,
> His sound views and honourable judgements,
> The strength of his body and the fire of his intellect,
> All these glorify the Earl Wulfnoth,
> Exile, prison, darkness, inclosure, chains,
> Receive the boy and forsake the old man,
> Caught up in human bonds he bore them patiently,
> Bound even more closely in service to God.[31]

King Harold's son Ulf also ended up in Norman custody. It has been suggested that he was another son of Harold and Queen Alditha, perhaps a twin with young Harold, but this seems unlikely and there certainly exists no evidence for it. It is more likely that he was another son of Harold and Edith, and if this is the case he would have been a youth, aged somewhere between thirteen and nineteen in 1066. This makes it more feasible that he could have been captured separately from his brothers, perhaps during the chaotic period immediately after Hastings, and taken to Normandy. Whatever the case, he too languished in prison during William's reign but was to prove more fortunate than his uncle Wulfnoth. When released in 1087, as part of the dying King William's amnesty, he fell into the hands of Robert 'Curthose', who as Duke of Normandy and excluded from the English throne had no fears about Ulf's claim. He not only released Ulf, but knighted him as well, after which he also departs from the pages of history.[32]

Thus in spite of the fall of King Harold and his brothers at Hastings, his remaining family, scattered and increasingly powerless as they were, remained a real and dangerous threat to William's occupation of the English throne. This was particularly the case in the period 1067–8, when they threatened to develop a rival power base in south-west England. A fearful William dealt ruthlessly with this resistance and thereafter, the direct influence of the family gradually declined. However, although King William's position in England was militarily secure by around 1070 and remained so in spite of further external threats, notably from the Danes in 1086, the legitimacy of his dynasty remained in a sense uncertain. Thus members of King Harold's family, even those in close custody of one form or another, remained a real threat and possible focus of opposition not only to King William I but also to his son and successor, William II. This surely is testimony to the insecurity of the original Norman claim to the throne and perhaps also to its lack of foundation. Indeed, it was only really in 1100 when William's younger son, Henry I, married Edith, daughter of St Margaret of Scotland, that the Norman hold on the throne gained wide acceptance among the English. She was a niece of *Atheling* Edgar of 'the true royal line of England', and brought with her the legitimacy bestowed by descent from King Alfred. This legitimacy in the end neither King Harold's descendants nor his Norman conquerors could match.[33]

CONCLUSION

Harold Godwineson was a remarkable man by any standards. He began his career with a number of important advantages. He was the second son of Earl Godwine of Wessex, the brother-in-law of King Edward of England, and Earl of East Anglia by the age of twenty-five. This early eminence had been secured for him as a direct result of his father's assiduous career in royal service first to Cnut and then to Edward. Therefore, he had witnessed the rewards of such service and benefited directly from it and this made a strong impression on him.

This impression would be reinforced by the events of 1051–2, when his father, after a period of increasing tension and disputes, usually involving his eldest son, Swein, found himself in direct conflict with the king. The disastrous results of this conflict, although soon overturned, convinced Harold to avoid any such conflict in the future. When the deaths of his elder brother and his father placed Harold at the head of his family and in the earldom of Wessex, he sought to minimize any future tensions and to make himself indispensable to King Edward.

As Harold had anticipated, his loyal service to Edward brought immense rewards in its wake. Harold himself became the king's lieutenant, and he and his family gained lands and position without equal. At the same time, Harold's service produced benefits for the king through a long period of relative peace and stability at home and victory against his enemies abroad. In the years from 1053 to 1066, when Earl Harold and King Edward worked together, there were only three rebellions against the king's peace, all of which were eventually resolved without open conflict and with Harold's assistance. In a carefully planned and conducted campaign, Harold completely crushed Gruffydd, the most powerful and most dangerous Welsh prince of the period. These actions secured the peace of England and cemented Harold's bond to the king. In 1065 he sacrificed his brother Tosti for the greater benefit of his family and of the kingdom, and thus avoided a bloody civil war. In contrast, his father, in similar circumstances, had supported Swein against the king and in doing so had almost brought about the ruin of the family in 1051.

In this way, Harold's career in royal service proved immensely rewarding and might have continued so under 'King Edgar' had he not visited Normandy in 1064. This visit revealed to Harold the ruthless ambition and dangerous claims to the throne of England of William of Normandy, the knowledge of which transformed Harold's intentions and brought him to consider for the first time the possibility of his own succession to the throne. Then, as King Edward's health ebbed away in late 1065, he contemplated the dangers of the succession of the youthful, weak and inexperienced *Atheling* Edgar. This boy could not be expected to defend the kingdom effectively and Harold therefore decided to attempt to ascend the throne himself.

It was now that Harold's long period of royal service proved really indispensable. He was by now so widely recognized as a royal deputy that many had no difficulty in accepting his rise to the throne. The great men whose support was essential to this process were either Harold's relations or his allies. Others who were not so convinced, Harold won over, using his remarkable powers of persuasion. The extent of his own lands and authority as Earl of Wessex meant that he would be completely familiar and at ease with governing England.

In his occupation of the throne, Harold was a usurper because he had put aside the rights of *Atheling* Edgar, but this action appears to have met with little opposition from the English in stark contrast to William's later rule. Indeed, Harold proved a very capable king despite the difficult circumstances he faced as a result of foreign invasions and his own lack of legitimacy. He was successful in government and victorious in war. Undaunted by two major foreign invasions in the space of one month, he completely defeated the great warrior Harald *Hardradi* of Norway, and was within an ace of defeating William of Normandy before his death on 14 October 1066 at Hastings.

Harold's career had been an astonishing success, but ultimately it ended in failure. If he had won at Hastings it seems likely that he would have been remembered as one of England's most successful kings. Instead, he was consigned to the footnotes of history as a supporting player in William of Normandy's triumph. With these antipodes of success and failure – how can we judge Harold?

In contemporary terms, Harold had been judged by God. The disastrous result of the battle of Hastings and his own death therein proved beyond doubt to his contemporaries that God had found him wanting. This fate must have been visited on Harold as a punishment for his sins. The search for the sin which brought about this dreadful divine retribution led naturally to the breach of his holy oath to William. Clearly, Harold had brought this destruction on himself by his failure to keep his oath once he had sworn it. This was the story which would be repeated in later medieval sources.

In modern terms, the position is less clear but the causes of Harold's fall have usually been sought in two main areas. Firstly, Harold usurped the throne in opposition to William, King Edward's chosen successor, and he was therefore unable to hold it against the true heir and the appeal of his natural right. Secondly, Harold was beaten at Hastings by a better man leading a better army.

In 1066 the true heir to the kingdom of England was in fact *Atheling* Edgar and none of the three contenders of 1066 had any legitimate claim. Harold succeeded to the throne because he had a power base and wide support in England and because he was able to convince the leading men to promote him in preference to Edgar. Harald of Norway launched an invasion in order to seize the throne by force, as had Swein and Cnut before him, but with less success against Harold. William had no true claim, no support and no power in England. Instead, he, like Harald of Norway, launched an aggressive war in order to claim the crown after failing to coerce Harold into helping him. These three men contended for a prize which should have been Edgar's.

Harold defeated his Norwegian namesake at Stamford Bridge then fought William for the crown at Hastings in a long and bloody battle. It was neither a walkover won by the use of cavalry against infantry nor a triumph of superior Norman training or tactics. A one-sided conflict like that would have been over much earlier in the day. It was in fact a tough battle between two very evenly matched armies, both led by excellent commanders. To suggest otherwise would not only reduce Harold's status but lessen William's achievement in staging his invasion, which was in fact immense. In these circumstances, it was naturally a long and hard battle and in the end only the element of chance could finally resolve it.

It was this element of chance which ultimately sealed Harold's fate and turned his success into failure. In 1064 Harold took the oath to William to ensure his own freedom and he later broke it. In 1065 he helped to ensure the exile of Tosti and a year later brought about his death in battle. In 1066 he ascended to the English throne, putting aside Edgar, the rightful heir. He then chose to defend his new kingdom against Harald and William in battle. All of these actions and decisions have been considered with hindsight as causes of Harold's downfall but all were, I would argue, the correct decisions for him to make at the time.

The truth is that Harold was an extraordinary man who was faced with an extraordinary crisis in autumn 1066. He faced this unprecedented crisis undaunted, and came within inches of surmounting it. In the end, he was simply overwhelmed by events and found that his luck deserted him at the very last. William's victory over Harold was indeed a tremendous feat but it was one in which luck played a significant part.

The remarkable nature of Harold's achievement is confirmed by the inability of his family after his death to play a major role in influencing subsequent events. They always represented a danger to his successors, but it was one which they were unable to realise without Harold's personal abilities.

THE MONK AETHELRIC

Aethelric the monk of Christ Church, Canterbury, who played a significant role in the events leading up to the great crisis of 1051–2, is a mysterious figure. He is only mentioned in one source, the *Vita Eadwardi*, but because this is a Godwine family tract and he is stated to be related to Godwine, its facts may perhaps be trusted. In this source, the exact nature of his relationship to Godwine is not made clear but it seems not to have been very close. He was perhaps a cousin rather than a nephew or grandson, for example. He had been a monk at Christ Church since childhood, but was nevertheless a good administrator, wise in the ways of the world. In an attempt to preserve control of their archbishopric, the other monks elected him to the office, probably as the most suitable candidate among them. In spite of the support of Aethelric's relative Earl Godwine, the scheme failed in the face of opposition from King Edward, who had his own candidate in mind. Thereafter, Aethelric disappears from the sources as suddenly as he had appeared. He has been assumed to be an unknown monk who made only this one brief appearance on the stage of history.[1]

However, there exists the possibility that this Aethelric is, in fact, the same as the Aethelric, also a monk of Christ Church, who was appointed Bishop of Sussex by King Edward in 1057, and who was consecrated to that see by Archbishop Stigand in 1058. The name of the two men is the same, although it is written 'Aelric', the usual Continental variant of Aethelric, by the Flemish author of the *Vita Eadwardi*. In this context, it should be noted that the Continental scribes of Domesday Book also record the Bishop of Sussex himself as 'Alric'. However, the name is a common one, and not sufficient to prove the identity of the two even given their common status as Christ Church monks. There does exist other evidence, though, which points strongly towards this.[2]

Aethelric, Bishop of Sussex, was deposed by King William at a synod on 24 May 1070 for unstated reasons and unjustly, according to a number of sources. It has been suggested that his deposition resulted from the fact that Archbishop Stigand had consecrated him but Siward, Bishop of Rochester, who was also consecrated by Stigand, retained his bishopric without incident until his death in 1075. If the Bishop of Sussex was the same man as Aethelric the monk of Christ Church, he could have been deposed because of his family relationship to King Harold. Such a purely political deposition would be uncanonical and would explain the letter written to Archbishop Lanfranc by Pope Alexander II complaining that the case against Aethelric was defective and that he should be reinstated and tried canonically. The Pope's request was ignored, and Aethelric languished in prison in Marlborough instead. Pope Alexander II may have been referring to Aethelric again in a further letter, in which he inquired anxiously about the fate of an imprisoned bishop whose liberation he had ordered. If this interpretation of the real political background to Aethelric's deposition is correct, it would explain why he was not restored but instead had his deposition confirmed at an English Church council held under William in Winchester at Easter 1076.[3]

A more solid link between the two men is provided by the report of a trial on Penenden Heath in Kent, in around 1072 or 1075/6. Aethelric, the former bishop of Sussex, 'a man of great age and very wise in the law of the land . . . was brought to the trial in a wagon', to explain ancient legal practice. If this Aethelric was the same man as had been considered mature enough to be proposed as a candidate for the archbishopric in 1050–1, then he would certainly be 'a great age' some twenty or so years later. The knowledge of the laws which he was required to explain at Penenden Heath also fits well with Aethelric, described as a 'man active in secular business' by the *Vita Eadwardi* in 1050–1. In addition, as the business in dispute at Penenden concerned Canterbury lands appropriated by Odo of Bayeux, Earl of Kent, the presence of Aethelric would be particularly apt and he may have provided evidence of Canterbury's ownership as well as legal advice.[4]

It would seem likely from this information that the two men were, in fact, one and the same. Although disappointed in his search for promotion in 1050–1, the monk Aethelric nevertheless bided his time. Subsequently, he was able to persuade King Edward to appoint him Bishop of Sussex, through the influence either of Archbishop Stigand, or of his relative Earl Harold. This area was, after all, the home territory of the family and an entirely suitable position for him, if lacking in the wealth of the archbishopric. He probably served in this position efficiently but without notice in the Chronicles until 1066, but after the conquest his relationship to King Harold became an embarrassment. Perhaps fearing his involvement in an attempt at a family restoration in 1070, King William deposed and imprisoned him. William cloaked his political actions, as always when dealing with the Church, in a religious guise, but in this case a patently thin one, which did not satisfy Pope Alexander in the least.

If accepted, this relationship can also provide an important key to one of the great puzzles surrounding the Norman Conquest. There apparently exists no contemporary English account describing Harold's visit to Normandy in 1064 or considering the reasons behind it. If Aethelric, the candidate for the archbishopric, is the same person as the later bishop of Sussex then we may have a contemporary source – Eadmer of Canterbury's later account of Harold's visit to Normandy. Eadmer himself informs us that he consulted Bishop Aethelric of Sussex when composing his life of St Dunstan. Therefore, it is possible that Aethelric was also the source of Eadmer's information on Harold's visit to Normandy. If so then his statement that its purpose was to free family hostages should perhaps carry considerable weight as the information came from a source within the family itself.[5]

THE ENGLISH EARLDOMS UNDER KING EDWARD

The English office of earl originated from that of the *ealdorman* of King Alfred's time, who was responsible for a single shire. The extent of the authority of these *ealdormen* grew with the expansion of Wessex and with the increasing sophistication of government, and by King Aethelred's time many *ealdormen* controlled areas which included several shires. This tendency continued under Cnut and Edward when, under Scandinavian influence, these men first began to be called earls.[1]

The earls were the leading men of the kingdom, who enjoyed viceregal powers in local areas in return for providing support to the king. The success or otherwise of their relationship with the king and of their interrelations with each other formed the basis of the politics of King Edward's reign.

In order to fully understand these relationships, it is important to know the extent of the earldoms held by these men and their relative size and location. Unfortunately, this is an extremely difficult task at this period because of the relative paucity of the records. Table 1, overleaf, summarizes what little firm evidence exists as to the extent and location of the authority of King Edward's earls, and on the basis of this evidence I have attempted to reconstruct the outlines of the English earldoms. This must remain speculative in many of its details, but nevertheless can shed considerable light on the background to King Edward's reign. The three great earls inherited by Edward from Cnut, namely Godwine, Leofric and Siward, and their successors will be considered first, and thereafter Edward's new earls.

NORTHUMBRIA

In 1042 Earl Siward certainly held authority both in Yorkshire and the rest of Northumbria to the north, as reflected by his role in the invasion of Scotland in 1054. This position is further confirmed by Gospatric's writ, which refers to Siward's authority in Cumbria also. It is known that Siward also held authority in Huntingdonshire sometime between 1050 and 1052, but since this county was held by Harold earlier in 1051, it seems likely that he governed this area only after the latter's exile in 1051. The extent of the later authority of Tosti and Morcar, as recorded below, may imply that Siward also controlled Lincolnshire, Derbyshire, Nottinghamshire and

Table 1: The Earldoms of King Edward's Reign

	Shire	Earl	Dating	Source
1.	Kent	Godwine	*c.* 1042–50	*ASW*, 38
		"	1051	*JW* 1051
		"	1051	*ASC* D 1051
		Harold	*c.* 1053–66	*ASW*, 35 and 39
2.	Sussex	Godwine	1051	*JW* 1051
3.	Surrey	Harold	*c.* 1053–66	*ASW*, 40–2
4.	Hampshire	Godwine	*c.* 1047–52	*A-S Charters*, No. CVII
		"	*c.* 1052–3	*ASW*, 111
		Harold	*c.* 1053–66	*ASW*, 85 and *A-S Charters*, No. CXIV
5.	Berkshire	Godwine	*c.* 1045–48	*ASW*, 3
		Swein	1051	*JW* 1051
		Harold	*c.* 1053–66	*ASW*, 5
6.	Wiltshire	[No data]		
7.	Dorset	Odda	1051	*ASC* E 1051
		Harold	*c.* 1053–66	*ASW*, 1 and 2
		"	Pre-1066?	*DB*, 1, 8
8.	Somerset	Swein	1051	*JW* 1051
		Odda	1051	*ASC* E 1051
		Harold	*c.* 1060–6	*ASW*, 64–70
9.	Devon	Godwine	*c.* 1045–46	*A-S Charters*, No. CV
		Odda	1051	*ASC* E 1051
		Harold	*c.* 1060–6	*ASW*, 120
10.	Cornwall	Odda	1051	*ASC* E 1051
11.	Middlesex	Leofwine	*c.* 1057–66	*ASW*, 88 and 89
		Harold?	*c.* 1065–6	*ASW*, 98
12.	Hertfordshire	Beorn	*c.* 1045–9	*ASW*, 78 and 79
		Leofwine	*c.* 1057–66	*ASW*, 90 and 91
13.	Buckinghamshire	[No data]		
14.	Oxfordshire	Swein	1051	*JW* 1051
		Ralph	*c.* 1053–7	*ASW*, 55
		Gyrth	*c.* 1057–66	*ASW*, 95, 103, 104
		Aelfgar	Pre-1062?	*DB*, B1
15.	Gloucestershire	Swein	1051	*JW* 1051
		Harold	*c.* 1062	*ASW*, 115
		"	Pre-1066?	*DB*, B1
16.	Worcestershire	Leofric	*c.* 1042	*A-S Charters*, No. XCIV
		"	*c.* 1051–2	*A-S Charters*, Nos CXI and CXII
		Aelfgar	*c.* 1062	*ASW*, 115–17
		Edwin	Pre-1066?	*DB*, C1
17.	Herefordshire	Swein	1043–6	*A-S Charters*, No. XCIX
		"	1051	*JW* 1051
		"	1051	*ASC* E 1051
		Ralph	1055	*ASC* C/D 1055
		Harold	*c.* 1057–66	*ASW*, 49 and 50
		"	Pre-1066?	*DB*, C12
18.	Cambridgeshire	Harold	1051	*JW* 1051
19.	Huntingdonshire	Harold	1051	*JW* 1051
		Siward	*c.* 1050–2	*ASW*, 59
20.	Bedfordshire	[No data]		
21.	Northamptonshire	Tosti	*c.* 1055–65	*ASW*, 62
22.	Leicestershire	[No data]		
23.	Warwickshire	Aelfgar	*c.* 1062	*ASW*, 115–17

	Shire	Earl	Dating	Source
		Edwin	Pre–1066?	*DB*, 1, 6
24.	Staffordshire	Edwin	*c.* 1065–6	*ASW*, 96
25.	Shropshire	Edwin	Pre–1066?	*DB*, 4, 1, 1
26.	Cheshire	Edwin	Pre–1066?	*DB*, S1
27.	Derbyshire	[No data]		
28.	Nottinghamshire	Tosti	*c.* 1060–5	*ASW*, 119
29.	Rutland	[No data]		
30.	Yorkshire	Tosti	*c.* 1060–5	*ASW*, 7 and 119
		"	1065	*ASC* C/D/E 1065
31.	Lincolnshire	Morcar	Pre–1066?	*DB*, T4
32.	Essex	Harold	1051	*JW* 1051
		"	*c.* 1052–3	*ASW*, 84
33.	Norfolk &	Harold	*c.* 1044–7	*ASW*, 13 and 14
	Suffolk	"	1051	*JW* 1051
		Aelfgar	*c.* 1051–2	*ASW*, 15–18
		"	*c.* 1053–7	*ASW*, 18–22
		Gyrth	*c.* 1065–6	*ASW*, 23–5

Northamptonshire, but although possible, this is not certain. He may have gained Northamptonshire, like Huntingdonshire, only after Harold's exile in 1051.[2]

In 1055 the Chronicle states that Tosti succeeded to Siward's earldom and it is known that Tosti's authority encompassed not only Yorkshire and Northumbria, but also Nottinghamshire and Northamptonshire. In addition, the Chronicle account of the rebellion against Tosti's rule in 1065 speaks of the insurgent Northumbrians and Yorkshiremen being joined by the men of Nottinghamshire, Derbyshire and Lincolnshire, surely an indication that Tosti's earldom extended to these shires. It might be argued that these three shires were part of Edwin's earldom, but the Chronicle clearly distinguishes them by saying that Edwin came to meet his brother and the men of these shires with the men of *his* earldom, which could not therefore encompass these shires. The *Vita Eadwardi* confirms Tosti's larger influence when it speaks of 'many slaughtered in the cities of York and Lincoln' during the rebellion against his rule. Thereafter, the rebels ravaged Northamptonshire, also held by Tosti, in order to bring home their opposition to his rule.[3]

In 1065 Earl Morcar succeeded to Tosti's authority, his rule extending certainly to Northumbria, Yorkshire and Lincolnshire. Morcar's role in the defence of York in 1066 indicates his authority there although Simeon of Durham suggests that he allowed Oswulf to deputize for him in Northumbria itself. Morcar likewise defended Lincolnshire against Tosti's attack in 1066, though he was assisted in this by his brother, Edwin. Although we cannot be certain, it seems likely that he also controlled Nottinghamshire and Derbyshire, though not apparently Northamptonshire, which perhaps fell to Earl Waltheof probably in 1066, when King Harold may have appointed him earl with authority in this area.[4]

MERCIA

In 1042 Earl Leofric probably held authority in Western Mercia with which his predecessors, Eadric *Streona* and Leofwine, appear to have been associated. The area he controlled certainly included a portion of the Welsh March as his brother Edwin was slain by the Welsh in 1039. It is clear that he did not control Herefordshire, which remained in other hands throughout this period. However, it seems that by 1055, if not before, Leofric controlled the rest of the Welsh border shires, as his son, Aelfgar, singled out Hereford for attack rather than oppose his father elsewhere. There is firm evidence that he controlled Worcestershire and, judging from the area governed by his successors, noted below, it seems likely that he also controlled Cheshire, Shropshire, Staffordshire, Warwickshire and possibly Leicestershire.[5]

The Chronicle records in 1057 that Aelfgar succeeded to the earldom that his father had held. This indicates that his authority extended over an area similar to that of his father and his authority over Worcestershire and Warwickshire, at least, is confirmed by the sources. Again, as his successor, Edwin, inherited his authority, it seems likely that Aelfgar also held Cheshire, Shropshire, Staffordshire and possibly Leicestershire. The possibility that Aelfgar held some authority in Oxfordshire will be discussed below.[6]

No source records Earl Edwin's succession to his father, but the extent of his authority is better reported. Thus we know from Domesday Book and elsewhere that Edwin's earldom included Cheshire, Shropshire, Staffordshire, Warwickshire, Worcestershire and possibly Leicestershire. In addition, the account of King William's reactions to the rebellions led by Earls Edwin and Morcar show him subduing them by constructing a castle at Warwick in 1068 and defeating their forces at Stafford the following year.[7]

WESSEX

In 1042 Earl Godwine certainly controlled a large area of southern England including Kent, Sussex and the region of Wessex incorporating, certainly, Hampshire, Devon and Berkshire, possibly Surrey and Wiltshire, and perhaps Somerset, Dorset and Cornwall. The dispute at Dover in 1051 confirms Kent as part of Godwine's earldom and the fact that he drew the support for his restoration in 1052 from Kent, Sussex and Surrey establishes his strong links with the area. The possible diminution of Godwine's area of authority in favour of his eldest son, Swein, will be discussed below.[8]

The exile of Earl Godwine in 1051 brought his earldom into King Edward's hands and the latter subsequently granted the shires of Somerset, Dorset, Devon and Cornwall to his kinsman Earl Odda. On his restoration in 1052 Earl Godwine was returned his earldom 'as fully and completely' as he had held it before. This seems to imply that Earl Odda lost the south-western shires, which were presumably returned to Earl Godwine and were certainly held by his successor Harold, though it is just possible that the latter may have gained them after Earl Odda's death in 1056.[9]

In 1053 Harold succeeded to his father's earldom, which certainly included Kent, Surrey, Hampshire, Berkshire, Dorset, Somerset and Devon and probably Sussex, Wiltshire and Cornwall. This earldom was extended in 1057 on the death of Earl Ralph, when Harold added the shires of Gloucester and Hereford to those covered by his authority. It appears that Harold retained this entire earldom in his own hands until he became king, when it provided him with a secure base for his rule.[10]

This discussion of the three main earldoms indicates a fairly clear pattern of succession to these earldoms, with only minor alterations or amendments. This leaves only a fairly narrow region from East Anglia to the Severn estuary and the Welsh border available for the new earls created by Edward. Allocating the few shires in this region to the new earls in a way which matches the established facts is a more difficult task. In view of the sparse evidence, the suggested outline that follows must remain just that, although it may provide a useful framework for the political structure of Edward's England.

THE OTHER EARLDOMS

King Edward appointed three new earls in the years immediately following his succession, namely Swein in 1043 and Beorn and Harold in 1045. Earl Swein certainly held Herefordshire from the start, as witness his invasion of Wales in 1046 and subsequent seizure of the abbess of Leominster. As John of Worcester mentions, it seems likely that Swein also controlled Gloucestershire and Oxfordshire. Although John also says Swein held Somerset and Berkshire in 1051, these must have been surrendered to him at a later date by Earl Godwine, because the latter held Berkshire between 1045 and 1048. In 1045 Swein may possibly have held Buckinghamshire and Middlesex instead. At this time Earl Beorn certainly held Hertfordshire, probably Huntingdonshire, and perhaps also Cambridgeshire, Bedfordshire and Northampton-shire. Earl Harold certainly held Norfolk and Suffolk, and probably also Essex.[11]

The exile of Earl Swein in 1047 disrupted this arrangement and authority over his shires was probably temporarily shared between Harold and Beorn, as implied by one of the Chronicle reports of Swein's return in 1049. Thereafter, the murder of Beorn, the renewed exile and subsequent restoration of Swein, and the appointment of King Edward's nephew, Ralph, to an earldom in 1050 produced a new pattern of earldoms by 1051. The exact process involved in this transformation is obscure, but some suggestions can be offered.[12]

According to John of Worcester, in 1051 Earl Harold held not only Norfolk, Suffolk and Essex, but also Cambridgeshire and Huntingdonshire. He presumably gained the latter shires after the murder of Beorn as compensation for his surrender either to Swein or to Ralph of his share of Swein's former earldom, perhaps Gloucestershire and Oxfordshire. Also according to John of Worcester, Swein was in control of

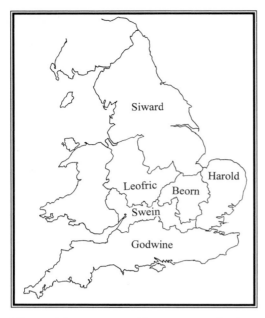

The earldoms, 1045. (© Ian W. Walker)

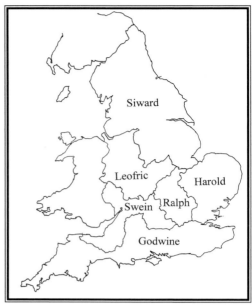

The earldoms, 1050. (© Ian W. Walker)

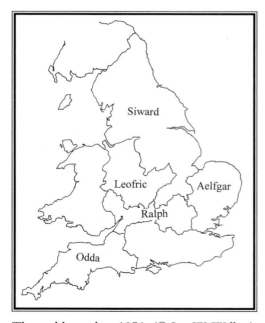

The earldoms, late 1051. (© Ian W. Walker)

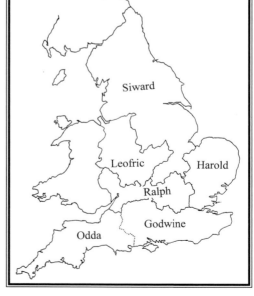

The earldoms, late 1052. (© Ian W. Walker)

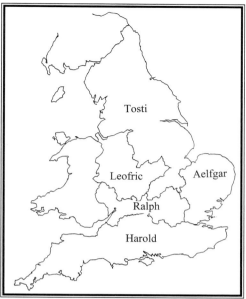

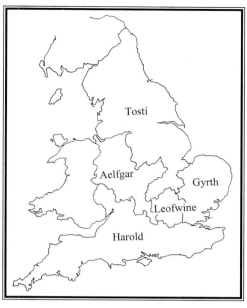

The earldoms, 1056. (© Ian W. Walker)

The earldoms, 1060. (© Ian W. Walker)

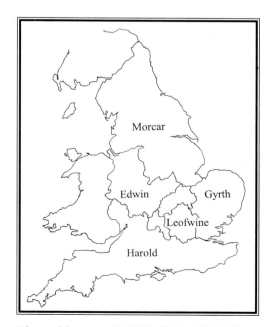

The earldoms, end 1065. (© Ian W. Walker)

Herefordshire, Gloucestershire, Oxfordshire, Somerset and Berkshire in 1051. This area consisted of Herefordshire, recovered from Earl Ralph who had established his Frenchmen in the shire, and Gloucestershire and Oxfordshire, recovered from either Earl Ralph or Earl Harold. However, it also included Somerset and Berkshire, probably donated by Earl Godwine himself in order to persuade King Edward and the other earls that Swein's restoration would be relatively painless. If these assumptions are correct, the earldom held by Ralph can now be deduced, by a process of elimination, as consisting probably of the remaining shires of Middlesex, Hertfordshire, Buckinghamshire, Bedfordshire and Northamptonshire. The Chronicle makes it clear that in spite of his loss of Herefordshire, on Swein's return Ralph still held territory from which he raised troops to support King Edward.[13]

The exile of the Godwine family in 1051 meant further upheavals, with both Swein and Harold deprived of their earldoms. Earl Harold's earldom was granted to Aelfgar, son of Leofric, who certainly controlled Norfolk and Suffolk, and probably Essex and Cambridgeshire, though not apparently Huntingdonshire. Earl Ralph resumed control of Herefordshire, and probably Oxfordshire, from Swein and possibly gained Gloucestershire, though he appears to have surrendered Northamptonshire. The two shires lost by these men apparently passed to Earl Siward, perhaps as a reward for supporting King Edward in the recent crisis.[14]

The restoration of the Godwine family a year later brought about further reorganization. Earl Harold recovered his earldom of East Anglia from Aelfgar, including Norfolk, Suffolk, Essex and Cambridgeshire, but possibly with the exception of Huntingdonshire, which may have been retained by Siward. Earl Swein's death later that year, before he could return to England, avoided any need to reorder Ralph's earldom in the west, which he continued to hold after this point. Thereafter, Earl Aelfgar resumed control of Harold's East Anglian earldom in 1053, when the latter succeeded to Wessex.[15]

The next rearrangement of the smaller earldoms arose following the consecutive deaths of Earl Leofric and Earl Ralph in 1057. Earl Aelfgar succeeded his father in Mercia and surrendered his earldom of East Anglia, which was subsequently passed unchanged to Gyrth. In contrast, the shires of Ralph's former earldom were redistributed to a number of other earls. As we have seen, Earl Harold certainly received Herefordshire and probably Gloucestershire. In addition, Earl Leofwine is known to have obtained Hertfordshire and Middlesex, but possibly also received Bedfordshire and Buckinghamshire. It would seem that Oxfordshire should also have fallen to Leofwine, but instead we have evidence that this shire was held by both Earl Aelfgar and Earl Gyrth. The solution to this difficulty would appear to be that Earl Aelfgar was granted Oxfordshire as his share of Ralph's earldom, but this shire later passed to Earl Gyrth, either as the price of Aelfgar's exile in 1058 or after his death in 1062.[16]

This summary of the succession to earldoms and the variations in their extent and composition is by no means final, but represents simply an account which fits the available evidence. The resultant pattern of earldoms over this time is illustrated in the series of maps on pp. 210–11. In light of the scarcity of this evidence, other interpretations remain possible and there remain some difficulties, for example, the fate of Earl Odda's earldom. Nevertheless, the framework presented is a valid one and has been employed to provide the background to this account of events in King Edward's reign.

ABBREVIATIONS

AB	*Adam of Bremen – History of the Archbishops of Hamburg-Bremen,* ed. F.J. Tschan (New York, 1959)
ASC	*The Anglo-Saxon Chronicle,* ed. D. Whitelock, D.C. Douglas, S.I. Tucker, rev. edn (London, 1961)
ASW	*Anglo-Saxon Writs,* ed. F.E. Harmer (Manchester, 1952)
BJRL	*Bulletin of the John Rylands Library*
CMCS	*Cambridge Medieval Celtic Studies*
DB	*Domesday Book,* ed. J. Morris, 34 vols (Chichester, 1975–86)
EER	*Encomium Emmae Regina,* ed. A. Campbell (London, 1949)
EHD I	*English Historical Documents, Volume I: c. 500–1042,* ed. D. Whitelock (London, 1979)
EHD II	*English Historical Documents, Volume II 1042–1189,* ed. D.C. Douglas and G.W. Greenway (Oxford, 1981)
EHR	*English Historical Review*
Flor	*Florence of Worcester's Chronicle,* tr. J. Stevenson (Lampeter, 1989)
JBAA	*Journal of the British Archaeological Association*
JRSAI	*Journal of the Royal Society of Antiquaries of Ireland*
JW	*The Chronicle of John of Worcester, Volume II,* ed. R.R. Darlington and P. McGurk (Oxford, 1995)
TEAS	*Transactions of the Essex Archaeological Society*
TRHS	*Transactions of the Royal Historical Society*
VER	[*Vita Eadwardi Regis*] *The Life of King Edward Who Rests at Westminster,* ed. F. Barlow, 2nd edn (Oxford, 1992)
WC	*The Waltham Chronicle,* ed. L. Watkiss and M. Chibnall (Oxford, 1994)
WJ	*The Gesta Normannorum Ducum of William of Jumieges, Orderic Vitalis and Robert of Torigni,* ed. E.M.C. Van Houts, 2 vols (Oxford, 1992 and 1995)
WP	*Guillaume de Poitiers – Histoire de Guillaume le Conquérant,* ed. Raymonde Foreville (Paris, 1952)

NOTES

INTRODUCTION

1. E.B. Fryde, D.E. Greenway, S. Porter and I. Roy, *Handbook of British Chronology*, 3rd edn (London, 1986), p. 29 for the length of Harold's reign. Only King Edmund 'Ironside' ruled for a shorter period at seven months twelve days.

2. P. Compton, *Harold the King* (London, 1961) and H.R. Loyn, 'Harold, Son of Godwine' in *1066 Commemoration Lectures* (London, 1966). F. Barlow, *Edward the Confessor* (London, 1979), D.C. Douglas, *William the Conqueror* (London, 1964) and D. Bates, *William the Conqueror* (London, 1989) all feature Harold but only in relation to their eponymous subjects.

3. P. Stafford, *Unification and Conquest* (London, 1989), pp. 83–100 for a new interpretation.

4. H.R. Loyn, *The Governance of Anglo-Saxon England 500–1087* (London, 1984), Chapters 4, 5, 6, F.M. Stenton, *Anglo-Saxon England* (Oxford, 1971), Chapter XV, pp. 545–56, D. Whitelock, *The Beginnings of English Society*, rev. edn (Harmondsworth, 1972), Chapters II, III, IV, and V, D. Crouch, *The Image of Aristocracy in Britain 1000–1300* (London, 1992), pp. 46–50, Stafford, *Unification*, Chapters 8, 9, 11, Barlow, *Edward*, Chapters III, VIII for more detail on the social and political background.

5. R. Fleming, *Kings and Lords in Conquest England* (Cambridge, 1991), pp. 52–4, R.A. Brown, *The Normans and the Norman Conquest* (London, 1969), pp. 78–84, P.A. Clarke, *The English Nobility under Edward the Confessor* (Oxford, 1994), pp. 162–3, E. John, 'Edward the Confessor and the Norman Succession', *EHR*, XCIV (1979), pp. 244–6 for the view of weak kingship and over-mighty earls. Barlow, *Edward*, pp. 286–8 for a more balanced view.

6. *ASC*, pp. xi–xxiv for the references in this book cited by Chronicle version year date. Ibid., pp. xvii–xviii. *EHD II*, No. 1, p. 103, Barlow, *Edward*, p. xviii, *The Norman Conquest*, ed. R.A. Brown (London, 1984), p. 51, *The Anglo-Saxon Chronicle*, ed. M. Swanton (London, 1996), pp. xxiii–xxviii for political bias in the different versions of the Chronicle. The new translation by Swanton appeared too late to be used in this book and I have relied on that of Whitelock *et al.* (see Abbreviations) throughout.

7. *JW* for the references in the book cited by the year date. R.R. Darlington and P. McGurk 'The *Chronicon ex Chronicis* of "Florence" of Worcester and its Sources for English History before 1066', *Anglo-Norman Studies*, V (1982), pp. 185–96, *EHD I*, p. 120 for the date and make up of this work. Unfortunately I have only been able to consult the single published volume of this new edition which ends in 1066. I refer to the older and less reliable translation of *Flor* for the years after 1066. The volume of the new edition covering the period after 1066 is now available.

8. *VER*, Introduction for the probable date and purpose of this work. E.K. Heningham, 'The Literary Unity, the Date and the Purpose of Lady Edith's Book: "The Life of King Edward Who Rests at Westminster"', *Albion*, 7 (1975), pp. 24–40 for another view of its purpose. *VER*, p. xlv for the focus on Tosti; Ibid., p. xxi for this confusion of purpose; and Ibid., p. 89 for its quote.

9. *WJ*, Volume I, pp. xxxii–xxxv, and pp. xlv–l, liii–liv for William of Jumieges' chapters on Duke William's claim and the Conquest, dated between 1067 and 1070.

10. *WP*, pp. xii–xx. R.H.C. Davis, 'William of Poitiers and his History of William the Conqueror' in R.H.C. Davis (ed.), *From Alfred the Great to Stephen* (London, 1981), pp. 101, 104, Brown, *Norman Conquest*, p. 15 and *EHD II*, No. 4, p. 230 for the dating of this work. I have referred to Foreville's French edition throughout but have added in parentheses references to English translations where these exist. Thus ( ) refers to the translation contained in Brown, *Norman Conquest*, pp. 15–41, and [ ] to that contained in S. Morillo (ed.), *The Battle of Hastings* (Woodbridge, 1996), pp. 3–15. A new English translation is now available in R.H.C. Davis and M. Chibnall, *The Guesta Guillelmi of William of Poitiers*, Oxford 1998.

11. D.M. Wilson, *The Bayeux Tapestry* (London, 1985), p. 12, *The Bayeux Tapestry*, ed. F.M. Stenton (London, 1965), pp. 9–11, and Brown, *Norman Conquest*, pp. 173–173 for the background. Wilson, *Bayeux*, pp. 17–18, Stenton, *Bayeux*, pp. 9–24, and D.J. Bernstein, *The Mystery of the Bayeux Tapestry* (London, 1986), pp. 114–15 for the allusiveness and difficulties of interpretation. The number of interpretations of Aelfgyva scene are legion. For example, Wilson, *Bayeux*, p. 178, Stenton, *Bayeux*, p. 10, Bernstein, *Mystery*, p. 19, J.B. McNulty, 'The Lady Aelfgyva in the Bayeux Tapestry', *Speculum*, 55 (1980), pp. 659–68 and R.D. Wissolik, 'The Saxon Statement: Code in the Bayeux Tapestry', *Annuale Mediaevale*, 19 (1979), pp. 81-8.

12. Davis, 'William of Poitiers', pp. 104–112 for the interrelationship of these three sources.

13. C. Morton, 'Pope Alexander II and the Norman Conquest', *Latomus*, XXXIV (1975), pp. 362–82, and H.E.J. Cowdrey, 'Bishop Ermenfrid of Sion and the Penitential Ordinance following the Battle of Hastings', *Journal of Ecclesiastical History*, XX (1969), pp. 225–42 for later Papal concerns about the Norman Conquest, and *EHD II*, No. 81, pp. 649–50 for the text of the penance imposed on those participating in the Conquest.

14. *DB*, Introduction to each volume. Brown, *Norman Conquest*, pp. 158–9, V.H. Galbraith, *Domesday Book* (Oxford, 1974), pp. 33-7 and H.C. Darby, *Domesday England* (Cambridge, 1977), pp. 3–9 for the process of its compilation. Galbraith, *Domesday*, pp. 175–9 for the clearest statement of this revisionist position, but it is evident throughout the text itself.

15. T.J. Oleson, *The Witenagemot in the Reign of Edward the Confessor* (Oxford, 1955), pp. 35–47, A. Williams, 'Land and Power in the Eleventh Century: The Estates of Harold Godwineson', *Proceedings of the Battle Conference on Anglo-Norman Studies, 1980* (1981), p. 171, Fleming, *Kings and Lords*, pp. 16–20, 47, and Barlow, *Edward*, pp. xxi–xxii for the scarcity of charters and the problems of reliability among those which do exist.

16. These sources are cited below where used.

17. Brown, *Norman Conquest*, p. xiv, Stafford, *Unification*, pp. 101–102, M. Chibnall, *Anglo-Norman England 1066–1166* (Oxford, 1986), p. 1 for the controversy about the impact of the conquest. Brown, *Normans*, pp. 121–4, Douglas, *William*, p. 169, Bates, *William*, p. 59, Barlow, *Edward*, pp. 107–8, 228, and John 'Edward the Confessor', pp. 241–67 for some assessments of the Norman claim.

CHAPTER ONE

1. *VER*, p. 11. (By permission of Oxford University Press)

2. *ASC* C/D/E 997 to 1005. The few exceptions were for justifiable reasons. Thus in 1000 and 1005 the Viking fleets withdrew to replenish in Normandy and Denmark respectively. While in 1002 they were paid off by the English with 24,000 pounds of silver. *ASC* C/D/E 1006 for the great fleet and 1007 for the payment.

3. *ASC* C/D/E 1008 and 1009.

4. S. Keynes, *The Diplomas of King Aethelred 'The Unready' 978–1016* (Cambridge, 1980), p. 212 for Eadric and Brihtric as *thegns* witnessing royal charters from 997 to 1007 and 997 to 1009 respectively. *ASC* C/D/E 1006 for Aelfhelm's murder and *JW* 1006 for Eadric's involvement, supported by Keynes, *Diplomas*, p. 212. *ASC* C/D/E 1007 for Eadric's elevation and Keynes, *Diplomas*, p. 213 for his marriage to Edith, which is recorded by *JW* 1009 in a way which suggests it had occurred before that date.

5. *ASC* C 1009 for Wulfnoth *Cild*, *ASC* D/E/F 1009 and *JW* 1008 for his Sussex origins and *ASC* F1009 for him as father of Earl Godwine. *JW* 1008 does not indicate that Wulfnoth the Sussex *thegn* is the same as Wulfnoth father of Earl Godwine in *JW* 1007 but since he makes the latter Wulfnoth a nephew of Eadric *Streona* and Brihtric, there appears to be confusion at this point in his account. Keynes, *Diplomas*, Tables 7 and 8 for Wulfnoth as a witness in only four out of fifty-four diplomas. N. Hooper, 'Some Observations on the Navy in Late Anglo-Saxon England' in C. Harper-Bill *et al.* (eds), *Studies in Medieval History for R. Allen Brown* (Woodbridge, 1989), pp. 206–7 for Kent and Sussex and the fleet. *ASC* C/D/E 994 Sussex was ravaged. *ASC* C/D/E 998 Danes 'got their food' from Sussex probably by plunder. *ASC* C/D/E 1006 they plundered 'every shire of Wessex'.

6. *ASC* C/D/E 1009. (Methuen and Co.)

7. *JW* 1008 for Brihtric's accusations as unjust and Keynes, *Diplomas*, Table 8 for Brihtric's disappearance from among the witnesses of Aethelred's diplomas in 1009. A. Williams, A.P. Smyth and D.P. Kirby, *A Biographical Dictionary of Dark Age Britain* (London, 1991), p. 65 for a late source suggesting Brihtric may have been murdered in Kent.

8. *EHD I*, No. 129, pp. 593–6 and Keynes, *Diplomas*, p. 267 for the date, and the latter for Godwine as Wulfnoth's son. M.K. Lawson, *Cnut* (London, 1993), pp. 77–8 considers Athelstan died on 25 June 1016. This fails to consider his brother Edmund's prominence in the accounts of 1015 and 1016, and the fact that he and not Athelstan succeeded Aethelred on 23 April 1016. This latter would have been impossible if Athelstan, the elder of his sons, had still been alive then.

9. *DB Sussex*, 11: 36. The other Sussex Compton was held in 1066 by Harold himself from King Edward. *DB Sussex*, 10: 23, this makes it less likely as the Compton concerned here.

10. *EHD I*, No. 129, pp. 595–6 This sword may be the same as that sent to Offa by Charlemagne in 796 and recorded in *EHD I*, No. 197, p. 849, and therefore a great heirloom.

11. Keynes, *Diplomas*, Table 1 where Edward began to witness his father's diplomas from 1011, *ASC* C/D/E 1014 for Edward acting as ambassador for his father and *VER* p. 13 for this supposed oath.

12. *EHD I*, No. 129, pp. 594–5, Williams *et al.*, *Dark Age Britain*, pp. 181, 214, 227 provides summaries of the careers of these men and with P. Stafford, *The East Midlands in the Early Middle Ages* (Leicester, 1985), pp. 126–7 indicates Sigeferth and Morcar's links to Aelfhelm.

13. *ASC* C/D/E 1015. Stafford, *Unification*, pp. 67–8 and Stafford, *East Midlands*, pp. 126–7.

14. *ASC* C/D/E 1015, *JW* 1015, Stafford, *Unification*, p. 68 and Williams *et al.*, *Dark Age Britain*, pp. 126–7 for all this.

15. *ASC* C/D/E 1015 and 1016. Stafford, *Unification*, p. 68 and Lawson, *Cnut*, p. 19.

16. *ASC* C/D/E 1016 and *VER*, p. 9 for Godwine active in war.

17. *ASC* C/D/E 1017 for the submission of all England to Cnut and K. Mack, 'Changing Thegns: Knut's Conquest and the English Aristocracy', *Albion*, 16 (1984), pp. 375–80, Lawson, *Cnut*, pp. 83–6 and Fleming, *Kings and Lords*, pp. 42–6 for the purge.

18. *VER*, p. 9 for Godwine, *EHD I*, No. 131, pp. 597–99 for this diploma in favour of Bishop Burhwold. *EER*, pp. 30–1 and Mack, 'Changing Thegns', p. 380 for this quote on loyalty. Loyalty is also among the qualities for which Godwine is praised in *VER*, p. 7, *ASC* C/D/E 1017, *JW* 1017 and *EER*, pp. 30–3 for Eadric's execution.

19. *ASC* C/D/E 1017 states that Cnut took 'Wessex for himself' but this probably represents an interim military government as in A. Williams, '"Cockles Among the Wheat": Danes and English in the Western Midlands in the First Half of the Eleventh Century', *Midland History*, 11 (1986), pp. 1–11 and Lawson, *Cnut*, p. 83. By 1018 he had appointed Godwine to control the central portion of Wessex. At this point Aethelweard still held the Western Shires of Wessex and possibly an Earl Sired ruled in Kent. Lawson, *Cnut*, p. 186 for the latter. *EHD I*, No. 131, pp. 597–9 for this diploma to Burhwold.

20. *ASC* C/D/E 1019, *ASC* C 1023, *VER*, pp. 5–6, 11, and Lawson, *Cnut*, pp. 89–91, and p. 94 for these expeditions and Godwine's promotion. S. Keynes, 'Cnut's Earls' in A. Rumble (ed.), *The Reign of Cnut* (Leicester, 1994), pp. 70–4, and pp. 84–7 for Godwine's promotion linked to the 1023 visit to Denmark. Williams *et al.*, *Dark Age Britain*, p. 144 for Godwine's brothers-in-law.

21. *Walter Map – De Nugis Curialium*, tr. M.R. James, Cymmrodorion Record Series 9 (1923), pp. 228–32, and *Knytlinga Saga*, tr. H. Palsson and P. Edwards (Odense, 1986), pp. 32–4 respectively for these apparently unrelated English and Danish legends.

22. Lawson, *Cnut*, p. 188 considers that Godwine was 'not the colossus of later years' under Cnut but his prominent position in the witness lists of Cnut's diplomas and his position as one of the three great earls on Cnut's death suggest otherwise. Williams *et al.*, *Dark Age Britain*, pp. 170–1 for Leofwine.

23. *ASC* C/D/E 1021, Stafford, *Unification*, p. 73, L.M. Larson, *Canute the Great, 995–1035* (London, 1912), pp. 146–7, Lawson, *Cnut*, pp. 174–5 for Thorkell's fall. *Anglo-Saxon Charters*, ed. P.H. Sawyer (London, 1968), p. 285–97 and Keynes, 'Cnut's Earls', p. 53, Table 4.1 for the charter or diploma evidence. Stafford, *Unification*, p. 74 reflects on the gaps in this evidence and suggests Cnut's absence as the explanation. Keynes, 'Cnut's Earls', pp. 54–8 and 82–4 for the other two earls. Lawson, *Cnut*, p. 186 and Keynes, 'Cnut's Earls', p. 76 for Earl Sired while the 1051 crisis shows Godwine governing Kent.

24. *ASC* E/F 1026. Stafford, *Unification*, pp. 74–5 and Keynes, 'Cnut's Earls', pp. 58–60, 62–4 for this rebellion, Lawson, *Cnut*, pp. 96–100 offers an alternative identification for the Ulf and Eilaf at Holy River. This relies on rather later sources and in any case does not invalidate the case for Godwine supporting Cnut, since Godwine did so even when the king subsequently had his brother-in-law, *Jarl* Ulf, killed at Roskilde. *William of Malmesbury – The Kings Before the Norman Conquest*, tr. J. Stevenson (Lampeter, 1989), p. 171 records Godwine's presence with Cnut on this occasion but on what authority is unclear and it may simply be a confusion with earlier expeditions.

25. *EHD I*, No. 53, pp. 476–8 for Cnut's letter. *Snorri Sturluson-Heimskringla, The Olaf Sagas*, tr. S. Laing, rev. edn (London, 1964), for Ulf. *JW* 1027. *EHD I*, No. 18, pp. 339–40. *ASC* F 1028 for Olaf. Larson, *Canute*, p. 237 for a runic inscription said to record Godwine's actions in Norway, which is however rejected by N. Lund, 'The Armies of Swein Forkbeard and Cnut', *Anglo-Saxon England*, 15 (1986), p. 118.

26. *EHD I*, No. 48, pp. 452–4 for Thorkell as regent. *EHD I*, No. 53, pp. 476–8 for the 1027 letter. *VER*, p. 11 and Stafford, *Unification*, p. 75 for Godwine's prominence.

27. Sawyer, *A-S Charters*, No. 970 for Polhampton. Lawson, *Cnut*, p. 188 for another view.

28. S.B.F. Jansson, *Runes in Sweden* (Varnamo, 1987), p. 77–9 for the likely origin of the name Tosti.

29. Williams *et al.*, *Dark Age Britain*, pp. 132, 150–1, 170–1, Keynes, 'Cnut's Earls', pp. 76, 84–7. Lawson, *Cnut*, p. 185 suggests Eilaf survived later than this.

30. Williams *et al.*, *Dark Age Britain*, pp. 169–70, 217. Stafford, *East Midlands*, pp. 74–5, G.N. Garmonsway, *Canute and his Empire* (London, 1964), pp. 18–25 and Lawson, *Cnut*, pp. 95–102 for Cnut's absences abroad.

31. *ASC* C/D/E/F 1035, *JW* 1035. Stafford, *East Midlands*, p. 127 for Harold's Midland connections through his mother, Aelfgifu of Northampton, perhaps already including Earl Leofric himself. Cnut's other son by Aelfgifu, Swein, had died probably in 1034.

32. *ASC* E/F 1036 and *JW* 1035. The Chronicle account refers to Harold's regency but *JW* 1035 and *EER*, pp. 38–9 make it clear this was an attempt on the throne. The rumours about Harold's birth were part of the propaganda put out by his opponents to discredit him. *EER*, p. 41 and F. Barlow, *The English Church 1000–1066* (London, 1979), pp. 43–4 for Archbishop Aethelnoth.

33. T. Talvio, 'Harold I and Harthacnut's Jewel Cross Type Reconsidered' in M.A.S. Blackburn (ed.), *Anglo-Saxon Monetary History* (Leicester, 1986), pp. 288–9 for the division of the coinage between Harold and Hardecnut reflecting the Chronicle's division at the Thames. *AB*, p. 108, *Saxo Grammaticus-Danorum Regum Heroumque Historia*, ed. E. Christiansen (Oxford, 1980), Volume 1, Books X–XVI, p. 46 and G. Jones, *A History of the Vikings* (Oxford, 1984), p. 398 for Magnus of Norway. *ASC* C/D 1035 for the seizure of Emma's treasure, which occurred sometime between Cnut's death and March 1036 but whether before or after the Oxford council is unclear. I have placed it after as this appears to coincide with the period when the power of Hardecnut's supporters began o wane.

34. Stafford, *Unification*, p. 79 and Talvio, 'Harold I and Hardecnut', pp. 283–9 for the change in control of the coinage south of the Thames.

35. *EER*, pp. 40–3 for the trap. *JW* 1036 attempts to reconcile the two versions. Barlow, *Edward*, p. 44 and Stafford, *Unification*, p. 79.

36. *WJ*, pp. 105–7 and *WP*, pp. 5–7 for Edward's invasion.

37. *ASC* C/D 1036, *VER*, p. 20, *EER*, p. 42–7, *WJ*, pp. 105–7 and *WP*, pp. 5–7 for Alfred. The lack of any mention of Edward's role in the English sources may reflect the wish to draw a veil over his failure. The Norman sources would wish to demonstrate the powerful support they provided and which later supposedly prompted Edward to bequeath his kingdom to William.

38. *ASC* C/D 1036, *JW* 1036, *EER*, pp. 42–7, *WJ*, pp. 105–7 and *WP*, pp. 5–11 for this.

39. *ASC* C/D 1036, *JW* 1036, *EER*, pp. 44–7, *WJ*, pp. 105–7, and *WP*, pp. 9–11 for the murder.

40. *ASC* C/D/E/F 1037, *JW* 1037 and *EER*, pp. 46–9.

41. *ASC* C 1039, *JW* 1039, *ASC* C/D/E/F 1040, *JW* 1040 and *EER*, pp. 48–53.

42. *ASC* C/D 1040 and *JW* 1040, J.M. Cooper, *The Last Four Anglo-Saxon Archbishops of York* (York, 1970), p. 15 and V. King, 'Ealdred, Archbishop of York: the Worcester Years', *Anglo-Norman Studies*, XVIII (1995), pp. 125–6 for Aelfric and Lyfing.

43. *ASC* C/D/E/F 1041, *JW* 1041, *EER*, pp. 52–3. Also Stafford, 'Unification', p. 81 and Barlow, *Edward*, pp. 48–52 for possible reasons. William of Poitiers' account of Norman support being responsible for Edward's return appears unlikely given the chaotic state of Normandy at this time, for which see Douglas, *William*, pp. 39–50. In contrast, *WJ*, p. 107 clearly attributes Edward's return to Hardecnut.

44. *ASC* C/D/E/F 1042, *JW* 1042. *VER*, p. 9. D. Hill, *An Atlas of Anglo-Saxon England* (Oxford, 1981), maps 154–163 and 167–169 for royal itineraries, and map 179 for royal lands.

45. *ASC* C/D/E 1043, *JW* 1043, K.E. Cutler, 'Edith, Queen of England 1045–1066' *Medieval Studies*, 35 (1973), p. 224.

46. *ASC* C/E 1044. Barlow, *English Church*, pp. 108–9. Fleming, *Kings and Lords*, p. 81 for these grants.

47. *ASC* C/E 1045. *ASW*, pp. 557, 563 for Beorn and Harold, and Barlow *Edward*, p. 74 for Swein.

CHAPTER TWO

1. *VER*, pp. 47–9. (By permission of Oxford University Press)

2. *ASW*, p. 563 for Harold as earl in diplomas. *EHD II*, No. 184, pp. 901–2 and *Anglo-Saxon Wills*, ed. D. Whitelock (Cambridge, 1930), pp. 80–4 for Thurstan,s will.

3. *ASC* D 1045.

4. *EHD II*, No. 184, pp. 901–2 and No. 187, pp. 903–4 for these wills.

5. *ASW*, Nos 13 and 14, pp. 157–8 for Harold, and Fleming, *Kings and Lords*, p. 97 for Colne.

6. *ASC* D 1044 and *JW* 1044 for Gunnhild and her sons, and *ASC* C/D/E 1046 for Osgod *Clapa*. Also Williams *et al.*, *Dark Age Britain*, p. 193 and Barlow, *Edward*, pp. 88–9. Fleming, *Kings and Lords*, p. 89 for Wroxall on the Isle of Wight.

7. Brown, *Normans*, pp. 113–20, Douglas, *William*, pp. 166–70 and M.W. Campbell, 'A Pre-Conquest Norman Occupation of England', *Speculum*, 46 (1971) for the theory of Norman infiltration but Stenton, *A-S England*, pp. 425–6 and H.R. Loyn, *The Norman Conquest*, 3rd edn (London, 1982), pp. 54–5 for a cautionary note.

8. Campbell, 'Norman Occupation', pp. 21–31 for this fifth column. Barlow, *English Church*, pp. 81–4 for foreigners as only seven out of twenty-nine appointees to bishoprics and Barlow, *Edward*, pp. 164–5 for only some four or five foreign nobles in total. *ASC* D 1051 and 1052 refer to the castle men only as Frenchmen. In contrast, *JW* 1051 and 1052 do refer to these men as Normans, but this may simply be analogous with the use of the generic term Norman to refer to William's followers in 1066 whether Breton, French or Norman. Clarke, *English Nobility*, pp. 224–6, 332–6 for the lands of Earl Ralph, Ralph the Staller and Robert fitzWimarch.

9. *ASC* C 1046, *JW* 1049, *Hemingi Chartularium ecclesiae Wigorniensis*, ed. T. Hearne (1723), Volume i, pp. 275–6, Barlow, *Edward*, p. 91 and K.L. Maund, *Ireland, Wales and England in the Eleventh Century* (Woodbridge, 1991), pp. 126–30. *DB Herefordshire*, 1: 14 and 38 n. 1, 10a for her lands in 1066, *EHD I*, No. 49, p. 463 where Cnut's laws lay down penalties for the abduction of nuns. *ASC* E 1047, *JW* 1049, *ASC* D 1049 for Swein's exile.

10. *ASC* C/D/E 1049 for the division of Swein's lands between Harold and Beorn.

11. *ASC* D 1047, *JW* 1049, *ASC* D 1049, *AB*, p. 108 and Jones, *Vikings*, p. 401 for Swein of Denmark's defeat.

12. *ASC* E 1046, Barlow,*Edward*, p. 97, Stafford, *Unification*, pp. 117–18, *ASC* C/D/E 1049, D. Nicholas, *Medieval Flanders* (London, 1992), p. 50.

13. *ASC* C/D/E 1049.

14. *ASC* C/D/E 1049, *JW* 1049.

15. *ASC* C/D/E 1049, P.G. Foote and D.M. Wilson, *The Viking Achievement* (London, 1970), p. 426 for Scandinavian use of this sentence, and R.I. Page, *Chronicles of the Vikings* (London, 1995), p. 145 for record of a similar act of *nithingswerk* on a Swedish rune-stone of this period.

16. *ASW*, p. 570 and A. Williams, 'The King's Nephew: The Family and Career of Earl Ralph of Hereford' in C. Harper-Bill *et al.*, *Studies*, pp. 330–8. Ralph appears as earl in diplomas dated to 1050 before the exile of Godwine and his family. Appendix Two for the earldoms at this time. *ASC* C 1052 for Swein's pilgrimage. *ASC* C/E 1050 for Swein's return. *JW* 1049, Cooper, *York*, p. 25 and King, 'Ealdred', p. 127 for Ealdred's role in this. *ASC* D/E 1051 for the disputes between the foreigners of Hereford and Earl Swein.

17. *VER*, p. 27, P. Stafford, *Queens, Concubines and Dowagers* (London, 1983), p. 82, Stafford, *Unification*, p. 92 and Cutler, 'Edith, Queen of England', pp. 222–31.

18. John, 'Edward the Confessor', p. 248 for Edward's celibacy. This suggestion is dismissed by Barlow, *Edward*, pp. 81–5. Edward himself may have been impotent but if so, why did he marry Edith, and Godwine consent to this? Clearly they both anticipated the birth of an heir. *The Leofric Missal*, ed. F.E. Warren (Oxford, 1883), p. 9a and *VER*, p. lxxv for Leofric's benediction. Sawyer, *A-S Charters*, Nos 1007–13 for Edith as witness, but Nos 1014 onwards for Edith's absence until No. 1026 of 1055 when she reappears. *ASC* C/E 1050 for the fleet, which had intervened on behalf of Harold 'Harefoot'.

19. Barlow, *English Church*, pp. 85–6.

20. *ASC* C/D/E 1050 and E 1051, *VER*, p. 31 and Barlow, *Edward*, p. 104.

21. *ASC* E 1051, and Barlow, *English Church*, pp. 47–8 for Spearhafoc. C. Morris, *The Papal Monarchy* (Oxford, 1991), p. 87, Barlow, *English Church*, p302 and *ASC* E 1050 for Ulf. M.F. Smith, 'Archbishop Stigand and the Eye of the Needle', *Anglo-Norman Studies*, XVI (1994), pp. 202, 208 for Stigand's support for Spearhafoc and the lack of any definite connection between the former and Godwine respectively.

22. *VER*, p. 33, N. Brooks, *The Early History of the Church of Canterbury* (Leicester, 1984), p. 304, Barlow, *English Church*, pp. 47–8. He may have even suggested that Godwine was plotting to kill King Edward himself.

23. *ASC* E 1051, H.J. Tanner, 'The Expansion of the Power and the Influence of the Counts of Boulogne Under Eustace II', *Anglo-Norman Studies*, XIV (1992), pp. 264–8, Douglas, *William*, pp. 391–2 for the date of this Norman-Flemish alliance through Duke William's marriage to Mathilda of Flanders.

24. *ASC* E1051 and *VER*, p. 35. *JW* 1041 for the attack on Worcester in which Godwine participated.

25. *ASC* D/E 1051, *VER*, p. 39, i.e. September 1051. Tanner, 'Eustace II', pp. 264–8.

26. *ASC* D 1051 for Ralph supporting the king. *ASC* D 1051, and *JW* 1051 for Eustace still in England in September when Godwine demanded his surrender. *ASC* D/E 1051 and *VER*, p. 35 for Leofric and Siward at Gloucester, the Chronicles state in support of King Edward.

27. *ASC* D/E 1051, *JW* 1051 and *VER*, p. 35, the last for a milder account but *ASC* D 1051 perhaps, reveals better Godwine's assessment of the strength of his position at this point.

28. *ASC* D/E 1051 reveal the tensions of this period, although these were resolved by negotiation.

29. *ASC* D/E 1051, *JW* 1051, *WP*, p. 32 (20) fails to name them, noting them only as the 'son and grandson of earl Godwine' but *Eadmer – Historia Novorum in Anglia*, tr. G. Bosanquet (London, 1964), p. 6 identifies them as Wulfnoth and Hakon. This is also suggested by F. Barlow, *William Rufus* (London, 1983), p. 66 which speaks of Wulfnoth's captivity beginning when still a boy. *ASC* C/D/E 1067 (recte 1068) for Harold's sons, both Godwine and Edmund were probably born before 1051.

30. *ASC* D/E 1051, *VER*, p. 35, *JW* 1051. Clarke, *English Nobility*, pp. 93–4.

31. *ASC* D/E 1051, *JW* 1051, *VER*, p. 35.

32. *ASC* C/D/E 1051, *JW* 1051, *VER*, pp. 35–7.

33. *ASC* D/E 1051, *VER*, pp. 37, 39–41. This account is to be preferred to that of the more distant Chronicle D, which names Thorney as their point of departure.

34. *ASC* D/E 1051, *JW* 1051, *VER*, p. 41. The latter for King Diarmait since the Chronicle fails to name him. *The Annals of Ulster to AD 1131*, ed. S. MacAirt and G. MacNiocaill (Dublin, 1983), 1052 for Diarmait's seizure of Dublin.

35. *ASC* D/E 1051, Williams, 'King's Nephew', p. 338 and Appendix Two. *DB Herefordshire*, 19: 3 records the gains of the Frenchmen of the castles at this time. Campbell, 'Norman Occupation', pp. 21–31.

36. *ASC* D/E 1051, *VER*, pp. 37, 45, *JW* 1051. *The Vita Eadwardi* is closest to Queen Edith and should know the truth. It is possible the Chronicle accounts which have her sent to Wherwell reflect where she was sent first, before moving to Wilton. Stafford, *Unification*, p. 92. for Edward's divorce plans.

CHAPTER THREE

1. *ASC* D 1052.

2. *ASC* D 1051, Brown, *Normans*, p. 121, for this connection but Douglas, *William*, p. 169 and Bates, *William*, p. 34, for its refutation.

3. *WJ*, p. 159, *WP*, p. 30 (20). *ASC* 1051 for Robert's promotion to the archbishopric and Barlow, *Edward*, p. 126 for the date of his death.

4. Brown, *Norman Conquest*, p. 2 and p. 17 for the purpose of these writers. *WJ*, p. 159 and *WP*, pp. 30–2 (19–20), 100 [4], 174–6 [11] for the basis of the claim. *WP*, pp. 174–6 [11] for Stigand's part. Barlow, *English Church*, p. 78 for Stigand's actual status. He did not become Archbishop of Canterbury until 1052, after Archbishop Robert fled into exile. Barlow, *Edward*, p. 108 for this as a simple error by William of Poitiers.

5. Douglas, *William*, p. 168, Bates, *William*, pp. 59–60 and Barlow, *Edward*, pp. 107–9.

6. *ASC* D/E 1051, *JW* 1051, Barlow, *Edward*, p. 108.

7. A. Williams, 'Some Notes and Considerations on Problems Connected with the English Royal Succession 860–1066', *Proceedings of the Battle Conference on Anglo-Norman Studies, 1977* (1978), pp. 144–67 for English succession practices.

8. Douglas, *William*, pp. 76–8, 391–5 and Bates, *William*, p. 100 for William's marriage. Douglas, *William*, p. 380 for Adelaide and Ibid., p. 419, Table 2 for Enguerrand's death in 1053. Douglas, *William*, pp. 58–69 for the Norman crisis of 1051–4.

9. Williams, 'King's Nephew', p. 327 for Ralph, Douglas, *William*, p. 418, Table 1 for William. Tanner, 'Eustace II', p. 263, Eustace of Boulogne had no claim since his first wife Godgifu, Edward's sister, died before 1049 without issue by him.

10. Barlow, *Edward*, pp. 28–53 and S. Keynes, 'The Aethelings in Normandy', *Anglo-Norman Studies*, XIII (1991), pp. 173–205 for Edward's early years.

11. *WJ*, p. 159 and *WP*, p. 30 (20) for the motivation for Edward's action. Douglas, *William* pp. 31–7 for these Dukes. Keynes, 'Aethelings', pp. 193–4, Barlow, *Edward*, pp. 51–2 and Bates, *William*, p. 59 for Robert's invasion plan. *ASC* C/D/E/F 1041, *JW* 1041, *EER*, p. 35, *WJ*, p. 107 and *WP*, p. 12 for Hardecnut inviting Edward to England. At this time William was in the midst of his difficult minority and in no position to assist anyone. Bates, *William*, p. 59 and Barlow *Edward*, p. 52 dismiss any suggestion of Norman aid. Keynes, 'Aethelings', pp. 173–205, Douglas, *William*, pp. 166–7 and Brown, *Normans*, pp. 111–16 for an alternative view.

12. *ASC* C/D/E 1052, *JW* 1052.

13. *VER*, pp. 39–41.

14. *Brut y Tywysogyon – Red Book of Hergest Version*, tr. T. Jones, 2nd edn (Cardiff, 1973), *VER*, p. 41, *ASC* E 1052. MacAirt and MacNiocaill, *Ulster* 1052. *The Annals of Tigernach*, tr. Whitley Stokes (Lampeter, 1993), 1052. M.T. Flanagan, *Irish Society, Anglo-Norman Settlers, Angevin Kingship* (Oxford, 1989), pp. 57–8. Maund, *Ireland*, p. 165. P.F. Wallace, 'The English Presence in Viking Dublin' in M.A.S. Blackburn (ed.), *Anglo-Saxon Monetary History* (Leicester, 1986), pp. 204–5 for the English earls as the inspiration behind Diarmait's conquest. *ASC* D 1052 for Gruffydd. Ralph was absent on duty with the fleet.

15. *ASC* C 1052, *JW* 1052.

16. *ASC* C/D/E 1052, Stafford, *Unification*, p. 86, Barlow, *Edward*, pp. 101–2, *ASC* E 1049 for Godwine, Harold, Swein and Tosti as captains of ships. *VER*, p. 41, *ASC* C/D/E 1052.

17. *ASC* C/D/E 1052, *VER*, pp. 41–3, Hooper, 'Some Observations', p. 206.

18. *ASC* C/D/E 1052, *VER*, pp. 41–3.

19. *ASC* E 1052.

20. *ASC* C/D/E 1052, *JW* 1052, *VER*, pp. 43–5, Stafford, *Unification*, p. 92.

21. Barlow, *Edward*, pp. 114–15 and Appendix Two for the earldoms of Odda and Ralph, E. Okasha, *Handlist of Anglo-Saxon Non-runic Inscriptions* (Cambridge, 1971), pp. 63–4 and Barlow, *Edward*, p. 125 for their retention as earls.

22. Barlow, *English Church*, pp. 77–81, Brooks, *Canterbury*, p. 305 and Smith, 'Stigand' for Stigand.

23. *ASC* D/E 1058 Stigand consecrated Aethelric and Siward. He also consecrated Bishop Remigius in 1067 under King William but otherwise his actions were carefully restricted.

24. *ASC* C 1053 and *ASC* E 1050, Barlow, *English Church*, pp. 215–6 for Wulfwig.

25. Stafford, *Unification*, p. 92, Barlow, *Edward*, p. 303, Barlow, *English Church*, p. 126, Brooks, *Canterbury*, p. 307.

26. *WJ*, p. 159, *WP*, pp. 30–2 (20), Stafford, *Unification*, p. 92, Douglas, *William*, p. 169, Bates, *William*, p.59, Brown, *Normans*, p. 122, Barlow, *Edward*, pp. 106–9 and Loyn, *Norman Conquest*, p. 57, all date it to 1051. Barlow, *Edward*, p. 126 and *WP*, p. xxv for Robert's death sometime between 9 January 1053 and 1055, perhaps closer to the former.

27. Barlow, *English Church*, p. 86, *WJ*, p. 159 and *WP*, pp. 30–2 (20), *WJ*, pp. xlvi, liii for the dating of this passage in William of Jumieges.

28. *ASC* C 1052, *JW* 1052, *ASC* C/D/E 1053, *JW* 1053.

CHAPTER FOUR

1. *WP*, p. 156 (27).

2. This chapter relies substantially on the essential groundwork on Domesday Book carried out by the following: R.H. Davies, 'The Lands of Harold, Son of Godwine, and their Distribution by William I', unpublished MA dissertation (Cardiff, 1967); Williams, 'Land and Power'; Fleming, *Kings and Lords*; R. Fleming, 'Domesday Estates of the King and the Godwines: A Study in Late Saxon Politics', *Speculum*, 58 (1983); and Clarke, *English Nobility*. I have not always followed the interpretation of the evidence by these writers but have drawn significantly on the data they have assembled.

3. Fleming, *Kings and Lords*, pp. xv–xvi, Whitelock, *Beginnings*, pp. 64–6 for the importance of land. Clarke, *English Nobility*, pp. 205, 220, Williams, 'Land and Power', pp. 171–3, Fleming *Kings and Lords*, pp. 58–71, Hill, *Atlas*, pp. 100–5 and J. Campbell, *The Anglo-Saxons* (London, 1991), pp. 216–17 for landholdings. *EHD II*, No. 172, p. 877 for the costs of feeding a slave-woman.

4. Williams, 'Land and Power', pp. 171–3, Fleming, *Kings and Lords*, pp. 11–20, 47, Barlow, *Edward*, pp. xxi–xxii, Clarke, *English Nobility*, pp. 1–12 for these problems. Williams, 'Land and Power', p. 177, Clarke, *English Nobility*, pp. 17–18 and Davies, 'Lands of Harold', pp. 6–17 for the problem of deceased owners.

5. Davies, 'Lands of Harold', Parts II and III, Clarke, *English Nobility*, pp. 18–23 and Fleming, *Kings and Lords*, Chapter 1 for possible sources of land.

6. *EHD I*, No. 129, pp. 593–6 for this will. *EHD I*, No. 51, pp. 468–9 for a *thegn's* minimum estate of 5 hides.

7. *DB Sussex* entries, Williams, *Land and Power*, pp. 176–7, Davies, 'Lands of Harold', pp. 29–31, Clarke, *English Nobility*, pp. 164–205 for Sussex.

8. Lawson, *Cnut*, p. 188 for Godwine's position under Cnut. Fleming, *Kings and Lords*, pp. 39–42 and Mack, 'Changing Thegns', pp. 375–87 for Cnut's actions.

9. Fleming, *Kings and Lords*, pp. 89–90, Clarke, *English Nobility*, pp. 169–91, Davies, 'Lands of Harold', pp. 19–23 and Williams, 'Land and Power', p. 175 for these earldom lands.

10. Whitelock, *Anglo-Saxon Wills*, pp. 22–5 and Fleming, *Kings and Lords*, pp. 42–7 for these bequests. *Chronicon Abbatiae Rameseiensis*, ed. W.D. Macray (London, 1886), p. 129. Williams *et al.*, *Dark Age Britain*, pp. 8,9, 12 for these nobles. *VER*, p. 33 for Folkstone.

11. Sawyer, *A-S Charters*, Nos 970 and 1022 for these grants. Fleming, *Kings and Lords*, pp. 90–5 and Davies, 'Lands of Harold', pp. 112–14 for the royal demesne. *DB Gloucestershire*, 1: 63 for Woodchester.

12. Whitelock, *Anglo-Saxon Wills*, pp. 84–7, Williams, 'Land and Power', pp. 173–4 for Harold in East Anglia.

13. Fleming, *Kings and Lords*, pp. 76, 91, 96–8, Clarke, *English Nobility*, pp. 181–91 for the lands in East Anglia. *The Waltham Chronicle*, ed. L. Watkiss and M. Chibnall (Oxford, 1994), pp. 25–7 for Athelstan.

14. The relevant *DB Suffolk*, *Essex*, *Huntingdonshire* and *Cambridgeshire* entries, Clarke, *English Nobility*, pp. 273–9 for Edith's lands. *DB Cambridgeshire* shows Harold in possession of land valued at £36 only.

15. *ASC* C 1049, *ASW*, Nos 78 and 79, pp. 345–6 for Beorn.

16. Clarke, *English Nobility*, pp. 181–2, 184–91 and relevant *DB Norfolk*, *Suffolk*, *Essex* and *Cambridgeshire* entries for Harold's men. *DB Essex*, 34: 28 for Wulfric. Williams, 'Land and Power', p. 179 for Leofwine of Bacton. *DB Norfolk*, 30: 16 and Williams, 'Land and Power', pp. 179–80 for Eadric the Steersman. *DB Suffolk*, 6: 92 for Stanwine.

17. *DB Essex*, 30: 16 for Leighs, *WC*, pp. 25–7 and Clarke, *English Nobility*, pp. 243–9 for Ansgar. *DB Suffolk*, 6: 92 and Clarke, *English Nobility*, pp. 283–302 for Eadric of Laxfield. *EHD II*, No. 187, pp. 903–4 for this bequest and *DB Norfolk*, 35: 16 for Fritton. *EHD II*, No. 189, pp. 905–6 and No. 184, pp. 901–2 for these bequests.

18. *ASC* C/D/E 1051 and 1052.

19. Williams, 'Land and Power', p. 177 for Gytha. *DB Hampshire*, 31: 1 for Polhampton. Williams, 'Land and Power', pp. 174–5, Fleming, *Kings and Lords*, pp. 89–90 and Davies, 'Lands of Harold', Part III for Harold in Wessex.

20. *ASC* C 1053, Fleming, *Kings and Lords*, pp. 98, 102, Davies, 'Lands of Harold', pp. 44–9 for retention of supposed comital estates. Fleming, *Kings and Lords*, p. 102 speaks of lands 'likely' to be so and Williams, 'Land and Power', p. 174 of lands 'presumably' so. *DB Suffolk*, 3: 55 for Gyrth. Fleming, *Kings and Lords*, pp. 41–2 for the disruption resulting from the Danish conquest.

21. Appendix Two for Ralph's earldom but Williams, 'King's Nephew', pp. 327–43 for a different view. Williams, 'Land and Power', p. 172, Davies, 'Lands of Harold', pp. 40–4 and Clarke, *English Nobility*, pp. 179–81 for Harold's lands. Fleming, *Kings and Lords*, p. 89 and Williams, 'Land and Power', pp. 174–5 for possible comital holdings.

22. *DB* relevant entries and Clarke, *English Nobility*, relevant entries. Williams, 'Land and Power', p. 180 and Fleming, *Kings and Lords*, p. 95 for these men.

23. *DB Kent*, p. 20, *DB Dorset*, 27: 2, Clarke, *English Nobility*, pp. 237–8, Williams, 'Land and Power', pp. 180–1 for these men.

24. *VER*, p. 33 and *DB Gloucestershire*, 1: 63 for this story and Whitelock, *Beginnings*, pp. 87–8 for the curse. However, it should be noted that King Edward himself held the lands of Berkeley in 1066 as noted in *DB Gloucestershire*, 1: 15. Davies, 'Lands of Harold', pp. 73–8, Williams, 'Land and Power', pp. 181–2, Fleming, *Kings and Lords*, pp. 84–6, and E.A. Freeman, *A History of the Norman Conquest of England*, 6 vols (Oxford, 1870), Vol. II, pp. 542–2 for these cases. *DB Cornwall*, 4: 21 and *ASW*, pp. 275–76 *DB Wiltshire*, 23: 7. *DB Dorset*, 1: 30. *DB Surrey*, 2: 3, and *DB Kent*, p. 20 for these phrases.

25. Williams, 'Land and Power', p. 182 and *DB Worcestershire*, App V, G14, 15, 17 and 20 for seizures of land from the bishopric of Worcester by Leofric and his family and followers. *DB Kent*, p. 20, *DB Dorset*, 19: 14, *DB Sussex*, 10: 63, *DB Surrey*, 2: 3, *DB Hertfordshire*, 1: 1, *DB Herefordshire*, 2: 8, 19: 8. Fleming, *Kings and Lords*, pp. 189–92 for cases of the misappropriation of church land by Normans including Odo Bishop of Bayeux, King William's own half-brother.

26. Fleming, *Kings and Lords*, pp. 84, 170 for the view that Harold seized this estate before Edward's death. *ASW*, pp. 275–6 and Lawson, *Cnut*, p. 149 for these lands as a personal gift by Cnut to Duduc his priest, who subsequently became Bishop of Wells and on his death bequeathed them to the bishopric. *ASW*, No. 71, pp. 284–5, *DB Kent*, p. 20, *DB Herefordshire*, 2: 8. Clarke, *English Nobility*, pp. 169–91 for these statistics.

27. Davies, 'Lands of Harold', p. 88, *DB Essex*, 30: 16 and *DB Suffolk*, 16: 35, 36: 8 and 16 for Scalpi. Williams, 'Land and Power', pp. 178–9, *DB Middlesex*, 8: 3, *DB Hertfordshire*, 17: 13 and *DB Essex*, 28, 1 and Fleming, *Kings and Lords*, p. 86 n. and p. 170 n. for Gauti. Davies, 'Lands of Harold', p. 83 and *DB Gloucestershire*, 1: 66 for Tofi. *DB Berkshire*, 1: 45 for Brihtward and *DB Surrey*, 5: 27 for Leofgar.

28. *DB Surrey*, 6: 5 for Pyrford, *VER*, p. 8, *ASC* D 1063, *JW* 1064 for the spoils of Harold's Welsh campaign and Stevenson, *Malmesbury – Before the Conquest* p. 216 for the spoils of Stamford Bridge.

29. *DB Essex*, 1: 26. *ASC* C/D/E 1056 for Leofgar.

30. *WP*, p. 224 (38) and *William of Malmesbury – A History of the Norman Kings*, tr. J. Stevenson (Lampeter, 1989), pp. 19–20 for the banner. *WC*, p. 33, Wilson, *Bayeux*, pls 3–6 and 27–31. *VER*, p. 21 and *JW* 1040 record equivalent gifts of fully equipped ships presented by Godwine to King Hardecnut and King Edward. *VER*, p. 87 and *ASC* D 1063 for the Welsh spoils and *ASC* D 1065 for the hunting lodge.

31. Williams, 'Land and Power', pp. 182–4 and Fleming, *Kings and Lords*, p. 51 for Harold's grants. *VER*, p. xlix n. and *William of Malmesbury – De Gestis Pontificum Anglorum*, ed. N.E.S.A. Hamilton (London, 1870), pp. 182–3, Fleming, *Kings and Lords*, p. 51 n. *The Chronicle of Hugh Candidus*, ed. W.T. Mellows (London, 1949), p. 70, Barlow, *English Church*, p. 60 n. Williams, 'Land and Power', pp. 183–4 for details.

32. *WC*, pp. 3–27. *Three Lives of the Last Englishmen*, tr. M. Swanton (London, 1984), pp. 5–10. Fleming, *Kings and Lords*, p. 57 for the history. Swanton, *Three Lives*, p. 5 for the miraculous cure. *WC*, pp. 33–7, Swanton, *Three Lives*, pp. 7–8, E.C. Fernie, 'The Romanesque Church of Waltham Abbey', *JBAA*, CXXXVIII (1985), pp. 48–87 and P.J. Huggins, K.N. Bascombe and R.M. Huggins, 'Excavations of the Collegiate and Augustinian Churches, Waltham Abbey, Essex 1984–87', *Archaeological Journal*, CXLVI (1989), pp. 476–537 for the church buildings.

33. *WC*, pp. 27–38 and Swanton, *Three Lives*, p. 8 for the staff. *WC*, pp. 29–31 and relevant *DB* entries for these lands. S. Keynes, 'Regenbald the Chancellor', *Anglo-Norman Studies*, X (1988), pp. 201–3 and R. Ransford, *Early Charters of the Augustinian Canons of Waltham Abbey, Essex 1062–1230* (Woodbridge, 1989), pp. xxiii–xxlv, 3–4 for a genuine source behind the later copy of Edward's confirmation charter of 1062. *WC*, p. 33 for these gifts and Swanton, *Three Lives*, p. 8 for the looting of many of them by William. *VER*, pp. 112–15 for Edward's gifts to St Peter's at Westminster. M.E.C. Walcott 'Inventory of Waltham, Holy Cross', *TEAS*, 5 (1873), p. 261 and Fleming, *Kings and Lords*, p. 57 n. 32 for the inventory.

34. *WC*, pp. xliii–xlviii and Swanton, *Three Lives* for their preservation of Harold's memory into the thirteenth century. Compton, *Harold*, p. 31 for these place-names.

CHAPTER FIVE

1. *ASC* C/D 1065.
2. *ASC* D 1051, *ASC* C/E 1049, *WJ*, p. 171 and *WP*, p. 10.
3. *ASC* C/D/E 1052, *VER*, p. 45.
4. *ASC* C/D/E 1016 and 1057, Stafford, *East Midlands*, p. 127.
5. *ASC* C/D 1054, *JW* 1054, Barlow, *Edward*, pp. 215–16. T. Reuter, *Germany in the Early Middle Ages 800–1056* (Harlow, 1991), p. 255, Z.J. Kozstolnyik, *Five Eleventh-Century Hungarian Kings* (New York, 1981), p. 75.
6. *ASC* C/D/E 1055, *JW* 1055, *VER*, p. 49, *ASC* D 1054.
7. Maund, *Ireland*, pp. 133–8, *Orderic Vitalis – The Ecclesiastical History*, ed. M. Chibnall (Oxford, 1969), Volume II, Books III and IV, pp. 138, 216. *DB Warwickshire*, 6: 5. *ASC* C/D/E 1055.
8. *ASC* C/D/E 1055, *JW* 1055, *ASC* C 1056, *JW* 1056.
9. *ASC* C/D/E 1055, *JW* 1055, Maund, *Ireland*, pp. 134–5, *Brut y Tywysogyon – Peniarth Ms 20 Version*, tr. T. Jones (Cardiff, 1952), p. 14, Williams *et al.*, *Dark Age Britain*, pp. 145–6, Maund, *Ireland*, pp. 64–8, D. Walker, *Medieval Wales* (Cambridge, 1990), p. 17. *DB Herefordshire*, 1: 49.
10. *ASC* C/D/E 1055, *JW* 1055.
11. *ASC* C/D/E 1055, *JW* 1055, *VER*, p. 51, C.N.L. Brooke, *The Church and the Welsh Border in the Central Middle Ages* (Woodbridge, 1986), pp. 10–11, 92–3 for the loss of Archenfield to Gruffydd, which I would date after the 1055 raid, rather than 1056. *DB Cheshire*, B7 for the lands beyond the Dee being given to Gruffydd by King Edward, no date is given for this, although 1055 is possible, 1058 would seem the more likely time.
12. *ASC* C/D 1056, *JW* 1056, *ASC* D 1049.
13. *ASC* C/D 1056.
14. *ASC* C/D/E 1056, *JW* 1056 record his death (C and D mistakenly naming him Cona) and both D and E have the return of Edward the Exile as their next entry. C has no further entries until 1065. Reuter, *Germany*, p. 255, Kozstolnyik, *Hungarian Kings*, P. Grierson, 'A Visit of Earl Harold to Flanders in 1056', *EHR*, LI (1936), pp. 90–7, *VER*, p. 53.
15. N. Rogers, 'The Waltham Abbey Relic-List' in Carola Hicks (ed.), *England in the Eleventh Century* (Stamford, 1992), pp. 165–6.
16. *ASC* D/E 1057. *ASC* p133 note 6 for this death as one of the unsolved mysteries of the period followed by Douglas, *William*, pp. 71–2, Brown, *Normans*, p. 126, and Stenton, *A-S England*, p. 571.
17. *VER*, pp. xxvi–xxvii, lxvi. and N. Hooper 'Edgar the Atheling: Anglo-Saxon Prince, Rebel and Crusader', *Anglo-Saxon England*, 14 (1985), p. 202 for a later tradition that Edward commended Edgar to the magnates as his heir. *ASC* D 1066.
18. *ASC* D/E 1057, *JW* 1057. *VER*, p. 51 suggests Gyrth may have initially received only Norfolk, because of his youth. He presumably gained all of East Anglia over time. *DB Middlesex*, 9: 1 for Harold, son of Ralph. Appendix Two for the fate of Ralph's earldom, and Williams, 'King's Nephew', pp. 331–9 for an alternative view.
19. Maund, *Ireland*, p. 138 places the marriage around 1057. Stenton, *A-S England*, p. 575, Stafford, *Unification*, p. 93, Loyn, *Norman Conquest*, p. 66, Douglas, *William*, p. 172, F. Barlow, *The Feudal Kingdom of England 1042–1216* 2nd edn (London, 1988), p. 70, Barlow, *Edward*, pp. 193–4 for varying views on whether or not any scheme existed on the part of Godwine's family to oust Leofric's family from power.
20. *ASC* D 1058, *JW* 1058, Jones, *Brut – Peniarth*, p. 14, Stokes, *Tigernach* 1058, *DB Yorkshire*, 1L1 for Amounderness, *DB Cheshire*, B7 for lands beyond the Dee. It is possible that Aelfgar received part of the spoils since *DB Oxfordshire*, B1 records him as earl before 1066 but this shire is more likely to have come into his hands on the death of Earl Ralph in 1057.
21. Ransford, *Early Charters*, pp. xiii–xxiv, 3–4. *WC*, pp. xxxviii–xliii, 31–9.
22. *ASC* D 1061, *JW* 1061, *VER*, pp. 34–7 and Swanton, *Three Lives*, p. 103 for Tosti's visit to Rome and *Simeon of Durham – A History of the Kings of England*, tr. J. Stevenson (Lampeter, 1978), 1061 for Malcolm's raid.
23. *ASC* 1058, Swanton, *Three Lives*, p. 104, *ASC* D 1063, *JW* 1063, *ASC* 1065 for this raid.
24. *ASC* D 1063, *JW* 1063.
25. *VER*, p. 87. (By permission of Oxford University Press)
26. *ASC* D/E 1063, *JW* 1063, *VER*, pp. 65, 87–8, *Gerald of Wales – Journey Through Wales/Description of Wales*, tr. L. Thorpe (Harmondsworth, 1978), p. 266.
27. *ASC* D/E 1063, *JW* 1063–4 and Jones, *Brut – Peniarth*, p. 15. MacAirt and MacNiocaill, *Ulster* 1064 names the murderer. Stafford, *Unification*, pp. 95, 121, K.L. Maund 'Cynan ap Iago and the Killing of Gruffydd ap Llywelyn', *CMCS*, 10 (1985), p. 65.
28. *DB Cheshire*, B7 and Brooke, *Welsh Border*, pp. 11, 93 for the restorations and *ASC* C/D 1065 for Harold's conquests. R.R. Davies, *The Age of Conquest: Wales 1063–1415* (Oxford, 1991), p. 26, Walker, *Medieval Wales*, pp. 18–19, Barlow, *Edward*, p. 212, Thorpe, *Gerald of Wales*, p. 266 and *Johannis Saresberiensis Episcopi Carnotensis Policratus*, ed. C.C.J. Webb (London, 1909), pp. 19–20.

CHAPTER SIX

1. Wilson, *Bayeux*, pls 25–6.
2. *WJ*, pp. 159–61, *WP*, pp. 100–14 [4–6] for the Norman version of events and Bosanquet, *Eadmer*, pp. 6–7 for an alternative version.
3. *WJ*, pp. 159–61, *ASC* D 1063 and *ASC* C/D 1065, *JW* 1064 records Gruffydd's death in 1064 but this appears to be an error. Douglas, *William*, pp. 174–5, 178–9.
4. *WJ*, pp. 159–61, *WP*, pp. 100–6 [4–5]. See Table 4 below. Douglas, *William*, pp. 174, 410, Bates, *William*, pp. 40–1. *VER*, p. 79.
5. *VER*, p. 51.
6. *VER*, p. 51, Douglas, *William*, pp. 174–5, Bates, *William*, pp. 41–2.
7. Wilson, *Bayeux*, pp. 201–12 and pl. 17, and Bernstein, *Mystery*, pp. 116–23 and pl. 1.
8. Thus Bosanquet, *Eadmer*, p. 8 and *WJ*, pp. 161, 263 in Orderic Vitalis' later additions to William's text. Wilson, *Bayeux*, pl. 17, *DB Buckinghamshire*, 4: 21 for a reference to Harold's 'sister', Aelfgyva.
9. Wilson, *Bayeux*, p. 117, Bernstein, *Mystery*, p. 19, Stenton, *Bayeux*, p. 178. *WJ*, pp. 161, 263 in Orderic Vitalis' later additions to William's text. I would reject the opinion that the Aelfgyva scene is merely a reference to a well known scandal, as every other picture in the Tapestry is essential to the story and therefore this one also must be related.
10. Stevenson, *Malmesbury – Before the Conquest*, p. 214. Wilson, *Bayeux*, pls 5–6.
11. *WJ*, p. 161, *WP*, pp. 100–2 [4], Wilson, *Bayeux*, pl. 7.
12. Bosanquet, *Eadmer*, pp. 6–7. A. Williams, *The English and the Norman Conquest* (Woodbridge, 1995), pp. 165–8, R.W. Southern, *St Anselm and his Biographer* (Cambridge, 1963), pp. 229–40 and R.W. Southern, *Saint Anselm: A Portrait in a Landscape* (Cambridge, 1990), pp. 404–21 for Eadmer and Christ Church. Barlow, *English Church*, p. 74 n.1 for the view that it was Aethelric I, an earlier Bishop of Sussex rather than this Aethelric, who supplied Eadmer with his information on St Dunstan. This appears unlikely since this man had died in 1034 and neither Eadmer nor his intermediary Aethelred/Nicholas prior of Worcester (for whom, see E. Mason, *St Wulfstan of Worcester, c. 1008–1095* (Oxford, 1990), pp. 221–22), who died in *c*. 1125 and 1124 respectively, can realistically have met him. Williams, *The English*, p. 159 n.19.
13. Bates, *William*, pp. 61–2, Douglas, *William*, p. 176 and Stenton, *A-S England*, p. 577.
14. *WJ*, p. 165, *WP*, p. 150 [7] and Wilson *Bayeux*, pls 35–7 for the need to construct a fleet and *WP*, p. 148 [6], 156–8 [8] for the barons reluctance to invade and the disparity between the duchy and kingdom.
15. *WJ*, p. 161, *WP*, pp. 100–2 [4] and Wilson, *Bayeux*, pl. 7 for Harold's capture and *WP*, p. 102 [4] for the prevalence of hostage-taking for ransom among the French.
16. *WJ*, p. 161, *WP*, p. 102 [4] and Wilson, *Bayeux*, pls 10–14, *WP*, p. 102 [4] for the importance of Harold and his reception in Normandy. Douglas, *William*, p. 176 for William's 'opportunity' and Bates, *William*, p. 61 for this 'masterly stroke'.
17. Wilson, *Bayeux*, pls 18–26, and *WJ*, p. 161, *WP*, pp. 100–14 [5–6] Bosanquet, *Eadmer*, p. 7 for the suggestion that Harold was duped.
18. *WP*, pp. 106–14 [5–6], Wilson, *Bayeux*, pls 18–24 and Douglas, *William*, pp. 177–9.
19. Bosanquet, *Eadmer*, p. 7, *WP*, p. 230 [38] and Stevenson, *Malmesbury – Before the Conquest*, p. 214 all mention this proposed marriage. Chibnall, *Ecclesiastical History*, pp. 119–313 and Douglas, *William*, pp. 174, 410, Bates, *William*, p. 40 for Count Walter. Bates, *William*, p. 61 and Douglas, *William*, p. 177 concede Harold's danger. *WJ*, · p. 161, *WP*, pp. 102–6 [4–5] and Wilson, *Bayeux*, pls 25–6 for the oath. *EHD I*, No. 49, p. 460 for oaths. D. Rollason, *Saints and Relics in Anglo-Saxon England* (Oxford, 1989), p. 191. Swanton, *Three Lives*, p. 100 for Wulfstan.
20. *WJ*, p. 161, *WP*, pp. 102–6 [23], Wilson, *Bayeux*, pls 25–6.
21. *WJ*, p. 161, *WP*, p. 176 [11] for the use of Harold's perjury as motivation. *WP*, p. 114 [6], Bosanquet, *Eadmer*, p. 6 for Wulfnoth.
22. *WP*, p. 114 [6], Wilson, *Bayeux*, pls 24–5, Bosanquet, *Eadmer*, p. 8 and Stevenson, *Malmesbury – Before the Conquest*, p. 216.
23. *VER*, p. 81 and *WP*, pp. 172 (30) and 148 (26).
24. Stafford, *Unification*, p. 97 for this possibility, *VER*, p. xxiii for the suggestion that this work was compiled in order to justify the succession to power of the Godwine brothers. If this is correct, then the dating of the work around 1064–5 suggests the possibility that the *Vita Eadwardi* itself may also be evidence for this new view on Harold's part.
25. Wilson, *Bayeux*, pl. 28, *ASC* C/D 1066, Bosanquet, *Eadmer*, p. 8. Wilson, *Bayeux*, pl. 28 shows Edward apparently remonstrating with Harold but as usual leaves us guessing about the reasons.

CHAPTER SEVEN

1. *VER*, p. 59. (By permission of Oxford University Press)

2. *VER*, p. 77.

3. W.E. Kapelle, *The Norman Conquest of the North: The Region and its Transformation 1000–1135* (London, 1979), pp. 87–9, Stenton, *A-S England*, p. 571, Barlow, *Edward*, pp. 234–9.

4. *Simeon of Durham – A History of the Church of Durham*, tr. J. Stevenson (Lampeter, 1988), pp. 67–9 for Copsi and his gifts to Durham. *DB Yorkshire*, C36, 6N36 and 23N1, and *DB Lincolnshire*, 36: 3–4 and CK28 for Copsi's lands. Stevenson, *Simeon: Church of Durham*, pp. 65, 66–7, W.M. Aird, 'St Cuthbert, the Scots and the Normans', *Anglo-Norman Studies*, XVI (1994), p. 9 for Durham and the Bishops but Kapelle, *North*, pp. 90, 98 for an alternative view. Stevenson, *Simeon: Kings of England* 1059 and 1061 for Tosti and King Malcolm.

5. *VER*, p. 79, Aird, 'St Cuthbert', p. 4 n. 20 for Tosti's justice. *Liber Vitae Ecclesiae Dunelmensis*, ed. J. Stevenson (London, 1841), p. 2 for Tosti and Godwine's names, later almost obliterated by erasure, possibly after the Conquest. Okasha, *Handlist*, pp. 87–8 for the sundial inscription.

6. *JW* 1058 for the Norwegian raid and *DB Yorkshire*, 1L1 for its effect. This devastation might also be due to William's harrying of the North in 1069–70. *ASC* D 1061, *JW* 1061, *VER*, pp. 53–7 for Tosti's visit to Rome. Stevenson *Simeon: Kings of England* 1061 for Malcolm's raid. There is no real evidence for raids in 1058 or 1059 as mentioned by Kapelle.

7. Kapelle, *North*, pp. 91–4, *VER*, p. 67, Kapelle, *North*, p. 88.

8. Whitelock, *Beginnings*, pp. 44–5, Kapelle, *North*, pp. 17–19 and Stenton, *A-S England*, p. 390 n. 1. *JW* 1065, Stevenson, *Simeon: Kings of England* 1065 for this incident. *ASW*, No. 121 for Gospatric's writ. Kapelle, *North*, p. 95. *ASC* C/D 1041, Stevenson, *Simeon – Church of Durham*, pp. 64–5, Kapelle, *North*, p. 25 for Siward.

9. *VER*, pp. 55–7, *ASC* D 1067 and 1069 and Table 13.

10. *ASC* Table 13, Kapelle, *North*, p. 95, MacAirt and MacNiocaill, *Ulster* 1054 for Dolfin as son of Thorfinn, *ASW*, No. 121.

11. *JW* 1065, Stevenson, *Simeon: Kings of England* 1065, Kapelle, *North*, pp. 95–6.

12. *ASC* C/D/E 1065, *JW* 1065, Stevenson, *Simeon: Kings of England* 1065, *VER*, p. 77, Kapelle, *North*, pp. 96–7 for the low assessment of the northern shires.

13. *DB Yorkshire* entries. Kapelle, *North*, pp. 96–8, *ASC* C 1065 and *VER*, p. 79.

14. *ASC* C/D/E 1065, *VER*, pp. 75–7, Kapelle, *North*, p. 98, P.J. McGurk and J. Rosenthal, 'The Anglo-Saxon Gospel Books of Judith Countess of Flanders: Their Texts, Make-Up and Function', *Anglo-Saxon England*, 24 (1995), p. 252.

15. *ASC* C/D/E 1065, *JW* 1065.

16. Stafford, *East Midlands*, p. 127, *ASC* Table 13, Kapelle, *North*, pp. 100–1, 108–9 for these men.

17. *VER*, pp. 77, 81 for Tosti as Edward's favourite. *JW* 1066, *WP*, p. 102 [4] for Harold's position.

18. *ASC* C/D/E 1065, *JW* 1065, *VER*, p. 77 for Lincolnshire. *ASW*, Nos 62 and 119 for Northamptonshire and Nottinghamshire. Also Appendix Two for Tosti's earldom.

19. *ASC* C/D/E 1065, *VER*, pp. 79, 81.

20. *ASC* C 1065, *JW* 1065, *VER*, p. 79 all highlight the great efforts made to reach a compromise and the stubbornness of the rebels.

21. *VER*, pp. 79–81. The author, even though sympathetic to Tosti makes clear his opinion that he did not believe the charge.

22. *VER*, pp. xxvi–xxvii, lxii–lxiii.

23. Stafford, *Unification*, p. 97 for this suggestion but Barlow, *Edward*, p. 238 rejects this possibility.

24. *VER*, pp. 81–3, *ASC* D 1065.

25. *ASC* C/D 1065 and *JW* 1065. The date of 28 October for this may have been used as it was the date of the council which decided the matter. *VER*, pp. 81–3 for Tosti's exile following after his expulsion from the earldom. *DB Hertfordshire*, 1: 18 and *DB Bedfordshire*, 54: 3 for the forfeitures.

26. *VER*, pp. 81–3 and *JW* 1065, *DB Shropshire*, 3d: 7 for this lawsuit.

27. *VER*, pp. 83, 119, Barlow, *Edward*, pp. 244–5, *WJ*, p. 161, *WP*, p. 146 [6], 100 [4].

28. *WP*, pp. 166–8 [9], *VER*, p. 77, Chibnall, *Ecclesiastical History*, p. 139.

29. *VER*, p. 119, Barlow, *Edward*, pp. 245–6, Smith, 'Stigand', pp. 199–219 and Cooper, *York*, p. 26.

30. Hooper, 'Edgar the Atheling', p. 204, Williams, 'English Royal Succession', pp. 166–7.

31. *ASC* C/D 1065, *ASC* E 1066, *JW* 1066, *VER*, pp. 123–5. The latter gives the date as 4 January possibly because Edward died during the night between 4/5 January. Wilson, *Bayeux*, pl. 30. *WP*, p. 172 [10] for the deathbed bequest.

32. *Ungedruckte Anglo-Normannische Geschichtsquellen*, ed. F. Liebermann (Strasburg, 1879), pp. 245–6. G. Garnett, 'Coronations and Propaganda: Implications of the Norman Claim to the Throne of England in 1066', *TRHS*, 5th Series, 36 (1986), pp. 91–116.

CHAPTER EIGHT

1.   *VER*, p. 49.

2.   Wilson, *Bayeux*, *passim*, *ASC* C/D/E 1056 for Leofgar, P. Seaby, *The Story of British Coinage* (London, 1985), p. 43, and H. Grueber and C. Keary, *English Coins in the British Museum* (London, 1970), Anglo-Saxon Series, Vol. II, pls XXXI and XXXII for the coins. *WP*, p. 160 (41) and Chibnall, *Ecclesiastical History*, p. 199 for Norman views on Anglo-Saxon hair styles. G.R. Owen-Crocker, *Dress in Anglo-Saxon England* (Manchester, 1986), pp. 168–9 for moustaches and beards.

3.   *VER*, p. 49, Wilson, *Bayeux*, pls 19–20, *ASC* D/E 1066.

4.   *VER*, pp. 47–53.

5.   *WP*, p. 224 (38) and Stevenson, *Malmesbury – Norman Kings*, pp. 19–20 for the banner. *Flor* 1068, *ASC* C/D 1056, C/D/E 1063 & C/D/E 1066, *WP*, p. 202 (15), 104 (23).

6.   Seaby, *Coinage*, p. 43, Grueber and Keary, *English Coins*, p. xcvii, M. Dolley, *Anglo-Saxon Pennies* (London, 1970), pp. 29–30 and S. Keynes, 'An Interpretation of the Pacx, Pax and Paxs Pennies', *Anglo-Saxon England*, 7 (1978), pp. 170–1 for the meaning behind these coins. *ASC* C 1055, 1056 & 1058. *ASC* C 1065 and *VER*, pp. 79–83.

7.   *WP*, p. 156 [8] himself mentions Harold's 'sapientia' or wisdom. *ASC* D1066.

8.   *VER*, pp. 48, 91, *WP*, pp. 102–4 [4–5], Bossanquet, *Eadmer*, pp. 6–7, *VER*, p. 81.

9.   *WP*, pp. 114 (24), 146 (26), 166 (29), *WJ*, p. 161.

10.   *WP*, pp. 100 [4], 102–6 [4–5].

11.   *JW* 1062, Swanton, *Three Lives*, pp. 100, 108–9 for Wulfstan. *VER*, p. 53 for Rome. Wilson, *Bayeux*, pl. 3 for Bosham. *WC*, p. 47 and Freeman, *Norman Conquest*, Vol. II, pp. 670–4 for Waltham.

12.   *WC*, pp. 31–3, Swanton, *Three Lives*, pp. 8-9, [3–40], Rogers, 'Relic-List', pp. 163–6.

13.   Williams, 'Land and Power', pp. 181–4, Fleming, *Kings and Lords*, pp. 84–5, 202–3.

14.   Barlow, *English Church*, p. 109, Douglas, *William*, pp. 170, 324 for Stigand as 'destined for deposition'. Stenton, *A-S England*, p. 659 for the suggestion that the prompting or his deposition came from the Papacy.

15.   *WP*, p. 234 (38), Barlow, *English Church*, pp. 78–81, Smith, 'Stigand', pp. 199–218, Brooks, *Canterbury*, p. 306 and *ASW*, pp. 572–3 for Stigand. *ASW*, Nos 13 and 14, pp. 157–8.

16.   Loyn, 'Harold', p. 32 for his 'odd' marital circumstances. *WC*, p. 55, Swanton, *Three Lives*, p. 34, *Chronica Johannis de Oxenedes*, ed. H. Ellis (London, 1859), p. 292 and Freeman, *Norman Conquest*, Vol. III, pp. 790–3 for Edith. *DB Kent*, C4 for 'Harold's concubine'. C. Fell, *Women in Anglo-Saxon England and the Impact of 1066* (London, 1984), pp. 138–40, Douglas, *William*, pp. 15, 37–44 and Bates, *William*, p. 22 for different marriage customs on the Continent.

17.   *ASC* D 1067 (recte 1068) for Harold's sons. Stafford, *East Midlands*, p. 127 for such alliances. Williams, 'Land and Power', p. 176 and Clarke, *English Nobility*, pp. 273–9 for Edith's landholdings.

18.   Fell, *Women*, p. 89, Williams, 'Land and Power', p. 176 for this link. J.R. Clark-Hall, *A Concise Anglo-Saxon Dictionary* (Cambridge, 1960), p. 50, H. Sweet *The Student's Dictionary of Anglo-Saxon* (Oxford, 1896), p. 25, and Fell, *Women*, p. 67 for female beauty. *DB Suffolk* 4: 17, *DB Suffolk*, 1: 61, *DB Suffolk*, 16: 10, *DB Warwickshire*, 6: 10 for these different women. E. Searle, 'Women and the Legitimization of Succession at the Norman Conquest', *Proceedings of the Battle Conference on Anglo-Norman Studies, 1979* (1980), pp. 167–9 emphasizes the real issues behind what had appeared to Southern *St Anselm*, p. 185, as 'a strange and passionate romance'. P.H. Sawyer, '1066–1086: A Tenurial Revolution?' in P.H. Sawyer (ed.), *Domesday Book: A Reassessment* (London, 1985), p. 78 for Alan's occupation of Edith's lands.

19.   *DB Cambridgeshire, Hertfordshire, Buckinghamshire* for her as *Faira*, fair, or *Pulchra*, beautiful. *DB Suffolk* for her as *Dives*, rich. *DB* entries recording her landholdings are summarized by Clarke, *English Nobility*, pp. 273–9. *DB Cambridgeshire*, 14: 66 for Grimbald, and Fell, *Women*, p. 97 for the gospel book. *Oxenedes*, p. 292 for this donation. Stafford, *Queens*, p. 40, Stafford, *East Midlands*, pp. 127, 151, and Stafford, *Unification*, pp. 68, 76–7 for Aelfgifu of Northampton.

20.   Swanton, *Three Lives*, p. 34 and *WC*, p. 55 for Edith. Stafford, *Queens*, pp. 40, 49 and Stafford, *Unification*, pp. 76–8 for Cnut's marriages.

21.   *JW* 1066 and Freeman, *Norman Conquest*, Vol. III, pp. 638–40 for Queen Alditha. Stevenson, *Malmesbury – Norman Kings*, p. 71 for Harold, son of Harold. Maund, *Ireland*, pp. 133–9 for Alditha's first marriage. M. Meyer, 'Women's Estates in Later Anglo-Saxon England: The Politics of Possession', *Haskins Society Journal*, 3 (1992), p. 120 for the suggestion of no marriage. Stafford, *Unification*, p. 77 where Cnut's second wife, Emma, claimed this about her son Hardecnut in 1035.

22.   *WP*, p. 230 (38) and Chibnall, *Ecclesiastical History*, p. 137 for the Norman bride and *JW* 1066 for Alditha.

23.   *DB Somerset*, 1: 14 and 16. *Flor* 1068 for Godwine, son of Harold.

24.   *ASC* 1067 (recte 1068) and 1069, *Flor* 1068 and 1069 for Harold's sons. *VER*, p. 23 for Edith at Wilton. Swanton, *Three Lives*, p. 118 for Gunnhild. Freeman, *Norman Conquest*, Vol. III, pp. 754–7 for Harold's children.

25. *ASC* 1053, *WP*, p. 204 (15), *VER*, p. 83 for Gytha. Clarke, *English Nobility*, pp. 164–9 for Godwine's lands.

26. *ASC* C/D 1056, Rogers, 'Relic-List', pp. 163, 166, King, 'Ealdred', pp. 127–9 and J.L. Nelson, 'The Rites of the Conqueror' in J.L. Nelson *Politics and Ritual in Early Medieval Europe* (London, 1986), pp. 389–95.

27. Swanton, *Three Lives*, pp. 100, 108–9, and Mason, *St Wulfstan*, pp. 65–7, 100–4.

28. *DB Middlesex*, 9: 1. Williams, 'King's Nephew', pp. 327–43.

29. *ASC* C/D 1065, Wilson, *Bayeux*, pls 2, 4, 9, 14, Whitelock, *Beginnings*, pp. 91–2, *DB Herefordshire*, 25: 9 for hunting. *DB Surrey*, 11: 1, C.H. Haskins, 'King Harold's Books', *EHR*, XXXVII (1922), pp. 398–400, R.M. Wilson, *The Lost Literature of Medieval England* (London, 1970), p. 69, L. Cochrane, *Adelard of Bath* (London, 1994), p. 53, J.A. Green, *The Government of England under Henry I* (Cambridge, 1986) for hawks.

30. *VER*, p. 23 for Edith, Green, *Henry I*, pp. 158–9 for literacy.

CHAPTER NINE

1. *ASC* C/D 1065

2. *ASC* E 1066, Wilson, *Bayeux*, pls 30–1, *JW* 1066 for Harold as sub-regulus. Mason, *St Wulfstan*, p. 3, Garnett, 'Coronations', p. 98 and Nelson, 'Rites', pp. 393–5 for the validity of Harold's consecration which caused difficulties for William's claim. *WJ*, p. 161, *WP*, p. 146 [6] and Wilson, *Bayeux*, pls 30–1 and p. 138 nn. where the reversal of the death and burial scenes is interpreted as implying haste. *ASC* C/D 1066 for word of William's invasion.

3. Nelson, 'Rites', pp. 389–95.

4. *WP*, p. 146 [6] and Wilson, *Bayeux*, pl. 31 for Harold's consecration contrasting with *JW* 1066. *ASC* C/D/E 1058 and 1059, *JW* 1062 and Swanton, *Three Lives*, p. 105 for Stigand and Ealdred as consecrators respectively. *ASC* C/D/E 1066 and *WP*, p. 220 for William's consecration by Ealdred.

5. *WP*, p. 165, Bosanquet, *Eadmer*, p. 8, *WP*, p. 150 [7] and Wilson, *Bayeux*, pls 35–9 for the Norman preparations.

6. Swanton, *Three Lives*, p. 109, M. Dolley, *The Norman Conquest and the English Coinage* (London, 1966), pp. 37–8, Barlow, *Feudal Kingdom*, p. 76, Douglas, *William*, p. 183, Kapelle, *North*, pp. 101, 105. D. Whitelock, 'The Dealings of the Kings of England with Northumbria in the Tenth and Eleventh Centuries' in P. Clemoes (ed.), *The Anglo-Saxons* (London, 1959), p. 88 and B. Wilkinson, 'Northumbrian Separatism in 1065–1066', *BJRL*, 23 (1939), pp. 504–26 and Stafford, *Unification*, p. 99.

7. Swanton, *Three Lives*, p. 109, *JW* 1066, *ASC* C/D 1066.

8. *ASW*, No. 71, pp. 284–5, Wilson, *Bayeux*, pl. 31, Bernstein, *Mystery*, pp. 37–50 for parallel illustrations.

9. Galbraith, *Domesday Book*, pp. 175–7, Garnett, 'Coronations', pp. 91–116, Stafford, *Unification*, p. 99, *EHD II*, No. 35, p. 461-2 and No. 77, pp. 644–6. There exists only one slip in Domesday Book where *DB Hampshire*, 1: 13 admits Harold's reign. *EHD II*, No. 33, p. 461 and No. 36, p. 462 and Brown, *Norman Conquest*, No. 174, p. 146.

10. *JW* 1066, *DB Hampshire*, 1: 12–14 and *DB Gloucestershire*: 1, 3–5.

11. Grueber and Keary, *English Coins*, pp. 460–74, Hill, *Atlas*, maps 221, 224 and 225, Dolley, *Coinage*, pp. 11–12, Dolley, *A-S Pennies*, pp. 29–30 and H.R. Loyn, *Anglo-Saxon England and the Norman Conquest* (London, 1962), p. 124.

12. *EHD II*, No. 223, p. 964 (Abingdon Chronicle) and D. Knowles, C.N.L. Brooke and V. London, *The Heads of Religious Houses, England and Wales, 940–1216* (Cambridge, 1972), p. 24 for Ealdred. *Liber Eliensis*, ed. E.O. Blake (London, 1962), p. 169, Knowles *et al.*, *Heads*, p. 45 for discussion on a dispute over the date of Wulfric's death which nevertheless makes it clear Thurstan was appointed by Harold.

13. *ASW*, No. 62, pp. 262–5 for an indication that Tosti ruled Northamptonshire which was later to belong to Waltheof. *ASC* D 1066 for the first mention of Waltheof as an earl. *DB Hampshire*, D11. *DB Bedfordshire*, 53: 20, 54: 3. *ASC* D/E 1065 gives 28 October for King Edward's agreement to the terms given by the Northumbrian rebels and *JW* 1065 adds that Tosti was exiled after 1 November. *JW* 1065 and *VER*, p. 81 both confirm that Edward's health declined from this time onward. F.S. Scott, 'Earl Waltheof of Northumbria', *Archaeologia Aeliana*, 4th Series, 30 (1952), pp. 158–60 correctly dismisses the possibility that William appointed Waltheof but fails to consider Harold, whose nine month reign provided sufficient time for such an appointment. The fact that Domesday Book records Waltheof as an earl *Tempore Regis Edwardi* probably merely reflects the inexactitude of its record.

14. Gaimar, *L'Estorie des Engles*, ed. T.D. Hardy and C.T. Martin (London, 1888), p. 222, K. Mack, 'The Staller: Administrative Innovation in the Reign of Edward the Confessor', *Journal of Medieval History*, 12 (1986), pp. 123–34 for Marleswein as a man holding lands similar in extent to known stallers. Clarke, *English Nobility*, pp. 322–4 for the lands.

15. Barlow, *English Church*, *passim*. Keynes, *Regenbald*, pp. 185–222 for Regenbald, Douglas, *William*, pp. 290, 292 and Mack, 'The Staller', pp. 123–34, for the stallers, and A. Freeman, *The Moneyer and the Mint in the Reign of Edward the Confessor 1042–1066* 2 vols (Oxford, 1985), pp. 27–40 for the moneyers.

16. *WJ*, p. 165, *JW* 1066, *ASC* D/E 1063, *WP*, p. 102 [4].

17. *ASC* C/D 1066, M. Biddle 'Seasonal Festivals and Residence: Winchester, Westminster and Gloucester in the Tenth to Twelfth Centuries', *Anglo-Norman Studies*, VIII (1985), pp. 51–72.

18. *ASC* C/D 1066, *JW* 1066, F. Stevenson and C.B.F. Walker, *Halley's Comet in History* (London, 1985), p. 57, Wilson, *Bayeux*, pl. 32, *WJ*, p. 163, *WP*, p. 208 (36).

19. *ASC* C/D 1066, *JW* 1066, *DB Hampshire*, 1: 14 and 5, and 9: 2 for Tosti's lands on the Isle of Wight. Ibid. records nine estates held by Tosti, all in the extreme west of the island, while *DB Sussex* lists only one and *DB Kent* none.

20. *ASC* C/D 1066, *JW* 1066, *ASC* C/D 1066, *WP*, p. 154 [7].

21. *ASC* C/D 1066, *JW* 1066, Galbraith, *Domesday Book*, p. 176, Hill, *Atlas*, maps 179 and 181 combined, reveal the extent of these holdings, C.W. Hollister, *Anglo-Saxon Military Institutions on the Eve of the Norman Conquest* (Oxford, 1962), p. 122 and Hooper, 'Some Observations', p. 22 for the fleet.

22. *ASC* C/D/E 1066, *JW* 1066, Hardy and Martin, *Gaimar*, p. 219, *DB Lincolnshire* 1: 65, 30: 1 for Tosti's lands and Ibid. 36: 3 for Copsi's lands.

23. *ASC* C 1066, *JW* 1066, *WP*, p. 154 [7], *DB Norfolk*, 10: 76 and 77. F.M. Stenton, 'St Benet of Holme and the Norman Conquest', *EHR*, XXXVII (1922), pp. 227, 233 and Hooper, 'Some Obsevations', pp. 24–5, *DB Sussex*, 5: 2. Douglas, *William*, p. 186.

24. *WJ*, p. 165, *WP*, pp. 156 [8], 186 [12], Brown, *Norman Conquest*, No. 171, pp. 134–44.

25. Douglas, *William*, p. 188, Barlow, *Feudal Kingdom*, p. 77, Brown, *Normans*, pp. 147–8.

26. *WP*, p. 154 [7], Genealogical Table 1 for Harold and Swein. *Annales Corbiensis in Monumenta Germaniae Historica, Scriptores*, ed. G.H. Pertz (Hannover, 1857), Vol. III, p. 6 and Wissolik, 'Saxon Statement', p. 71.

27. *WP*, pp. 152–4 [7], Douglas, *William*, pp. 187–8, Stenton, *A-S England*, p. 586, Brown, *Normans*, pp. 148–9, Barlow, *Feudal Kingdom*, pp. 78–9.

28. Morton, 'Pope Alexander', pp. 362–82], H.E.J. Cowdrey, *The Age of Abbot Desiderius* (Oxford, 1983), pp. 118–22 for the political scene.

29. *EHD II*, No. 81, pp. 649–50 for the Penitential Ordinance, Douglas, *William*, p. 187, Bates, *William*, p. 65, Brown, *Normans*, p. 148, Barlow, *Feudal Kingdom*, p. 79, Stenton, *A-S England*, p. 586 for other views. Stevenson, *Malmesbury – Norman Kings*, p. 17 for Harold's lack of response.

30. *WP*, pp. 158–160 [8], Bates, *William*, p. 65 for this date. There exists no clear date for this event. Douglas, *William*, p. 193, 398 places it on 12 September, but based on a later source. Douglas, *William*, p. 193, Bates, *William*, p. 66, Stenton, *A-S England*, p. 588.

31. *ASC* C 1066, *JW* 1066, N. Hooper 'The Anglo-Saxons at War' in S.C. Hawkes (ed.), *Weapons and Warfare in Anglo-Saxon England* (1989), p. 195, Douglas, *William*, p. 192, Brown, *Normans*, p. 144, Barlow, *Feudal Kingdom*, p. 80, Stenton, *A-S England*, p. 588, R.A. Brown, 'The Battle of Hastings', *Proceedings of the Battle Conference on Anglo-Norman Studies, 1980* (1981), p. 7, J. Gillingham, 'William the Bastard at War' in C. Harper-Bill *et al.*, *Studies*, pp. 156–7 disagrees with this opinion. If Douglas' dating is correct, it was in fact less than two full months.

32. *ASC* C/E 1066, *DB Essex*, 6: 9.

33. *JW* 1066. *ASC* C 1014.

CHAPTER TEN

1. *ASC* D 1066.

2. B. and P. Sawyer, *Medieval Scandinavia* (Minneapolis, 1993), pp. 54–8 and P.H. Sawyer, 'The Wealth of England in the Eleventh Century', *TRHS*, 5th Series, 15 (1965), pp. 145–64.

3. *AB*, pp. 107–8, Jones, *Vikings*. pp. 400–5.

4. *AB*, p. 124, *King Harald's Saga*, tr. M. Magnusson and H. Palsson (Harmondsworth, 1966), pp. 9–39, K. Skaare, *Coins and Coinage in Viking Age Norway* (Oslo, 1976), pp. 65–8.

5. *AB*, pp. 124, 127–9, Jones, *Vikings*, pp. 405–6, Magnusson and Palsson, *Harald's Saga*, pp. 48–63 for the saga account. S. Blondal and B.S. Benedikz, *The Varangians of Byzantium* (Cambridge', 1978), pp. 54–102, and H.R.E. Davidson, *The Viking Road to Byzantium* (London, 1976), pp. 207–29 for the historical basis.

6. Magnusson and Palsson, *Harald's Saga*, pp. 68, 70, where Thjodolf's verses indicate a warlike stance between the two Norwegians followed by the sharing of the kingdom, and p. 73, a verse by Bolverk, which admits Harald made payment to Magnus for a share of the kingdom. *AB*, pp. 122–4 for an account heavily biased in favour of Swein of Denmark who of course did *not* control either England or Norway. Magnusson and Palsson, *Harald's Saga*, pp. 79–80, 122–4 for verses on this war. Skaare, *Coins*, pp. 106–8, Magnusson and Palsson, *Harald's Saga*, pp. 62–6, P. Grierson, *Coins of Medieval Europe* (London, 1991), pp. 74–5, Skaare, *Coins*, pp. 65–8 for Harald's wealth and coinage.

7. *WP*, p. 166 [9], *AB*, pp. 158–9 and Magnusson and Palsson, *Harald's Saga*, pp. 135–6, Jones, *Vikings*, pp. 406–8.

8. Magnusson and Palsson, *Harald's Saga*, pp. 127–9 in Thjodolf's verses, Hardy and Martin, *Gaimar*, p. 164, *ASC* C 1066, *JW* 1066.

9. Stokes, *Tigernach* 1058 for this earlier invasion. *AB*, p. 128, *ASC* C 1066, *JW* 1066 for this surprise and *ASC* D 1045, *JW* 1045 for knowledge of Magnus's invasion plans. Stenton, *A-S England*, p. 588, Barlow, *Feudal Kingdom*, p. 76, Douglas, *William*, p. 180 and Brown, 'Hastings', p. 7, *WP*, p. 166 (29), Magnusson and Palsson, *Harald's Saga*, p. 137 for the Norwegian claim.

10. *ASC* C/D 1066 where Tosti submits to King Harald.

11. *ASC* C/D/E 1066, *JW* 1066, Stevenson, *Simeon – Kings of England* 1066 names the landing place.

12. *ASC* D/E 1066, Kapelle, *North*, pp. 103–4 errs in placing the fall of York before the battle of Fulford. Stenton, *A-S England*, p. 589, Douglas, *William*, p. 193, Brown, *Normans*, p. 155, Barlow, *Feudal Kingdom*, p. 80.

13. *ASC* C 1066, *JW* 1066, Magnusson and Palsson, *Harald's Saga*, p. 144 for mention of Waltheof. *DB Yorkshire*, C28 for Fulford, Kapelle, *North*, p. 104 for the folly.

14. *ASC* C/D/E 1066, *JW* 1066, Magnusson and Palsson, *Harald's Saga*, pp. 143–4.

15. *ASC* C 1066, *JW* 1066, Douglas, *William*, p. 193, Stenton, *A-S England*, p. 589, Brown, *Normans*, p. 156, Whitelock, 'Dealings of the Kings', p. 88 for Northumbrian separatism but *EHD I*, No. 52, p. 476, Wilkinson, 'Separatism', pp. 516–26 and F.M. Stenton, 'The Danes in England' in D.M. Stenton (ed.), *Preparatory to Anglo-Saxon England* (Oxford, 1970), p. 161 for another view.

16. *ASC* C/D/E 1066 and *JW* 1066 imply that word of the Norwegian landing at York was sent to Harold, but he was probably already aware of their earlier progress along the coast. *DB Worcestershire*, 26: 16, *DB Essex*, 6: 15, Barlow, *Edward*, p. 262 for this story recorded by Osbert of Clare in 1138.

17. R.P. Abels, *Lordship and Military Obligation in Anglo-Saxon England* (London, 1988), pp. 160–70 and N. Hooper 'Anglo-Saxon Warfare on the Eve of the Conquest: A Brief Survey' *Proceedings of the Battle Conference on Anglo-Norman Studies, 1977* (1978), pp. 84–6, N. Hooper, 'The Housecarls in the Eleventh Century', *Anglo-Norman Studies*, VII (1984), pp. 161–76 for huscarls. I favour Hooper's initial view of the housecarls as distinct from *thegns* and the *fyrd*. Hollister, *A-S Military Institutions*, pp. 38–102, Abels, *Lordship*, pp. 176–84 and Hooper, 'A-S Warfare', pp. 87–9 for the *fyrd*.

18. *ASC* C 1066. *ASC* D/E 1066 relate events in a compressed form which omits this distinction. *EHD I*, No. 49, Item 71 and R.H.C. Davis, *The Medieval Warhorse* (London, 1989), pp. 74–5 for extra horses. Hooper, 'A-S Warfare', pp. 84–93 but also R. Glover, 'English Warfare in 1066', *EHR*, LXVII (1952), pp. 1–18 for use of horses in war. B.S. Reilly, *The Kingdom of Leon-Castille under Alfonso VI* (Guildford, 1988), p. 149 and B. Bachrach, 'The Angevin Strategy of Castle Building in the Reign of Fulk Nerra, 987–1040', *AHR*, 88 (1983), p. 542 for the rates of travel.

19. *DB Kent*, D3 for mounted royal messengers.

20. *ASC* C/D 1066, Kapelle, *North*, pp. 104–5, Brown, *Normans*, p. 156 and Whitelock, 'Dealings of the Kings', p. 88 for Northumbrian separatism but refuted by Wilkinson, 'Separatism', pp. 504–26.

21. *ASC* C 1066, *JW* 1066, *DB Yorkshire*, 4E2 for Catton.

22. Stenton, *A-S England*, p. 590 and Jones, *Vikings*, pp. 413–14.

23. *ASC* C/D/E 1066, I. Atkinson, *The Viking Ships* (Cambridge, 1979), p. 26, *Mariani Scotti Chronicon – Monumenta Germaniae Historica Scriptores* ed. G.H. Pertz (Hannover, 1844), Vol. V, p. 559.

24. Magnusson and Palsson, *Harald's Saga*, pp. 150, 152.

25. *ASC* C/D 1066, *JW* 1066, Magnusson and Palsson, *Harald's Saga*, pp. 151–52, Hooper, 'A-S at War', p. 200 but Glover, 'Warfare', pp. 1–18 for an alternate view.

26. Magnusson and Palsson, *Harald's Saga*, p. 153. (Reproduced by permission of Penguin Books Ltd)

27. Jones, *Vikings*, p. 413.

28. *VER*, p. 89 This poem was subsequently turned into a form more critical of Harold and particularly of his role in Tosti's death. *WP*, pp. 170 [10], 202 [15] for a Norman appreciation of this victory. Barlow, *Feudal Kingdom*, pp. 80–1, Douglas, *William*, p. 194.

29. Brown, 'Hastings', pp. 7–8 and Hooper, 'A-S at War', p. 193 for the impressive nature of English military organization, but also Brown, 'Hastings', pp. 6–7.

CHAPTER ELEVEN

1. Wilson, *Bayeux*, pl. 71.

2. *JW* 1066, *ASC* D 1066, *WJ*, p. 167 and *WP*, pp. 160–4 [89].

3. *WP*, pp. 160–2 [8], Gillingham, 'William', pp. 155–7, Douglas, *William*, pp. 193–6, Bates, *William*, p. 66.

4. *WJ*, p. 167, *WP*, p. 168 [9–10], *ASC* D/E 1066, *JW* 1066, Wilson, *Bayeux*, pls 42–51, Gillingham, 'William', pp. 157–8.

5.   Stenton, *A-S England*, p. 592 and Bates, *William*, p. 67, Gillingham, 'William', pp. 148–54. Douglas, *William*, pp. 213–15, 219–20 for William's use of mobility on other occasions.

6.   *WP*, p. 170 [10], *DB Sussex*, 5: 1.

7.   *ASC* E 1066 where Harold came from the 'north' to the battle. *JW* 1066.

8.   Knowles *et al.*, *Heads*, p. 81 for Abbot Aelfwig and *ASC* E 1066 for Abbot Leofric. *EHD II*, No. 223, pp. 964–8 (Abingdon Chronicle) for the men of Abingdon including Thurkill of Kingston and Sheriff Godric. *DB Huntingdonshire*, D7 for those of St Benets and *EHD II*, No. 238, p. 983 for Bury's tenants. J. Backhouse, D.H. Turner, L. Webster (eds), *The Golden Age of Anglo-Saxon Art* (London, 1984), p. 198 where a twelfth-century martyrology of St Augustine's records a tradition of the fall of Harold with 'very many of our brethren'. This last may refer to men of the abbey but perhaps simply to fellow Englishmen. *DB Suffolk*, 76: 20, 31: 50 and *DB Hampshire*, 69: 16 for these men.

9.   *JW* 1066, *ASC* D 1066, Hardy and Martin, *Gaimar*, p. 222, Kapelle, *North*, p. 105, *JW* 1066 but here the later compiler of this source seems to draw an inference not found in the more contemporary Chronicles.

10.   *ASC* D 1066.

11.   *ASC* D/E 1066, *JW* 1066, Brown, 'Hastings', p. 8, Stenton, *A-S England*, p. 592, Douglas, *William*, pp. 196–8, Bates, *William*, p. 68.

12.   *JW* 1066, *WP*, p. 180 [11], reinforced by even later accounts like that of Stevenson, *Malmesbury – Norman Kings*, p. 18. Darby, *Domesday England*, pp. 243–5 for the effect of Norman raids in Sussex.

13.   *WJ*, p. 167, *WP*, pp. 172–8 [10–11], 180 [11], Gillingham, 'William', pp. 159–60.

14.   Douglas, *William*, pp. 216–17, Bates, *William*, pp. 76–7, Barlow, *Feudal Kingdom*, pp. 87–8, Brown, *Normans*, pp. 43–5 and Gillingham, 'William', pp. 155–6 for the Breton expedition.

15.   *WP*, p. 180 [11] for the fleet. Gillingham, 'William', p. 157, Hooper, 'A-S at War', p. 198, Barlow, *Feudal Kingdom*, p. 82 almost appreciates this point.

16.   *ASC* D 1066 for this landmark. *DB Sussex*, 9: 21 for this estate. C.H. Lemmon 'The Campaign of 1066' in D. Whitelock, D.C. Douglas, C.H. Lemmon and F. Barlow, *The Norman Conquest* (London, 1966), p. 97 places it, not implausibly, on nearby Caldbec Hill. *WP*, pp. 172–4 [10], 178–80 [11], R. Bartlett, *Trial by Fire and Water* (Oxford, 1988), p. 104.

17.   *WJ*, p. 167 and *WP*, p. 180 [11].

18.   *ASC* D/E 1066, *JW* 1066.

19.   *WJ*, p. 169 and *WP*, p. 184 [12], Brown, 'Hastings', p. 9 and Lemmon, 'Campaign', p. 102.

20.   *WP*, p. 224 (38), Wilson, *Bayeux*, pls 54–5, Stevenson, *Malmesbury – Norman Kings*, pp. 19–20 and *The Chronicle of Battle Abbey*, ed. E. Searle (Oxford, 1980), p. 40 for Harold's banner, which was raised on the spot where Battle Abbey was later built. Hooper, 'A-S Warfare', pp. 91–3 and 'A-S at War', pp. 199–200 for the English battle tactics. Wilson, *Bayeux*, pls 61–2 for the shield wall. Douglas, *William*, pp. 198–9, Brown, 'Hastings', pp. 9–10, Lemmon, 'Campaign', p. 100 for the strength of Harold's position. Lemmon, 'Campaign', p. 100 suggests he reconnoitred the position during the summer of 1066, while he awaited the invasion. Brown, 'Hastings', p. 9 where it is suggested Harold adopted this position on the spur of the moment, which is more unlikely.

21.   Hooper, 'A-S Warfare', pp. 85–7, Hooper, 'Housecarls', pp. 169–72 and Abels, *Lordship*, pp. 160, 167–70 for the *huscarls*. Hooper, 'A-S Warfare', pp. 88–9 and Abels, *Lordship*, pp. 175–9 for the *fyrd*.

22.   *WP*, pp. 184–6 [12], Brown, 'Hastings', pp. 11–12 and Lemmon, 'Campaign', pp. 104–5 for William's army, and *WP*, pp. 182–4 [12] for his speech.

23.   *WJ*, p. 208, *JW* 1066 both state that the battle began at the third hour, which Lemmon, 'Campaign', p. 105, places at this time. *WJ*, p. 169 says it began early in the morning. *WP*, pp. 186–90 [12-13] and Wilson, *Bayeux*, pls 60–5 for the course of the battle.

24.   *WP*, pp. 190–2 [13], Brown, 'Hastings', p. 14 n. 87 and Douglas, *William*, pp. 200–1, Lemmon, 'Campaign', pp. 107–8, Wilson, *Bayeux*, pls 63–4 and *WP*, p. 204 [15] for Harold's brothers.

25.   *WP*, p. 190 [13], Wilson, *Bayeux*, pls 66–7.

26.   *WP*, pp. 190–2 [13], *WJ*, p. 169 and *JW* 1066, Lemmon, 'Campaign', pp. 107–8, Barlow, *Feudal Kingdom*, p. 83 for the condemnation of Harold. Gillingham, 'William', pp. 145–8, R.C. Smail, *Crusading Warfare 1097–1193* (Cambridge, 1972), pp. 15–16 and P. Contamine, *War in the Middle Ages* (Oxford, 1984), pp. 255–9.

27.   *WP*, pp. 192–4 [13].

28.   *WP*, p. 194 [13–14], Lemmon, 'Campaign', pp. 109–10 disputes the tactic, but see Brown, 'Hastings', pp. 14–16 for its use, here and elsewhere, by trained troops.

29.   Wilson, *Bayeux*, pls 68–70 where large numbers of arrows also appear in English shields and bodies. *WP*, p. 194 [14], Brown, 'Hastings', pp. 16–17, *WJ*, p. 169 mentions only that Harold fell in 'the last shock of the battle' as amended, surely correctly by Gillingham, 'William', p. 148 n. 36 from the incorrect form 'the first shock of battle'.

30. Wilson, *Bayeux*, pl. 71. N.P. Brookes and H.E. Walker, 'The Authority and Interpretation of the Bayeux Tapestry' *Proceedings of the Battle Conference on Anglo-Norman Studies, 1978* (1979), p. 33 for confirmation of the figure with the arrow in his eye as Harold. It would be interesting to know whether the archer whose arrow felled the king fulfilled the penance laid down by the Papal legate in 1070 of penance as for 3 Lents (see *EHD II*, No. 81, p. 650). Whatever reward he may have received after the conquest could not be enough. Wilson, *Bayeux*, pls 71–2, *WJ*, p. 169, and Searle, *Battle Abbey*, p. 38.

31. Wilson, *Bayeux*, pl. 71 for the figure falling beneath a Norman knight. Brookes and Walker, 'Bayeux Tapestry', pp. 32–3 for this also representing Harold. Stevenson, *Malmesbury – Norman Kings*, pp. 20–1 relates the story of the cowardly action of striking the fallen Harold. *WJ*, p. 169 and *WP*, pp. 204 [15], 224 (38), Hooper, 'A-S Warfare', p. 93, Lemmon, 'Campaign', pp. 110–11, Brown, 'Hastings', pp. 17–18, Stenton, *A-S England*, pp. 595–6, Barlow, *Feudal Kingdom*, p. 84, Douglas, *William*, p. 201 for the decisive importance of Harold's fall.

32. *ASC* D 1066, *WP*, pp. 200 [15], 204 [15], *JW* 1066, *DB Huntingdonshire*, D7, Knowles *et al.*, *Heads*, p. 81, and *DB Suffolk*, 76: 20 for these men. Davis, 'William of Poitiers', p. 113 considers this account may have been inspired by the story of Achilles and Hector's body in the Iliad. Stevenson, *Malmesbury – Norman Kings*, p. 23 and Swanton, *Three Lives*, p. 34, *WC*, pp. 51–7for Edith 'Swan-neck'.

33. Swanton, *Three Lives*, pp. 38–40, Thorpe, *Gerald of Wales*, pp. 198–9, Jones, *Brut – Peniarth*, 1332, p. 127, Wilson, *Lost Literature*, pp. 58–9 and Rollason, *Saints*, pp. 218–19 for Harold as a hermit in Chester and M. Ashdown, 'An Icelandic Account of the Survival of Harold Godwineson' in Clemoes, *The Anglo-Saxons*, pp. 123–4 for him as a hermit at Canterbury. C. Kightly, *Folk Heroes of Britain* (London, 1984), p. 110 and Ashdown, 'Icelandic Account', pp. 134–5 for Harold as folk hero.

CHAPTER TWELVE

1. *ASC* D 1067 (recte 1068).

2. B. Hudson 'The Family of Harold Godwineson and the Irish Sea Province', *JRSAI*, 109 (1979), pp. 92–100 provides a good account of the fate of Harold's family but my opinion differs in several respects. In particular, the references to Tosti, son of Swein, depend on a late source and this individual is mentioned nowhere else so I have discounted him. It is of course just possible he represents a distant memory of Hakon, son of Swein. *ASC* D 1066, *WP*, pp. 208–16 (36–37), *The Carmen de Hastingae Proelio of Guy, Bishop of Amiens*, ed. C. Morton and H. Muntz (Oxford, 1972), pp. 38–42 for the period after Hastings.

3. *ASC* D 1066, *JW* 1066 and *WP*, pp. 214–16 (36–37), Morton and Muntz, *Carmen*, pp. 41–3 for Edgar's position.

4. *JW* 1066, Morton and Muntz, *Carmen*, p. 40 for Edith. Support for such a view might be found in *WP*, pp. 166–8 [9] and *VER*, p. 54 but is discounted by Barlow, *Edward*, p. 242.

5. *ASC* D 1066, *WJ*, pp. 171–3, *JW* 1066, *WP*, pp. 216–46 (37–40).

6. *EHD II*, No. 81, p. 649 for the Ordinance. M. Chibnall, *The World of Orderic Vitalis* (Oxford, 1984), p. 11 for Orderic's feelings on the foreign speech of the Normans, *ASC* D 1066 for castles, *EHD II*, No. 81, p. 649 for the looting of churches, *ASC* E 1066 for land seizures. R.H.C. Davis, 'The Norman Conquest' in Davis (ed.), *Alfred to Stephen*, pp. 59–60 for a general view.

7. *WJ*, pp. 177–9, *WP*, pp. 262–4(41), Swanton, *Three Lives*, p. 110, 'It was as if the whole strength of the country had fallen with Harold'.

8. *ASC* D 1067 (recte 1068). *WJ*, p. 181. J. Allan, C. Henderson and R. Higham, 'Saxon Exeter' in J. Haslam *Anglo-Saxon Towns in Southern England* (Chichester, 1984), p. 385 for Exeter's status (after London, York and Winchester) with *c.* 2,000 citizens and 400 houses. For the family lands in the region see the relevent entries in *DB Devonshire, Somerset* and *Cornwall* but conveniently summarized by Clarke, *English Nobility*, pp. 164–205. Flanagan, *Irish Society*, p. 59 for the Godwine family counter offensive, but I consider Harold's sons were also present. Also Williams, *The English*, pp. 19–21.

9. *DB Devonshire*, 1: 50, Hamilton, *William of Malmesbury, De Gestis*, p. 204 and Knowles *et al.*, *Heads*, p. 72 for Sihtric, *EHD II*, No. 223, pp. 964–8 (Abingdon Chronicle) and Knowles *et al.*, *Heads*, p. 24 for Ealdred. M. Lapidge, 'Surviving Booklists from Anglo-Saxon England' in M. Lapidge and H. Gneuss (eds), *Learning and Literature in Anglo-Saxon England* (Cambridge, 1985), pp. 58–9 for Saewold, Sawyer, 'Tenurial Revolution?', p. 73 for Brihtric and Chibnall, *Ecclesiastical History*, pp. 211, 215.

10. *ASC* D 1066, Flor 1067, Chibnall, *Ecclesiastical History*, pp. 194–6, J. Le Patourel, *The Norman Empire* (Oxford, 1976), p. 41.

11. *ASC* D 1067 (recte 1068).

12. Chibnall, *Ecclesiastical History*, pp. 210–12, Flor 1067, *ASC* D 1067, Douglas, *William*, pp. 216–17.

13. *Flor* 1067, Chibnall, *Ecclesiastical History*, p. 214, *ASC* D 1067 (recte 1068). *WJ*, pp. 181–3, Chibnall, *Ecclesiastical History*, p. 224, Wallace, 'Viking Dublin', p. 205 and Maund, *Ireland*, p. 167 for Diarmait. *The Annals of Inisfallen*, ed. S. MacAirt (Dublin, 1951) 1068, *WP*, p. 224 (38) and Wilson, *Bayeux*, pl. 71 for these standards.

14. *ASC* D 1067 (recte 1068). *DB Somerset*, 1: 14 and 16 for Godwine's lands and Hill, *Atlas*, map 225 for the Taunton mint. *Flor* 1069, Chibnall, *Ecclesiastical History*, p. 224 and these spoils. Freeman, *Norman Conquest*, Vol. III, pp. 788–90 for Harold's sons.

15. *ASC* D 1069, *Flor* 1069, *WJ*, pp. 181–3, Chibnall, *Ecclesiastical History*, p. 224 and Flanagan, *Irish Society*, p. 60. *DB Devonshire*, 17: 41 and Darby, *Domesday England*, pp. 238–9 for wasted lands.

16. *ASC* D 1069, *Flor* 1069, *WJ*, pp. 181–3, Chibnall, *Ecclesiastical History*, p. 224.

17. *ASC* D 1067 (recte 1068), *Flor* 1067, *WJ*, p. 183, Chibnall, *Ecclesiastical History*, p. 244.

18. Brown, *Normans*. p. 191, Barlow, *Feudal Kingdom*, pp. 89–90, Douglas, *William*, pp. 213, 267, Stenton, *A-S England*, pp. 600, 602, Stafford, *Unification*, pp. 103–4, Loyn, *Norman Conquest*, p. 105, Chibnall, *Anglo-Norman England*, p. 16 for views.

19. Chibnall, *Ecclesiastical History*, p. 224 for Flanders. P. Grierson, 'Relations between England and Flanders before the Norman Conquest', *TRHS*, 4th Series, 23 (1941), p. 109, Lapidge, 'Booklists', p. 39 and Rogers, 'Relic-List', p. 167 for these bequests.

20. Douglas, *William*, pp. 224–5 for the Flemish situation. Appendix One for Aethelric. J.F.A. Mason, 'William the First and the Sussex Rapes' in *1066 Commemoration Lectures* (London, 1966), pp. 37–58.

21. Christiansen, *Saxo*, p. 58, Fell, *Women*, p. 183, *ASC* D/E 1069 and D/E 1070, Chibnall, *Ecclesiastical History*, pp. 224–34 and *AB*, p. 160 for Danish invasions. Christiansen, *Saxo*, pp. 58, 228 n. 20, *Snorri Sturluson-Heimskringla*, tr. S. Laing (London, 1930), p. 236 and *The Russian Primary Chronicle*, ed. S.H. Cross and O.B. Sherbowitz-Wetzor (Cambridge, 1973), p. 214 for Gytha's marriage supported by B. Rybakov, *Kievan Rus* (Moscow, 1989), p. 224, D. Obolensky, *Six Byzantine Portraits* (Oxford, 1988), pp. 89–90 and G. Vernadsky, *Kievan Russia* (London, 1973), pp. 96, 336.

22. J. Martin, *Medieval Russia 980–1584* (Cambridge, 1995), pp. 57–89, Vernadsky, *Kievan Russia*, pp. 99–209, S. Franklin and J. Shepard, *The Emergence of Rus 750–1200* (London, 1996), pp. 278–319 for the Russian background.

23. Cross and Sherbowitz-Wetzor, *Russian Chronicle* 1076–1107, pp. 211–14 and Obolensky, *Portraits*, pp. 85–104.

24. Cross and Sherbowitz-Wetzor, *Russian Chronicle* 1076 and pp. 206–15, Obolensky, *Portraits*, pp. 104–14, Cross and Sherbowitz-Wetzor, *Russian Chronicle*, pp. 211, 214–15.

25. Cross and Sherbowitz-Wetzor, *Russian Chronicle* 1107 and p. 214 for her death. This would make her aged over fifty, which links with the Laing, *Heimsk*, p. 292 description of her as 'Gytha the Old'. *Chronicle of Novgorod 1016–1471*, tr. R. Mitchell and N. Forbes (London, 1914) 1113 for Vladimir's rule in Kiev. Cross and Sherbowitz-Wetzor, *Russian Chronicle* 1076 and p. 211 for Msistislav's birth and Laing, *Heimsk*, pp. 236–92 for his Norse name Harold. Mitchell and Forbes, *Chron. Novgorod* 1132, Laing, *Heimsk*, pp. 236, 292 for this genealogical information. Although late, this Icelandic source of *c.* 1240 is fairly accurate on genealogies, which were central to the culture of Iceland, J.L. Byock, *Medieval Iceland* (London, 1988), pp. 14–18.

26. Chibnall, *Ecclesiastical History*, pp. 214–18, Ibid., p. 228, Ibid., pp. 138 and 216, Maund, *Ireland*, pp. 137–40 and Williams, *The English*, p. 53 for this lady. The suggestion that she was buried in the Abbey of La Chaise Dieu in France appears unlikely. The 'Queen Edith' who paid for the construction of the abbey's dormitory is more likely to be Harold's sister and the story of the later burial was perhaps no more than an attempt to associate a famous lady with the place. G. Beech 'England and Aquitaine in the Century before the Norman Conquest', *Anglo-Saxon England*, 19 (1991), pp. 94–5 for details. Stevenson, *Malmesbury – Norman Kings*, pp. 33, 71. Olaf is called Magnus in error. Laing, *Heimsk*, p. 263 refers to the fatal arrow in some skaldic verse but does not mention young Harold's presence.

27. Swanton, *Three Lives*, p. 118, Mason, *St Wulfstan*, pp. 224–25. S.J. Ridyard, *The Royal Saints of Anglo-Saxon England* (Cambridge, 1988), pp. 172–3 for Wilton as a place of refuge for noble English ladies and as a guardian of English tradition.

28. Southern, *St Anselm*, pp. 185–93, Southern, *Portrait*, pp. 262–4, Searle, 'Women', pp. 167–9, Mason, *St Wulfstan*, pp. 226–8 and Barlow, *William Rufus*, pp. 313–14 for alternative views.

29. Searle, 'Women', pp. 167–9 and Sawyer, 'Tenurial Revolution?', p. 78.

30. *WP*, p. 32 (20) for Wulfnoth as a hostage in 1051–2. Bosanquet, *Eadmer*, pp. 6–7 for Harold's attempt to gain his release in 1064. *Flor* 1087 for William's deathbed release of Wulfnoth followed by his reincarceration by William Rufus.

31. Barlow, *William Rufus*, pp. 65–6.

32. *Flor* 1087.

33. *ASC* 1100.

APPENDIX ONE

1. *VER*, pp. 18–19, Barlow, *Edward*, p. 104, Barlow, *English Church*, pp. 104, 209 n. and Brooks, *Canterbury*, pp. 303, 305 for Aethelric the monk.

2. *ASC* D 1057, *ASC* D/E1058, *JW* 1057 and 1058 for Bishop Aethelric. *VER*, pp. xlii–xliii for its Flemish author. *DB Sussex*, 9: 11 and 60 for Bishop Aethelric's lands.

3. *JW* 1070 and *Letters of Lanfranc, Archbishop of Canterbury*, ed. H. Clover and M. Gibson (Oxford, 1979), pp. 62–3 for his deposition. *ASC* D/E 1058, Barlow, *English Church*, pp. 221–22, for Siward. Barlow, *English Church*, pp. 113–14 for the Papal letters. Stenton, *A-S England*, p. 671 n.1. for the church council.

4. *EHD II*, No. 50, pp. 481–3 for the trial. *VER*, p. 18 for Aethelric's skill in affairs.

5. Williams, *The English*, p. 158 n.19, Barlow, *English Church*, p. 74 n. 1 for Bishop Aethelric as a source for Eadmer's Life of St Dunstan, and Mason, *St Wulfstan*, pp. 117 n. 36, 221 for his intermediary.

APPENDIX TWO

1. Loyn, *Governance*, pp. 31–133 and Freeman, *Norman Conquest*, Vol. II, pp. 555–69.

2. *ASC* C/D 1054 for Siward's responsibility for warfare in Scotland. *ASW*, No. 121 for his control of Cumbria. *ASW*, No. 59 for a writ addressing Earl Siward in Huntingdonshire, but *JW* 1051 for Harold's earldom encompassing this shire.

3. *ASW*, Nos 7 and 119 for Tosti in Yorkshire and the latter for Nottinghamshire also, and *ASW*, No. 62 for Northamptonshire. *ASC* D/E 1065, for these shires and the devastation of Northamptonshire. *VER*, p. 77.

4. *ASC* C/D/E 1066, Stevenson *Simeon –Kings of England* 1072, *DB Lincolnshire*, T4 shows Morcar in receipt of the earl's third penny for the city of Lincoln. *ASC* C 1066 and *JW* 1066 indicate that he drove Tosti's raiding force out of Lindsey with his brothers' help, although other versions of the Chronicle attribute this action to Earl Edwin alone. Barlow, *Edward*, p. 194 n. 3 for Waltheof's later authority in Northamptonshire, as indicated by Chibnall, *Ecclesiastical History*, p. 263, perhaps originating at this time.

5. Williams, *The English* pp. 169, 170–1, and pp. 113-14 for Leofric and his predecessors. *ASC* C 1039 and *JW* 1039, *ASC* C/D/E 1055 for Leofric and the Welsh Border, *Anglo-Saxon Charters* ed. A.J. Robertson (Cambridge, 1939), Nos XCIV, CXI, CXII for Leofric holding Worcestershire.

6. *ASC* D/E 1057, *ASW*, Nos 115–17 for Aelfgar's authority in these shires confirmed by his role in the appointment of Bishop Wulfstan of Worcester as recorded in Swanton, *Three Lives*, p. 104.

7. *ASW*, No. 96 for Edwin and Staffordshire and *DB Shropshire*, 4, 1, 1, *DB Cheshire*, S1, *DB Warwickhire*, 1: 6 and *DB Worcestershire*, C1 for these other shires. Chibnall, *Ecclesiastical History*, p. 219 for the construction of Warwick castle to subdue Earl Edwin in 1068 and Ibid., p. 229 for the defeat at Stafford in 1069.

8. *ASW*, Nos 38, 111, 3 for Kent, Hampshire and Berkshire respectively. Robertson, *A-S Charters*, No. CV for Devon and No. CVII for Hampshire. *JW* 1051 for Godwine's authority in Kent, Sussex and Wessex. The possibility of his authority extending to Surrey, Dorset and Somerset reflects Harold's later responsibilities. *ASC* D/E 1051 for Dover and *ASC* C/D 1052 for his supporters in 1052. The latter also refers to support from Essex, perhaps in favour of Harold rather than his father, since it is unlikely that Godwine's authority extended beyond the Thames.

9. *ASC* E 1051, *ASC* C/D/E 1052, Barlow, *Edward*, p. 125 n. 2 for a possible transfer of Earl Odda's earldom to perhaps encompass Worcestershire or Gloucestershire. However, this appears to conflict with Earl Leofric's authority in Worcestershire. Earl Odda's appearance in Robertson, *A-S Charters*, Nos CXI and CXII may relate instead to his links with Pershore.

10. *ASW*, Nos 35 and 39 for Kent, Nos 40–2 for Surrey, No. 85 for Hampshire, No. 5 for Berkshire, Nos 1 and 2 for Dorset, Nos 64–70 for Somerset and No. 120 for Devon. The inclusion of Sussex which was held by Godwine seems very likely and that of Wiltshire and Cornwall probable. *ASW*, No. 115 for Gloucestershire held by Harold in 1062 and *ASW*, Nos 49 and 50 for Herefordshire. *ASW*, p. 567 for spurious writs indicating his brother Leofwine as earl in Kent or Surrey which have been ignored in this discussion.

11. *ASC* C 1046 and Robertson, *A-S Charters*, No. XCIX for Swein in Herefordshire perhaps in succession to Earl Hrani of Cnut's time, for whom see Williams *et al.*, *Dark Age Britain*, p. 206. *JW* 1051 for Gloucestershire and Oxfordshire but also Somerset and Berkshire in spite of *ASW*, No. 3. *ASW*, Nos 78 and 79 for Hertfordshire. *ASW*, Nos 57 and 58 for Earl Thuri holding Huntingdonshire, which presumably fell to Beorn as his successor, according to Williams *et al.*, *Dark Age Britain*, p. 227. *ASW*, Nos 13 and 14 for Norfolk and Suffolk and *ASW*, No. 84 and *JW* 1051 for Essex.

12. *ASC* E 1047 for Swein's exile and *ASC* C 1049 for the possibility that Harold and Beorn expected to lose if Swein was restored.

13. *JW* 1051, *ASC* E 1051 for the Frenchmen and their castle established in Earl Swein's province undoubtedly by Earl Ralph. *ASW*, No. 3 for Earl Godwine holding Berkshire in the period 1045–1048. *ASC* D 1051 for Ralph.

14. *ASC* D/E 1051 for Aelfgar. *ASW*, Nos 15–17 for Norfolk and Suffolk, but *ASW*, No. 59 for Earl Siward holding Huntingdonshire at this time. *ASC* C/D 1055 shows Ralph responsible for the defence of Herefordshire in 1055 and it seems likely that King Edward would wish to restore it to Earl Ralph as soon as possible after being forced to deprive him of it in 1050. *ASW*, No. 55 for his control of Oxfordshire. *ASW*, No. 59 for Huntingdonshire in Siward's hands at this time and Northamptonshire, although not so recorded, subsequently passed to his successor Tosti.

15. *ASC* C/D 1052 for Harold's restoration and *ASW*, No. 84 for Essex. Barlow, *Edward*, p. 125 n. 2 suggests the possibility that Odda may have gained some of Earl Ralph's shires to replace the south western shires restored to Earl Godwine. *ASC* C/D/E 1053 for the exchange of East Anglia.

16. *ASC* D/E 1057, *ASW*, Nos 23–5 for Gyrth's authority in Norfolk and Suffolk. *VER*, p. 50 for the suggestion that he received only Norfolk initially. *ASW*, Nos 88 and 89 for Leofwine in control of Middlesex and *ASW*, Nos 90 and 91 for Hertfordshire. *DB Oxfordshire*, B1 indicates that Aelfgar held the third penny of Oxford but *ASW*, Nos 95, 103, 104 show the shire controlled by Gyrth.

BIBLIOGRAPHY

PRIMARY SOURCES

Adam of Bremen – History of the Archbishops of Hamburg-Bremen, tr. Francis J. Tschan (New York, 1959)

Anglo-Saxon Charters, ed. P.H. Sawyer (London, 1968)

Anglo-Saxon Charters, ed. A.J. Robertson (Cambridge, 1939)

The Anglo-Saxon Chronicle, ed. D. Whitelock with D.C. Douglas and S.I. Tucker, rev. edn (London, 1961)

The Anglo-Saxon Chronicle, ed. Michael Swanton (London, 1996)

The Anglo-Saxon Chronicle, ed. G.N. Garmonsway (London, 1953)

Anglo-Saxon Wills, ed. Dorothy Whitelock (Cambridge, 1930)

Anglo-Saxon Writs, ed. F.E. Harmer (Manchester, 1952)

Annales Corbiensis – Monumenta Germaniae Historica, Scriptores, Vol. III, ed. G.H. Pertz (Hannover, 1857)

The Annals of Inisfallen, ed. Sean MacAirt (Dublin, 1951/1977)

The Annals of Tigernach, tr. Whitley Stokes (Llanerch, 1993)

The Annals of Ulster (to AD1131), ed. Sean MacAirt and Georoid MacNiocaill (Dublin, 1983)

The Bayeux Tapestry, ed. David M. Wilson (London, 1985)

The Bayeux Tapestry, ed. F.M. Stenton (London, 1965)

Brut Y Tywysogyon Peniarth MS. 20 Version, ed. Thomas Jones (Cardiff, 1952)

Brut Y Tywysogyon Red Book of Hergest Version, ed. Thomas Jones (Cardiff, 1955)

The Carmen de Hastingae Proelio of Guy Bishop of Amiens, ed. Catherine Morton and Hope Muntz (Oxford, 1972)

Chronica Johannis de Oxenedes, ed. H. Ellis (London, 1859)

The Chronicle of Battle Abbey, ed. Eleanor Searle (Oxford, 1980)

The Chronicle of Hugh Candidus, ed. W.T. Mellows, (London, 1949)

The Chronicle of John of Worcester, Vol. II, ed. R.R. Darlington and P.J. McGurk (Oxford, 1995)

Chronicle of Novgorod 1016–1471, tr. Robert Mitchell and Nevill Forbes (London, 1914)

Chronicon Abbatiae Rameseiensis, ed. W.D. Macray (London, 1886)

Domesday Book, ed. J. Morris, 34 vols. (Chichester, 1975–86)

Eadmer – Historia Novorum in Anglia, tr. G. Bosanquet (London, 1964)

The Ecclesiastical History of Orderic Vitalis, ed. M. Chibnall, 6 vols. (Oxford, 1969–80)

Encomium Emmae Reginae, ed. Alistair Campbell (London, 1949)

English Historical Documents: Vol. I, c. 500–1042, ed. Dorothy Whitelock (London, 1979)

English Historical Documents: Vol. II, 1042–1189, ed. David C. Douglas and George W. Greenway (Oxford, 1981)

Facsimiles of English Royal Writs to AD 1100, ed. T.A.M. Bishop and P. Chaplais (Oxford, 1957)

Florence of Worcester's Chronicle, tr. Joseph Stevenson (Lampeter, 1989)

Gaimar, L'estoire des Engles, ed. T.D. Hardy and C.T. Martin (London, 1888)

Geffrei Gaimar: L'Estoire des Engleis, ed. Alexander Bell (Oxford, 1960)

Gerald of Wales: Journey Through Wales/Description of Wales, tr. Lewis Thorpe (Harmondsworth, 1978)

T*he Gesta Normannorum Ducum of William of Jumieges, Orderic Vitalis and Robert of Torigni*, ed. E.M.C. Van Houts, 2 vols, (Oxford, 1992 and 1995)

Guillaume de Poitiers – Histoire de Guillaume le Conquérant, ed. Raymonde Foreville (Paris, 1952)

Hemingi Chartularium ecclesiae Wigorniensis, Vol i, ed. T. Hearne (1723)

Johannis Sareberiensis episcopi Carnotensis Policratus, ed. C.C.J. Webb (London, 1909)

King Harald's Saga, tr. Magnus Magnusson and Hermann Palsson (Harmondsworth, 1966)

Knytlinga Saga, tr. Hermann Palsson and Paul Edwards (Odense, 1986)

The Leofric Missal, ed. F.E. Warren (Oxford, 1883)

Letters of Lanfranc, Archbishop of Canterbury, ed. H. Clover and M. Gibson (Oxford, 1979)

Liber Eliensis, ed. E.O. Blake (London, 1962)

Liber Vitae Ecclesiae Dunelmensis, ed. J. Stevenson (London, 1841)

The Life of King Edward Who Rests at Westminster, ed. Frank Barlow, 2nd edn (Oxford, 1992)

Mariani Scotti Chronicon – Monumenta Germaniae Historica Scriptores, Vol. V, ed. G.H. Pertz (Hannover, 1844)

The Norman Conquest, ed. R. Allen Brown (London, 1984)
Orkneyinga Saga, tr. Hermann Palsson and Paul Edwards (London, 1978)
Recueil des Actes des Ducs de Normandie (911–1066), ed. Marie Fauroux (Caen, 1961)
The Russian Primary Chronicle, ed. S.H. Cross and O.P. Sherbowitz-Wetzor (Cambridge, Mass., 1973)
Saxo Grammaticus Danorum Regum Heroumque Historia, Books X–XVI, Vol. I, ed. Eric Christiansen (Oxford, 1980)
Simeon of Durham: A History of the Church of Durham, tr. Joseph Stevenson (Lampeter, 1988)
Simeon of Durham: A History of the Kings of England, tr. Joseph Stevenson (Lampeter, 1987)
Snorri Sturluson-Heimskringla, tr. Samuel Laing (London, 1930)
Snorri Sturluson-Heimskringla: The Olaf Sagas, tr. Samuel Laing (London, 1964)
Three Lives of the Last Englishmen, tr. Michael Swanton (London, 1984)
Ungedruckte Anglo-Normanische Geschichtsquellen, ed. F. Liebermann (Strassburg, 1879)
Walter Map – De Nugis Curialium, tr. M.R. James (Cymmrodorion Record Series 9, 1923)
The Waltham Chronicle, ed. L. Watkiss and M. Chibnall (Oxford, 1994)
William of Malmesbury: De Gestis Pontificum Anglorum, ed. N.E.S.A. Hamilton (London, 1870)
William of Malmesbury – A History of the Norman Kings, tr. Joseph Stevenson,. (Lampeter, 1987)
William of Malmesbury – The Kings before the Norman Conquest, tr. Joseph Stevenson (Lampeter, 1989)

SECONDARY SOURCES

Books

Abels, R.P. *Lordship and Military Obligation in Anglo-Saxon England*, London, 1988
Atkinson, I. *The Viking Ships*, Cambridge, 1979
Backhouse, J., Turner, D.H., Webster, L. (eds). *The Golden Age of Anglo-Saxon Art*, London, 1984
Barlow, F. *Edward the Confessor*, London, 1979
——. *The English Church 1000–1066*, London, 1979
——. *William Rufus*, London, 1983
——. *The Feudal Kingdom of England 1042–1216*, 2nd edn, London, 1988
Barrow, G.W.S. *Feudal Britain*, London, 1971
Bartlett, R. *Trial by Fire and Water*, Oxford, 1988
Bates, D. *Normandy Before 1066*, Harlow, 1982
——. *William the Conqueror*, London, 1989
Bernstein, D.J. *The Mystery of the Bayeux Tapestry*, London, 1986
Blackburn, M.A.S. (ed.). *Anglo-Saxon Monetary History*, Leicester, 1986
Blair, P.H. *An Introduction to Anglo-Saxon England*, Cambridge, 1959
Blondal, Sigfus, and B.S. Benedikz. *The Varangians of Byzantium*, Cambridge, 1978
Bradbury, J. *The Medieval Archer*, Woodbridge, 1985
Brooke, C.N.L. *The Church and the Welsh Border in the Central Middle Ages*, Woodbridge, 1986
Brooks, N. *The Early History of the Church of Canterbury*, Leicester, 1984
Brown, Michelle P. *Anglo-Saxon Manuscripts*, London, 1991
Brown, R.A. *The Normans and the Norman Conquest*, London, 1969
——. *The Normans*, Woodbridge, 1984
Burton, Janet. *Monastic and Religious Orders in Britain 1000–1300*, Cambridge, 1994
Butt, Ronald. *A History of Parliament: The Middle Ages*, London, 1989
Byock, J.L. *Medieval Iceland*, London, 1988
Byrne, Francis John. *Irish Kings and High Kings*, London, 1973
Campbell, J. *The Anglo-Saxons*, London, 1991
Chibnall, M. *The World of Orderic Vitalis*, Oxford, 1984
——. *Anglo-Norman England 1066–1166*, Oxford, 1986
Clark-Hall, J.R. *A Concise Anglo-Saxon Dictionary*, Cambridge, 1960
Clarke, Howard. *Medieval Dublin*, Dublin, 1990
Clarke, P.A. *The English Nobility Under Edward the Confessor*, Oxford, 1994
Clemoes, P. (ed.). *The Anglo-Saxons*, London, 1959

Cochrane, L. *Adelard of Bath*, London, 1994
Contamine, P. *War in the Middle Ages*, Oxford, 1984
Cooper, J. *The Last Four Anglo-Saxon Archbishops of York*, York, 1970
——. *The Battle of Maldon*, London, 1993
Coss, Peter. *The Knight in Medieval England 1000–1400*, Stroud, 1993
Cowdrey, H.E.J. *The Age of Abbot Desiderius*, Oxford, 1983
Darby, H.C. *Domesday England*, Cambridge, 1977
Davidson, H.R.E. *The Viking Road to Byzantium*, London, 1976
Davies, R.R. *The Age of Conquest*, Oxford, 1991
Davies, Wendy. *Wales in the Early Middle Ages*, Leicester, 1982
——. *Patterns of Power in Early Wales*, Oxford, 1991
Davis, R.H.C. (ed.). *From Alfred the Great to Stephen*, London, 1981
——. *The Medieval Warhorse*, London, 1989
De Vries, Kelly. *Medieval Military Technology*, Ontario, 1992
Dodwell, C.R. *Anglo-Saxon Art, A New Perspective*, Manchester, 1982
Dolley, M. *The Norman Conquest and the English Coinage*, London, 1966
——. *Anglo-Saxon Pennies*, London, 1970
Douglas, D.C. *William the Conqueror*, London, 1964
——. *The Norman Achievement*, London, 1969
Duby, Georges. *France in the Middle Ages 987–1460*, Oxford, 1991
Dubabin, Jean. *France in the Making 843–1180*, Oxford, 1985
Fell, C. *Women in Anglo-Saxon England and the Impact of 1066*, London, 1984
Flanagan, M.T. *Irish Society, Anglo-Norman Settlers, Angevin Kingship*, Oxford, 1989
Fleming, R. *Kings and Lords in Conquest England*, Cambridge, 1991
Fletcher, R. *Who's Who in Roman Britain and Anglo-Saxon England*, London, 1989
Foote, P.G., and Wilson, D.M. *The Viking Achievement*, London, 1970
Franklin, S., and Shepard, J. *The Emergence of Rus 750–1200*, London, 1996
Freeman, A. *The Moneyer and the Mint in the Reign of Edward the Confessor 1042–1066*, 2 vols, BAR 1985
Freeman, E.A. *A History of the Norman Conquest of England*, 6 vols, Oxford, 1870–9
Galbraith, V.H. *Domesday Book*, Oxford, 1974
Garmonsway, G.N. *Canute and his Empire*, London, 1964
Green, J.A. *The Government of England under Henry I*, Cambridge, 1986
Grierson, P. *Coins of Medieval Europe*, London, 1991
Grueber, H., and Keary, C. *English Coins in the British Museum*, Anglo-Saxon Series, Vol. II, London, 1970
Haslem, Jeremy (ed.). *Anglo-Saxon Towns in Southern England*, Chichester, 1984
Hawkes, S.C. (ed.). *Weapons and Warfare in Anglo-Saxon England*, Oxford, 1989
Hicks, Carola (ed.). *England in the Eleventh Century*, Stamford, 1992
Higham, N.J. *The Kingdom of Northumbria 350–1100*, Stroud, 1993
Hill, D. (ed.). *Ethelred the Unready*, Oxford, 1978
——. *An Atlas of Anglo-Saxon England*, Oxford, 1981
Hollister, C.W. *Anglo-Saxon Military Institutions on the Eve of the Norman Conquest*, Oxford, 1962
Holt, J.C. (ed.). *Domesday Studies*, Woodbridge, 1987
Jansson, S.B.F. *Swedish Vikings in England*, London, 1966
——. *Runes in Sweden*, Varnamo, 1987
Jones, Gwyn. *A History of the Vikings*, 2nd edn, Oxford, 1984
Kapelle, William E. *The Norman Conquest of the North*, London, 1979
Keynes, S. *The Diplomas of King Aethelred 'The Unready' 978–1016*, Cambridge, 1980
Kightly, Charles. *Folk Heroes of Britain*, London, 1984
Knowles, D., Brooke, C.N.L., and London, V. *The Heads of Religious Houses, England and Wales, 940–1216*, Cambridge, 1972
Kozstolnyik, Z.J. *Five Eleventh-Century Hungarian Kings*, New York, 1981
Lancaster, J.C. *Godiva of Coventry*, Coventry, 1967
Lapidge, M., and Gneuss, H. (eds). *Learning and Literature in Anglo-Saxon England*, Cambridge, 1985
Larson, L.M. *Canute the Great, 995–1035*, London, 1912
Lawson, M.K. *Cnut*, London, 1993
Le Patourel, John. *The Norman Empire*, Oxford, 1976

Loyn, H.R. *Anglo-Saxon England and the Norman Conquest*, London, 1962

——. *The Norman Conquest*, 3rd edn, London, 1982

——. *The Governance of Anglo-Saxon England 500–1087*, London, 1984

Martin, J. *Medieval Russia 980–1584*, Cambridge, 1995

Mason, E. *St Wulfstan of Worcester c. 1008–1095*, Oxford, 1990

Maund, K.L. *Ireland, Wales and England in the Eleventh Century*, Woodbridge, 1991

Moltke, Erik. *Runes and their Origin*, Copenhagen, 1985

Morillo, S. (ed.). *The Battle of Hastings*, Woodbridge, 1996

Morris, C. *Marriage and Murder in Eleventh Century Northumbria*, York, 1992

Morris, C. *The Papal Monarchy*, Oxford, 1991

Nelson, J.L. *Politics and Ritual in Early Medieval Europe*, London, 1986

Nicholas, David. *Medieval Flanders*, London, 1992

Norwich, John Julius. *The Normans in the South*, London, 1967

O'Corrain, Donncha. *Ireland Before the Normans*, Dublin, 1972

Obolensky, D. *Six Byzantine Portraits*, Oxford, 1988

Okasha, E. *Hand-List of Anglo-Saxon Non-Runic Inscriptions*, Cambridge, 1971

Oleson, T.J. *The Witenagemot in the Reign of Edward the Confessor*, Oxford, 1955

Ortenberg, Veronica. *The English Church and the Continent in the Tenth and Eleventh Centuries*, Oxford, 1992

Page, R.I. *Chronicles of the Vikings*, London, 1995

Ransford, Rosalind. *Early Charters of the Augustinian Canons of Waltham Abbey, Essex 1062–1230*, Woodbridge, 1989

Raw, Barbara C. *Anglo-Saxon Crucifixion Iconography*, Cambridge, 1990

Reilly, Bernard F. *The Kingdom of Leon-Castille under King Alfonso VI*, Princeton, 1988

Reuter, Timothy. *Germany in the Early Middle Ages 800–1056*, Harlow, 1991

Reynolds, Susan. *Kingdoms and Communities in Western Europe 900–1300*, Oxford, 1984

Ridyard, S.J. *The Royal Saints of Anglo-Saxon England*, Cambridge, 1988

Rollason, D. *Saints and Relics in Anglo-Saxon England*, Oxford, 1989

Ronay, Gabriel. *The Lost King of England*, Woodbridge, 1989

Round, J.H. *Feudal England*, London, 1964

Rumble, A. (ed.). *The Reign of Cnut*, Leicester, 1994

Rybakov, Boris. *Kievan Rus*, Moscow, 1989

Saul, Nigel. (ed.) *England in Europe 1066–1453*, London, 1994

Sawyer, Birgit and Peter. *Medieval Scandinavia*, Minneapolis, 1993

Sawyer, P. (ed.). *Domesday Book: A Reassessment*, London, 1985

Scragg, D. (ed.). *The Battle of Maldon AD 991*, Oxford, 1991

Seaby, Peter. *The Story of British Coinage*, London, 1985

Searle, E. *Predatory Kinship and the Creation of Norman Power*, London, 1988

Skaare, K. *Coins and Coinage in Viking Age Norway*, Oslo, 1976

Smail, R.C. *Crusading Warfare 1097–1193*, Cambridge, 1972

Southern, R.W. *Saint Anselm and his Biographer*, Cambridge, 1963

——. *Saint Anselm: A Portrait in a Landscape*, Cambridge, 1990

Stafford, P. *Queens, Concubines and Dowagers*, London, 1983

——. *The East Midlands in the Early Middle Ages*, Leicester, 1985

——. *Unification and Conquest*, London, 1989

Stenton, D.M. (ed.). *Preparatory to Anglo-Saxon England*, Oxford, 1970

Stenton, F.M. *Anglo-Saxon England*, Oxford, 1971

Stevenson, F., and Walker, C.B.F. *Halley's Comet in History*, London, 1985

Strickland, M. (ed.). *Anglo-Norman Warfare*, Woodbridge, 1992

Sweet, H. *The Student's Dictionary of Anglo-Saxon*, Oxford, 1896

Vernadsky, George. *Kievan Russia*, London, 1973

Walker, David. *The Norman Conquerors*, Swansea, 1977

——. *Medieval Wales*, Cambridge, 1990

Whitelock, D. *The Beginnings of English Society*, Harmondsworth, 1972

Whitelock, D., Douglas, D.C., Lemmon, C.H., and Barlow, F. *The Norman Conquest*, London, 1966

Williams, A. *The English and the Norman Conquest*, Woodbridge, 1995

Williams, A., Smyth, A.P., and Kirby, D.P. *A Biographical Dictionary of Dark Age Britain*, London, 1991

Wilson, Alan J. *St Margaret, Queen of Scotland*, Edinburgh, 1993

Wilson, R.M. *The Lost Literature of Medieval England*, London, 1970

Woods, J.D., and Pelteret, D.A.E. (eds). *The Anglo-Saxons*, Ontario, 1985

Wright, C.E. *The Cultivation of Saga in Anglo-Saxon England*, 1939

Articles

Aird, W.M. 'St Cuthbert, the Scots and the Normans', *Anglo-Norman Studies*, XVI (1994), pp. 1–20

Ashdown, M. 'An Icelandic Account of the Survival of Harold Godwineson' in P. Clemoes (ed.), *The Anglo-Saxons* (1959), pp. 122–36

Bachrach, B. 'The Angevin Strategy of Castle Building in the Reign of Fulk Nerra, 987–1040', *AHR*, 88 (1983), p. 542.

Barlow, F. 'Edward the Confessor's Early Life, Character and Attitudes' *EHR*, LXXX (1965), pp. 225–51

——. 'Edward the Confessor and the Norman Conquest' *1066 Commemoration Lectures* (1966), pp. 5–18

Beech, G. 'England and Aquitaine in the Century before the Norman Conquest', *Anglo-Saxon England*, 19 (1991), pp. 81–101

Bernstein, D.J. 'The Blinding of Harold and The Meaning of the Bayeux Tapestry', *Anglo-Norman Studies*, V (1982), pp. 40–64

Biddle, M. 'Seasonal Festivals and Residence: Winchester, Westminster and Gloucester in the Tenth to Twelfth Centuries', *Anglo-Norman Studies*, VIII (1985), pp. 51–72

Brookes, N.P., and Walker, H.E. 'The Authority and Interpretation of the Bayeux Tapestry', *Proceedings of the Battle Conference on Anglo-Norman Studies, 1978* (1979), pp. 1–84

Brown, R.A. 'The Battle of Hastings', *Proceedings of the Battle Conference on Anglo-Norman Studies, 1980* (1981), pp. 1–21

Brown, S.A. 'The Bayeux Tapestry: History or Propaganda?' in J.D. Woods and D.A.E. Pelteret (eds), *The Anglo-Saxons* (1985), pp. 11–25

Campbell, J. 'Some Agents and Agencies of the Late Anglo-Saxon State', *Domesday Studies* (1987), pp. 201–18

Campbell, M.W. 'The Encomium Emmae Reginae: Personal Panegyric or Political Propaganda?', *Annuale Mediaevale*, 19 (1979), pp. 27–45

——. 'The Anti-Norman Reaction in England in 1052: Suggested Origins', *Medieval Studies*, 38 (1976), pp. 428–41

——. 'Queen Emma and Aelfgifu of Northampton: Cnut the Great's Women', *Medieval Scandinavia*, 4 (1971), pp. 66–79

——. 'A Pre-Conquest Norman Occupation of England', *Speculum*, 46 (1971), pp. 21–31

——. 'Earl Godwine of Wessex and Edward the Confessor's Promise of the Throne to Duke William', *Traditio*, 28 (1972), pp. 141–58.

——. 'The Rise of an Anglo-Saxon "Kingmaker": Earl Godwin of Wessex', *Canadian Journal of History*, 13 (1978), pp. 17–33

Cowdrey, H.E.J. 'Bishop Ermenfrid of Sion and the Penitential Ordinance following the Battle of Hastings', *Journal of Ecclesiastical History*, XX (1969), pp. 225–42

Cutler, K.E. 'The Godwinist Hostages: The Case for 1051', *Annuale Mediaevale*, 12 (1971), pp. 70–7

——. 'Edith, Queen of England 1045–1066', *Medieval Studies*, 35 (1973), pp. 222–31.

Darlington, R.R., and McGurk, P. 'The *Chronicon ex Chronicis* of "Florence" of Worcester and its Sources for English History before 1066', *Anglo-Norman Studies*, V (1982), pp. 185–96

Davis, R.H.C. 'The Norman Conquest' in R.H.C. Davis (ed.), *From Alfred the Great to Stephen* (1981) pp. 59–60

——. 'William of Poitiers and his History of William the Conqueror' in R.H.C. Davis (ed.), *From Alfred the Great to Stephen* (1981) pp. 101, 104

Douglas, D.C. 'Edward the Confessor, Duke William of Normandy, and the English Succession', *EHR*, LXVIII, pp. 529–45

Dumville, D.N. 'The Aetheling: A Study in Anglo-Saxon Constitutional History', *Anglo-Saxon England*, 8 (1979), pp. 1–33

Dvornik, F. 'The Kiev State and its Relations with Western Europe', *TRHS*, 4th Series, 29 (1947), pp. 27–46

Fell, C. 'The Icelandic Version of the Anglo-Saxon Emigration to Byzantium', *Anglo-Saxon England*, 3 (1974), pp. 179–96

Fernie, E.C. 'The Romanesque Church of Waltham Abbey', *JBAA*, CXXXVIII (1958), pp. 48–78

Fleming, R. 'Domesday Estates of the King and the Godwines: A Study in Late Saxon Politics', *Speculum*, 58 (1983), pp. 987–1,007

Garnett, G. 'Coronations and Propaganda: Implications of the Norman Claim to the Throne of England in 1066', *TRHS*, 5th Series, 36 (1986), pp. 91–116

Gillingham, J. 'William the Bastard at War' in C. Harper-Bill *et al.* (eds), *Studies in Medieval History for R. Allen Brown* (1989), pp. 141–58

——. 'Thegns and Knights in Eleventh Century England: Who was then the Gentleman?', *TRHS*, 6th Series, 5 (1995), pp. 129–53

Gillmor, C.M. 'Naval Logistics of the Cross Channel Operation 1066', *Anglo-Norman Studies*, VII (1984), pp. 105–31

Glover, R. 'English Warfare in 1066', *EHR*, LXVII (1952), pp. 1–18

Grierson, P. 'A Visit of Earl Harold to Flanders in 1056', *EHR*, LI (1936), pp. 90–7

——. 'Relations between England and Flanders before the Norman Conquest', *TRHS*, 4th Series, 23 (1941), pp. 71–112

Haskins, C.H. 'King Harold's Books', *EHR*, XXXVII (1922), pp. 398–400

Heningham, E.K. 'The Literary Unity, the Date, and the Purpose of Lady Edith's Book: "The Life of King Edward Who Rests at Westminster"', *Albion*, 7 (1975), pp. 24–40

Hooper, N. 'Anglo-Saxon Warfare on the Eve of the Conquest: A Brief Survey', *Proceedings of the Battle Conference on Anglo-Norman Studies, 1977* (1978), pp. 84–93

——. 'The Housecarls in England in the Eleventh Century', *Anglo-Norman Studies*, VII (1984), pp. 161–76

——. 'Edgar the Atheling: Anglo-Saxon Prince, Rebel and Crusader', *Anglo-Saxon England*, 14 (1985), p. 202

——. 'The Anglo-Saxons at War' in S.C. Hawkes (ed.), *Weapons and Warfare in Anglo-Saxon England* (1989), pp. 191–202

——. 'Some Observations on the Navy in Late Anglo-Saxon England' in C. Harper-Bill *et al.* (eds), *Studies in Medieval History for R. Allen Brown* (1989), pp. 203–13

——. 'Military Developments in the Reign of Cnut' in A. Rumble (ed.), *The Reign of Cnut* (1994), pp. 89–100

Hudson, B. 'The Family of Harold Godwineson and the Irish Sea Province', *JRSAI*, 109 (1979), pp. 92–100

Huggins, P.J., Bascombe, K.N., and Huggins, R.M. 'Excavations of the Collegiate and Augustinian Churches, Waltham Abbey, Essex 1984–87', *Archaeological Journal*, CXLVI (1989), pp. 476–537

Hunt, J. 'Piety, Prestige or Politics? The House of Leofric and the Foundation & Patronage of Coventry Priory' in G. Demidowicz (ed.), *Coventry's First Cathedral* (1994), pp. 97–117

Hunter Blair, C.H. 'Seal of Harold's College at Waltham, Holy Cross', *TEAS*, 16 (1922), pp. 131–2

John, E. 'Edward the Confessor and the Norman Succession', *EHR*, XCIV (1979), pp. 241–67

Keats-Rohan, K.S.B. 'William I and the Breton Contingent in the Non-Norman Conquest 1060–1087', *Anglo-Norman Studies*, XIII (1991), pp. 157–72

Keynes, S. 'An Interpretation of the Pacx, Pax and Paxs Pennies', *Anglo-Saxon England*, 7 (1978), pp. 165–73

——. 'The Crowland Psalter and the Sons of King Edmund Ironside', *Bodleian Library Record*, 11 (1985), pp. 359–70

——. 'Regenbald the Chancellor', *Anglo-Norman Studies*, X (1988), pp. 185–222

——. 'The Aethelings in Normandy', *Anglo-Norman Studies*, XIII (1991), pp. 173–205

——. 'Cnut's Earls' in A. Rumble (ed.), *The Reign of Cnut* (1994), pp. 43–88

King, V. 'Ealdred, Archbishop of York: the Worcester Years', *Anglo-Norman Studies*, XVIII (1995), pp. 123–37

Lapidge, M. 'Surviving Booklists from Anglo-Saxon England' in M. Lapidge and H. Gneuss (eds), *Learning and Literature in Anglo-Saxon England* (1985), pp. 58–9

Lemmon, C.H. 'The Campaign of 1066' in D. Whitelock *et al.*, *The Norman Conquest* (1966), pp. 77–122

Lewis, C.P. 'The Early Earls of Norman England', *Anglo-Norman Studies*, XIII (1991), pp. 207–24

Loyn, H.R. 'Harold, Son of Godwine', *1066 Commemoration Lectures* (1966), pp. 19–36

——. 'Abbots of English Monasteries Following the Norman Conquest' in D. Bates *et al.* (eds), *England and Normandy in the Middle Ages* (1994), pp. 95–103

Lund, N. 'The Armies of Swein Forkbeard and Cnut', *Anglo-Saxon England*, 15 (1986), pp. 105–18

Mack, K. 'Changing Thegns: Knut's Conquest and the English Aristocracy', *Albion*, 16 (1984), pp. 375–87

——. 'The Staller: Administrative Innovation in the Reign of Edward the Confessor', *Journal of Medieval History*, 12 (1986), pp. 123–34

Mason, E. 'Change and Continuity in Eleventh-Century Mercia', *Anglo-Norman Studies*, VIII (1985), pp. 154–76

Mason, J.F.A. 'William the First and the Sussex Rapes', *1066 Commemoration Lectures* (1966), pp. 37–58

Maund, K.L. 'Cynan ap Iago and the Killing of Gruffydd ap Llywelyn', *CMCS*, 10 (1985), pp. 57–65

——. 'The Welsh Alliances of Earl Aelfgar of Mercia and his Family in the Mid-Eleventh Century', *Anglo-Norman Studies*, XI (1988), pp. 181–90

McGurk, P. J., and Rosenthal, J. 'The Anglo-Saxon Gospel Books of Judith Countess of Flanders: Their Texts, Make-up and Function', *Anglo-Saxon England*, 24 (1995), pp. 251–308

McNulty, J.B. 'The Lady Aelfgyva in the Bayeux Tapestry', *Speculum*, 55 (1980), pp. 659–68

Meyer, M. 'Women's Estates in Later Anglo-Saxon England: The Politics of Possession', *Haskins Society Journal*, 3 (1992), pp. 111–29

——. 'The Queen's "Demesne" in Later Anglo-Saxon England' in M. Meyer (ed.), *The Culture of Christendom* (1993), pp. 75–114

Morillo, S. 'Hastings: An Unusual Battle' in S. Morillo (ed.), *The Battle of Hastings* (1996), pp. 220–7

Morton, C. 'Pope Alexander II and the Norman Conquest', *Latomus*, XXXIV (1975), pp. 362–82

Nelson, J.L. 'The Rites of the Conqueror', in J.L. Nelson, *Politics and Ritual in Early Medieval Europe* (1986), pp. 389–95

Oleson, T.J. 'Edward the Confessor's Promise of the Throne to Duke William of Normandy', *EHR* LXXII (1957), pp. 221–8

Raraty, D.G.J. 'Earl Godwine of Wessex: The origin of his power and his political loyalties', *History*, LXXIV (1989), pp. 3–19

Rogers, N. 'The Waltham Abbey Relic-List' in Carola Hicks (ed.), *England in the Eleventh Century* (1992), pp. 157–81

Ross, M.C. 'Concubinage in Anglo-Saxon England', *Past & Present*, 108 (1985), pp. 3–34

Sawyer, P.H. 'The Wealth of England in the Eleventh Century', *TRHS*, 5th Series, 15 (1965), pp. 145–64

——. '1066–1086: A Tenurial Revolution?' in P.H. Sawyer (ed.), *Domesday Book: A Reassessment* (1985), pp. 71–85

Scott, F.S. 'Earl Waltheof of Northumbria', *Archaeologia Aeliana*, 4th Series, 30 (1952), pp. 149–215

Searle, E. 'Women and the Legitimization of Succession at the Norman Conquest', *Proceedings of the Battle Conference on Anglo-Norman Studies, 1979* (1980), pp. 159–70

——. 'Emma the Conqueror' in C. Harper-Bill *et al.* (eds), *Studies in Medieval History for R. Allen Brown* (1989), pp. 281–8

Smith, M.F. 'Archbishop Stigand and the Eye of the Needle', *Anglo-Norman Studies*, XVI (1994), pp. 199–220

Stafford, P. 'Women in Domesday', *Reading Medieval Studies*, 15 (1989), pp. 75–94

——. 'The Reign of Aethelred II' in D. Hill (ed.), *Ethelred the Unready* (1978), pp. 15–46

Stenton, F.M. 'St Benet of Holme and the Norman Conquest', *EHR*, XXXVII (1922), pp. 227–33

——. 'The Danes in England' in D.M. Stenton (ed.), *Preparatory to Anglo-Saxon England* (1970), pp. 135–65

——. 'Pre-Conquest Herefordshire' in D.M. Stenton (ed.), *Preparatory to Anglo-Saxon England* (1970), pp. 193–202

Strickland, M. 'Slaughter, Slavery or Ransom: the Impact of the Conquest on Conduct in Warfare' in Carola Hicks (ed.), *England in the Eleventh Century* (1992)

Talvio, T. 'Harold I and Harthacnut's Jewel Cross Type Reconsidered' in M.A.S. Blackburn (ed.), *Anglo-Saxon Monetary History* (1986), pp. 283–9

Tanner, H.J. 'The Expansion of the Power and Influence of the Counts of Boulogne under Eustace II', *Anglo-Norman Studies*, XIV (1992), pp. 251–86

Van Houts, E.M.C. 'The Gesta Normannorum Ducum: A history without an end', *Proceedings of the Battle Conference on Anglo-Norman Studies, 1979* (1980), pp. 106–18

Walcot, M.E.C. 'Inventory of Waltham, Holy Cross', *TEAS*, 5 (1873), pp. 257–64

Wallace, P.F. 'The English Presence in Viking Dublin' in M.A.S. Blackburn (ed.), *Anglo-Saxon Monetary History* (1986), pp. 201–22

Whitelock, D. 'The Dealings of the Kings of England with Northumbria in the Tenth and Eleventh Centuries' in P. Clemoes (ed.), *The Anglo-Saxons* (1959), pp. 70–88

Wilkinson, B. 'Northumbrian Separatism in 1065–1066', *BJRL*, 23 (1939), pp. 504–26

Williams, A. 'Some Notes and Considerations on Problems Connected with the English Royal Succession 860–1066', *Proceedings of the Battle Conference on Anglo-Norman Studies, 1977* (1978)

——. 'Land and Power in the Eleventh Century: The Estates of Harold Godwineson', *Proceedings of the Battle Conference on Anglo-Norman Studies, 1980* (1981), pp. 171–87

——. '"Cockles Among the Wheat": Danes and English in the Western Midlands in the First Half of the Eleventh Century', *Midland History*, 11 (1986), pp. 1–22

——. 'The King's Nephew: The Family and Career of Earl Ralph of Hereford' in C. Harper-Bill *et al.* (eds), *Studies in Medieval History for R. Allen Brown* (1989), pp. 327–43

Wissolik, R.D. 'The Saxon Statement: Code in the Bayeux Tapestry', *Annuale Mediaevale*, 19 (1979), pp. 69–97

Unpublished Thesis

Davies, R.H. 'The Lands of Harold, Son of Godwine', unpublished Ph.D. thesis, Cardiff, 1967

INDEX

Aachen, Germany 82

Aarhus, Denmark 153

Abingdon Abbey (Oxon.) xxiv, 29, 71–2, 125, 168, 188

Adam of Bremen 153, 154

Adelaide, sister of William of Normandy 39

Adelard, the schoolmaster 72, 125

Adeliza, daughter of William of Normandy 94, 99

Aelfric of Eynsham 193

Aelfgar, Earl of Mercia 35–6, 49, 53, 56, 65, 76–80, 83, 85–6, 87–8, 91, 104, 107, 110, 111, 122, 123, 128, 129, 130, 133, 206–7, 208, 212

Aelfgifu, of Northampton, wife of Cnut 6, 12, 128, 129, 130, 187

Aelfgifu, sister of *Ealdorman* Aethelweard 59

Aelfgifu, wife of Earl Aelfgar 103, 128, 129

Aelfgyva, sister of Harold II Godwineson 12, 93, 94

Aelfheah, *Ealdorman* 8, 60

Aelfhelm, *Ealdorman* of York 1, 3, 6, 103

Aelfhere, *Ealdorman* 60

Aelflaed, Lady 62

Aelfnoth, Sheriff of Herefordshire 80

Aelfric *Cild* 60

Aelfric of Brookethorpe 140

Aelfric of Yelling 181

Aelfric, Archbishop of York 16, 46, 133

Aelfric, *Ealdorman* 9

Aelfstan, the *Staller* 142

Aelfwig, Abbot of New Minster, Winchester 158, 168, 181

Aelfwine, Abbot of Ramsey 158

Aelfwold, Abbot of St Benet of Holme 145

Aethelmaer, *Ealdorman* 8

Aethelnoth *Cild* 66, 67, 68, 69

Aethelnoth, Abbot of Glastonbury 139

Aethelnoth, Archbishop of Canterbury 13, 16

Aethelred II, 'the Unready', King of England 1, 3, 5, 6–7, 8, 10, 11, 12, 13, 33, 39, 58, 59, 60, 106, 121, 144, 205

Aethelric of Kelvedon 150

Aethelric, Bishop of Durham 104

Aethelric, Monk of Christ Church and Bishop of Sussex 27, 49, 80, 95, 136, 193, 203–4

Aethelthryth 107

Aethelweard, *Ealdorman* 8, 10, 59

Aethelwig, Abbot of Evesham 80, 158

Aethelwine, Bishop of Durham 104, 108, 188

Agatha, mother of Edgar *Atheling* 117

Agnes of Poitiers, Regent of the Empire 81

Ailey (Heref.) 134

Alan the Black, brother of Alan the Red 196

Alan the Red, Earl of Richmond 129, 196

Aldan-Hamal 104

Aldbourne (Wilts.) 60

Aldermaston (Berks.) 59, 65

Aliditha, Queen of Harold II Godwineson 77, 85, 116–17, 129–30, 131, 138–9, 169, 182, 185, 192, 195, 197

Alexander II, Pope 148–9, 154, 203, 204

Alfred of Marlborough 67

Alfred, *Atheling* xxv, 5, 14–15, 16, 17, 30, 32, 33, 39, 41, 74, 96, 124, 136

Alfred, King of Wessex 115, 136, 138, 149, 187, 198, 205

Allerdale (Cumb.) 105, 106

Amounderness (Lancs.) 85, 104, 105

Amund, *huscarl* of Tosti 108

Andrew I, King of Hungary 81

Anglesey, Isle of 88, 195

Angmering (Suss.) 60

Anjou, County of 147

Anselm, Archbishop of Canterbury 196

Ansgar, the *Staller* 62–3, 142, 183

Archenfield (Heref.) 78, 80, 81, 89

Arnor, skald to King Harald 164

Ashington (Essex) 7, 8, 9

Ashtead (Surr.) 66

Ashton–under–Hill (Glos.) 66

Athelstan, *Atheling* 5–6, 39, 56, 58, 59

Athelstan, Bishop of Hereford 80

Athelstan, son of Tofi the Proud 61, 63, 72

Avon, River (Som.) 35, 191

Azur, a royal *thegn* 60, 66

Bacton (Suff.) 62

Baldwin V, Count of Flanders 24, 30, 32, 35, 43, 81, 93, 114, 144, 147

Baldwin VI, Count of Flanders 192, 193

Baldwin, Abbot of Bury St Edmunds 119

Banwell (Som.) 68

Barcwith, *huscarl* of Tosti 104

Barnstable (Devon) 191

Battle Abbey (Suss.) 179

Bavaria 82

Bayeux, Normandy 100

Bayford (Herts.) 114

Beaurain, Ponthieu 96

Bedfordshire 72, 206, 209, 212

Benedict X, Pope 50, 137

Beorhtweald of Wokefield 69

Beorn, Earl of East Midlands xxiv, 18, 22, 24–5, 60, 62, 132, 206, 209

Berkeley Abbey (Glos.) 67

Berkhampstead, (Herts.) 66, 185

Berkshire 72, 206, 208, 209, 212

Beverstone (Glos.) 32, 33

Bigbury Bay (Devon) 191

Billingsley (Shrops.) 79

Bishophill (Yorks.) 138

Blakeney (Norf.) 62

Bleddyn ap Cynfyn 89

Bondi, the *Staller* 142

Bonneville-sur-Toques, Normandy 100

Bosham (Suss.) 21, 24, 35, 125

Boulogne, County of 14

Breme, freeman of King Edward 168

Brian, Count 192

Brightlingsea (Essex) 61

Brihtric, brother of Eadric *Streona* 1, 3

Brihtric, son of Aelfgar 188

Brinsop (Heref.) 36

Bristol (Som.) 35, 43, 88, 133, 145, 191

Britford (Wilts.) 108

Brittany 40, 41, 91, 97–8, 172, 176, 196

Brompton Regis (Som.) 59

Brookethorpe (Glos.) 140

Brown, R. Allen xxvi

Bruges, Flanders 15, 22, 25, 42–3, 44, 193

Buckinghamshire 61, 128, 206, 209, 212

Bulgaria 153

Burghill (Heref.) 36, 66

Burhwold, Bishop of Cornwall 9

Burnham, River (Norf.) 145

Bury St Edmunds (Suff.) 127, 168

Byrthnoth, *Ealdorman* 19

Byzantine Empire 153

Caen, Normandy 149

Caldbec Hill (Suss.) 173, 174

Cambridgeshire 20, 35, 61, 128, 206, 209, 212

Canterbury (Kent) xxiv, 21, 30, 45, 49–50, 67, 80, 95, 127, 129, 167, 182, 183, 204
Cassel, Flanders 193
Catherington (Hants.) 60
Catton (Yorks.) 161, 162
Cavendish (Suff.) 168
Chalton (Beds.) 114, 141
Chalton (Hants.) 59, 60
Charlemagne, Emperor 122
Chernigov, Russia 194
Cheshire 207, 208
Chester (Ches.) 78, 88, 130, 182, 185, 195
Christ Church, Canterbury 27, 60, 67, 95, 131, 203
Cnut *Lavard* of Denmark 195
Cnut, King of England xxix, 5, 6, 7–12, 13, 14, 19, 20, 21, 24, 39, 49, 58–60, 61, 65, 75, 76, 83, 99, 103, 114, 115, 122, 125, 128, 129, 130, 131, 152, 153, 160, 187, 199, 201, 205
Colne (Essex) 19
Cologne, Germany 76, 81, 82
Compton (Suss.) 3, 5, 56, 58
Conan II, Duke of Brittany 97–8
Congresbury (Som.) 68
Constantinople 43, 52, 154
Copsi, lieutenant of Tosti 103, 110, 154
Cornwall 67, 187, 190, 191, 206, 208, 209
Corvey Abbey, Saxony 147
Cosham (Hants.) 6
Couesnon, River 97, 121
Coventry (Warwicks.) 71, 125
Crowhurst (Suss.) 174
Cumbria 105, 205
Cynan ap Iago 89
Cynesige, Archbishop of York 87, 133, 138
Cypping 66

Danube, River 81
Dartmouth (Devon) 24
Dee, River 86, 89

Deerhurst (Glos.) 71, 125
Denmark 9, 10, 11, 12, 13, 19, 22–3, 24, 25, 122, 152, 153–4, 155, 157, 181, 187, 193
Derbyshire 205, 207
Derwent, River (Yorks.) 161, 162
Devon 187, 191, 206, 208, 209
Diarmait Macmael-Na-Mbo, King of Leinster 35, 43, 131, 190, 191
Dinant, Brittany 98
Dives, River 149–50
Dol, Brittany 97–8
Dolfin, son of Thorfinn 105
Dorset 206, 208, 209
Douglas, William 37
Dover (Kent) xxiv, 14, 30, 32, 44, 59, 66, 68, 100, 167, 183, 188, 208
Down Hatherley (Glos.) 140
Drogo, Count of the Vexin 40
Dublin 35, 42, 43, 78, 190, 191, 195
Duduc, Bishop of Wells 68
Dungeness (Kent) 44
Dunstan, son of Aethelnoth 107–8
Durham (Dur.) 71, 103–4, 108

Eachmargach, King of Dublin 43
Eadmer *Atre* 66
Eadmer of Canterbury xxvii, xxviii, 93, 95, 96, 123, 204
Eadmer of Haresfield 140
Eadnoth, the *Staller* 66, 142, 191, 192
Eadric *Streona, Ealdorman* of Mercia 1, 3, 6–8, 10, 208
Eadric the Deacon 168, 181
Eadric the Steersman 62, 145
Eadric of Laxfield 62, 63
Eadsige, Archbishop of Canterbury 18, 27, 29
Eadwig, *Atheling* 5, 10, 39
Eadwulf, Earl 103, 105
Ealdgyth, wife of King Edmund 'Ironside' 6, 76, 128
Ealdred, Abbot of Abingdon 140, 187

Ealdred, Bishop of Worcester and Archbishop of York 25, 35, 50, 68, 76, 80, 81, 87, 117, 127, 132–3, 136, 183–5

East Anglia 7, 19, 20, 21, 34, 49, 56, 60–3, 65, 66, 76–7, 79, 83, 87, 130, 142, 168, 188, 209, 212

East Midlands 21, 66, 141

Eaton Bishop (Heref.) 67

Edgar, *Atheling* 83, 92, 95, 102, 112–13, 114–16, 117, 119, 136, 183–5, 187, 189, 192, 195, 196, 198, 199, 200, 201

Edith, Abbess of Leominster 22

Edith, daughter of King Aethelred II 1

Edith, sister of Harold II Godwineson and Queen of Edward the Confessor xxv, 12, 18, 22, 27, 36, 39, 47, 52, 60, 72, 74–5, 76, 83, 87, 105, 106, 111, 112, 113, 116, 118, 121, 131–2, 133–5, 184, 195

Edith Canmore, daughter of King Malcolm 196, 198

Edith 'Swan-neck', wife of Harold II Godwineson (*Edith the Fair*) 20, 61, 72, 127–30, 131, 187, 194, 197

Edmund, *Atheling* 75

Edmund, son of Harold II Godwineson 6, 121, 131, 187, 189–94

Edmund 'Ironside', King of England 5–6, 7–8, 9, 13, 39, 40, 58, 59, 75, 76, 122, 128

Edward, *Atheling* 40, 75–6, 81–3, 117, 133

Edward I, King of England 89

Edward the Confessor, King of England xxi, xxii–xxiii, xxv, xxvii–xxviii, 56, 58, 99, 120, 122, 123, 125, 127, 133, 134, 158, 159, 176, 190, 199, 200, 205, 213

  Atheling 5, 14–15, 16–17, 39, 96

  King of England 17–18, 19–21, 22–3, 24–5, 27, 29–30, 32–4, 35–6, 37, 38, 39–41, 43–4, 46–7, 49–53, 59–61, 63, 65, 69, 71, 72, 74–7, 78–81, 82–3, 85, 87, 88–90, 91–2, 102, 104, 105, 108, 110–14, 116–19, 136, 138, 139, 140, 141, 142, 144, 149, 152, 203, 204, 208, 209, 212

  lands and wealth 54–5

  the succession to the English throne 27, 30, 36, 37–42, 50–1, 74–6, 81–3, 91–2, 102, 114–19

  illness, death and legacy 114, 116, 118–19, 136, 142, 144

Edwin, brother of Earl Leofric 208

Edwin, Earl of Mercia 85, 87, 103, 110–11, 112, 114, 115, 116, 133, 138, 145, 155, 157–8, 169, 183, 184, 192, 195, 206–7, 208

Eilaf, Earl 8, 10, 11, 12

Elizabeth, wife of Harald *Hardradi* 153

Ely (Camb.) 15

Emma, Queen of King Aethelred II and Cnut 8, 12, 13–15, 18, 40, 49, 129

English Channel 24, 44, 45, 96, 144, 145–6, 150–1, 158, 164, 166, 188, 193

Enguerrand, Count of Ponthieu 40

Erik, Earl 8, 10, 12

Erminfrid, Bishop of Sion xxvii, 148

Essex 19, 20, 24, 61, 62, 72, 128, 160, 165, 207, 209, 212

Estrith, sister of Cnut 10

Eu, Ponthieu 96

Eustace, Count of Boulogne xxiv, 14, 30, 32, 33

Evesham Abbey (Worcs.) 158

Exe, River (Devon) 190

Exeter (Devon) 25, 43, 131, 187, 188, 189–90, 191, 192

Faringdon (Berks.) 60

Fecamp Abbey, Normandy 21, 145, 167

Five Boroughs 6, 7

Flanders 25, 30, 32, 40, 43, 81, 82, 92, 114, 144, 188, 192, 193

Flatholme, Isle of 190, 192
Folkstone (Kent) 60, 67
Fordwich (Kent) 59
Fritton (Norf.) 20, 63
Fulford (Yorks.) 142, 155, 157, 160, 161, 162, 169, 184, 186

Gamal, father of Orm 106
Gamal, son of Orm 105, 106
Gamelbearn 107–8
Gauti, *huscarl* of Harold II Godwineson 69, 70
Geoffrey, Count of Anjou 98
Geffrei Gaimar xxviii
George, Grand Prince of Kiev 194
Gerald of Wales 88, 90
German Empire 76, 181
Giso, Bishop of Wells 67, 68, 139
Ghent, Flanders 82
Glasbury on Wye (Heref.) 80
Gloucester (Glos.) 32, 34, 88
Gloucestershire 66, 83, 206, 209, 212
Gluniarn, son of Heardwulf 107–8
Godfrey of Cambrai 197
Godgifu, sister of Edward the Confessor 14, 40
Godgifu, wife of Earl Leofric 128
Godric, *Ealdorman* 8
Godric, Sheriff of Berkshire 168
Godwine of Soberton 140
Godwine, Earl of Wessex xxiii, xxiv, xxv, 3, 12, 36, 41, 42, 44, 54, 56, 71, 74, 83, 103, 104, 107, 114, 122, 132, 144, 147, 199, 203
   early career 5, 6, 7–8, 10, 56, 58
   Earl of Wessex 8–18, 19, 20, 21–5, 27, 29–30, 32–4, 37, 38, 39, 49–53, 58–9, 63, 74–5, 77, 80, 205, 206, 208, 209, 212
   exile in Flanders 35–7, 42–3, 44, 45–7
   lands and wealth 56, 58–60, 63, 65, 66, 67, 132

death and legacy 52–3, 63, 65, 74–5, 83, 132
Godwine, son of Harold II Godwineson 128, 131, 187, 188, 189–94
Goscelin of St Bertin xxv
Gospatric, son of Maldred 105, 106, 107, 108, 110, 155
Gospatric, son of Uhtred, Lord of Allerdale 105, 106–7, 110, 155, 205
Great Barrington (Glos.) 69
Grimbald, goldsmith of Edith 129
Gruffydd ap Llwelyn, Prince of Wales 22, 43, 68, 70, 77–81, 83, 85–6, 88–9, 91, 111, 116, 122, 123, 130, 138, 171, 195, 199
Gruffydd ap Rhydderch, Prince of South Wales 78
Guildford (Surr.) 15
Gunnhild, daughter of Harold II Godwineson 70, 129, 131, 195–6
Gunnhild, sister of Harold II Godwineson 12, 35, 190, 192–3
Gunnhild, niece of Cnut 19, 20
Guy of Amiens xxviii
Guy, Count of Ponthieu 96, 99
Gyrth, Earl of East Anglia 12, 35, 65, 79, 83, 87, 111, 113, 115, 116, 132, 145, 159, 168, 169, 176, 180, 183, 192, 206–7, 212
Gytha Countess, mother of Harold II Godwineson 10, 12, 21, 35, 55, 59, 60, 65, 67, 103, 113, 128, 132, 181, 187–8, 190, 192–3, 194
Gytha, daughter of Harold II Godwineson 131, 190, 193–5
Gytha, wife of Earl Ralph 134

Hakon, Earl 8, 12
Hakon, son of Earl Swein 33, 37–8, 42, 47, 50, 99, 101, 132
Halley's Comet 143
Hampshire 9, 14, 21, 66, 168, 172, 186, 188, 206, 208, 209

Harald *Hardradi*, King of Norway 24, 85,
    122, 123, 153–5, 157–8, 163–4, 165,
    166, 168, 171, 172, 174, 177, 200,
    201
Harald, son of Earl Thorkell 19, 20
Hardecnut, King of England 11, 12–17,
    32, 39, 41, 130, 155
Harescombe (Glos.) 140
Haresfield (Glos.) 140
Harewood (Yorks.) 138
Harold I 'Harefoot', King of England
    12–15, 16, 39, 58, 130, 187
**Harold II Godwineson, King of
    England** xxi, xxiii–xxix, 1, 6, 12,
    14, 22, 38, 53, 54, 56, 58, 60, 65–6,
    76, 77, 78, 83, 86, 91, 103, 107,
    110, 120, 152, 154, 155, 183–5,
    187–98, 199–201, 203, 204, 205,
    206, 207, 208, 209, 212
career, chronologically
    appointed earl of East Anglia 18, 19–21
    marries to Edith 'Swan-neck' 20, 61,
        127–8, 129–30, 187
    benefits from fall of his brother Swein 22
    serves with the fleet 23–4
    opposes return of Swein 24
    persuaded to accept Swein's restoration
        25
    joins Godwine's rebellion 32
    no hostages demanded from him
        33–4
    deserted by his *thegns* 34
    flees to Ireland 35
    wins support of Diarmait of Leinster
        35, 43
    loses earldom to Aelfgar 35
    returns from Ireland to raid Somerset
        44–5
    joins Godwine's fleet 45–6
    restored to earldom of East Anglia 49,
        52, 212
    succeeds Godwine as Earl of Wessex
        52–3

relationship to King Edward in 1053
    74–5
supports Tosti's appointment as Earl of
    Northumbria 76
role in Aelfgar's exile 1055? 77
campaigns in Wales and secures peace
    78–9
his personal chaplain Leofgar becomes
    Bishop of Hereford 80
Leofgar killed by Welsh 80–1
defends Welsh Border and secures
    peace 81
mission to secure the English
    succession? 81–2
succeeds to part of Ralph's earldom 83
role in Aelfgar's exile 1058? 85
attends dedication of Holy Cross
    College, Waltham 86–7
raids Gruffydd's palace at Rhuddlan
    87–8, 171
campaigns against Gruffydd of Wales
    88–9, 171
defeated Welsh submit to him 89–90
visits Normandy 91–6, 204
captured by Guy of Ponthieu 96
released by William of Normandy
    96
participates in William's Breton
    campaign 97–9, 172
swears oath of fealty to William 99–101
returns to England 101–2
negotiates with Northumbrian rebels
    111–12
advises concessions including deposition
    of Tosti 112–14
persuades King Edward to accept terms
    and Tosti is exiled 113–14
King Edward falls ill and Harold
    contemplates the succession 114–15
canvasses support for his own
    succession 115–17
designated to succeed King Edward
    118–19

coronation at Westminster 136–8

rejects William's claim 138

calms unrest in Northumbria 138–9

marries to Alditha 138–9

Halley's Comet 143

repulses Tosti's raids 144

summons forces to defend the coast 144–5

prepares defences against Norman threat 145

Norman awareness of his strength 147

Norman diplomatic and military preparations 147–50

disbands defence forces 150

naval clash in the Channel? 150–1

assessment of the situation, September 1066 151

Norwegian invasion and battle of Fulford 155, 157

receives word of Norwegian invasion 158

summons army to oppose the Norwegians 158

advances rapidly north to York 159–60

surprises Norwegians at Stamford Bridge 160–1

at battle of Stamford Bridge 162–5

celebrates his victory at York 166

Normans land in Sussex 166–7

they learn of Harold's victory at Stamford Bridge 167–8

learns of the Norman landing 168

summons army to oppose the Normans 168–9

advances rapidly south to Hastings 169–71

reasons for haste 171–2

preparations for battle at Hastings 173–4

assessments of the situation by the opposing commanders 173–4

deployment of opposing forces 174

composition of opposing armies 174–5

tactics in opening phases of battle 176–8

tactics in subsequent phases of battle 178–9

dies and his army is defeated 179–80

summary of battle 180–1

burial traditions 181, 183

cult of martyr and survival traditions 181–2

loss of his leadership 183–4

reaction of his family 187

pursuit of their claim to the throne 187–92

character and reputation

character 74, 121–5, 135

contemporary reputations xxiii, 88–9, 121, 123–4, 164, 168, 200

Danish heritage 11–12, 121–2, 127–8, 130–1

diplomatic skills 35, 80, 81, 82, 111–14, 115–18, 138–9

education 134–5

interest in sports of the chase 134–5

later reputation xxi, xxviii–xxix, 72–3, 89–90, 181–2, 200–1

military skills 45, 78–9, 87–8, 88–90, 97–9, 121–2, 144–5, 151, 152, 158–65, 166–81; his banner 70, 121, 180, 190

physical appearance 120–1

religious views 67–8, 70–3, 80–1, 125, 127, 129–31; holy oath 99–101, 123, 124–5, 182, 200; relics 35, 82, 125

sources xxiii–xxviii, 55–6, 90, 91–4, 169–70, 179

government and administration

coinage 120–1, 122, 140

justice 140

royal appointments 140–2

royal army 144–5, 158–60, 165, 168–9, 174

royal estates 144

royal fleet 144–5, 150–1

royal officials 142
royal title 140
writs and charters 139–40
lands and wealth
East Anglia, earldom of 19–20, 60–1
East Anglia, lands in 61
East Anglia, supporters in 62–3, 65
expenses 69–70
full extent of [lands and wealth] 54–5
gifts to church 70–2
gifts to Holy Cross, Waltham 70, 71,
72–3, 125
gifts to laymen 70
Harold and church lands 67–8, 125, 127
inherited lands 60, 63, 65
lands granted to supporters 69
lands in Wales 89
lifestyle 69–70, 86–7
links between his landholding and his
authority as earl 56
revenues 69
Wessex, earldom of 65–6
Wessex, lands in 65–6
Wessex, supporters in 66
personal relations with
Alditha, his second wife 116–17,
129–31, 138–9
Beorn, his cousin 25, 132
Ealdred, Archbishop of York 46, 117,
132–3, 136–8
Edith 'Swan-neck', his first wife, 20,
61, 127–31
Edith, his sister, xxv, 113, 116, 132
Edward the Confessor 25, 33–4, 53,
74–5, 83, 113–14, 118–19, 199–200
Godwine, his father, 24, 32, 52–3, 74, 132
Gyrth, his brother 113, 116, 132
Gytha, his mother 132
Leofwine, his brother 35, 113, 116, 132
Ralph, Earl 133–4
Swein, his brother 24, 74, 132
Tosti, his brother 76, 88–9, 112–13,
132, 166

Wulfnoth, his brother, and Hakon, his
nephew 95, 96, 101, 132
Wulfstan, Bishop of Worcester 125,
127, 133, 138
political relations with
Aelfgar, Earl of Mercia 77, 85
Diarmait of Leinster 35, 43
Edwin and Morcar 112, 114, 115–17,
145, 157, 169
Gruffydd of Wales 43, 78–80, 81, 86,
87–8, 88–90
Stigand, Archbishop of Canterbury 24,
50, 117, 127, 136–8
William of Normandy 96–8, 99,
101–2, 138, 144–5, 168–80, 181
Harold's Park, Nazeing (Essex) 73
Harold's Wood, Romford (Essex) 73
Harold, son of Earl Ralph 83, 85, 92,
133–4
Harold, son of Harold II Godwineson
130, 131, 138, 182, 192, 195, 197
Harston (Camb.) 62
Hastings (Suss.) xxi, xxvi, xxvii, xxix, 35,
44, 55, 60, 72, 113, 117, 125, 129,
130, 131, 132, 142, 147, 159, 162,
167–82, 183, 186, 187, 190, 192,
197, 200, 201
Haversham (Bucks.) 59
Hawkhurst (Kent) 66, 68
Hayling Island (Hants.) 140
Hedeby, Denmark 153
Henry I, King of England 198
Henry III, Emperor of Germany 24, 76, 81
Henry IV, Emperor of Germany 81,
147–8
Henry I, King of France 91
Hereford (Heref.) 21, 30, 47, 66, 67, 68,
78, 83, 122, 133, 208
Herefordshire 22, 25, 32, 33, 35–6, 47, 66,
78, 83, 87, 100, 206, 208, 209, 212
Hereman, Bishop of Ramsbury 21, 71
Herleve, mother of William, of
Normandy 128

Hertfordshire 56, 61, 62, 69, 72, 128, 206, 209, 212
Hitchen (Herts.) 61
Holy Cross, Waltham (Essex) 55, 70, 71, 72, 125, 133, 138, 181
Holy River, Sweden 11
Houghton (Suff.) 62
Hrani, Earl 8, 12
Hugh the Frenchman 21
Hugh, Earl of Shrewsbury 195
Humber, River 145, 155, 157, 164
Hungary 75, 76, 81–2, 117
Huntingdonshire 35, 61, 141, 205, 206, 207, 209, 212

Iaroslav, Prince of Novgorod 152, 153
Ingebiorg, daughter of Msistislav I 195
Ipswich (Suff.) 65
Ireland 35, 43, 44, 78, 187, 191, 192
Islington (Dorset) 66
Italy 148

Jerusalem 25, 43, 52
John of Salisbury 90
John of Worcester xxiv, 3, 14, 15, 16, 17, 20, 22, 47, 88, 89, 105, 107, 114, 130, 131, 138, 140, 143, 154, 155, 157, 168, 170–1, 184–5, 190, 209
Judith of Flanders, wife of Tosti 32, 35, 93, 103, 108, 192, 193

Kapelle, William 105
Kent 11, 21, 44–5, 59, 66, 67, 172, 183, 186, 188, 206, 208, 209
Ketel, son of Wulfgyth 61, 63, 127
Kiev, Russia 194–5
Kingsbridge Estuary (Devon) 191
Kingston Bagpuise (Oxon.) 72
Kirkdale (Yorks.) 104, 105, 107

Lambeth (Surr.) 17, 61
Lancashire 103
Land's End (Cornwall) 45

Lanfranc, Archbishop of Canterbury 196, 203
Langford Budville (Som.) 191
Lawford (Essex) 61
Laxfield (Suff.) 62
Leckhampstead (Berks.) 72
Leicestershire 206, 208
Leighs (Essex) 62, 63, 69
Leo IX, Pope 29, 50
Leofgar of Thames Ditton 69
Leofgar, Bishop of Hereford 68, 70, 80–1, 120, 122, 125, 133
Leofman of Hayling Island 140
Leofric, Abbot of Peterborough 72, 158, 168
Leofric, Bishop of Exeter 25, 27
Leofric, Earl of Mercia 12, 17, 20, 22, 32–4, 37, 38, 44, 46–7, 49, 53, 55, 56, 67, 71, 72, 76, 77, 78–9, 81, 82, 83, 125, 128, 205, 206, 208, 212
Leofwine of Bacton 62
Leofwine, Earl of East Midlands 12, 35, 65, 83, 111, 113, 115, 116, 132, 168, 176, 180, 183, 192, 206, 212
Leofwine, *Ealdorman* 8, 10, 12, 208
Leominster (Heref.) 22, 209
Lexden (Essex) 61
Limpsfield (Surr.) 134
Lincoln (Lincs.) 207
Lincolnshire 21, 56, 66, 103, 111, 142, 145, 205, 207
Lindisfarne 87, 104
Lizard (Cornwall) 191
London xxiv, 3, 7, 13, 14, 21, 27, 29, 33, 34, 35, 38, 44, 46–7, 82, 116, 140, 143, 144, 150–1, 160, 166, 168, 169, 172, 173, 183, 184, 185, 190
Lotharingia 40, 72
Louis the Pious, Emperor 5
Lycia 43
Lyfing, Bishop of Worcester 16

Macbeth, King of Scots 105
Magnus 'Barelegs', King of Norway 195
Magnus Haraldsson of Norway 85, 154
Magnus Olafsson, King of Norway 13, 15, 18, 19, 20, 22–3, 24, 122, 152, 153, 155
Magnus, son of Harold II Godwineson 122, 131, 187, 189–91
Maine, County of 91, 92
Malcolm *Canmore*, King of Scots 76, 78, 87, 104–5, 106, 145, 154, 196
Malmesbury Abbey (Wilts.) 6, 71, 125
Marianus Scotus 162
Marlborough (Wilts.) 203
Marleswein, Sheriff of Lincolnshire 142, 169
Mathilda, wife of William of Normandy 149, 188
Melcombe Horsey (Dorset) 67
Mercia 7, 13, 20, 83, 85–7, 111, 133, 157, 208, 212
'Merclesham' (Kent) 66, 68
Mersey, River 85
Metz, France 82
Middlesex 69, 206, 209, 212
Midlands 12–13, 196
Milverton (Som.) 191
'Moran' (Norf.) 63
Morcar, Earl of Northumbria. 103, 110–11, 112–13, 114, 115, 116, 133, 138, 141, 142, 145, 155, 157–8, 169, 183, 184, 192, 195, 205, 207
Morcar, *thegn* of Danelaw 5–6
Moretonhampstead (Devon) 59, 65
Morton, Catherine 148
Msistislav I, (Harold) Grand Prince of Kiev 194–5
Much Cowarne (Heref.) 66
Murchad, son of King Diarmait 43, 190

Necton (Norf.) 61
Nettlecombe, (Som.) 191
Newport (Essex) 61

Newton (Suff.) 62
Norfolk 19, 61, 63, 65, 207, 209, 212
Normandy xxiii, xxvii, xxix, 14, 21, 27, 30, 37, 38, 40–1, 50–1, 85, 91, 92–102, 116, 123–5, 134, 166–8, 169, 170, 171, 172–80, 185, 188, 196, 197, 199, 204
Northampton (Northants.) 111, 114
Northamptonshire 111, 141, 206–7, 209, 212
Northman, *Ealdorman* 8, 10
Northumbria xxv, 7, 13, 20, 76–7, 79, 80, 85, 103–8, 110–14, 116, 117, 123, 132, 133, 138–9, 141, 145, 155, 157–8, 160, 161, 169, 188, 205, 207
Norway 11, 19, 85, 105, 147, 152, 153–5, 157–8, 160–5, 166, 168, 171, 195
Nottinghamshire 111, 205, 207
Novgorod, Russia 194, 195
Noyon, France 82

Odda, Earl 35, 43–5, 46, 49, 71, 85, 125, 206, 208, 213
Odo, Bishop of Bayeux xxvi, 92, 100, 148, 204
Offa, King of Mercia 5
Olaf I Tryggvason, King of Norway 152
Olaf II (St) Haraldsson, King of Norway 11, 154
Olaf III Haraldsson, King of Norway 123, 164, 195
Old Cleeve (Som.) 59, 65
Old Minster, Winchester 53, 59–60
Oleg of Chernigov 194
Orderic Vitalis xxviii, 94, 97, 100, 169, 188, 190, 191
Ordric, Abbot of Abingdon 72, 140
Ordgar 62
Orkney Islands 154
Orm Gamalsson 104, 105, 106
Osbeorn, son of Earl Siward 76, 83
Osbern 'Pentecost' 21

Osbern the Priest 21
Osgod *Clapa* 20–1, 42, 43–4, 45
Oswulf, son of Eadwulf 104, 110, 207
Ouse, River (Yorks.) 155, 157, 161
Over Wallop (Hants.) 59
Oxford (Oxon.) 12, 111
Oxfordshire 86, 206, 208, 209, 212

Paglesham (Essex) 158
Parrett, River 191
Paul, Earl of Orkney 164
Peasenhall (Suff.) 62
Penenden Heath (Kent) 204
Pereyaslavl, Russia 194
Peterborough Abbey (Camb.) 71, 125
Pevensey (Suss.) 24, 44, 151, 166
Philip I, King of France 147
Plunkers Green (Essex) 62
Polhampton (Hants.) 11, 60, 65
Ponthieu, County of 94, 96
Porlock (Som.) 44
Portland (Dorset) 44–5
Portskewet (Gwent) 70, 89, 91, 134
Potton (Beds.) 141
Princes Risborough (Bucks.) 59
Puddleton (Dorset) 59, 65
Pyrford (Surr.) 69

Ralph the *Staller* 21, 142
Ralph, Earl 21, 25, 30, 32, 35, 40, 43–4,
    46, 49, 65–6, 68, 76, 78–9, 80,
    83–5, 92, 133, 206, 209, 212
Ramsey Abbey (Hunts.) 59, 158, 160
Ravenswart *huscarl* of Tosti 108
Regenbald, Chancellor 140, 142
Regensburg, Bavaria 81, 82
Remigius, Bishop of Dorchester 148
Rennes, Brittany 98
Rheims, France 82
Rhiwallon ap Cynfyn 89
Rhiwallon of Dol 97–8
Rhuddlan (Clwyd) 88, 171
Riccall (Yorks.) 155, 160, 161, 164

Richard Fitzscrob 21
Richard II, Duke of Normandy 41
Robert Fitzwimarch the *Staller* 21, 142
Robert I, Duke of Normandy 41, 96,
    128
Robert II 'Curthose', Duke of
    Normandy 93, 197
Robert of Hastings 167
Robert of Jumieges, Archbishop of
    Canterbury xxv, xxvi, 21, 27, 29–30,
    32, 35–6, 37–8, 41, 47, 49, 50–1,
    91, 95, 101
Robert, Count of Mortain 67
Robert of Romney 67
Robert the Frisian, Count of Flanders
    193
Rome 11, 25, 29, 38, 50, 70, 82, 87,
    113, 125, 148
Rotherbridge (Suss.) 66
Rotherfield (Suss.) 60
Rouen, Normandy 96, 100
Russia 152, 194–5
Rye (Kent) 145

Saewold, Abbot of Bath 188
St Augustine's, Canterbury 168
St Benet of Holme, Norfolk 72, 129,
    168
St Bertin's, Flanders 193
St Brigit of Kildare 35
St Cuthbert's, Durham 103
St Donation's, Bruges 35, 193
St Dunstan 95, 129, 131, 204
St Gregory's, Kirkdale 104
St Margaret of Scotland 194, 198
St Martin's Dover 66, 67, 68
St Omer, Flanders 81, 82, 192
St Oswine 108
St Paul's, London 136
St Peter's, Westminster 158
St Petroc's, Cornwall 67
St Riquier, France 82
St Valery-sur-Somme 149–50, 166

St Vladimir 194
Sandford on Thames (Oxon.) 60
Sandhurst (Glos.) 140
Sandwich (Kent) xxiv, 1, 3, 19, 23–4, 43, 44, 144, 150
Sawston (Camb.) 62
Saxo Grammaticus 193
Scalpi, *huscarl* of Harold II Godwineson 63, 69, 70
Scandinavia xxix, 11, 95–6, 152
Schleswig, Denmark 153
Scotland 47, 83, 107, 145, 154, 155, 157, 205
Senlac Ridge (Suss.) 174, 178
Severn, River 44, 209
Shaftesbury (Dorset) 12
Shrewsbury (Shrops.) 195
Shropshire 1, 207, 208
Sicily 153
Sigeferth, *thegn* of Danelaw 5–6, 76, 128
Sihtric, Abbot of Tavistock 187, 190
Silchester (Hants.) 66
Simeon of Durham 207
Sired, Earl 11, 12
Siward, Abbot of Abingdon 18
Siward, Bishop of Rochester 137, 203
Siward, Earl of Northumbria 12, 13, 17, 20, 32–4, 35, 37, 38, 46–7, 76, 103, 105, 110, 205–7, 212
Siward, nephew of Earl Siward, 76
Smolensk, Russia 194
Snorri Sturluson 153
Snowdonia 89
Soberton (Hants.) 140
Somerset 49, 67, 131, 187, 191, 206, 208, 209, 212
Southampton (Hants.) 14
Southwark (Surr.) 46, 59
Spearhafoc, Abbot of Abingdon 29, 35–6
Stafford (Staffs.) 195, 208
Staffordshire 207, 208

Stamford Bridge (Yorks.) 89, 117, 123, 142, 158, 160–5, 167, 168, 169, 171, 173, 174, 178, 181, 186, 195, 201
Stanwine of Peasenhall 62, 63
Steyning (Suss.) 21, 67, 68, 145
Stigand, Archbishop of Canterbury 34, 37, 38, 46–7, 49, 75, 87, 117, 127, 133, 136, 148–9, 183–5, 203, 204
Stonham (Suff.) 62
Suffolk 19, 20, 61, 62, 63, 65, 69, 128, 207, 209, 212
Surrey 206, 208, 209
Sussex 1, 3, 7, 9, 21, 44–5, 56, 58, 60, 66, 95, 167, 169–71, 172–174, 181, 193, 203, 204, 206, 208, 209
Sussex Weald 169, 173
Sweden 11, 152
Swein, Earl 12, 18, 20, 22, 23, 24–5, 27, 30, 32–5, 43, 47, 49, 52, 53, 60, 62, 63, 66, 74, 78, 132, 199, 206, 208, 209, 212
Swein 'Forkbeard', King of Denmark xxix, 39, 115, 152, 201
Swein Ulfson, King of Denmark 22–3, 24, 27, 147–8, 152, 153–4, 188, 192, 193–4

Tadcaster (N. Yorks.) 160, 163, 171
Taunton (Som.) 191
Taw, River 191
Tees, River 105, 107
Temple Newsham (Yorks.) 107
Thames Ditton (Surr.) 69
Thames, River 11, 13, 17, 34, 46, 144, 183, 184
Thorbert of Ashton 66
Thorfinn Macthore 106
Thorgils of Ashtead 66
Thorkell of Rotherbridge 66
Thorkell the Tall, Earl of E. Anglia 3, 7, 8, 9, 10, 11, 12, 19, 20, 61
Thorney Abbey (Camb.) 129

Thurbrand, *thegn* of Yorkshire 5–6
Thurgarton (Norf.) 72
Thurkill White 66
Thurstan, Abbot of Ely 140
Thurstan, son of Wine 19, 20, 61, 63
Tofi the Proud 61, 72
Tofi, *huscarl* of Harold II Godwineson 69, 70
Tofi, Sheriff of Somerset 139
Toirdelbach, King of Munster 190
Tosti, Earl of Northumbria xxv, 12, 24, 32, 35, 53, 56, 65, 66, 74, 76–7, 79, 80, 83, 85, 87, 88–9, 93, 95, 103–8, 110–14, 115, 116, 122, 123, 125, 132, 133, 138–9, 141, 144–5, 147, 152, 154–5, 158, 161, 164, 166, 199, 205–7
Trondheim, Norway 154
Tyne, River 155
Tytherley (Hants.) 168

Uhtred, *Ealdorman* of Northumbria 6, 7, 8
Uhtred of Houghton 62
Ulf, Bishop of Dorchester 21, 29, 47, 49, 50
Ulf, *Jarl* of Denmark 10, 11
Ulf, son of Dolfin 105, 106
Ulf, son of Harold II Godwineson 131, 197
Ulfkell *Snilling, Ealdorman* 19

Vercelli, Italy 29
Vexin, County of 14, 21
Victor II, Pope 81–2
Valdemar I, King of Denmark 195
Vladimir II *Monomakh*, Grand Prince of Kiev 194–5
Wales xxiv, 22, 66, 68, 70, 72, 77–81, 82, 85–6, 88–90, 95, 105, 107, 111, 112, 122, 134, 142, 144, 157, 208, 209
Wallingford (Oxon.) 183, 185
Walter, Count of Vexin 14, 40, 76, 92, 99
Waltham (Essex) xxviii, 50, 55, 61, 70, 71–3, 82, 87, 129, 181

Waltheof I, *Ealdorman* 106–7, 108.
Waltheof, Earl 76, 83, 110, 141, 157, 207
Warrington (Devon) 187
Warwick (Warwicks.) 208
Warwickshire 7, 206, 208
Wells (Som.) 67
Wessex 1, 7, 9, 10, 11, 13, 15, 16, 17, 18, 20, 25, 34, 35, 46, 49, 53, 56, 59, 60, 65, 74, 83, 87, 102, 142, 183, 188, 190, 205, 208–9, 212
Westbourne (Suss.) 5
Westminster Abbey (M'sex) 16, 71, 72, 116, 125, 136, 139, 142–3, 185
Whatlington (Suss.) 172, 174
Wickham Skeith (Suff.) 62
Wiflet of Harescombe 140
Wight, Isle of 44–5, 144, 145, 150
William of Normandy xxi, xxiii, xxv–xxvii, xxviii–xxix, 103, 123, 124–5, 127, 128, 131, 139, 199–201
Duke of Normandy 14, 21, 30, 36, 39–40, 47, 75, 91–102, 112, 114, 115, 118, 136–8, 142, 144–5, 147–51, 152, 155, 158, 165, 166–82, 183–5
'claim' to the throne of England 37–9, 40–2, 50–2, 91–2, 96–7, 99–101, 114, 115, 118
invasion and conquest of England 144–5, 147–51, 152, 166–82, 183–92, 195
King of England xxiii, 49, 67, 68, 105, 106, 140, 141, 145, 149, 185–98, 200, 203–4, 208
William II *Rufus*, King of England 196, 197, 198
William Malet 181
William of Jumieges xxv–xxvii, 14, 15, 37–9, 41, 51, 91, 97, 99, 149, 179, 192
William of Malmesbury xxviii, 94, 149, 187, 195

William of Poitiers xxiii, xxv–xxvii, 14, 15, 37–9, 40–2, 50, 91, 92, 97, 98, 99, 114, 116, 119, 122, 123–5, 142, 147–50, 155, 166, 167, 171, 172, 173, 176–181, 183

William, Bishop of London 21, 35–6, 47, 49

Willisham (Suff.) 62

Wilton (Wilts.) 36, 70, 129, 131, 195–6

Wiltshire 9, 206, 208, 209

Winchcombe (Glos.) 66

Winchester (Hants.) 13, 14, 25, 34, 38, 49–50, 53, 167, 184, 188, 197, 204

Wissant, Boulogne 14

Witton (Worcs.) 158

Wokefield, (Berks.) 69

Woodchester (Glos.) 60

Worcester (Worcs.) 16, 32, 50, 68, 80, 87, 125, 133

Worcestershire 16, 160, 165, 206, 208

Worms, Germany 82

Writtle (Essex) 61, 70

Wroxall (Hants.) 21

Wulfgyth, Lady 20, 61, 63

Wulfnoth Cild, thegn of Sussex 1, 3, 5, 11, 12, 36, 56, 58

Wulfnoth, brother of Harold II 12, 33, 37–8, 42, 47, 50, 85, 99, 101, 196–7

Wulfric, Abbot of Ely 140

Wulfric the Priest 62

Wulfric Spott 103

Wulfstan, Bishop of Worcester 87, 99, 125, 127, 133, 138

Wulfwig, Bishop of Dorchester 49, 50

Wulfwine, Dean of Waltham 72, 125

Wulfwine, goldsmith of Edith 129

Wulfwold, Abbot of Bath 140

York (Yorks.) 7, 76, 108, 110, 133, 139, 142, 155, 157–8, 159, 160, 161, 162, 165, 168, 169, 170, 171, 207

Yorkshire 56, 66, 103, 107, 108, 111, 158, 161, 166, 205, 207